SHERIFF ANDREW JAMESON

The Life of Effie Gray's Uncle

Douglas Gourlay

Published by

MELROSE BOOKS

An Imprint of Melrose Press Limited
St Thomas Place, Ely
Cambridgeshire
CB7 4GG, UK
www.melrosebooks.co.uk

FIRST EDITION

ISBN   978-1-909757-62-2

Printed and bound in Great Britain by:
4edge Limited
7a Eldon Way, Eldon Way Industrial Estate
Hockley, Essex
SS5 4AD

CONTENTS

ACKNOWLEDGMENTS

First and foremost I must thank my brother-in-law, James Neil St Clair Jameson, for permitting me full access to the Jameson archive. It contains not only documents relating to seven generations of his family's direct association with the legal profession but it is also a treasure trove of legal history of the eighteenth and nineteenth centuries.

When an undergraduate at St Andrews University, Andrew Jameson kept a diary, and when he wished to enter something that was particularly personal and private, he would render it in Latin. While I retain a rudimentary knowledge of Latin, I have been dependent upon the assistance given me by a fellow student of my own St Andrews days, Mr Michael Wilson, formerly head of classics at Robert Gordon's College, Aberdeen. In addition, being entirely bereft of classical Greek, I relied upon Mr Wilson to explain to me the nature and content of the classical Greek syllabus at St Andrews on those occasions when Andrew Jameson described the manner of his approach to the study of that language.

Fluent in French, German, Italian and Spanish, Andrew Jameson often introduced passages in these languages to his letters and diaries. I must therefore thank my near neighbour, Mrs Anabel Stewart, for her assistance, more times than I can remember, with occasional French words and phrases used by Andrew Jameson in his correspondence. In particular, she composed for me a letter of thanks to M. Denis Johnston, Président Directeur Général de Nathaniel Johnston & Fils, Bordeaux. M. Johnston had, in his turn, assisted me by providing the correct names and titles of the persons whom Andrew Jameson met, when invited by his ancestor, Nathaniel Johnston, the founder of the wine-making firm, to spend a weekend at Belsito, his country house outside Bordeaux. (See pages 185–188 for an account of this visit.) In his courtship of Margaret Hotchkis, his second wife, Andrew Jameson wrote her a love poem in Italian that Dr Mary Dargie of the Aberdeen branch of the Dante Alighieri Society kindly translated for me. A letter to Andrew Jameson from Fedele Betti, a protestant from Tuscany, was written in very old-fashioned Italian and I am grateful to Dr Domenic Zanré for the trouble that he took in translating it.

Revision of the civil and criminal codes of Maltese law was an important part of Andrew Jameson's career. I am most grateful to Dr Joseph Grima, a former Deputy Head of Education for Malta, for advising me on the historical and social background of the island, at the time when Andrew Jameson was carrying out his work on behalf of the British government.

Between 1833 and 1849 Andrew Jameson was severely troubled by what is now known as dysphonia, a throat complaint that affected his speech. I must thank Dr Ronald McAndrew and Mr Howard Young for explaining to me the nature of this illness.

The following students on the Robert Gordon University postgraduate course leading to the award of Master of Science in Information and Library Studies assisted me with literature reviews carried out as part of their assessment for their degrees. Fiona Fox (Sligo), Monika Ligocka (Camberwell), Elizabeth Mortimer (Cranfield), Frances Richardson (Lerwick) and Kaitlyn White (Toronto).

Two distant family connections of the Jameson family provided me with information that I would not have found elsewhere. Mrs Lynette Gray, of Esperance, West Australia, widow of a direct descendant of George Gray, who emigrated to Australia, gave me some details of her husband's family history. George Gray was a nephew of Andrew Jameson. Mrs Rachel Godfrey (née Ogilvie) of Henderson, North Carolina, is a direct descendant of Rachael Ogilvie, sister of Andrew Jameson (Senior) and thus an aunt of Andrew Jameson. I learned a lot about her Ogilvie ancestors and this was particularly helpful since the two cousins, Andrew Jameson and John Ogilvie, were close friends and fellow students at both St Andrews and Edinburgh Universities.

Thanks are due also to three other family members, whose assistance was invaluable. Mrs Jean Hotchkis of Bath (previously St Andrews) has carried out her own research on her late husband's family. Mr James Hotchkis of Nairn sent me copies of the highly detailed family tree compiled as a labour of love by his father, the late Mr Dunmore Hotchkis. Mr Ronald Rankine, a great-great-grandson of Andrew Jameson, helped me with information about the marriage of Andrew Jameson and Margaret Hotchkis.

I am indebted to the co-operation of the following from whom I have sought and received information. Mrs Eva Adamson (Dumfries and Galloway Family History Society), Mr John Ballantine (Gorebridge and District Local History Society), Miss Yvonne Boni (Cupar Library), Rev. Donald Campbell (Dumfries), Mr Douglas Campbell (Rector, Bell Baxter High School, Cupar), Mrs Helen Chavez (Archivist, Arbuthnot Museum, Peterhead), Mr Rob Close (Ayrshire Archaeological & Natural History Society), Mr S. Connelly (Archivist, Perth and Kinross Council), Mr Jeremy Duncan (Local Studies Librarian, Perth and Kinross Council), Mrs Irene Ferguson (Edinburgh University Library), Professor Angelo Forte (Aberdeen University), Professor Robert Frost (Aberdeen University), Dr Christopher Grech (Columbia University, Washington, D. C.), Professor Stephen Halliwell (St Andrews University), Mrs Rachel Hart (Archivist, St Andrews University Library), Rev. Dr A. Scott Hutchison (formerly minister of Ceres Church, Fife), Mr Tom Hutton, (Langholm Archive Group), Mrs Erica Johnson (Ewart Library, Dumfries), Professor Keith Kendle (Robert Gordon University, Aberdeen), E. J. Lawson (Dunfermline), Miss Jean McMillan (Buteshire Natural History Society), Miss Pam McNicol (Archivist, Stirling Council), Dr Jan Merchant (Archivist, Perth and Kinross Council), Miss Jane Petrie (Archivist, Stirling Council), Dr Norman Reid (Head, St Andrews University Library), Mr B. C. Scroggie (Robert Gordon University), Rev. Calum Smith (Free Church, Dumfries), Miss Alison Wainwright (Signet Library) and Mr David Weir (Renfrewshire Central Library).

Acknowledgment must be made of those who gave me special

assistance. Mr Donald Abbott of Invergowrie, a distant connection of George Gray, sent me a history of the Gray family from mediaeval times. The Rev. Dr Andrew Wilson (formerly minister of Rubislaw Parish Church, Aberdeen) was very helpful in providing me with material concerning Andrew Buchanan. The Rev. Dr Henry Sefton (formerly Senior Lecturer, Christ's College, Aberdeen University) gave me a lot of valuable information about Thomas Chalmers and the educational role of the foreign missionaries of the Free Church, such as Alexander Duff. Mr Malcolm Selkirk of Crieff drew my attention to a gross error in the Memoir concerning Captain Alexander Leith. Far from fighting at Culloden and subsequently evading capture for a few weeks, there is documentary evidence that he was captured at Carlisle some months before the battle. Two members of the Faculty of Advocates Library, Miss Andrea Longson, Senior Librarian, and Dr David Parratt, Curator, gave me both documents and advice that allowed me to give an accurate account of Andrew Jameson's public examination for acceptance as a member of the Faculty of Advocates. In particular, I must thank Mrs Diane Scott of Daviot in Aberdeenshire for drawing up the genealogical tables.

Finally, my thanks to so many younger colleagues at Robert Gordon University for coming to my assistance when things went wrong on account of my weakness with modern computer practice. Dr Simon Burnett, Mr George Cheyne, Miss Jane Kidd and Dr Farid Ullah have helped on countless occasions. Mr Alan Hunt has never failed to answer my request for assistance in formatting. However, my greatest thanks must go to Mr Ian Calder, Learning Technologist, who, as late as March 2014, retrieved my whole text when I thought that it had been lost forever down some computer black hole.

FOREWORD

The distinguishing feature of Andrew Jameson was his attractive manner. People to whom he was introduced for the first time were immediately glad to have made his acquaintance and to offer him their full trust and confidence. John Ruskin invited Andrew Jameson to accompany him for two days as they explored Turin, although they had met only the previous evening, and Sir Thomas Acland, wealthy landowner and politician, having entered into conversation with him on the quayside of St Jean de Luz, invited him, there and then, to join his family aboard his yacht as it sailed along the Basque coast.

The great scholars of the Scottish Enlightenment, such as David Hume, Adam Smith and William Cullen had died before Andrew Jameson was born, but he and his contemporaries were the beneficiaries of the pattern of teaching they had laid down in Scottish universities. This included close personal communication between professors and their students, but for the latter to benefit fully from this special relationship it was necessary for them to reciprocate in an appropriate manner. Had Andrew Jameson not possessed this trait to the full, it is unlikely that Thomas Chalmers would have taken any interest in him nor that Douglas Cheape, who occupied the chair of Scots law at Edinburgh University, would have invited him, but 18 years old, to a dinner where the other guests included two prominent advocates (later Lord Colonsay and Lord Robertson), who had represented William Burke, the resurrectionist, at his trial for murder, Thomas Chalmers and John Wilson, Professor of Moral Philosophy, who wrote for *Blackwood's Edinburgh Magazine* under the pseudonym of Christopher North.

Once established as a sheriff-substitute, Andrew Jameson became a familiar figure in Edinburgh society. His acquaintanceship was not confined to legal circles but spread far beyond it to include such luminaries as Sir Noel Paton, the artist, Sir David Brewster, the Principal of the university, and Sir James Young Simpson, the pioneer in the field of anaesthetics. This friendship established with Simpson was continued by their descendants down to the present day.

However, the most lasting outcome of Andrew Jameson's ability to attract favourable attention came during a brief visit to Malta during the winter of 1840/41. In the course of three weeks he was invited three times to dine with the Chief Secretary and once with the Governor. So impressed were they with the character and intellectual depth of the young Scottish lawyer that he was invited to revise, on behalf of the British Government, the criminal code (and later the civil code) of the island. He made so fine a job of this that in the 1870s the criminal and civil codes of Maltese law were adopted in their entirety by the government of Italy. How and why he was selected for this task was unknown to modern Italian legal historians, until the author of this work, using documents discovered in the Jameson family archive, published an account in a historical journal.

Although it had no effect upon the career of Andrew Jameson, the fact that he was the uncle of Euphemia (later known as Effie) Gray adds a very interesting dimension to his life because it connected him closely with the *cause célèbre* of the mid-Victorian era. The decree of nullity that Effie obtained from her first husband, John Ruskin and her subsequent marriage to John (later Sir John) Millais, the renowned painter and illustrator, shocked society and appalled no less a personage than Queen Victoria. The circumstances of Effie's life brought her into a prominence that she did not deserve and has prompted the publication of a series of books about her, the latest one in 2013. The letters that she wrote to her uncle as a schoolgirl and later as a young bride and wife are published here for the first time.

After their first meeting in 1841 in Turin, Andrew Jameson corresponded regularly with John Ruskin until the very public dissolution of Ruskin's marriage with his niece inevitably brought all further contact between the two men to a sudden halt. Several previously unpublished letters from Ruskin to Andrew Jameson have been discovered in the Jameson family archive. All demonstrate the tremendous breadth of Ruskin's learning, whether he is assessing the political situation in Piedmont, giving an amusing account of his honeymoon in the Lake District or sympathising with Andrew Jameson on the death of his wife.

CHAPTER ONE

Early History of the Jameson Family

The name Jameson originates from Caithness, where, by the fourteenth century, the Gunns had established themselves as the most powerful clan. They claimed descent from Guni, a son of the King of Denmark, who came to Caithness in the eleventh century, but documentary evidence of this is totally absent and other myths relate that Guni was of Norwegian royalty. Their chieftain was known as the Crowner and, during the fifteenth century, one son of a Crowner of that period was James, or Sheamus. His son was known as MacSheamus-Chataich, or Jameson of Caithness, and so became the progenitor of the Jamesons.

The earliest ancestor that Andrew Jameson[1] could trace of his particular branch of the family was a William Jameson, who was born around 1680. He was described as a portioner[2] of Middletown of Wester Luscar[3] in the parish of Carnock, which lies a few miles to the west of Dunfermline. In his "Outline of Family History"[4] the author notes that the name Jameson was not uncommon in the nearby towns of Alloa and Clackmannan and in the village of Torryburn, which was within easy walking distance of Carnock. It seems likely that William Jameson's immediate ancestors came from this area and it may be more than a coincidence that Graycraig,[5] the home that Miss Jameson bought and from which she took her designation, was near Carnock.

When the laird of Dollarbeg in Kinrossshire died in about 1705, his widow, Jean Burn,[6] was left far from destitute. Under her husband's

---

[1] v. p. 438 infra.

[2] i.e. tenant farmer. This was how he was described in a document when he received a loan from the local church. v. p. 2 infra.

[3] By the nineteenth century it had become known as Burnside, but the name is retained today by the adjacent Craigluscar Hill, about 700 feet high.

[4] v. p. 440 infra.

[5] v. p. 11 infra.

[6] The name of this family is also given as Burne in the Memoir.

will she inherited the life-rent of some property at Dollarbeg and, in addition, she already had life-rent of land at Wester Luscar. How this came to her is not known. We know nothing of the physical charms or domestic virtues of this woman but her property may well have been her major attraction for William Jameson, tenant of the adjacent farm of Middletown of Wester Luscar. They were married sometime in 1707 and the following year she presented her husband with a son, Andrew.

She already had several children by her previous husband, whose name was Scotland.[7] Her eldest daughter married William's brother, an unusual but perfectly legal union that meant that her brother-in-law was also her son-in-law. Alexander Jameson, the son of this marriage, was therefore both her grandchild and her nephew by marriage, and so Alexander and Andrew, her son by William Jameson, were double cousins. As events turned out this double cousinhood did not enhance family harmony.

Jean Jameson, as she now was, did not need to move from her home at Dollarbeg because her second husband and she lived there until her eldest son, Thomas, was of age. Parish records show that Andrew, son of Thomas Scotland, laird of Dollarbeg, was baptised on 8th February 1719, a clear indication that by then Thomas had married and moved into his inheritance. Around that time the Jamesons moved to Wester Luscar and in 1722 William was able to purchase a third part of the property. The memoir gives such imprecise accounts of the property that it is unclear if the land which he purchased in 1722 was the farm of which he had been a tenant, the property of which his wife had the life-rent, some other adjacent property or indeed whether he had been the tenant of his wife's land. On that same day William Jameson granted to Thomas Scotland of Wester Dollarbeg a heritable bond over these lands for 5850 merks. In 1728 the kirk session of Carnock Parish Church loaned him 200 merks for some unspecified purpose, and later that year the same kirk session appointed "Jean Burn, Spouse to William Jameson of the Middletown of Luscar" to go with two other

---

[7] The Memoir does not give a Christian name.

females to examine a woman charged with being with child.

Meanwhile their son Andrew, who was to bring the family from obscurity to local prominence, had grown to full manhood. His parents sold their lands[8] of Wester Luscar in 1740 and went to live with their son, at Craighall,[9] near Ceres, where Jean Jameson died in 1744. According to their granddaughter, Miss Jameson of Graycraig, her husband lived on for several years before dying in a house at Largo belonging to a family called Durham.

William Jameson's wife was the sister of James Burn, factor[10] for the Duke of Argyll's property of Castle Campbell, near Dollar.[11] When his parents moved from Dollarbeg to Wester Luscar, Andrew remained in the area, probably living with his uncle, the factor. He served some sort of informal apprenticeship in his uncle's office and became familiar with the complicated deeds of inheritance and property required by the feudal law of Scotland. His uncle, to whom he must have been very indebted for the foundation he provided for his career, also made provision for him to study the classics, and Andrew's grandson[12] recalled that, as a schoolboy in Saline, his grandfather occasionally spoke to him in Latin.

Andrew must have spent some time in Edinburgh during his youth and probably took classes in law at Edinburgh University. He may have stayed with a wool merchant, John Scotland, a connection through his mother's first marriage. This man bound himself as Andrew's

---

[8] The Memoir gives the plural and so perhaps there were two properties to dispose of: William Jameson's original tenancy that he had purchased in 1722 and his wife's life-rented property.

[9] In the Memoir the name is Grayshall. I have spoken to the Rev. Dr A. Scott Hutchison, a native of Cupar and former minister of Ceres, and he has never heard of Grayshall. Mr Selkirk (v. footnote 24 infra) suggests that Miss Jameson of Graycraig, from whom the information came, confused the name of the house with her own. There is a Craighall in the parish of Ceres.

[10] In one of the documents concerning Dollarbeg he is designated "Clerk to the Regality of Campbell".

[11] By the nineteenth century Castle Campbell had ceased to be in the possession of the Dukes of Argyll.

[12] The father of the author of the Memoir. The Memoir relates that "Our father and uncle lived some time with him and attended the village school of Saline." It can only be suggested that since their parents had given a home to orphaned cousins, the Dysart house had become overcrowded and that they were sent to Barnhill, near Saline, where his aunt and grandfather were then living. v. p. 10 infra.

"Cautioner",[13] when, on 3rd November 1733, he was admitted as a notary public. We know that he finished his practical education under Alexander Orme, a Writer to the Signet, son of a David Orme of Balvaird near Arngask in Glenfarg, who was probably known to James Burn.

Andrew Jameson began to practise as a lawyer in the small Fife town of Strathmiglo. At Arngask House in the neighbouring parish there was now living a Miss Gib,[14] daughter of John Gib and granddaughter of Sir Patrick Gib of Old Meldrum. John Gib's sole heirs were two daughters, Christian by his first wife and Margaret by his second. He arranged for his lands at Couland to be inherited by Christian and those at Arngask by Margaret, although by some complicated arrangement Christian had to pay to her father £2,125 Scots on her marriage to Robert Murray for full possession of the Couland estate. John Gib died in 1725, and since his second wife did not long survive him Margaret was now living alone with her servants at Arngask. Through his connections with both the Orme family and his uncle the young lawyer was first introduced to Miss Gib at Balvaird. The memoir states that he would often walk the four miles across the hills dividing the rivers Eden and Miglo to see Margaret Gib at Arngask House. The young woman was not averse to his visits but not yet ready for any permanent relationship until a most alarming incident demonstrated a need for protection greater than what could be provided by her servants.

Another suitor for the hand of Miss Gib was the Master of Inchbrachie (now known today as Inchbrakie). He had lands in Upper Strathearn and was the son of Patrick Graham, who in 1695 had killed the Master of Rollo in a quarrel, been banished for life but allowed to return in 1720. Respect for civilised behaviour was just as absent in his son who, finding that he was making no inroads upon the affections of Miss Gib, arrived one night at Arngask House with thirty retainers and a clergyman and abducted her. One of the Arngask

---

[13] In Scots Law one who becomes bound as caution or surety for another, for the performance of any obligation or contract contained in a deed.

[14] Her name is sometimes given as Gibb.

servants escaped to let Andrew Jameson know what had happened. Together with as many tenants and others as he could muster he set off in pursuit of Inchbrachie and caught up with him three days later. Overawed by superior numbers, Inchbrachie surrendered his prize, who had resolutely refused to marry him, to her rescuers and there was therefore no addition to the number of rough wooings that figure in Scottish history.[15]

Andrew Jameson and Margaret Gib were married on 20th August 1735 at Couland, the home of her stepsister, Christian Murray. The bridegroom is described as "Writer in Strathmiglo and portioner of Wester Luscar", which suggests some property of his parents there had been transferred to him. Under the marriage settlement his bride conveyed to him her lands at Arngask together with the £2,125 Scots which her sister had had to pay for possession of Couland. So Andrew Jameson, just as his father, was not the loser by his marriage. The Ormes, father and son, were responsible for the execution of the settlement.

What the author of the Memoir calls the conflagration of the family records[16] makes it difficult to follow Andrew Jameson's career for the next few years. Sometime before 1738 he moved to Craighall in the parish of Cupar, and the parish records mention him as Factor for the Barony of Teasses.[17] As stated above, his parents came to live at Craighall in 1740 and parish records show that his mother was living there when she died in 1744. Presumably he kept possession of Craighall after he moved to Leven on the Fife coast in about 1744 but there is no further mention of the place after his mother's death. If Miss Jameson of Graycraig is correct concerning the last few years

---

[15] Miss Jameson of Graycraig gave the graphic details of her mother's abduction to the author of the memoirs when she was ninety years old. It is impossible to verify the story now but it is interesting that in 1828, when he was sheltering from the rain, the author of the memoirs met a woman in Arngask who related the same story about the abduction of whom she called "the leddy of Arngask". Furthermore, on another occasion, he met a woman who claimed to be the granddaughter of the one servant Inchbrachie had allowed Miss Gib to take with her and her account tallied in the main with the other two.

[16] v. 439 infra.

[17] Dr Hutchison confirms that there is a place of this in name in the parish of Ceres. He believes, however, that it is pronounced rather differently from what the spelling here suggests.

of William Jameson,[18] it may be that he moved from Craighall to the Leven area on his wife's death because Largo is adjacent to Leven.

Meanwhile the former Margaret Gib was enduring the lot of almost all other wives at this period: constant childbearing. Their first child, William, did not survive long but Jean, born in 1738, lived to be 93 and is the Miss Jameson of Graycraig on whom her grandnephew Andrew Jameson relied upon for family history of the eighteenth century. There followed another William in 1740, as short-lived as the previous one, Janet born that same year, John in 1741, and James in 1743. These last three survived to adulthood but six children in eight years were too great a strain on Andrew Jameson's wife and by 1744 he was a widower.

He did not grieve long, nor was that common at the time, especially when a professional man had four children under the age of seven to care for. On 2nd March 1745 Andrew Jameson, described as a Writer in Leven, and Betty Kay, eldest daughter of the provost of Kirkcaldy, were married at Old Greyfriars Church in Edinburgh.

Two months later, Andrew Jameson secured a loan of 500 merks on his own bond from the parish of Kennoway to assist him in the purchase from a Captain Braimer,[19] at a price of £1,000 sterling, the lands of West Newton that lay within the parish. The memoirs make the Delphic comment that the distance of Arngask from his place of business was now inconvenient but makes no further reference to that property. The name of the vendor is mentioned here solely on account of a curious coincidence. The agreement for entry into West Newton by Whitsunday 1746 was signed in August 1745 at Prestonpans where, a few weeks later, Captain Braimer, an officer of Cope's army, was killed in the battle to which the town gave its name.

---

[18] v. p. 3 supra.

[19] The name is sometimes given as Brymer by the memorialist and the property as Westernewton. Captain Braimer (or Brymer) is described as "of Edrom". This is a village between Chirnside and Duns in Berwickshire and the *Scots Magazine* of October 1741 records the marriage of "Capt David Brymer of Edrom, in Col. Long's regiment, to Miss Congalton of Congalton." (Congalton is near Dirleton in East Lothian.) Captain Braimer, to give him the spelling favoured by his family, was already 56 years old. His grandfather, Lieutenant-Colonel James Braimer had served under General Alexander Leslie, Earl of Leven, and on marriage to Leslie's half-sister in 1647 at Dysart had bought Westernewton. Shortly afterwards he took up land at Edrom and styled himself Braimer of Edrom.

Andrew Jameson was no Jacobite and played a small role during the rebellion as a loyal supporter of King George II. The Jacobite leaders, although they controlled little more than the city of Edinburgh, attempted to inaugurate some form of civil administration. After the rout of the government army at Prestonpans they ordered all collectors of land tax throughout Scotland to come to Holyrood with their account books and any payments currently held by them. Andrew Jameson must have been one of those concerned because he did travel to Edinburgh with his account books and such land tax as he held. However, these he delivered not to the rebel administration in Holyrood but to the governor of Edinburgh Castle, which held out for the government until the Jacobite retreat the following year into the Highlands. Since government ships controlled the Firth of Forth and blockaded Edinburgh it was not difficult for Andrew Jameson to explain his purpose and secure a passage to Edinburgh, but there is no account of how he was able to enter and leave Edinburgh Castle.

Though not known or connected to the Jameson family at that time, an Alexander Leith did favour the Stewart cause and received a commission in Gordon of Glenbuchat's regiment, consisting of men from Strathdon, Strathavon and Glenlivet. The Memoir states that Leith fought at Culloden, escaped to the home of his sister, a Mrs Anderson, whose husband farmed land near Aberdour in Fife, attempted to flee the country disguised as a woman but was apprehended. He was subsequently tried for treason in London and hanged on 29th November 1746 together with Sir John Wedderburn and three others on Kennington Common, near what is now Surrey County Cricket Club's ground. The author of the Memoir writes that in 1831 he visited Culloden and spoke to a local inhabitant, mentioning his relationship with Captain Leith. As the Memoir states, the man said, "Yes, he commanded Glenbucket's[20] Regiment and I will point out the spot where they stood."

Unfortunately, this account is considerably at variance with documentary evidence. Leith certainly marched south with the Jacobite

[20] The anglicised version of the correct spelling of Glenbuchat.

7

army to Derby but records show that on the retreat to Scotland he was left as one of the garrison at Carlisle Castle, where later he was captured. His subsequent fate is exactly as given in the memoirs.

Let us compare the provenance of the information about Captain Leith. The family version came from Mrs Normand[21] of Dysart, a daughter of Sophia Jameson by her first husband, John Anderson. She claimed to have learned it from her mother, who was a niece of the rebel captain. Is it possible that the tale of Captain Leith seeking to escape in the guise of a woman was confused with that of the Young Pretender, who adopted a similar ruse but with greater success? The other version, that he was captured at Carlisle, is stated in two standard works of reference: *Prisoners of the '45*[22] and *Jacobites of Aberdeenshire and Banffshire in the Forty-Five*.[23]

It is, of course, possible that the official records are incorrect. Captain Leith may have been sent (or escaped) from Carlisle to join his regiment in the north of Scotland but this can be no more than conjecture. It seems, however, probable that the more prosaic account, substantiated by written documents, is the one that should be believed, rather than one based upon oral tradition.[24] There is, nevertheless, no doubt about the visit of Andrew Jameson to Culloden in 1831 and his meeting with whom he calls a "Highland peasant". This local, who appeared out of a hut in the middle of the battlefield, could well have been a self-appointed guide to the site and been accurate about where the various clans stood in the line of battle. Yet, did he really recall the name of Leith, or did he feel that it was in his interests to say so?

As stated below at page 439, the manner in which the Memoir is written is infuriating. This is no more so than when one comes across the third marriage of Andrew Jameson with no reference to the death of his

---

[21] v. p. 14 infra.

[22] Seton, Sir Bruce Gordon, and Arnot, Jean Gordon, (1928/29) *Prisoners of the '45*. Edinburgh Scottish History Society, vol 3.

[23] Tayler, A., and Tayler, H., (1928) *Jacobites of Aberdeenshire and Banffshire in the Forty-Five*. Milne and Hutchison, Aberdeen. A copy is available in Aberdeen Public Library.

[24] I am grateful to Mr Selkirk of Crieff, an authority on the Jacobite rebellion of 1745/46, for drawing to my attention the official account of the capture, trial and death of Captain Leith.

second wife.[25] He married Rachel Wilson, widow of Dr David Russell, described as a "Chirurgeon Apothicary", at Kennoway in September 1748, and thus his second marriage had been of short duration. Again, Andrew Jameson married to his advantage. In addition to the life-rent of her late husband's house in Kennoway, where she was probably living when Andrew Jameson moved to neighbouring West Newton, she was able to assign 1,000 merks to her second husband. Her father had given her a dowry, or to use its delightful old Scottish name of tocher, of 5,000 merks on the occasion of her first marriage with the constraint that 1,000 merks should return to her if she was left widowed and childless.

The death of Captain Braimer at Prestonpans so soon after entering into the agreement to sell West Newton to Andrew Jameson interfered with the smooth transfer of the property. Braimer's heir was a minor and the executors of his father's will disputed the sale under some old but still valid aspect of Scottish feudal law. In addition, Andrew Jameson had been tardy with his payment, perhaps not surprisingly since he would not have wanted to hand over money while his right to the property was under challenge. It was not until 1750 that the conveyance of West Newton to Andrew Jameson was finally settled and that at the cost of the lands of Arngask. Even then there had to be special conditions that seem bizarre to us today but were then part and parcel of Scotland's feudal law. Arngask had been settled upon John Jameson, the elder surviving son of Andrew Jameson's first wife, Margaret Gib. Nevertheless, Andrew Jameson was able to sell Arngask to someone called Whyte with the agreement that his son would ratify the sale when he came of age; meanwhile Whyte would hold West Newton as security until that time. Accordingly, when John Jameson became 21, his father persuaded him to assent to the transaction and the lands of Arngask were lost to the family. This was the first but not the only occasion when the father sought his own financial salvation at the expense of his son.

---

[25] Rev. A. B. Duncan, writing on 30th July 1847 to his cousin Andrew Jameson, said their grandfather had been married twice. Perhaps his second marriage, which Leven parish records authenticate, was so short that Mr Duncan was unaware of it. *See also* footnote 28 below.

The two decades 1750 to 1770 were years of peace and prosperity for Scotland, but for the Jameson family peace was not attended by prosperity. Andrew Jameson and his wife may have enjoyed a comfortable lifestyle and been accepted as their social equals by the principal (and richer) families of the neighbourhood but this required a financial outlay that the husband's earnings could not sustain. Had they lived more modestly their life might not have descended into financial ruin but the foremost cause of Andrew Jameson's bankruptcy was that while his business was extensive he was financially inept. Perhaps he felt that it was not gentlemanly to press his clients for payment or, as his great-grandson, the writer of the Memoir discovered, he too often accepted title deeds to small properties in lieu of fees but did not foreclose on them. He also had to pay a considerable sum of money as a result of going surety for some financial transactions entered into by his cousin, Alexander, the son of that unusual union between his mother's daughter by her first marriage and his father's brother. Alexander then departed for the West Indies, sent some form of legal document promising to leave all his future property to his cousin but neither money nor Alexander were heard of again.

In 1773 Andrew Jameson had to convey all his property to an accountant in Edinburgh, John Hay, the trustee for his creditors. He had to sell West Newton, which had been bought at the expense of Arngask, and he retired to live with his daughter Jean at Barnhill, near Saline.[26] As the Memoir records, "There he spent the rest of his days in peaceful retirement and in the humble and frugal manner, which became a man who was unable to pay his debts."[27] There is no mention of his third wife, who, presumably, had died. He was assisted in his retirement by subventions from his youngest son James, now resident in India and making a very successful career not only as a merchant but also as an officer in the army of the East India Company, having first formed and later commanded the Bombay Grenadiers. Andrew Jameson died in 1782 and was buried in Dollar churchyard in the parish

---

[26] A village situated between Clackmannan and Kelty and not far from Wester Luscar.
[27] Memoir p. 49.

where he had been born and where he had set out upon his career in the office of his maternal uncle. Some time later his son James died in India, leaving a considerable fortune which enabled his unmarried sister to purchase Graycraig and live in a manner that allowed her to be designated "Miss Jameson of Graycraig". The Memoir states that "Graycraig is the only representative" of James Jameson's fortune although the Rev. A. B. Duncan, like the memorialist, a grandnephew of Miss Jameson, believed John Jameson, Andrew Jameson's elder son, had also been a beneficiary.[28] John was now practising as a lawyer in the royal burgh of Dysart.

As was common at the time, John Jameson had attended St Andrews University at an age where today he would be still in a secondary school. He was then sent to complete his education at Edinburgh. These are the bare details as recorded in the Memoir with the additional information that in 1765 he was studying civil law in the capital and attending the office of that same Mr Orme with whom his father had been so closely associated. The Memoir records that "A family copy of *Corpus Juris Civilis* which has already served three generations bears his name with that date."

Sometime around the end of 1768 John Jameson obtained the appointments of Town Clerk of Dysart and factor for a local landowner, Colonel St Clair. The former incumbent, a John Anderson, who left a widow and several children, had also held these offices in concert. His relict, Sophia, is reported to have been comely, and when she received from John Jameson a proposal of marriage, it is not surprising, on account of the children she had been left to support, that she found it acceptable. Born in 1738, and therefore a few years older than her second husband, she was the daughter of John Anderson of Kirkton, Burntisland, and Janet Leith of Aberdeen. Her first husband had

---

[28] The Rev. A. B. Duncan of Culross wrote to Andrew Jameson on 30th July 1847. Mr Duncan was a grandson of John Jameson's sister, Janet Bethune, and thus, like the memorialist, a grandnephew of Miss Jameson of Graycraig (which he spelled Greycraig). Mr Duncan believed Captain Jameson also left money to his brother John but there is no mention of this in the memoir and John Jameson's continual struggle to remain solvent argues that he was not a beneficiary of his younger brother's will.

been an Anderson cousin. It was through Sophia Anderson that the Jamesons became connected with Captain Leith of the '45 because her mother was his sister. Miss Jameson of Graycraig considered that her brother's choice of wife had encumbered him with responsibilities that were too heavy for a man at the beginning of his working life and she made some insinuations to the discredit of her sister-in-law. Her grandnephew, the author of the memoir, writes that it "can serve no good purpose to record" her comments and one can only presume that it was the great age of his grandaunt that caused her to forget that she was talking about his grandmother.

The couple married in January 1770 and their first child, Andrew, later the father of the author of the Memoir, was born on 30th October the following year. It must have been a very busy household because in addition to the children of her first marriage, Sophia Anderson presented her second husband with seven children in addition to Andrew, four (including twins) not surviving beyond infancy. Heaping Pelion on Ossa, some of the children of John Jameson's sister, Janet, who had married the Rev. Neil Bethune of Kennoway, had become orphans by the mid 1770s and for a time they were given a home with their cousins in Dysart.

Sadly, John Jameson, like his father, was poorly equipped financially to cope with the demands of his extended family. "He had great experience of men and business and was a person of sense and shrewdness in regard to all affairs but his own, being careless and easy to a fault. He lent his money or credit with an undue facility and was very negligent in what was due to him."[29] He was also the loser through his father's inability to adhere to common-sense business practice, including the wilful involvement of his recently qualified son in his own disastrous financial dealings. For the whole of his career John Jameson struggled to keep his head above the financial waters that seemed ever to be closing in upon him. As late as 1812 he had not escaped from one of the legal morasses into which his father had so thoughtlessly led him. This is best explained by quoting directly from the memoir.

---

[29] Memoir p. 117.

There is an interesting paper, preserved among our dear Father's papers, which records the decline of our Ancestor's fortunes. It is entitled – Memorial for John Jameson, eldest son of the deceast Andrew Jameson of Wester Newton respecting a claim against him, by the heirs and representatives of the also deceased Mr John Fair, writer in Colinsburgh. 1812. This paper gives some particulars about the failure, though it does not allude to the causes which led to it. It shews how the son became entangled in endeavouring to relieve the difficulties of his father. A sort of entail, which has unfortunately continued to be kept up in the family.

This Memorial states – that the Memorialist had not been long settled at Dysart, before he was repeatedly applied to by his Father for assistance, and being still ignorant of the real situation of his affairs and anxious to do what was in his power to serve him, the Memt. borrowed several sums upon his own credit, which with other sums advanced from time to time, were wholly applied to his father's use, but which although it brought the Memorialist into the greatest difficulties were quite inadequate to his Father's relief.[30]

It is very difficult to follow the life of John Jameson since the Memoir is not written in chronological order for this period of the family history and information about him appears at such irregular intervals that we know less about him than about his father and grandfather. His first wife died in 1788 and his sons, Andrew and James, were sent away to continue the excellent education they had already received from the parish schoolmaster, William Wilson,[31] who is described in the Memoir as "greatly superior to the mass of parish schoolmasters of that period". Andrew went to St Andrews University and James to Perth Academy.

---

[30] Memoir p. 47.

[31] He wrote *Elements of Navigation*, the second edition of which was published in Edinburgh in 1784. It has been suggested that this stimulated the interest of James Jameson, who had a successful career with the East India Company Maritime Service.

In 1790 John Jameson married Mary Spittal[32] and his daughter, Sophia, after some hesitation, accepted the hand of James Thomson, a writer in Cupar, because she was not happy living with her stepmother.[33] In 1805, Rachael, his second daughter, married a Dundee writer, James Ogilvie. The memorialist refers to John Jameson's second wife as "a wasted and broken-hearted woman, struggling with a large family and poverty brought on by her husband's folly and misconduct". She bore John Jameson a daughter, a son and three other sons, who died in infancy. According to the Memoir, this son, whose name is not given, was educated at Doncaster,[34] became dissipated, went out to the West Indies and died there. The daughter, Harriet, married James Swine (later known as Swayne), a banker in Dysart. Janet, daughter of his first wife by her previous husband, married a Captain Normand[35] and they and her unmarried sister, Margaret Anderson, also lived in Dysart. These women are occasionally mentioned in correspondence and in the Memoir.

In June 1799 a fire broke out in the business room of John Jameson's house and, although his clerk was arrested on suspicion of fire-raising, there was insufficient proof for him to be brought to trial. In his efforts to extinguish the flames his hands were severely burned and many of his clients' records were lost. He suffered financially from this disaster and also appears to have experienced a period of depression. One client whose records were saved was Sir James St Clair, the heir of Colonel St Clair, who had died in 1789, and it can be no criticism of John Jameson if he made a special effort to ensure that, whatever happened to the papers concerning his other clients, those of his most prestigious one were rescued.

Two years later, through the agency of Sir James St Clair, the office of Sheriff-Substitute of Fife was offered to John Jameson. He asked if, instead, it could be offered to his elder son, Andrew, who had

---

[32] She died in 1802.

[33] A daughter of this union, Elizabeth Thomson, came to figure prominently in the early life of the memorialist.

[34] This is surely a mistake made when the Memoir was typed. The family had no connections with Doncaster in Yorkshire, the only place of that name in this country.

[35] A direct ancestor of the twentieth-century Scottish judge, Lord Normand (1884–1962).

completed his legal apprenticeship satisfactorily in 1798. This was a very generous act because the father could certainly have improved his own sad financial position had he accepted. Sir James agreed and Andrew Jameson (Senior) was able to set out on a career in the legal profession that, in contrast to that of his father and grandfather, was attended with considerable success.

CHAPTER TWO
Childhood and Education

Andrew Jameson (Senior) had had an undistinguished career at St
Andrews University because, according to his son, "He did not make
great proficiency in the dead languages."[1] His proficiency at golf was
more highly regarded and he claimed to have driven a ball over the top of
the college steeple.[2] It was a different matter when he went to Edinburgh
in 1789 and was apprenticed to John Ferrier, a Writer to the Signet
and a friend of his father. He attended classes at Edinburgh University
in Scots Law and according to his son was "a diligent student".[3] He
remained with Ferrier for nine years, a remarkably long time since he
does not appear to have been remunerated, although for one whole year,
1793–94, he was unwell and had to live at home in Dysart.[4] Another
apprentice there was an Alexander Campbell[5] with whom he developed
a close friendship that continued for the rest of their lives.

It was during this year of absence from Edinburgh that he found
himself attracted to a young woman, whom he had known since their
schooldays. Euphemia Chalmers, known to her intimates as Femy,
was a young woman of good family but poor financial circumstances,
who had been brought up in or near Dysart by her grandmother. She

---

[1] Memoir p. 53.

[2] Considering the golf clubs and balls of that time and the height of the steeple of St Salvator's
Chapel, this seems an unlikely achievement.

[3] Memoir p. 55.

[4] He had some chest complaint and the treatment advised was regular bathing in the sea
throughout the winter together with frequent doses of Glauber salt. He followed this treatment
and remained healthy for the rest of his life. Glauber salt is hydrated sodium sulphate, one of the
minerals formed in salt lakes. It was formerly used as a laxative like Epsom salts (magnesium
sulphate), which acts by retaining water in the bowel and thus producing a bulk laxative effect.
Frequent doses in a restricted amount of water, however, can produce dehydration of the body,
an effect much like modern diuretics although by a different mechanism. This may have been of
some benefit in some heart diseases. (Information kindly supplied by Professor Keith Kendle.)

[5] He was appointed Sheriff-Substitute of Renfrewshire in May 1802.

was some connection of Dr Thomas Chalmers (1780–1847) who was appointed to his first charge, Kilmany, in 1803. This parish bordered that of Cupar, and Euphemia and her husband often gave the young minister hospitality at Barony House, their first home, in the Millgate, Cupar. The Memoir tells us no more than that her grandmother was a Mrs Melville, that her parents were dead and that her father had squandered his inheritance. Her uncle, John Melville, appears to have been unbusinesslike and a poor trustee of the small inheritance left to Euphemia by her mother because he hauled himself out of debt by using some of this money. Andrew Jameson, therefore, was seeking a union that brought him no material advantages.

Mrs Melville's maiden name had been Orme and since this is not a common name it is possible, perhaps probable, that she was connected with those same Ormes who had assisted Andrew Jameson's father and grandfather when they were studying in Edinburgh.[6] We can only guess but here again we have another aggravating example of the failure of the Memoir to provide fuller information about persons connected with the family.

France declared war on Britain in 1793 and the following year William Pitt, the Prime Minister, invited men to join their local militias. Campbell and Jameson joined the Edinburgh Regiment but apart from some occasional drilling do not appear to have become engaged in any serious preparation for actual combat. By the end of 1797 Andrew Jameson had completed his apprenticeship and was ready to take his examinations for acceptance as a Writer to the Signet but his father was unable to afford the necessary fees. He applied for a commission in the 5th (Fifeshire) Regiment of Militia and in April 1798 was gazetted a Lieutenant, being designated as "late of the Edinburgh Volunteers".

For the next three years he was with his regiment either on garrison duties in Perth, Stirling, Aberdeen and Fort George or on route marches to these places. In June 1801 he was on a route march in the north-east of Scotland, when he received a letter from his father giving him the

---

[6] v. pp. 4 & 11 supra.

news of his appointment as Sheriff-Substitute of Fife.[7] Presumably he wrote to his father acknowledging receipt of the good news but the appointment had another important consequence; it made it possible for him to marry Euphemia Chalmers with whom he had now had "an understanding" for some years.

That theirs was a true love affair is demonstrated by this letter Andrew Jameson wrote to Euphemia from Aberdeen. It is given here in full.

My most adored   21 June 1801
And beloved Femy   Abdn Barracks

What is it? Yes, my dearest love, I have the inexpressible happiness to tell you that I am appointed Sheriff-Substitute of the County of Fife – Oh God of infinite Goodness be praised – This good fortune has a thousand charms because my Femy will partake of it – I feel more ardent love for my friend and feel my heart cling closer to the heart of my beloved Femy – I told you the Sun would soon shine upon us. I have hardly time to say more – My father in communicating this most agreeable piece of intelligence says "I would have written Femy but did not know her directions but I did not forget to mention it to the Bailie,[8] who would no doubt write to her". My Residence will be in Cupar – do you think you will like it Oh my tender love? I am overjoyed and can hardly take pen to write – I suppose I will see you in about 14 days.

  Strange – oh stranger – what will Mrs M[9] say to all this –

---

[7] v. p. 15 supra.

[8] Presumably some local magistrate known to both families. Until the middle of the twentieth century bailies were local councillors, who, after a period of service, were chosen to hold office for six years instead of the usual three with the object of providing some continuity for council business. They also acted as magistrates for petty offences committed within the burgh. England and Wales had similar appointees known as aldermen.

[9] One would have presumed that this referred to her grandmother had Mrs Melville not recently died. It may have been the wife of her uncle, the unsatisfactory trustee with whom she may have been living since her grandmother's death, but that is the merest conjecture.

I hope you are safe in Dysart by this time. I must conclude
[there follow a few indecipherable words]
    Ever your most faithful
    Andrew Jameson

Wisely, Andrew Jameson allowed himself over a year to settle into his new post at Cupar before embarking upon matrimony. As well as the usual duties associated with a sheriff-substitute, he had certain responsibilities for public safety nowadays exercised by the police. This was a time when there were real, albeit wildly exaggerated, fears of French armies landing on British coasts. Obviously, were the French to attempt this, it would be along the south and east coasts of England, but the possibility of a French incursion on a Scottish coast was not discounted. In January 1802 there was a rumour of a French landing in Fife, and Andrew Jameson, about to go to Dysart for two days, sent a letter to a Captain Thomson[10] asking him to "inform me by an Express on horseback if the Volunteers are called to arms". Almost two years later the Lord Advocate[11] wrote to David Monypenny,[12] a relation of the Earl of Leven, asking him to alert the local authorities of the possibility of a French spy being in the county. As Sheriff-Substitute of Fife, Andrew Jameson was also informed.

---

[10] Possibly James Thomson, the husband of his sister Sophia (v. p. 14 supra), but Thomson is too common a name for certainty.

[11] This was Charles Hope, a distinguished member of the Scottish bar, who was later Lord Justice Clerk and Lord President of the Court of Session. He considered that it was his duty to encourage vigilance against even the remotest possibility of French revolutionary ideas being implanted within Scotland. The extravagant terminology used by Hope in the excerpt from his letter that appears below is a good example of how he interpreted his duty to the crown. That same year he carried his enthusiasm for a patriotic outlook to extraordinary lengths in the Morison case. Morison was a farmer in Banffshire who dismissed a servant for absenting himself without permission to attend a parade of the local volunteers of which he was a member. Hope was appalled at what he considered to be a rank injustice suffered by a man in humble circumstances, who was prepared to take up arms in the defence of his country. He said that the farmer's action "could only have arisen from a secret spirit of disaffection and disloyalty" and ordered the Sheriff-Substitute of Banffshire that "on the first Frenchman landing in Scotland, you do immediately apprehend and secure Morison as a suspected person, and you will not liberate him without communication with me". In his *Memoirs of his Time* Lord Cockburn described Hope as a man whose "hot temperament was not cooled by a sound head".

[12] He was later, as Lord Pitmilly, a member of the Itinerant Judiciary of the Northern Circuit of the High Court.

The Lord Advocate's letter states that a Frenchman is alleged to have been in the Fife coastal towns and the recipient of the letter is to investigate. In particular he is to visit one Rodgers who keeps a public house on St Monance Quay. The Lord Advocate writes that Rodgers "is well known to be one of the most notorious Jacobins and Republicans in Scotland. I know that he will deny that the Frenchman was in his House but I have positive information that he was there, and that he wrote the word 'Bonaparte' under a print of our Brother Muir of seditious memory which hung at the side of the looking glass in one of Rodger's Rooms." Muir of Huntershill was an unfortunate lawyer who in 1793 was sentenced to transportation for sedition (he had merely expressed too freely his support for some aspects of the French revolution) and, after years of vicissitudes, died while returning to his native country.[13]

Andrew Jameson and Euphemia Chalmers were married in the Inn at Kinross in October 1802. He was eight days short of his thirty-second birthday and, if Euphemia was even four years younger[14] than her husband, theirs was, by contemporary standards, a somewhat late marriage. Their first child (born 1803) was baptised John St Clair Jameson "in honor of Sir James St Clair, who had so long been the friend and patron of the family". The name has been continued through subsequent generations down to the present day.[15] Seven more children followed of whom the sixth was Andrew, the memorialist of the family, born on 30th April 1811. Apart from a visit to Miss Jameson of Graycraig in 1807 with her husband's uncle, James, who had a long and distinguished career in the Honourable East India Company's Maritime Service,[16] the Memoir makes no further mention

---

[13] The trial and conviction of Thomas Muir of Huntershill is regarded as a black mark in the history of the Scottish legal system. It occurred in the middle of a scare about revolutionary influence from France but that was poor excuse for this travesty of justice. For a history of the case and details of Muir's life see Bewley, C., *Muir of Huntershill*, Oxford University Press, 1982.

[14] There is no reference to her age in the Memoir or any correspondence but notice of her death (4th January 1815) was inserted in the *Scots Magazine*.

[15] Sir James St Clair later became Earl of Rosslyn.

[16] A history of this brother of Andrew Jameson (Senior) was written by the author of this work and published in May 2002 by The Robert Gordon University, Aberdeen.

of Euphemia Jameson until her death in 1815. On the other hand when her husband was away in London, pursuing on behalf of his fellow sheriff-substitutes an increase in their emoluments, she always received letters couched in the most affectionate terms.

We know little of the domestic life of Sheriff-Substitute Jameson and his wife apart from their moving in about 1810 from Barony House to "a lofty house in the main street or Crossgate – which went by the name of the Puddintour, a jocular allusion to the calling of a butcher who built it".[17] While it would be wrong to claim that Andrew Jameson and his family lived in penury, his position was poorly remunerated in relation to his responsibilities. On 8th February 1806 he sought the assistance of the Earl of Rosslyn[18] in his application for the appointment as Distributor of Stamps[19] for Fife and gave the poor salary of a sheriff-substitute – a mere £100 per annum – as his principal reason for seeking this additional employment. His application was unsuccessful.

He had, however, an additional source of income. On his appointment as sheriff-substitute he had resigned his commission in the Fife Militia but in April 1803 he sought, successfully, a commission as captain of a company of the newly raised Cupar Volunteers. He was promoted to major and later lieutenant-colonel. His emoluments from this post were not inconsiderable and his son reckoned that they brought his annual income up to about £250. This did not remove his sense of the injustice at the poor remuneration of sheriff-substitutes and by 1810 he had become one of their spokesmen in negotiations with the government. They claimed, with a considerable degree of justice, that their salaries bore small relationship to the duties that they were required to perform. The Memoir informs us that in June 1810 Andrew Jameson was in London as a member of a delegation that sought to persuade the government to increase their salaries and

---

[17] Memoir pp. 108 & 144.

[18] Formerly the Sir James St Clair through whose connection with his father he had obtained his sheriff-substitute post. v. p. 15 supra.

[19] Perhaps the most famous Distributor of Stamps was William Wordsworth, who was appointed for Westmorland.

with his colleagues secured an interview with the Prime Minister, Spencer Percival. Their salaries were increased to amounts varying with the county to which they were appointed, that of the sheriff-substitute of the county of Edinburgh being raised from £150 to £200. Andrew Jameson's salary was increased from £100 to £140. A further fourteen years with several visits to London were to pass before the sheriff-substitutes were awarded salaries that more truly reflected their responsibilities.[20]

Four years later, on 26th July 1814, we find Andrew Jameson writing to his father "that he is much distressed for want of money" but since John Jameson's life continued to be a perpetual struggle to keep afloat financially, he was an unlikely source of any subvention.[21] Andrew Jameson was in difficulty because he had allowed himself to be inveigled into an unwise financial transaction by Robert Thomson,[22] a full cousin of his wife. Thomson had inherited what is described in the Memoir as "a moderate fortune". He appears to have used it to buy Drums, near Freuchie in the parish of Falkland, a large house overlooking the valley of the River Eden and enjoying beautiful views south and east. The memorialist describes him as a genial but improvident man although a couple of gentlemen, who had visited him when he still owned Drums, described him as "a drunken beast or sot".[23] Thomson ingratiated himself with Andrew Jameson to the extent of persuading him to underwrite various financial transactions on the security of the Drums property. Rather surprisingly, since he must have known the financial problems that had accrued to his father and grandfather through similar arrangements, Andrew Jameson agreed to Thomson's request, accepting without question Thomson's estimate on the value of the house and land. When unbridled extravagance brought Thomson to the point of bankruptcy, Andrew Jameson found himself

---

[20] There is in the Jameson Family Archive (v. p. 438 infra) a large bundle of letters concerning the claims by the sheriff-substitutes for improved remuneration. They await the attention of a legal historian.

[21] v. p. 12 supra.

[22] Robert Thomson was not, as far as can be ascertained, related to James Thomson, writer in Cupar, who married Sophia Jameson, sister of Sheriff-Substitute Jameson.

[23] Letter to Andrew Jameson, dated 11th October 1815, from a D. Johnston.

mired in the same debt, because Thomson had grossly exaggerated the value of the Drums property. Moreover, Thomson was publicly claiming that his financial distress had been brought about by his association with him.

Salvation came through the intervention of his brother, Captain James Jameson, who was enjoying a successful career with the East India Company's Maritime Service. In what was clearly an act of fraternal support, Captain Jameson purchased Drums from Robert Thomson. This allowed Thomson to satisfy his creditors and simultaneously bring Andrew Jameson out of his financial predicament. Then, throughout his brother's long absences abroad, first at sea and finally at Calcutta, Andrew Jameson acted as factor for Drums (receiving appropriate remuneration) and developed the estate according to the instructions of James Jameson. Although Thomson went to Canada and there is no further mention of him, the memorialist considered that his father felt the "consequences of this ruinous connection during the rest of his life".

On 4th January 1815, when her husband was paying a visit to Miss Jameson of Graycraig, Euphemia Jameson gave birth to her eighth child. Whether the birth was premature can only be guessed but in view of Andrew Jameson's undoubted affection for his wife it seems unlikely that he would have been away from home had he believed the birth was imminent. James Thomson wrote from his home in Cupar[24] to tell his brother-in-law that his wife had given birth to a daughter but was very unwell. He sent this letter by express to Drums, now the home of Captain and Mrs Jameson, "with a request to send it forward by a servant, lest you may have been prevailed upon to prolong your stay another day". It is unlikely that Andrew Jameson managed to reach his wife before she died in the early hours of the 5th January 1815. The child was named Euphemia after her mother.

Andrew Jameson had to face immediately the matter of caring for his eight children, of whom the eldest was aged eleven. At that time it was quite common for a widower, after what was considered to be an appropriate period of mourning, to take a second wife or to come

---

[24] The letter bears no date other than "Wednesday, seven o'clock pm".

to some arrangements with a brother or sister to have his children brought up in their household. This was what happened when the children of John Jameson's sister Janet were orphaned in the 1770s and were brought up by her brother's wife with their cousins.[25] Andrew Jameson's sister-in-law, Betsey Jameson, wife of Captain Jameson, offered to look after his two elder daughters, Elizabeth (Betsey) and Sophia, at Drums. Since she was childless and thus had no experience of bringing up children it is not surprising that she did not offer to give a home to all eight of them. Andrew Jameson, however, preferred to keep his family together and having sought "a respectable discreet Lady somewhat advanced in years, who would attend to the children, take care of the house and sit at table",[26] he appointed a Miss Baird from Errol, a village between Dundee and Perth. This woman was in straitened circumstances on account of her brother's improvidence and, in the words used by one of her charges, Andrew Jameson, when he came to write the history of his family, "her disposition had not been improved by the reverses she had sustained".[27]

How the bereaved father became aware of the availability of Miss Baird to help him in his sad predicament can only be guessed. He may already have known the Grays of Perth, with whom Miss Baird was acquainted, and learned from them of the woman's circumstances. It is equally possible that he had heard about her through some other channel, possibly his father. His father wrote to him on 22nd February 1815 that Harriet "has made her short excursion to Dundee to see Rachel and also she will have the opportunity to see Miss Baird". From this we learn that Miss Baird was currently living in Dundee. (Harriet was John Jameson's daughter by his second wife and Rachael his youngest child by his first wife.[28]) Although of no significance whatsoever in 1815, the appointment of Miss Baird was the start of a continuing connection between the Grays and the Jamesons that, almost forty years later, was to lead to an *affaire célèbre* of no small notoriety.

---

[25] v. p. 12 supra.

[26] Memoir p. 112.

[27] Memoir p. 112.

[28] v. p. 14 supra.

The first mention of young Andrew Jameson comes in a letter written on 24th February 1817 by his father to Mrs James Jameson at Drums. There was at this time severe illness among the children, the main concern being John, the eldest. His grandfather, John Jameson at Dysart, was urging his son to take the boy to Edinburgh to see a Dr Bryer, who today would be called a consultant. The letter goes on to say that "Andrew and Melville are coming on very well and Robert is recovering more slowly. Femy is also laid up with measles and so my house is at present a complete Hospital almost. Miss Baird who is always so kind and attentive fortunately keeps her health which is an immense comfort to the Children and to me. If any of them should have the appearance of becoming worse I cannot leave them on Thursday but the doctor says they are all in a fair way at present and that he thinks I may safely leave them if they are no worse." On this occasion all the children recovered but illness and death were later to attend the family to a greater extent than was common even at that time.

John Jameson, father of Andrew Jameson and his brother Captain James Jameson, died in 1819. He had been suffering from a bowel complaint and paid a visit to the Wells of Pitkeathly, a spa near Perth with an undeserved reputation for curing a variety of ailments. There he consumed large draughts of these waters that did him no good but much harm, and he died on 16th August, aged 78.

Before 1820 the two elder sons of Andrew Jameson had already left home to begin their careers. Captain James Jameson used his influence with the East India Company's Maritime Service to secure a position for his nephew James on one of the company's vessels, *Scaleby Castle*, Captain Sotheby. Service in the maritime arm of the company could begin as young as twelve, although thirteen was more normal. Professional skills were therefore learned almost entirely "on the job", to use a term applied to manual training of craftsmen. Obviously a child of thirteen could not be given any executive role aboard ship and so young people aspiring to rise in the maritime service of the East India Company were enrolled for their early voyages as seamen. Consequently, those who survived the rigours of a seaman's life at that early age and showed promise could look forward to command of a vessel by their late twenties. James left home on 1st March 1818. The memoir states that he "sailed from Dundee in a smack, had a passage of 13 days of which he was sick four days".[29] However, by 18th March, he had joined the *Scaleby Castle* and in April was sailing down the English Channel. He was back in Cupar the following year and was still there when John left for London: this was the last time the five brothers were together.

Service in the East India Company's army began at a less tender age. In early December 1819, John St Clair Jameson, who had not yet reached his seventeenth birthday, travelled to London from Edinburgh by coach, arriving frozen to the marrow since he had been seated on top for the whole of the three days. He was met by his uncle, Captain James Jameson, who had arranged for him to stay with the Alleys, friends to whom his father had been introduced when he had been in London in 1810. James Jameson had secured for his nephew a cadetship in the army of the East India Company and took him on his third and final voyage as master of *Earl of Balcarras*[30] bound for Bombay and Whampoa. John kept a diary[31] of that voyage that eventually found its way to his brother, the memorialist. In it he makes clear his admiration for his uncle, who, others told him, was a "model of a Commander in knowledge of his profession in the maintenance of strict discipline and in the dignified courtesy and frankness of his demeanour".[32] His uncle introduced him to the most prominent people in Bombay, an indication of the captain's standing in his profession. He also presented his nephew with a fine Arabian horse.

John St Clair Jameson was soon promoted to a lieutenancy but apart from meeting, at Madras in 1830, his brother James, who was now following the same career as their uncle, nothing is written in

---

[29] Memoir p. 119.

[30] The memorialist uses the correct spelling of *Balcarres*.

[31] This diary is extant in almost pristine state. It has survived mainly because it is protected by stout hard covers. The calligraphy of John St Clair Jameson is worthy of praise since it enables one to read the diary as easily as if it was the clearest typescript. Unfortunately his father had not the same facility with his pen and his correspondence is often difficult to decipher.

[32] Memoir p. 119.

the Memoir about him. From considerable correspondence that has survived, we know that he came home on extended leave in 1836, married in 1839, returned to Bombay, took part in Napier's campaign against the mirs of Sind and contracted a fever there from which he died at Bombay in 1848.[33] The Memoir states that John St Clair Jameson had reached Bombay with his uncle "on 30th April 1820 [when] he caught the first sight of that land and city, where he was to die".[34]

Earlier in this chapter reference was made to visits by Andrew Jameson (Senior) to London as a member of delegations, consisting presumably of other sheriff-substitutes, seeking an improvement in their salaries. Since the family correspondence over the two years from 1822 is interrupted in mid 1824 with detailed information about the eventual settlement of this claim, it will be appropriate to deal with it separately.

In May 1824 Andrew Jameson wrote to his son Andrew about his meeting with Robert Peel, the Home Secretary, and of his other experiences in London. The father writes from the Globe Coffee House, Fleet Street, London, which may account for the poor quality of the paper and consequent difficulty in deciphering its contents. It is, on the other hand, so interesting that most of it will be given here. After apologising for not having written earlier, the father continues thus.

> I have been with Mr Peel and some other of the great folks on my business here. I am very happy to tell you that our case is looking well. The Home Secretary is disposed to be liberal and with the scale of Increase which [will be such[35]] as to ameliorate our conditions in a material degree. You may tell Mr Husband and Mr Paton[36] that I am very

---

[33] Chapter Six includes an account of John St Clair's leave in Scotland, marriage and subsequent career.

[34] Memoir p. 119.

[35] At this point in the letter the paper is torn and the script indecipherable and to give continuity the three words in parenthesis have been interpolated.

[36] The script is so poor that the name could just as well be Paterson.

sanguine of succeeding in my mission but I will write my Brethren the particulars when I know them.

I have been in high life lately. I had the good luck to go into the Palace and to see the company at the Drawing room and to see them alight from their splendid carriages under the Arcade. I then had the honor of being introduced to the King of the Sandwich Islands[37] – he is a stout man apparently about 36 years of age of a copper colour but of gentlemanly and mild manner and apparently supporting an intelligent mind. I asked him to come and see the Kingdom of Fife: he bowed politely and upon coming towards me he gave me a cordial shake by the hand. I am coming back another day to be introduced to his Queen and his Sister along with Mr Thomson.

By 9th July 1824, Andrew Jameson (Senior), now back from London, writes to his son Andrew from the New Inn, Cupar. He reports that his mission to London has been "crowned with success. It is most gratifying to me to be able to say that my exertions have contributed so much to the amelioration of the conditions of my Brethren. My [illegible word] quota is an increase of £110[38] and I have besides succeeded in obtaining from the finances a retrospect of the Increase to pay expenses, which is very fortunate for me. The new salary commences from 1 January." The letter concludes with the words "Mr Peel was particularly kind to me". Thus, through patient and constant application to the objective of winning from the Crown a level of remuneration appropriate to the duties and position that they held in the dispensation of justice in Scotland, Andrew Jameson had performed a signal service on behalf of his fellow sheriff-substitutes.

The arrangements for the early education of the five Jameson boys are far from clear. There is no mention of any school attended by

---

[37] Now Hawaii, 50th state of the USA.

[38] Presumably per annum. It raised his salary to £350. There must have been some small increments between 1810 and 1824.

James. John had spent a year at St Andrews University before leaving for India. In September 1819 Andrew was sent to St Andrews, where there was a grammar school headed by David Moncur, a fine classical scholar, and here Andrew began instruction in Latin and Greek. Robert had already been a pupil there for a year and he and his brother boarded with the Misses Jervis in Market Street. Melville certainly attended a school called Cupar Academy because there is an entry in the Almanack stating that in July 1825 he won first prize for Greek there. In the summer of 1820 Moncur was appointed Rector of Perth Grammar School and since Sheriff-Substitute Jameson considered that Andrew should continue his education under his tutelage he enrolled his son there in September 1820. Robert continued at the school in St Andrews. As regards the three daughters the Memoir merely states that "During this winter of 1820–21 Betsey [now aged 16] went to Edinburgh to her Aunt's in Dundas Street[39] and Sophia and Euphemia attended the Schools at Cupar."[40] There is a letter from which we learn that "our Mathematical Teacher has begun a course of chemical lectures and has about 50–60 students male and female. Sophia and Jane Thomson have taken tickets and I go sometimes to encourage them."[41]

It is difficult to follow the academic career of Robert. The Almanack for 1820 includes the brief comment "Ro – to St Andrews", which indicates that he remained at the St Andrews school. In a letter of May 1822 Andrew Jameson (Senior) told his son Andrew that Robert had returned to St Andrews to take "Mr Crake's Greek class for the summer in order to prepare himself for the second Greek class next September". Craik[42] was the name of two brothers, who succeeded Moncur at the St Andrews school. The Almanack for 1823 contains the simple statement "Robert ailing". The following year, in a letter of Andrew Jameson (Senior), dated 29th November 1824, to his son

[39] Captain James Jameson either bought or rented a house in Dundas Street, Edinburgh, for many years and his wife appears to have stayed there often, especially when her husband was away with his ship.
[40] Memoir p. 121.
[41] Andrew Jameson (Senior) to Andrew Jameson at Perth, 6th March 1824.
[42] This is the spelling given in the Memoir.

Andrew, who had by then matriculated at St Andrews University, the father writes that "Robert has this day entered as a student at our Accademy" (*sic*). One must conclude, therefore, that the unfortunate Robert, now aged 15, was attending Cupar Academy. We learn from the letters of Andrew Jameson (Senior) during the 1820s that Robert always struggled with both his health and studies and it is not difficult to conclude that his two younger brothers were much healthier and much brighter than him.

There is a curious entry in the Almanack for 7th January 1819. It states "obtains Ramsay Bursary for *1825–9* years – G. D. Gillespie of Mountquharie". It does not give the name of the beneficiary but Andrew Jameson writes in the Memoir that "I held one of the Ramsay Bursaries amounting to £25 p. annum. This I retained for nine years and it was a great assistance to my father as in some years it was sufficient to defray all my expenses during the college session."[43] Thus at seven years of age Andrew Jameson was awarded a bursary that would assist his father to pay the expenses of both his school and university.

Miss Baird arranged for Andrew to stay in Perth with her friend, Miss Jane Gray, at 1 The Crescent. Perth Grammar School and Perth Academy had different origins with the former able to date its foundation as far back as 1150 while the Academy had been founded by the Town Council in 1760. From 1807, however, they shared accommodation at Rose Terrace in what has been described as a "splendid edifice".[44] The salary of the Rector of the Grammar School consisted of £50 per annum together with two thirds of the class fees of twelve shillings and sixpence paid by each pupil per quarter. Also appointed at the same time as Moncur was William Cameron, whose title was Usher.[45] We can infer from correspondence that Andrew got on well with both men.

Today one can travel to Perth from Cupar in thirty minutes and it is interesting to learn the manner in which Andrew Jameson travelled

---

[43] Memoir, p. 125.

[44] Smart, E., *History of Perth Academy*. Milne, Tannahill and Methven, Perth, 1932.

[45] This title appears to have signified second master.

there in September 1820 to continue his education at the Grammar School. "In those days there was as yet no Steamboat on the Tay – and I remember well, that Miss Baird and my brother Robert accompanied me to Newburgh, where we embarked in a small row boat with a covered cabin something like a Venetian Gondola, in which we were slowly carried up the magnificent river to the South Inch of Perth."[46]

The earliest extant family correspondence[47] confirming that Andrew was being educated at Perth is a letter from Robert, who wrote in April 1822 to him there from St Andrews. In the Almanack there is an entry for 1821 stating that Captain Jameson "went to Andrew at Perth in July". Robert's letter to Andrew of April 1822 had been written at St Andrews and was conveyed first to Cupar by Dr Chalmers, now a member of the university staff. In his letter Robert supposes that Andrew will become a bejant[48] at St Andrews the following year but, even in an age when boys scarcely into their teens went up to university, a child of twelve years would probably have been considered too young.[49] Indeed two years were to pass before Andrew matriculated at St Andrews University. Robert did not receive a reply until almost three weeks later and this was in part because Dr Chalmers, whom Robert had asked to take the letter to Cupar, had probably forgotten about it.[50]

In May 1822 Andrew Jameson (Senior) sent his son some books including a Latin bible for which he had a "particular regard" and asked him to preserve it carefully, since it was about 200 years old. It included the "Psalms set to music as used in the Church of England which you will not like as you are no friend of Episcopalianism". He sent him also the Greek testament and the Buchanan Psalms along with a Latin book "for your perusal when you are at leisure". The father goes on to say

---

[46] Memoir p. 121.

[47] i. e. as distinct from the Memoir.

[48] From French *bec jaune*, a name still given to first year students at St Andrews University.

[49] Thomas Chalmers had matriculated in United College, St Andrews, at the age of eleven. This was in 1791, more than thirty years earlier, and his subsequent career suggests that his extraordinary intellect had already equipped him for university life at this remarkably young age.

[50] This, at least, was Robert's belief as stated in his letter of 10th May 1822 to Andrew.

that he hopes that his son is "keeping [his] grounds in [his] different classes – I shall be much disappointed if I do not see the examination this year and I am certain your uncle will accompany me".

Today it is difficult for us to imagine that a father would send a book in Latin to an eleven-year-old son with the suggestion that he look at it in his leisure time. It is even more unlikely that he would send him a copy of the New Testament in Greek. In order to demonstrate the level of academic attainment already reached by Andrew Jameson only eleven years after his birth, one needs to go no further than a quotation from the standard work on George Buchanan,[51] the most outstanding sixteenth century Scottish scholar, where it refers to Buchanan's translation of the psalms into Latin verse. The author writes "Buchanan's style here is a good example of what the Pléiade[52] was aiming at in the 1550s: erudite, elevated, but nevertheless managing to avoid arid obscurity. Vocabulary, with the use of periphrasis, carefully chosen, apt epithets, and noble terms, has an important role in this, along with the use of metaphors and extended similes, and grand-sounding proper nouns."[53] Two years later, Andrew and his brother Melville were in correspondence about the use of periphrasis[54] in Latin composition and thus his younger brother was equally advanced in his understanding of the classics.

Accompanying his father's letter was one from Melville. This is the first extant letter of Melville and the two brothers were henceforth to correspond regularly. Melville tells him that the family have heard from their eldest brother, John, who is now at Poona in the Bombay Presidency and where he has witnessed the effects of a serious plague

[51] George Buchanan (1506–1582) was tutor to a son of James V (1513–1542), to his daughter, Mary, Queen of Scots (1542–1587) and to his grandson James VI (1566–1625). On account of his adherence to the principles of the Reformation, he was forced to flee to France during the minority of Queen Mary. While in France he was recognised as one of Europe's greatest scholars and taught the essayist Michel de Montaigne. He later lived in Portugal before returning to Scotland in 1561.

[52] The Pleiades in classical myth were the seven daughters of Atlas and Pleione, sisters of the Hyades. Pleiad was a name frequently given to groups of seven illustrious persons. The French Pleiad, the Pléiade, was a group of seven French poets, who wrote their verses in the metres and style of the ancient Greeks and Romans. Their leader was Ronsard (1524–1585).

[53] Ford, P. J., (1982) George Buchanan, Aberdeen University Press, p. 93.

[54] The Concise Oxford Dictionary (Fourth Edition 1950) defines periphrasis as "Roundabout way of speaking, circumlocution: roundabout phrase e.g. did go = went".

causing hundreds of deaths among the natives. He then writes about shooting rabbits with Robert. While the standard manner of concluding a letter in those days was highly formalised, Melville ending his letter with the words "My dear Andrew, your most affectionate brother, Melville Jameson" demonstrates there was clearly considerable fondness between the two brothers as the letters they exchanged down the years were to show. Family affection was more openly expressed at this period but, in addition, it must be recalled that there was a difference of just over a year in their ages and that by the time Andrew was boarding in Perth with Miss Gray their two eldest brothers were already launched on their careers, John in India and James in the East India Company's Maritime Service. The other brother, Robert, as stated earlier, was at St Andrews. It is, therefore, not surprising that they felt a special kinship for each other and followed similar pursuits normal to boys of their own age.

In October 1822 Mr Moncur either committed suicide or died of a stroke. Andrew was clearly upset by this and received kind letters of support from both Melville and Robert, Melville mentioning that he hoped (correctly as it turned out) that Mr Cameron[55] would succeed Moncur. Tragedy had already struck the Jameson family in February of that year with the death from whooping cough of Euphemia. Then in March 1823 they suffered a further loss through the sudden death of their sister Elizabeth (Betsey). Thomas Chalmers wrote this letter from Glasgow[56] to Andrew Jameson (Senior).

> My dear Sir,
>   I received the mournful intelligence of your daughter's death, which I took not just personally but in which along with all your and their family I felt an interest both for your and for their mother's sake. I have the most interesting remembrance of her and still look forward with affection to

---

[55] According to the Memoir he ran the school well until he took to drink and had to be dismissed.
[56] The letter is dated simply "March 1823". At that time Chalmers was minister of the parish of St John in Glasgow and may have already known that he was about to return to St Andrews to take up the chair of moral philosophy. This may be why he states in the letter that he was looking forward to having intercourse with Andrew Jameson (Senior) "in my native county".

the prospect of having continual intercourse with yourself in my native county.

But then such memorials of our frailty should teach us to look further than to any earthly anticipation whatever. It is my prayer that this conviction should now take deep root in your heart softened by afflictions and exercised in the lesson of our mortality. There is, be assured, a sad derangement of our Nature that we so cling to the world, under most touching demonstrations of the world's vanity – and nothing will avail us, but that well grounded hope of immortality which a Faith in the gospel of Jesus Christ alone can inspire.

Do believe me, my dear sir, Yours very affectionately

Thomas Chalmers

When next we hear of Andrew it is towards the end of 1823, when he won a prize at school. This shows that he had been working assiduously at his lessons from the beginning of his time at Perth Grammar School, but this had involved him in studying up until midnight and then early in the morning before leaving for school. Miss Gray became so concerned at what she considered to be this lack of balance in the life of a boy, who, it must be remembered, was only twelve years old, that she wrote to her friend Miss Baird on the matter. The letter was shown to Robert, who wrote a kindly letter[57] to his brother saying that it was all very well "to be attentive and studious but it is *just riding on the rigging*[58] and besides it may hurt your health afterwards". He rebukes Andrew for his failure to write to any member of his family. Robert's letter accompanied one of the same date from his father, who says that he is pleased to learn how well he is progressing with his studies. He wonders, however, if the tasks set him by his teacher may be rather beyond his competence at his age and that, while education is important, he must have regard to his health. He

---

[57] Robert Jameson to Andrew Jameson (Junior), 4th December 1823.

[58] Robert underlines these words and it must have been a metaphor common at that time.

suggests that Miss Gray asks his teacher, Mr Cameron, to give him less to do although he concedes that "it is difficult to meddle with a teacher".

We learn from both these letters about Andrew's four brothers. The father reports that Robert "is now regaining his strength"[59] and that Melville, showing promise as a Latin scholar, is dux of his class. In his letter Robert tells Andrew that they have had three letters from John, who is still acting as adjutant for his corps and that James has been appointed sixth mate of the *Canning*, an East India company vessel, but that he would not sail until February 1824.

Andrew Jameson left Perth Grammar School in July 1824 and matriculated at St Andrews University in early November. On 15th January 1824 he had been staying at the house of the Misses Jervis[60] in St Andrews. Robert[61] wrote to him there that the family had been disappointed by Andrew's absence from home in Cupar over the New Year vacation and that he was expected to be with them on the first Monday of February. Robert writes that a Miss Mary Gray, whom he describes as "a very fine agreeable girl", has been with them since Christmas but is about to leave. He also writes that "Miss Gray is very much astonished at you not writing to her" and one must presume that this is Andrew's landlady in Perth and not the Miss Gray[62] who had attracted such favourable comment from him.

Since the sessions at the University of St Andrews ran from late October to May[63] it seems likely that Andrew was simply visiting the town. He was certainly back in Perth soon after this because Melville wrote[64] to him there at Miss Gray's. Melville wrote to him again in May 1824 and after discussing the use of periphrasis[65] in Latin composition he goes on to request Andrew to desist from sending him presents

---

[59] v. p. 29 supra.

[60] This family's name is spelled both "Jarvis" and "Jervis" in correspondence.

[61] Robert Jameson to Andrew Jameson (Junior), 15th January 1824.

[62] Possibly a relation of Andrew's landlady although the genealogical tables of the family of George Gray, who was to marry Sophia Jameson, do not contain a Mary until 1836.

[63] Cant, R. G., (1946) *University of St Andrews*, p.103. Oliver and Boyd, Edinburgh.

[64] Melville gives the date as just "Saturday morning" but at a later date someone, probably Andrew Jameson (Junior) when he was arranging the correspondence prior to writing his Memoir of the family, has added "ab initio anni 1824".

[65] v. p. 32 supra.

since he is unable to reciprocate. The next month there is another letter from Melville, again commenting on periphrasis and adding that their father is about to leave London. In November 1824 Andrew Jameson (Senior) writes to his son at St Andrews where he is again staying with the Misses Jervis along with his Dundee cousin, John Ogilvie. It is possible that his stay with them in January of that year had been a preliminary visit to see the town and, possibly, to arrange to board with the Misses Jervis, although, if so, he was making very early enquiries in that direction.

The Almanack for 1824 states "June 10. Miss Baird left us this day to the regret of us all, having been here ten years & two months." Then the Almanack for the following year repeats this information in similar words. "June 10. Miss Baird left us this day having been with me 10 years & 2 months." The latter year is the more probable because Miss Baird came to Sheriff-Substitute Jameson's home some weeks after the death of his wife in January 1815. This separation was not permanent because for the next few years she paid occasional visits to the family.

The university records show that Andrew had matriculated as a Secondar at the university in October of that year when still some months short of his fourteenth birthday. However, before writing about his years at St Andrews it is necessary to make some brief reference to the university where he was about to spend five years of his life.

St Andrews was founded in 1413 and thus is the oldest university in Scotland. In 1617 it received a visit from the king and became recognized as the centre of Scottish educational life. Members of the nobility sent their sons[66] to St Andrews, and it was about this time that students, on matriculation, were first ranked as "Primars", "Secondars" or "Ternars" and wore gowns that indicated their status. Primars were students from the nobility, Secondars came from successful merchant, professional and small landowning families (lairds), while the manse, farm or burgh shop was the background of the Ternars. This segregation

---

[66] They included Montrose and Argyll, who would later support different sides in the civil wars and pay the supreme penalty, and Lauderdale, who governed Scotland during the early part of the reign of Charles II.

of students by social background was still in operation during Andrew Jameson's undergraduate years and is almost certainly the reason for his outburst, at the end of his final year, against the university's "detestable servility to power, family and wealth".[67]

Despite its earlier promise St Andrews had fallen on sad times at the start of the eighteenth century with few students, dilapidated buildings and professors noted more for indolence than for learning. A Commission of Visitation was sent in 1718 and while it paid scant attention to the academic aspects of the university's life, it did, at least, put the financial arrangements on a sounder footing. This was but a temporary reprieve for by the 1730s the number of students had declined to the point where the survival of the university was imperilled. The situation was so bad that "even the lethargic masters of St Andrews were compelled to consider what might be done to save the university from utter ruin".[68] The proposed solution was to unite the three colleges of St Salvator, St Leonard and St Mary under a single administration. Although St Mary's, the divinity college, preferred to retain its independence the other two, following parliamentary approval, combined in June 1747 to become "The United College of Saint Salvator and Saint Leonard in the University of Saint Andrews". This title has remained to the present day as has the independence (within the university) of St Mary's College.

From that date there was better government of the university resulting in improvement in both the care and maintenance of its properties and in the academic standards of its staff. Significant appointments were that in 1772 of George Hill, as Professor of Greek, and, in 1778, of John Hunter, as Professor of Humanity.[69] Both were young men at the time of their first appointment, Hill[70] becoming the

---

[67] v. p. 75 infra.

[68] Cant, R. G., op cit. p. 87.

[69] In Scottish universities this is the term used elsewhere for Latin.

[70] Hill was especially dominant within the university after he became Principal of St Mary's, a post he held from 1791 to 1819. In an age when nepotism was elsewhere in decline he arranged for six of the thirteen posts in the University Senate to be held by close members of his family. It was said at the time that the most popular psalm sung in University Chapel was the 121st ("I to the hills will lift mine eyes, from whence doth come my aid.")

outstanding theologian of his day and Hunter, more than fifty years later, Principal of United College. In the mid 1820s Hunter would have Andrew Jameson in his class.

Andrew Jameson's years at St Andrews almost coincided with a four year period (1826–1830) when a Royal Commission on the Scottish Universities investigated all aspects of life in the four[71] universities. It is quite incorrect to say that the Royal Commission found the same degree of indolence and mismanagement as the 1718 Commission of Visitation had discovered[72] and, indeed, in the first quarter of the nineteenth century the university had continued with the improvements, both academically and administratively, that were already in train during the last two decades of the previous century. The most prominent among the innovators was Thomas Chalmers, who lectured on a variety of topics including political economy and mathematics, as well as combining this with his Church of Scotland living at the nearby parish of Kilmany. An interesting area where Chalmers sought reform was abandonment of the award of degrees in medicine. This was quite understandable at the time because throughout the eighteenth century degrees from St Andrews in medicine had been awarded *in absentia*, simply on the receipt of testimonials from two physicians and this at a period when the Faculties of Medicine in Edinburgh and, to a lesser extent Glasgow, were leading the world.[73] One purchaser of a St Andrews degree in medicine was the French revolutionary Jean-Paul Marat. From 1799 when some proof of appropriate medical training was sought together with examination by the university the supply of applicants declined to little more than an average of three each year.

Since the report of the Royal Commission was not published until the year after Andrew Jameson had left St Andrews, his time there would not have differed essentially in its curriculum or manner of instruction from that experienced by someone fifteen to twenty years

---

[71] Until 1860 there were five, because King's and Marischal Colleges in Aberdeen led separate existences before uniting in 1860.

[72] Cant, R. G., op cit p. 100.

[73] Benjamin Franklin encouraged young students of medicine in North America to complete their training at Edinburgh.

previously. We know exactly how a St Andrews undergraduate of the 1820s lived because his years there overlapped with those of Duncan Dewar, a man from a financial background not dissimilar to his own. Dewar kept a detailed record of all his financial transactions. His expenditure for each six month session was £14, which sufficed for lodgings (all found), purchase of books and class fees.[74]

According to R. G. Cant, the most recent historian of the university, the curriculum for an arts degree had hardly changed for a hundred years.[75] The first year consisted of Junior Greek and Junior Humanity and these subjects were taken again in the second year but at Senior[76] level and with the addition of Logic and Mathematics. In their third year the undergraduates studied Moral Philosophy and Mathematics, while in the fourth year there was added Natural Philosophy.[77] Students who had completed these four years satisfactorily could proceed in their fifth year to the degree of BA, securing either a pass or an honours award. A sixth year of study in the more modern subjects of Chemistry, Natural History and Political Economy could lead to the degree of MA.[78]

In 2005 St Andrews University published its *Biographical Register*.[79] This gives biographical sketches of all staff and students associated with the university between 1747 and 1897. It shows that the subjects taken by Andrew Jameson differ slightly from those suggested by Cant. In his first year he took Junior Humanity and Junior Greek and he repeated these subjects at senior level with the addition of Junior Mathematics; there is no mention of Logic unless this was a sub-set of mathematics. In his third year he continued with Humanity and Greek with the addition of Ethics, which is probably the Moral Philosophy of the Cant curriculum. The *Biographical Register* states that he studied

---

[74] Lang, Sir Peter Scott, (1926) *Duncan Dewar, a Student of St Andrews 100 Years Ago, His Accounts.* St Andrews University.
[75] Cant, R. G., op cit p. 107.
[76] The term used by the university was *provectior*, which can be translated as "more advanced".
[77] More widely known today as physics.
[78] By 1839 three years of study were all that were required for a BA and four for an MA. In 1861 the BA was abolished.
[79] The author was Robert Smart.

Political Economy and Mathematics 2 (senior?) but presumably he kept his classical languages going as well. For his fifth and final year the *Biographical Register* lists Humanity and Greek again with the addition of Natural Philosophy.

Andrew Jameson was not unusual in matriculating at the age of thirteen, but few of his contemporaries can have rivalled him in the depth and breadth of the learning he already possessed on going up to university. Even although he was living at a period when people entered upon adult life much earlier than today, anyone reading his diaries must make an effort to recall that they were being written by someone who today would be considered little more than a child. His diaries are less a narration of day-to-day activities than a general commentary on undergraduate life replete with references to contemporary and classical literature and history. Although these diaries are the prime source of his years at St Andrews and provide an early indication of the vast learning that was the foundation of his later career, their composition sometimes makes it difficult to follow his life in any regular sequence.

Unfortunately, there are no diaries earlier than that of 4th October 1826 to 4th April 1827. It is unlikely that Andrew Jameson did not begin to keep a diary until he entered his third year at university because he makes no mention on 4th October 1826 of a decision to start keeping a diary; indeed, the first entry reads like a continuation from a previous one. Earlier diaries, assuming they existed, may be lost. There is a third possibility for the absence of any diaries for 1824–26 and this is that at a later date they were destroyed. In the diaries that have survived there are individual pages where parts have been subsequently torn out and, sometimes, a few consecutive pages neatly cut out close to the binding. Since the diaries do not make for thrilling reading, it is rather frustrating when excisions occur, especially when they seem to be just at the point when something more interesting may have been written. One example is from March 1827 when he writes "there being a party in our house – delightful singing from Mr Grahame – It is my duty to record" and what was recorded has been excised.

Nothing that Andrew Jameson may have written about his first two years at St Andrews University has survived, other than a thin notebook with some comments headed "Notes of Dr Hunter's observations in the Session 1824–25". Since these notes are concerned entirely with the use of Latin by Sallust and his interpretation of some Roman customs such as manumission, they tell us nothing about the young student. Even correspondence between him and his family is scant, consisting but of four letters during his first year. In November 1824 his father[80] agrees to his request for a watch. This letter reveals two, possibly closely related, characteristics of Andrew Jameson (Senior). Some excerpts of the letter deserve to be quoted.

> As to the watch I have no objections to give you one for the reasons you mention and I always feel much pleasure in complying with the wishes of any of my dear Children particularly when they do so well to deserve it by their attention to their education and improvement. But I want to be in cash before presenting you with this article for the regulation of time.

> I am disappointed at your losing one of your numbers in the genders – I still hope however to hear that you are a Conqueror over your Antagonist and that I will again have the satisfaction of seeing your name in the Newspapers as the Winner of a prize at the University of St Andrews.

As already stated, the remuneration of sheriff-substitutes was not generous. In an earlier letter[81] from Robert to Andrew we learn that their father, when he heard that a landlady at St Andrews was asking £4 for accommodation for the first session of the academic year 1822/23, had instructed Robert to offer her £3:10. Secondly, Andrew Jameson (Senior)

---

[80] A. Jameson (Senior) to A. Jameson (Junior), 29th November 1824.
[81] 25th October 1822. This is the letter already referred to on p. 33 supra, where Robert commiserates on the death of Mr Moncur.

states that he is strapped for cash, and one reason may have been that the reimbursement of the expenses of his visits to London had yet to be paid. According to the Memoir[82] Sheriff-Substitute Jameson was awarded in October 1824 what would then have been the very large sum of £936 9s. 6d "for his trouble and expenses". Moreover, the improvement in salaries obtained as a result of that visit did not come into effect until the following year.[83] For that reason Andrew would have to wait for his watch. The winning of prizes at St Andrews would relieve some of the financial burden of supporting his son and so it was quite natural for Andrew Jameson to encourage his son in the manner he did.

In this letter of 29th November 1824 Andrew Jameson (Senior) looks forward to seeing his son and John Ogilvie on the next Saturday and that Andrew must not fail to call upon a Mr Gillespie. Mr Gillespie was the Dr Gillespie who lectured in humanity and whose class Andrew would be attending in his third year. Andrew and Melville[84] Jameson were fortunate in the acquaintances that their father had within the university. In addition to Dr Gillespie there were Dr Hunter and Dr Chalmers. Dr Hunter had been his father's tutor, was now Professor of Humanity, and as stated earlier, later became the Principal of the United College. Dr Chalmers took a keen interest in the Jameson brothers and the reason was his remembrance of their mother.[85] The memorialist had this to say of their association:

> Her kindness at this period[86] was never forgotten by Chalmers. Indeed his remembrance of her was accompanied by a peculiar tenderness, which often surprised me. Often in the midst of his triumphs of his later years, when Scotland rang with his fame, have I been stopped by him in the street and after his usual warm salutation, he would become abstracted – his features assume a dreamy aspect

---

[82] Memoir, p.126.

[83] v. p. 28 supra.

[84] Melville went up to St Andrews in 1827.

[85] v. p. 17 supra.

[86] i.e. the early years of his ministry at Kilmany. v. p.17 supra.

and then he would ask with pathetic interest "Do you remember your mother?" I could only reply "Alas, no: I only remember her funeral." And then he would seem to think and again ask about her children. This he did often and seldom did he meet me, without putting the same question. And in the last note I had from him, on our beloved father's death, he referred to the kindness and friendship of that early period. It was owing to this intimacy that at St Andrews two of her children were invited to the Sabbath School, that he assembled in his house and that he took a sort of peculiar charge over us, when at College.

Melville added a small postscript to his father's letter of 29th November, saying that their hawk died on Tuesday. A few days later Robert Jameson wrote from Cupar to ask his brother to return his (Robert's) black portfolio that was in the trunk he took to St Andrews and to "get one of your own". He refers to the dead hawk and said it died of starvation. "If Melville had not time to feed it, it ought to have been given away." He concludes with the hope that Andrew "will succeed in the Genders", clearly a reference to what their father had said in his letter of a few days earlier.

Apart from two letters in April 1825 from Andrew Jameson (Senior) to his son at St Andrews there is no extant correspondence until August of the following year. One of the two letters asks that accommodation be arranged for him at St Andrews because he is attending a "Jubilee Dinner" for Professor Hunter. The other letter is very short and says "I have received yours and approve of your plans – I have no time to say more – you can pay all your debts when you get your bursary from Mr Hunter, [presumably Professor Hunter] which you will do upon your return." He adds the briefest of comments that his second son, James, is about to sail for China.

In the absence of any other information about Andrew Jameson's first two years at St Andrews University, we must assume that he followed the curriculum already described.[87] It is possible that he did

---

[87] v. p. 39 supra.

succeed "in the Genders".[88] He was certainly in receipt of a bursary at the end of his first year and although there is no reference to its provenance or amount, it appears to have covered what debts he had incurred and were still owed at the end of the session.[89]

Although the Memoir tells very little about these first two years of his university life, there is a most interesting account of social life in Cupar at this period.

> The year 1825 was disastrous to the town of Cupar and its neighbourhood. The Fife Bank stopped payment and many of the principal inhabitants became insolvent. The Directors were much blamed by the public and I believe they had helped themselves to the capital. Sober men were inclined to think that this disaster was the natural consequence of the sensual indulgence that had degraded the society of Cupar for many years. Certain it is that this little town had acquired an unenviable character for the excess to which eating and drinking and card playing were carried on. The presence of a considerable number of French officers in the town during the late war, as prisoners on their parole, had not improved the tone of morals. The doctrines of the Gospel were not preached in the pulpits. The blight of unbelief was on the place and the fruits were seen in the preference given to animal indulgences and the pursuits and amusements of the world.

The author did not exclude his own father from his censure.

> Our father's hospitable disposition and easy friendly temper exposed him particularly to the temptations of this style of society, and his brother-in-law Mr James Thomson, a great card player, sometimes brought parties to the house without

---

[88] In February 2011 the author wrote to the Professor Stephen Halliwell, who occupied the chair of Classics at St Andrews University, asking if he could throw any light on "the Genders". In a courteous reply he said that neither he nor any colleague could identify "the Genders".
[89] This was almost certainly the Ramsay Bursary. v. p. 30 supra.

being invited. The evenings were spent in drinking Whiskey [sic] toddy and playing at whist. Many a weary night were the family deprived of domestic quiet and comfort by the inroads of these poor bon vivants, not a few of whom came to a poor end afterwards. Many unhappy youths followed the pernicious example of these bad times and ruined both their health and their character. The ruin of the Fife Bank put an end to much of that bad style of social life and was so far a blessing to the place.[90]

By contrast with the scanty information that he supplied about his first two years at St Andrews University, Andrew Jameson gave detailed accounts of two walking tours that he undertook in the summers of 1825 and 1826. Walking was the commonest means of getting about before the arrival of the railways unless one owned a horse, either for riding or for pulling a conveyance such as a gig, and the Jamesons did not have one. Andrew always travelled between his home and St Andrews on foot and so a walking tour presented no problems to him. Indeed, over the next few years he would make many excursions on foot, including travel in Europe and would write copious notes on what he had seen and done.

In early August 1825 he went first to Dysart, where he stayed with Captain Normand and his wife Janet.[91] Mrs Normand was a daughter of his paternal grandmother Sophia Anderson by her first husband, John Anderson, town clerk of Dysart. On his early death he had been succeeded in that position by John Jameson, who shortly afterwards married his relict.[92] Andrew continued his tour on to Burntisland, where he received hospitality from a Mr Aitken and his two unmarried sisters. All that is known of them is that they were "connected" with the Andersons[93] and they are mentioned here only because the elder

---

[90] Memoir pp. 130–31.

[91] She was also known as Sophia, according to a genealogical table kindly supplied to the author by Mr Christopher Normand of Worthing, Sussex. Her husband is described as a shipmaster. v. p. 14 supra.

[92] v. p. 11 supra.

[93] Sophia Jameson, his grandmother, was the daughter of a John Anderson of Kirkton, Burntisland.

of the two sisters left a legacy of £100 to Andrew Jameson's sister Sophia.[94] He went on to Dunfermline where he met two brothers called Russel "brothers-in-law to Mr Gray of Perth"[95] and then journeyed on to Graycraig, the home of his grandaunt, the formidable Miss Jameson. After a few days there he returned home to find Robert ill and his brother's condition did not improve until the following summer.

All that the Memoir tells us of Andrew Jameson's second session at St Andrews is that "After a winter of pretty hard study I got several prizes at the end of the Session in April."[96] There follows a long account of his walking tour of North East Scotland.

From both the Memoir and letters home together with a document written soon after his return to Cupar on 23rd September 1826, we know all the places he visited on this tour. It is a most detailed itinerary and states at what points he travelled on foot, where he used the public coach service and where he hired a horse. He calculates that he travelled 414 miles on foot, 234 by carriage and 109 on horseback. He estimates the cost of travel as 1¼ pence per mile. The same document gives the itinerary of a much shorter walking tour undertaken by Melville through Fife, Clackmannanshire and Kinrossshire, during which he walked 82 miles, used the public coach service for 61 miles and hired a horse for 16 miles. The cost of Melville's tour, which included two visits to their grandaunt Miss Jameson of Graycraig and another two to their aunt at Drums, was calculated to cost one farthing per mile cheaper than his elder brother's. This scrupulous account of the travels of the two brothers is highly informative and would be replicated in the future, when Andrew journeyed in the Scottish borders and, later, in Europe.

Andrew Jameson left his Cupar home on 3rd August 1826 and the early part of his journey was uncomfortable because he was wearing new shoes. After spending a night at Broughty Ferry he found it less painful to walk barefoot along the seashore and links to Arbroath, where

---

[94] The Almanack records her death in May 1827 and the legacy to Sophia. Andrew Jameson(Senior) attended her funeral.

[95] Presumably some connection of George Gray, who was to marry his sister Sophia, although the genealogical tables do not record any Gray connections with persons called Russel.

[96] Memoir p. 133.

he visited the abbey. He went on to Montrose by coach. He carried with him an instruction, dated 3rd August 1826, from an Alexander McNab of Cupar to the guard of the Union Coach from Dundee to Aberdeen, that "Mr Jameson of this place is on a walking tour and should he present this to any Guard of the Union Coach I request that they give him a ride free of charge and I will explain to them at Cupar why this should be done." After McNab's signature there comes a further instruction, this time from an Archibald Rhuich, presumably also of Cupar, who writes "In case the Bearer presents this to the Guard of the Star coach from Elgin to Inverness, he is to ride free."[97]

At Aberdeen he stayed a few days with a Professor Davidson, who "was related to some of my relatives and was intimate with the Graycraig and Dundee families of my kin".[98] On the 10th August he set off for Ellon. After he had crossed the River Don at what he called the "Auld Brig of Don", now known as the Brig o' Balgownie,[99] he caught up with another young man, who was travelling in the same direction. They breakfasted together at Ellon and before they parted Andrew Jameson was invited by his new acquaintance to spend a few days at Aden,[100] his father's country seat that was by the village of Old Deer. Andrew went on to Peterhead and the following day walked down to Aden, where he was warmly greeted by Peter Russel[101] and Mary, one of his sisters. We can judge from three letters to his sister Sophia[102] that Andrew must have stayed about five days at Aden during which it is clear that he enjoyed the luxury of this great country house and the company of some of his new friend's six brothers and five

---

[97] From the itinerary we learn that he interspersed travel by coach with walking. For example, he walked from Dundee to Arbroath, took the coach to Montrose, walked from there to Stonehaven and then reached Aberdeen by coach. The pattern was similar for the rest of his tour.

[98] Memoir p. 136.

[99] One of the oldest bridges in Europe, it was built in the 13th century but extensively renovated in 1605. It is open now for pedestrian traffic only.

[100] Pronounced as if it had two ds and not as the famous place of barren rocks on the Yemeni coast. Aden is now owned by Aberdeenshire County Council and known as Aden Park: it is open to the public.

[101] After 1835 the family spelled their name Russell.

[102] Unfortunately, all three were written on the same piece of paper. Part of the third letter is written at right angles to the first, making this third letter virtually illegible.

sisters. In the second of his three letters he writes that he had left Aden the previous day "and I need not say with what regret. Indeed the whole seems like a dream. However you may expect to see some of the young men during Winter on their way to Edinburgh and I am sure you'll find them agreeable. They are to write to me first." From a letter Russel wrote to Andrew Jameson on 21st August 1826 we learn that, on leaving Aden, Andrew had been accompanied by his friend first to Troop Head, a rocky outcrop on the Banffshire coast, and thence to Banff. The memoir states that they parted on the next morning at 4.00 a.m. and this otherwise mundane comment demonstrates how early, compared with this century, a day began. Aden lies 25 miles from Banff but Russel wrote that although he had walked all day "I was not so much tired so that I could not take a game of cricket, which I did with great pleasure being so long absent from it. There is to be a great match at cricket tomorrow for a wager."[103]

On the 19th August Andrew Jameson had reached Elgin and looked back with a degree of wonder on his stay at Aden. "What changes!! Helping out soup at Aden on Tuesday drinking wine and eating bride's Cake in Gordon Castle on Friday and finishing a letter to my sister in a writer's office Elgin, the city of the Moffats.[104] God be praised I am in good health and as you may see by my letter in excellent spirits. Oh nothing like walking and that by oneself, what a feeling of independance [sic] and conciousness [sic] of [illegible word]. I expect a letter from you at the Bairds, which you must write whenever you receive this." After the usual affectionate farewell there is a postscript. "I hope you will favour me with a long letter. It is astonishing how well I like you, when I am trudging along a dreary road. I am perfectly certain that it is exceedingly favourable for the exercise of the Social

---

[103] The letter is peripheral to any research on Sheriff Jameson but it has information about the Russels that is of interest to Mrs Helen Chavez, Archivist at the Arbuthnot Museum in Peterhead, who is carrying out research on the Russels. The mention of the cricket match is of particular interest both to Mrs Chavez, because she is trying to locate the cricket field at Aden, and to Mr Neil Leitch, the official historian of the Scottish Cricket Union. Both Mrs Chavez and Mr Leitch have been sent copies of Peter Russel's letter, which provides incontrovertible evidence that cricket was being played in north-east Scotland as early as the 1820s.

[104] Presumably some distant family connection or friends.

affections. Give my kind Comps to Papa, Bob and Melville and Miss Baird and Elizabeth Thomson and sister."

After a short stay with a widow in Forres, a friend of his uncle Captain James Jameson, he set off for Arabella Farm, which lay between Nigg and Tain and was tenanted by Alexander Baird, a brother of the Miss Baird who had been responsible for bringing up the children of Andrew Jameson (Senior) after the death of his wife. Awaiting him at Arabella Farm[105] was a long letter from his father[106] giving him advice on where to travel and whom to see. He was welcomed as a member of the family and after resting a few days resumed his walking tour, accompanied by Thomas Baird, one of Alexander's sons.

Their route took them west from Arabella Farm on horse to Dalmore on the Cromarty Firth and thence by a gig north to Invershin from where they walked up through Lairg to Altnaharra. It is interesting to recount what Andrew Jameson says in his memoir about his journey through country that was now almost uninhabited on account of the "Clearances" that had occurred just a few years earlier.

> Next day we marched to Tongue on the Northsea coast, having seen during these two days nothing but a succession of green hills and valleys without one inhabitant. But we noticed many sad vestiges of former homesteads and cottages, from which the noble peasantry of Sutherland had been driven to make a solitude for sheep and thus encrease [sic] the rents of the proprietor. Once or twice we talked with a passing wayfarer and were told these very straths

[105] Andrew Jameson (Senior) had addressed this letter to his son "care of Mr Alexander Baird, Cromarty Mains, Cromarty". Peter Russel had addressed his letter "care of Mr Baird, Arabella Farm, Rossshire". Did Mr Baird own or rent two farms that were on different sides of the Cromarty Firth? We know from the itinerary that Andrew Jameson called at Cromarty, having previously been at Fort George, and stated that the journey between these two places was only ten miles. He must, therefore, have taken a boat from Fort George across the very narrow strait of the Moray Firth to either Fortrose or Rosemarkie and walked up to Cromarty. The itinerary then shows that he walked only seven miles from Cromarty to Arabella Farm that was located between Nigg and Tain. Consequently he must have taken a boat across the equally narrow entrance to the Cromarty Firth, and then have walked on to Arabella Farm, now known as Arabella Holdings.

[106] Andrew Jameson (Senior) to Andrew Jameson (Junior), 11th August 1827.

used to maintain and turn out hundreds of armed men. Cruel
and I believe suicidal policy! Which the descendants of the
oppressor, may, as well as the country, yet rue, lamenting
the want of such men as formed the Sutherland Highlanders.

They then walked eastwards along the coast through Melvich to Thurso,
where they hired horses to take them to first to John O'Groats and then
south to Keiss. Their homeward route was through Wick, Berriedale,
Brora and, again, to Arabella Farm, where they found Alexander Baird
ill in bed.[107] Andrew then walked by way of Dingwall to Inverness,
whence he took the coach to Perth and covered the 22 miles from there
to Cupar on foot.

Nine days after his return home Andrew Jameson was back in St
Andrews. From this date, 2nd October 1826, we have a continuous
series of diaries and consequently a personal and detailed account of his
undergraduate life. The content of these diaries is very different from
what one might expect to find in one written by an undergraduate today
because in addition to fairly standard entries on classes taken, essays
submitted and intercourse with other students, there is a great deal of
self-criticism of a painfully agonising kind. Although applying to his
studies a strictly imposed code of continual and dedicated attention
that would be daunting to almost all modern undergraduates, he often
writes at some length in a manner reminiscent of the line "O'er my own
shortcomings weep with loathing" in Paraphrase xx. It would be both
tedious and pointless to reproduce these many entries, and that which
he wrote on 4th October 1826 will suffice as an example of the genre:

> The lusts of the flesh were daily gaining ground, and if I did
> not endeavour to stem the current of corruption in time, I
> might soon be unfitted for staying it for ever. This, with the
> considerations that it was my duty both to my Creator and
> myself to live so as to be prepared for that awful change,
> wherewith all flesh must undergo, God only knows how

---

[107] He died a few weeks later and, as the Memoir relates, "the family were scattered".

soon, and that, if I was spared to a good old age, the remembrance of a virtuous life, of the performance of my duty to
God and Man, would be my only consolation, when standing
on the brink of eternity; and would alone fit me for heaven;
all urged me to bestir my self, and consider my latter end.
There was a time, when this however solemn, would have
had no effect upon me but now by the blessing of God it has.
May he in his infinite wisdom and mercy complete what he
has begun, that he may guide me in the way I should go, and
enable me to believe sincerely in the saviour, and imitate, as
far as Mortal can, his noble character.

The concept with which the young Andrew Jameson was wrestling was
the deadly sin of sloth. Today sloth is thought of usually in its physical
sense but its true and original sense is entirely spiritual. The other six
deadly sins – pride, envy, wrath, avarice, gluttony and lust – are believed
to combine in such a manner as to weaken the senses and thus render them
first slow to respond to the commands of God before ultimately sending
them into a permanent sleep of complacency. The virtue that contends
with sloth is zeal, the persistent endeavour to remember and fulfil God's
commands to mortals. It was in passages such as that immediately above
that Andrew Jameson would sometimes confess what he believed to be
a decline in the full and proper attention to his studies that zeal required
and this backsliding was therefore contrary to his duty to God, his Maker.

In his first entry in the diary on 2nd October 1826 Andrew Jameson
writes that he had promised his father to return from his walking tour
to the north "a month previous to the commencement of the Session;
and redeem by close application the time, that I had thrown away in
the late summer months". His books and clothes had already been
sent on 30th September, and on his first day back he was reading the
fifth book of Homer and the second and fifth of Juvenal's satires. He
also promises himself to set aside for each day 13 hours for study and
11 for "sleep, exercise and meals".

On 20th October Lord Melville was installed as Chancellor of St

Andrews University and he gave an account of this ceremony in his diary. This particular entry is an excellent example of how Andrew Jameson was already able to employ both clarity of expression and economy of words to present an account that is brief but fully descriptive of an important event.[108]

> The meeting was opened with the usual act of solemnity by the rector in his robes of office. He then requested his Lordship in the name of the Senatus to take the chair; which having accepted and the rector stationed at the foot of the table, both sides lined with the professors in their gowns, the two principals and professors of Divinity in cocked hats. His Lordship was addressed by Dr Buist, rector, in an appropriate and well expressed speech; in which the origin of the University was briefly noticed; and the characters of her former chancellors given at some lenth [sic]; and concluded with several wishes, hopes and compliments in more particular reference to the august personage addressed.
>
> He (the Chancellor) delivered a neat and tout á propos reply, extempore, and embraced every subject quod a partibus. The ceremony was concluded by a blessing from the rector and splendid copies of the Catalogue of the University Library being presented to the Chancellor (Lord Melville) and also Sir Henry Jardine and Dr Lee.
>
> The University gave a public dinner on this joyous occasion and more than a hundred guests sat down to table. My father was one of the number; in the course of the day he introduced me to Lord Pitmilly.[109] (Friday the 20th of October, 1826 A. D.)

---

[108] This was in all probability a result of his close acquaintance with the classics. The tortured and convoluted prose that is now commonplace can be attributed, at least in part, to the almost total absence of classics from school curricula.

[109] As David Monypenny he was one of the persons, along with Andrew Jameson (Senior), whom the Lord Advocate urgently requested to investigate the possibility of a French spy being at a hostelry in St Monans, Fife. v. p.19 supra.

Andrew Jameson (Senior) would have been a guest of the university on account of his appointment as Sheriff-Substitute of Fife at Cupar.[110] There would be other occasions when his position entitled him to be associated formally with St Andrews University and, as mentioned earlier,[111] this must have been of some advantage to his sons.

The university term commenced on 9th November 1826. Andrew Jameson had thus obeyed his father by spending a month in preparation for his entry into the third year of his studies. We learn from the diary that his preparation included reading the life of Count Vittorio Alfieri (1749–1803), the Italian poet and dramatist. Whether this biography was in Italian or a translation into English is not stated but one can hazard the guess that it was in Italian because he writes that he is "well satisfied with my application this week". Was this an early example of his command of foreign tongues? Although there is no mention of him studying Italian, it was his proficiency in that language that enabled him two decades later to revise the Criminal and Civil Codes of Malta. He also read a life of Alexander Pope and of a Eustace Bagwell, otherwise unknown to English literature.[112] Here we return to Andrew Jameson's concern about his relationship with God for he writes of Bagwell as "a melancholy example of the baneful effect of yielding to passion in the first place and neglecting religion in the second. Bagwell gradually descended into vice and misery and left this world an infidel and a Suicide." This unhealthy and unnatural introspection by one so young, had it continued in this vein, could well have had a deleterious effect on his future mental balance had there not been a reduction in its influence as he grew to more mature years.

He enrolled in the following classes: Moral Philosophy, Natural History, Senior Greek and Senior Latin. He is pleased that his friend James Wilson of Perth, "whom I had known intimately and with pleasure since the end of 1821", had returned to the university. He goes on to say that they had many conversations and when at Perth

---

[110] He was also a Freeman of the town, having been awarded this honour in 1815.

[111] v. p. 42 supra.

[112] There is no entry in the *Dictionary of National Biography*.

went on excursions into the neighbourhood. Andrew muses on the friendship and mentions Wilson "was some years older and I moved in a much higher state of Society and perhaps our companionship might have been improved had we resembled each other in these points. For he wanted that cultivation, which is only to be got in the better spheres of life and the refinements and amenities or courtesies of which are so powerful auxiliaries of an agreeable companionship." This may well have been true and, although it was a somewhat priggish comment to make, one must remember that the contents of a diary, unless specifically written with publication in mind, are essentially the private and personal thoughts of the author.

The young student may have been a model student but he was not above forgetting that his physical comforts emanated from a devoted domestic background. Soon his sister Sophia, now 16, and undertaking many of the household duties normally performed by a wife, was writing to rebuke him for not returning his washing on time. Tuesday was washing day and he must send it on Saturdays, "other wise it is both inconvenient for yourself and us".[113]

She also tells him that she is about to go to Edinburgh to stay with Mrs Jameson, her uncle's wife. She will be taking singing lessons and will meet many people because "Mrs Jameson has a very numerous acquaintance and in a very genteel circle." From this it is almost certain that her aunt was about to give her a season in the capital that was part of the process of coming out. She goes on to say that she has had a visit from George Gray who had business at Luthrie.[114] In discussions with him her father had said that Andrew was "speaking of studying some law books and might become a lawyer", George Gray gave it as his opinion that it was wrong for Andrew to divide his attention between his current studies and thoughts of a career in law. Nevertheless "after that Mr Gray had said that he had some books which he had read and which were of no use to him now, and he thought they might be useful to you – he would send them to you and along with them he would

---

[113] Sophia Jameson to Andrew Jameson, 24th November 1826.

[114] A village between Cupar and Newport.

write you a letter giving you advice about studying law". The books duly arrived and included *The Wealth of Nations*. Finally, she says that a letter had been received from John in India and that he had been appointed adjutant to the 18th Regiment. She notes that his letter was dated 20th June 1826 "which is very recently".

Two days later Sophia wrote again to her brother. She says that she had discussed with their father whether or not the books sent by George Gray had been a present or a loan and they had decided that Gray who "always does these things in such a handsome way" had left it to her brother to decide when he would return them. She goes on to say that she hopes that Andrew has got into the Debating Society. In a long farewell she writes "I expect to hear from you by the return of post tell me what you thought and about everything that comes uppermost".

Every first Monday in a month was a university holiday and on the preceding Friday Andrew would walk to Cupar to spend two nights with his family. The journey took about three hours and the diaries tell how much he enjoyed walking with only the moon and stars to illuminate his way. We learn from a letter of his father[115] that after one visit in mid-December 1826 he missed by one hour an opportunity to have a lift with Dr Chalmers in his chaise. His father had found himself sharing a coach from North Queensferry with Dr Chalmers and was pleased to report that Dr Chalmers had told him that his son had "an attitude of an attentive student" and that this, coming from such a source, had much gratified him. This letter concludes with the hope that the family will see him over Christmas "if you get any vacation over the Holy days". This is an interesting sidelight on the virtual absence at that time of any celebration of Christmas Day in Scotland.[116]

He did walk home on 23rd December. This must have served as a welcome, perhaps necessary, break in the programme of study that he imposed on himself that month. He finds that Greek "has taken up so

[115] Andrew Jameson (Senior) to Andrew Jameson (Junior), 16th December 1826.
[116] It may be recalled that the trial of Burke and Hare took place on 24th December 1828 with sentence delivered on the following day. Christmas Day did not become an official public holiday in Scotland until about 1960.

much of my time and with little improvement that I have had but too little for other and as necessary studies. I should not have entered into it had it not been for the honour which situated as I am I must maintain quantum posuit.[117] Last week, the second of December I have been up on an average at 5 o'clock running over the books of Homer, at which I have begun to have a dislike. The examination shall likely be at the end of this week. I have little hopes of succeeding from any state of preparation, or, I should say, want of it."[118] In an entry headed "Journal of Monday 18th of Dec. 1826" he writes that he rose at 5.00 a.m. and learned 40 lines of the third book of Homer, read about the buildings of Athens, walked 7.30 to 8.00 a.m., attended his Latin class, read Gibbon which he did for leisure "but was too often tempted to transgress on the hours of rigid study by the fascinating subject". He hears a very good lecture from Dr Chalmers "but cannot perceive the connection with his immediate subject of benevolence. Indeed, I am quite disappointed in this class from the want of precision and logical arrangement in all the enquiries of the eloquent lecturer. I thought that of all things this would not be a desideratum in a class the subject of which, to have clear and true notion of it, must be freed from all extraneous matter and at least be treated with perspicuity; or in a Professor, whose known proficiency in the strictest of all reasoning would argue propriety in all other points." After 6.00 p.m. he prepared some grammatical work on Greek pronouns for his professor. James Wilson called "and interrupted me for some time" before he turned his attention to the fifth book of Livy. A look at Tacitus followed. Finally, "Not satisfied nor dissatisfied with this day; hope, shall make some improvement tomorrow." He went to bed at midnight and intended to rise at 6 a.m.

Unsurprisingly he did not wake until just before 8 a.m. Although apparently working equally hard all that day he considers that he has behaved badly since he has done less than the day before and consequently asks God for assistance.[119] Possibly to compensate for

---

[117] It is possible that he is referring to a bursary that he holds.

[118] The date for this entry in the diary is 18th December 1826, but this must be a mistake for a slightly earlier date because the subsequent entry is also dated 18th December 1826.

[119] Diary entry 19th December 1826.

his late awakening that day he was up before 5 a.m. the next morning (20th December 1826) and studied assiduously all that day. He found some encouragement from the high approval he received from Dr Chalmers for an essay on gratitude that he had submitted.

Having returned to St Andrews on 26th December 1826, he immediately settled down to some study of Juvenal and, for some unexplained reason, went home again two days later. One wonders why he had come to St Andrews and not remained at Cupar. Still, he did not allow living at home to interfere with his studies for he used the opportunity to prepare some Latin and to read Horace with Melville. There is no reference to any celebration of the new year but perhaps that was delayed until the 2nd January 1827 because his entry for that day reads "Came to St Andrews in the evening with 3 other companions; behaved ill, swore, fell into a passion; oh how weak I am!" The following part of the entry has been roughly torn from the page but it is good to read that he was not always the paragon of virtue that a casual reading of his diaries might suggest. Nevertheless, the more austere aspect of his character was resumed on the following day, when he remained awake at his studies until 3.00 a.m.

Meanwhile Melville had been enjoying the new year with Captain and Mrs Jameson in Edinburgh where Sophia was still staying. They went to the theatre and Melville was most impressed by the party travelling there by coach from the house. On 31st December 1826 they stayed up until midnight and "got some posset which is customary on the last night of the year". Next day he went with his uncle to the "tavern where Mr Thomson lived and asked him to dinner". (The name Thomson occurs frequently in correspondence. Was this Thomson a brother – or other close connection – of the Thomson who lived at Eden Park, just outside Cupar, and was married to Sophia, sister of Sheriff-Substitute Jameson?)[120] Melville's comment on Thomson suggests the man was not entirely *persona grata* with the family because he writes "Mr Thomson was smooth as butter before Mrs Jameson." The following day their

---

[120] He cannot have been Robert Thomson, the former owner of Drums, from whom Captain Jameson purchased Drums.

uncle took Sophia and Melville to the museum where they "were highly gratified". On 5th January 1827, Melville "came over" this being the term used for returning to Fife across the Firth of Forth.

Andrew's unswerving attention to his studies had been prompted by the approach of an examination on the twelve books of the Illiad. The examination would consist of two papers, one on a Tuesday and one on the subsequent Saturday in the middle of January 1827. It is difficult to discover from the diary if this was a competition for a prize, which would explain his careful preparation, or simply a test that excited the competitive element in his character. Since there were only six students involved and he refers to them as candidates, it seems likely that some prize was involved. In common with students of today he decided to "spot" two areas, the ninth and the twelfth book, whereon he believed the examination was likely to concentrate. To his delight he found that his "spotting" had been correct. On the Tuesday the candidates were examined on the first three lines of the 9th book and he came first with only six mistakes while two men, Connel and Lee, whom he refers to as his opponents, both made seven. On the Saturday the questions were more difficult and more numerous but he found that he had again spotted correctly. That morning he had risen early, had looked over the first hundred lines of the twelfth book of the Illiad and when he was handed the examination paper had found that the passage was from the thirteenth to the thirty-second line. He writes that if the examination had been based upon a passage "which I had not prepared, I would have undoubtedly been ruined". He was not ruined, but when the results were published on 15th February 1827 he found that he had come second to Lee.

For the next few weeks he led a life that was less academically arduous than that to which he had committed himself before the examination. His father visited him in St Andrews and stayed overnight on the weekend of 17th/18th February, and a week later Andrew went over for a night to Dundee "where I found all well".[121]

---

[121] His father's sister Rachael had married James Ogilvie, a writer, who was a partner in the Dundee legal firm, J. & J. Ogilvie. v. 14 supra.

Disembarking from the ferry at Newport the following day, he met his father unexpectedly and then walked back to St Andrews, where he attended the Literary Society in the evening. Throughout this period, however, his diary reveals that he was tormented with religious doubt and on 18th February he wrote "I have now lived one month without God in the world." Thankfully, the requirement to concentrate his thoughts upon preparation for another intellectual challenge gradually replaced this unhealthy spiritual contemplation. This was the Greek Competition and he started serious study for it on the last day of February. Meanwhile, however, he had already sought assistance from a new quarter, Dr Grace, Rector of Cupar Academy.

Melville attended this establishment until he went up to St Andrews. If Andrew had been a pupil there, it can have been only for a brief period before he was sent to the grammar school at St Andrews.[122] On the other hand Andrew Jameson must have known the rector well enough to write sometime in January 1827 asking for advice on the study of classical literature. On 28th January Dr Grace replied with a very long letter full of the most erudite comment and displaying a vast knowledge of classical literature, philosophy and history. It is all the more extraordinary that Dr Grace begins by saying that some Glasgow business had "prevented me making the requisite investigations for the subjects you mention. Any hints therefore which I can offer must be very crude and must wear the flimsiness and irregularity of conversational remarks rather than the depth and order of well digested thought." There follows three and a half closely written pages on foolscap-sized paper and although the comments are obviously extempore the whole letter combines a lucidity and coherence that are remarkable. The many references to classical history and philosophy and to the debt of the Romans to Greek civilization indicate that Dr Grace knew the depth and extent of the fifteen-year-old Andrew Jameson's level of understanding in this area of learning. It is also a comment on the standard of erudition possessed by Scottish schoolmasters of that era.

---

[122] v. p. 29 supra.

As already demonstrated from earlier correspondence,[123] his father was anxious for his son to win prizes for academic excellence. Writing to his son on 12th February 1827, Andrew Jameson gave arguments for the importance of prizes for excellence of learning and from the nature of the language it seems possible that his son had argued against their worth. He makes reference to the award by the President of the Board of Control for India of a position in India to the best scholar of the two senior classes at Westminster College, London, "so I hope you will be convinced upon due reflection that prizes are useful and favorable to the progress of education and not against it". The letter continues with some family gossip[124] and then, as some afterthought, he has scrawled across the first page a list of prizes won by a Thomas Lewis at the last 1826 examination at Addiscombe College.[125] It would be interesting to know the financial position of Andrew Jameson (Senior) at this period. He was maintaining one son at university, another was soon to go up and their ailing elder brother was still dependent upon him as was his remaining daughter. It is difficult to argue that the father's advocacy of the value of prizes was anything other than their immediate financial benefit rather than their long term effect in the securing of appointments.

On the first day of March Andrew resumed his customary pattern of dedicated study and began his preparation for the Greek Competition. He worked hard on the 2nd and 3rd March and left for Cupar on the evening of the 3rd, walking through snow drifting in a north-east wind, and reached home at 7.00 p.m. The diary continues with the words "It is my duty to record that" and the top half of the next page has been torn out. Did he think better of committing something to paper that might not have been in the family interest? The second half of the torn page states he returned on the Sunday night to St Andrews. It is not possible to give a date of the next entry because of the torn page and the first word on the second part of that page is "Thursday".

---

[123] v. p. 41 supra.

[124] Sophia was still having her season in Edinburgh.

[125] No Thomas Lewis appears in the surviving documents. Addiscombe College, Croydon, was where the East India Company trained its army cadets.

It is reasonable to assume that this is an entry for 15th March 1827, where he writes that he is mentally and physically relaxed and that on the Friday and Saturday he had studied Demosthenes for the Greek Competition that took place at 10.00 a.m. on that Saturday. After the competition he walked on the West Sands, a form of relaxation that continues among students of today.

He then allowed himself another few weeks of release from his normal grind of study. Later that month he read an essay to the Literary Society on "the influence of government upon the advancement of the arts Sciences and literature, which met with a very favourable reception". He took another weekend at Cupar during which he read and enjoyed Byron's famous satire "English Bards and Scotch Reviewers".[126] He also found time to "write to Wilson, poor fellow. He left St Andrews at Christmas and has been detained at Perth by indisposition. I have to regret and feel the want of his excellent companionship." Wilson had written to him on 15th February and it is clear that he had been far from well during the previous term at St Andrews. "You can form no adequate conception of the misery [a strong word] mental and bodily which I endured the last month I staid at St Andrews." The reply from Andrew Jameson demonstrates his better side than when he confided to his diary his thoughts on Wilson's social inferiority.[127]

On Tuesday, 3rd April 1827 he admits that "I have not studied a syllable this fortnight, but have spent it in trifling among the students rooms and perusing works of fiction". The previous Friday (presumably 30th March) he was examined on the first ten Satires of Juvenal and Seneca *de providentia et de brevitate vitae*. "I was formerly [he must have meant "formally"] examined on Tacitus 2 first books of the History and the Germania. I am sorry I have not wrote [sic] Chalmers' Prize Essay on the origins, the rights and advantages of Property."

---

[126] In 1807 Byron had published his poem "Hours of Idleness". It was criticised with such sarcasm by Brougham in an article printed in the *Edinburgh Review* that Byron was driven to a riposte, "English Bards and Scotch Reviewers". It made a considerable impact upon literary circles at that time and for that reason has remained a significant event in the history of literary reviewing. The article had been anonymous and Byron was dead before it was revealed that Brougham had been the author.

[127] v. p. 54 supra.

However, he determines to return to the narrow path of righteousness and continues "This ensuing month I have to spend with diligence, improvement and satisfaction – I propose to write two essays with one exercise and to prepare well for the Greek." Four days later he rebukes himself because "I have as yet acted so far against this good resolution as to spend the whole of last week in novel reading. I have finished Woodstock, read The Antiquary and some other tales: and my mind is unstrung, my habits interrupted and my conscience offended."

The receipt of two letters from his brother Robert brought perhaps their father's rather than his brother's opinion of how a third-year student should be behaving. In the first[128] Robert says "be sure and get before the other fellows this last examination and carry off the first prize but I would advise you to take care of 'Taught at Perth'.[129] I expect to hear from Sophia every day – I will let you know when I hear from her – It[130] is to take place in June". Six days later Robert writes again to his brother and, after telling him that Sophia is expected home by the end of May, refers to an essay prize worth one hundred guineas (an enormous prize in 1827 when the average wage was under a pound per week) to be presented by His Majesty's Commissioners for visiting the Colleges for the best essay "On the national character of the Athenians and the causes of those peculiarities by which it was distinguished". Robert must have been referring to the Commissioners who were visiting all Scottish universities at this period[131] but there is no mention of such a prize competition in his younger brother's diaries.

From April 1827 there is a gap of almost two years in the surviving correspondence, apart from a letter (4th March 1828) from a Robert Birrell inviting Andrew Jameson (Senior) to the funeral of his son David. We are, therefore, dependent on the diaries and the Memoir for discovering what took place during this period in the life of Andrew Jameson (Junior).

The university year ended on the 30th April 1827, the day he

---

[128] Robert Jameson to Andrew Jameson (Junior), 5th April 1827.

[129] What this can mean can only be guessed.

[130] This is her wedding to George Gray.

[131] v. p. 38 supra.

entered his seventeenth year. The last three weeks of the month were not the happiest for the student because he was unwell throughout this period and he found that he had performed less successfully in the prize competitions than he had hoped. He came third in both moral philosophy and Latin and second in Greek. Apparently recovered in health, he spent the second week of May on a visit to his grandaunt, Miss Jameson of Graycraig, and then on 18th June there was the marriage of his sister Sophia to George Gray of Perth.

George Gray was a nephew of the Miss Gray, with whom Andrew had boarded when he was at Perth Grammar School, and Gray had always taken an interest in him. As he writes in his diary, "Her husband, George Gray, is an old acquaintance. He paid me much kind attention from the first, when I went to Perth, which he continued to the end of my residence in that city. I have twice received munificent presents from him; the first a fine edition of Langhorne's Plutarch, which I had often, whilst in Perth, borrowed from his library; and the second, this session, a number of books[132] connected with moral philosophy."

The marriage took place in the family home at Cupar. Her father had already made a present to Sophia of £100,[133] a considerable sum for someone who only five years earlier had asked Robert to reject an offer of rooms at St Andrews at £4 per academic term and negotiate for £3 10s.[134] In the forenoon Andrew and Melville walked out to Carslogie, just west of Cupar, "breaking off the richest branches of Hawthorn we could find to decorate the lobbies of the Auld Pudintour".[135] The diary records that "the exhortation of the officiating clergyman was solemn and energetic, though short. The parties concerned, after partaking of a slight repast in another room, set off for Perth in a carriage. The rest of the Company enjoyed an elegant dinner and excellent wines with much conviviality, and the evening was altogether spent in a manner appropriate to the occasion."

---

[132] v. p. 54 supra.

[133] The Almanack for 1827 states simply "24th May £100 to Sophia".

[134] v. p. 41 supra.

[135] The name occasionally and affectionately given to their home by the younger Jamesons. v. p. 21 supra.

George Gray had purchased Bowerswell House for his family home. The Memoir describes it as a "prettily situated villa on Kinnoull Hill overlooking the majestic Tay and the ancient city of Perth. Robert wrote me, the previous April, 'Papa thinks that Bowerswell is a very good looking place.'" It certainly was and remains so, but it would be more accurate to say that it was at the foot of Kinnoull Hill. This house would become well known in literary history because of its previous association with the Ruskin family and the ill-fated marriage of Euphemia, the first child of George and Sophia Gray, to the art critic John Ruskin.

For the rest of the summer the diary of Andrew Jameson mentions nothing apart from commentaries on books he was reading. This reading ranged widely over the classics, general history and recent novels and was thus a broadening experience as well as preparation for his fourth year at university. However, three pages of the memoir recall a walking tour undertaken in August by Melville and himself, which will be here recorded in some detail since they met several persons, who were to become well acquainted with them in later life.

They set off on 10th August 1827 and spent the first night under the roof of Captain and Mrs Normand, from whom Andrew had received similar hospitality almost exactly two years previously.[136] "Our other aunts next door tried to get us to stay" but the brothers were anxious to pursue their journey. The "other aunts" could have been Margaret Anderson, unmarried sister of Mrs Normand and Harriett Swine, who was married to a Dysart banker, both, like Mrs Normand, half-sisters of their father.[137] Their route took them through Dunfermline to Kincardine-on-Forth, where they crossed the river and came to Falkirk but not before they "inspected the great iron works of Carron, where the immense machinery, the prodigious furnaces and the large body of workmen about 800 or 900, struck our minds with astonishment".[138] From Falkirk they travelled to Glasgow by canal boat and thence walked to Paisley where they were welcomed by Sheriff-Substitute

---

[136] v. p. 45 supra.

[137] v. p. 14 supra.

[138] Memoir p. 145.

Campbell, an old friend of their father.

Although he was Sheriff-Substitute of Renfrewshire, Alexander Campbell lived in Dunbartonshire at Barnhill, a fine property at the foot of the Kilpatrick Hills that he had recently inherited from a maternal uncle called Colquhoun. He took his young guests in a small sailboat from Paisley down the River Cart to its confluence with the River Clyde and then along the Clyde to Dumbarton Rock from where they walked up to his home. There they met the sheriff-substitute's family. His two sons Neil and Robert were contemporaries of Andrew and Melville Jameson and "we soon formed an intimacy, destined to last during life. The three elder sisters were grown up and Margaret and Fanny were in the bloom of youthful loveliness. The three youngest were still little girls, Lexy being only seven."[139] The other two were Susan and Elisabeth.[140]

They spent a few days enjoying the Dunbartonshire countryside. Melville left on 20th August to visit their Dundee cousins and Andrew accompanied him part of the way. They crossed Loch Lomond to Inversnaid, climbed Ben Lomond and walked on to Aberfoyle, where they spent the night at an inn. Next day they called at the manse, where Dr Graham, a friend of the Campbells, welcomed them and introduced them to Dr Macfarlane, Principal of Glasgow University.[141] The brothers then parted and Andrew walked all the way back to Barnhill. A few days later he departed Barnhill, reaching home by the most circuitous route of Arochar, Inverary, Taynuilt, Oban, Lochgilphead and Greenock.

By the end of October 1827 his thoughts were turning to the resumption of the university session and possible entry into the competition for the Gray Prize. This required competitors to write Latin and English translations of the second Olynthiac[142] of Demosthenes,

---

[139] Memoir p. 147.
[140] The reason for giving what might seem unnecessary details about the Campbells is that Andrew Jameson was to marry Lexy and that references to other members of her family crop up in the diaries and correspondence.
[141] Principal Macfarlane and Andrew Jameson were later to meet on several occasions.
[142] These were orations by Demosthenes (384–322 BC) aimed at rousing the Athenians to resist the growing power of Philip of Macedon.

but after completing the first part he found himself to be "so deficient in Latin composition as to make writing the other almost a hopeless task". So, instead, he went off to Perth with Melville and enjoyed a week at Bowerswell, the home of their sister Sophia and her husband. On 7th November 1827 his fourth university session commenced at St Andrews, where he was now joined by Melville. They persuaded their father to allow them to rent furnished accommodation rather than board with the Misses Jervis.

At this point the Memoir introduces the names of two fellow students with whom Andrew Jameson remained friendly for the rest of his life. One was a slightly older student from England called Robert Lee,[143] with whom Andrew had been vying in competition for university prizes since both came up. He occupied furnished rooms in Toul West, a lane[144] running between Market Street and South Street, immediately next door to the Jameson brothers. He became a minister of the Church of Scotland and although he remained within the Established Church at the Disruption their friendship was retained. The other was Patrick Stirling, with whom he became particularly intimate for the rest of his life.

His diary now becomes less detailed than that which covered the period October 1826 to April 1827. All that is worth stating here is that he enrolled for classes in English Reading and Composition, French, Greek, Latin, Political Economy and Mathematics. On New Year's Day 1828 the four brothers, James (home on leave from the East India Company Maritime Service), Andrew, Melville and Robert, along with their father, were entertained by Captain and Mrs Jameson at Drums and two days later classes resumed at St Andrews. Just before Christmas students had learned the subject of a prize essay in political economy "On the respective parts which agriculture and commerce bear in the progress and stability of national wealth." It had to be submitted by 1st April 1828 and Andrew writes that he has "already begun to collect material".

---

[143] Already mentioned in the diaries. v. p. 58 supra.
[144] If it still exists, it has today a different name.

He had become very interested in political economy, no doubt stimulated by the lectures of Dr Chalmers, who had introduced this subject to the curriculum.[145] He comments at length upon an essay on the future of agriculture that he had to prepare for reading in class before Dr Chalmers and was pleased to receive the comment "that it was a very good essay". On Saturday, 19th January both Andrew and Melville were invited by Dr Chalmers to take breakfast with him in his rooms at St Leonard's College, and, as stated earlier, this connection with so distinguished an academic and theologian can have done them no harm. This friendship was not one-sided because the Jameson family became staunch supporters of Chalmers when, in 1843, he persuaded about one third of the ministers of the Church of Scotland to abandon their livings and establish the Free Church of Scotland.

The breadth of Andrew Jameson's reading is shown by his attention to another subject, French. Chalmers had introduced his students to the work of Horne Tooke,[146] a leading radical who had opposed the Enclosure Acts and advocated parliamentary reform. Andrew noticed a reference by this author to a treatise, *De la Formation Mécanique des Langues*, by President de Brosses.[147] He got hold of a copy and found it useful in composing a short philological exercise that sought "to prove that the abstract terms, expressions of several principal moral qualities in certain languages, have been formed upon the system of utility. I am far, however, from subscribing to the doctrines of this mercantile scheme of morality as well as of beauty." One has always to bring to mind that the age of the student who was discussing these philosophical matters was only seventeen.

On Friday, 1st February 1828 Andrew and Melville walked home to attend a farewell party for James, who was about to leave Cupar to join his ship at London. The diary tells us that this party "was distinguished

---

[145] v. p. 38 supra.

[146] John Horne Tooke (1736–1812).

[147] Charles de Brosses, usually known as President de Brosses, because he was President of the Parliament of Burgundy. This must have been mainly an honorific post because he lived many years in Rome during the middle of the eighteenth century. A learned scholar, he published many letters and treatises that were not published until late in that century. The particular treatise to which Andrew Jameson refers was written in 1765.

far more for scenes which I deprecated" and then the rest of the page is torn out, so that the nature of the scenes can never be known.

Over the second weekend of the following month there was a visit from their father and Robert. The three brothers had an enjoyable Saturday together "golfing, walking and putting". Andrew and Melville spent the following weekend at Cupar and the diary gives an account of how the family passed the two days. The brothers took an opportunity to fish under the walls of Dairsie Castle *en route* to Cupar but were unsuccessful. Their father had invited some gentlemen to dinner and they played cards while Melville and Andrew read by the fireside. Next day, Saturday, at 8.00 a.m., Mr Clephane, the sheriff,[148] came to breakfast. That afternoon Andrew went fishing and "hooked a very fine grilse". Robert was in Perth, presumably visiting their sister Sophia, and the two youngest boys had the company of their father all evening. On Sunday the family went to church both in the morning and the afternoon and "after dining sumptuously and making ourselves very comfortable we walked in here[149] very agreeably by ½ past 8".

The entry in the diary of 2nd April 1828 is full of self-criticism for what he calls "the most despicable use of my time". Certainly, he had made more visits home than usual and, while he was reading widely across his subjects, he does not appear to have devoted the same amount of time to his studies as in his third year. In particular, he had made no effort to gather material for the prize essay[150] on political economy that had to be submitted by the first day of April. From 25th to 28th March he made several attempts to draft out an essay but "everything promised a complete failure". However, he became more resolute by 29th March, worked steadily over the weekend and handed in his essay, with little hope of success, on the evening of the

---

[148] It must be remembered that Andrew Jameson (Senior) was a sheriff-substitute and that the Sheriff of Fife was an advocate in practice in Edinburgh. The term sheriff-substitute remained until the middle of the twentieth century when it was replaced with that of sheriff and sheriffs became sheriffs principal, who lived in the area for which they were responsible.

[149] Their lodgings at St Andrews. The time of arrival and the knowledge that it took three hours to walk from Cupar to St Andrews is an illustration of how early (in comparison with today) dinner was taken in households at that era.

[150] v. p. 66 supra.

last possible day for acceptance.

Three days later he set off to visit Sophia, walking the thirteen miles to Newburgh in time to catch the steamboat[151] that brought him to Perth at 5 p.m. While there he read Boswell's *Life of Johnson*, and although he deplored the egotism of the man and felt repugnance at his "rudeness and coarse manner", he nevertheless admired "the vigorous mind of Johnson and the entertaining and piquante details of Boswell". He breakfasted early on the Monday, took the steamboat back to Newburgh, walked to Cupar, dined with his father and Melville and walked back to St Andrews on Tuesday morning in time for his class in political economy.

The session was now approaching its conclusion and on the evening of 17th April 1828 Andrew "called upon Dr Gillespie, the assistant and future successor of the professor of humanity, and spent some pleasant hours with him". Whether he had been invited or whether he just called in the hope of seeing him must be left to conjecture. It does, however, conjure up a delightful picture of a bygone age when a member of the university staff and one of his students could discuss classical literature almost as equals. On the following Saturday, Dr Chalmers, who was leaving the university to take up the chair of Divinity at Edinburgh University, gave a breakfast to Andrew and some other students, during which "he took occasion to confute in a very animated manner the vulgar notion that a high mathematical intellect was inconsistent with great imaginative powers". This does not seem to be a proposition that needed much evidence for its refutation, but since mathematics was one of the many subjects for which Dr Chalmers was highly reputed, he was perhaps very sensitive to this slight, real or imagined. Breakfast over, Dr Chalmers showed his garden to his students as well as the garden of the adjoining house that had formerly been part of St Leonard's College. Dr Chalmers also pointed out, in what Andrew Jameson somewhat oddly describes as "the eastmost domicile of the building", the study of George Buchanan, who had been Principal of St Leonard's from 1566–1570.

---

[151] This must have been one of the earliest steamboats on the Tay.

On this pleasant note Andrew Jameson completed his fourth university year, although there were still class examinations to take. These he "easily passed", winning second prize in political economy.[152] He chides himself, however, for his want of attention to diligent study and consequently this year "has been least marked by improvement". He came home on 3rd May and spent five weeks intermingling his reading of classical texts with excursions to Strathearn for fishing, one day catching a one-and-a-quarter-pound trout. He was with the family at Perth on 7th June for the christening of Euphemia Chalmers Gray,[153] the little girl named after her grandmother and her mother's short-lived sister.

He spent much of the summer on visits to relations. First he went to his aunt and uncle at Drums and engaged in several fishing expeditions. On the 1st July 1828 he walked over twenty miles to the home of his grandaunt, Miss Jameson of Graycraig, and remained with her for six weeks. Now a nonagenarian, she was in full possession of all her faculties and her young grandnephew "endeavoured to elicit all kinds of information about my ancestry from so good an authority and it was with as much honest pride as regret that I learned the family had fallen rather than otherwise". It is probable that this refers to the career of her father, Andrew's great-grandfather, who had dissipated the advantages he had enjoyed from an advantageous marriage and an established legal practice through his financial ineptitude and subsequent bankruptcy.[154] His son, her brother John, Andrew's grandfather, had also been beset with financial problems throughout his career. While at Graycraig her grandnephew enjoyed "the attractive society of my cousins who are models of ladylike conduct". Unfortunately, he did not give their names,[155] and perhaps it was one of them whom he found particularly attractive. "I had for the most part of my stay an affair of the heart in hand and was punished duly

---

[152] This, he says, was by the votes of his fellow students. It must be assumed that he did not win the essay prize in political economy.

[153] Born 7th May 1828.

[154] v. p. 10 supra.

[155] It is possible they were daughters of his father's sister Sophia, who had married James Thomson, the writer in Cupar. If so, the girl whom Andrew Jameson found so attractive might well have been Elizabeth, who was later to feature prominently in his diary.

by all its anxieties and vanity." He walked home to Cupar towards the end of August and then "vegetated for two months".

He and Melville returned to St Andrews at the beginning of November 1828 where they had taken new lodgings,[156] each with his own room in order that private study would be uninterrupted. The first entry in his diary reads "I may say I have lost a summer" and that "it is long, by far too long, since I have subjected my mind to that course of ardent and mental exercise that can deserve the name". He determines to address himself more conscientiously to his studies and recognises that this will require "strenuous exertion to overcome the dangerous habits of superficial thinking". He enrolled for classes in Latin, Greek, political economy, moral philosophy and natural philosophy.

In mid-November he went back to wrestling with his religious conscience. For two years now he had "continued in a state of irreligion", dating from November 1826 "when my mind took a decidedly serious turn in much solitary meditation". He was still, two years later, full of doubt about the existence of a God and remained "in such a state as it was easy to live in, but most appalling to die in. It was not belief nor unbelief: it is a state of uncertainty and indifference worse than rational infidelity, if there be such a thing."

By the end of November 1828, however, he was in a happier frame of mind because his time has been "properly employed" and he hopes that by following "a still more regular and rigorous course of study I may perfect what I have commenced". He makes no secret that he is finding it hard to keep up with the class in natural philosophy and that his difficulties arise out of his "utter want of advanced mathematics". Moreover, he cannot spare any time remedying this defect through private study because that would encroach upon the time necessarily devoted to other subjects that were now at an advanced level. Latin and Greek, in contrast to natural philosophy, were areas where success shone abundantly.

On Tuesday, 30th December 1828 classes ceased for seven days, another example of how Christmas was not regarded in Scotland as

---

[156] In the Memoir he describes it as "a comfortable house near the west end of North Street".

a holiday. He was still struggling with natural philosophy and states bluntly in his diary that the class had "been engaged in abstract and complex investigations concerning Rotation for some time, but I don't understand it". Nevertheless, having been examined on this day in natural philosophy, he writes that he "got off tolerably". Christmas had not been allowed to pass without some celebration and Melville and he had what he describes as "a select party to supper". It does not appear to have been the most sober of occasions because one guest called Mar was "rather elevated" and had to be seen home by Andrew. Then on the following night Andrew made what he called his "debut" at the Assembly and "danced with several young ladies". He follows this information with the most unromantic comment that "I saw or felt nothing however to make me regret that I had studiously abstained from the four preceding sessions. When one thinks of the whole scene there is a great deal of frivolity and vanity mixed up with it." On his last night in St Andrews before returning to Cupar he read a book, *L'Amoroso*, that described very vividly the deplorable state of manners in Naples and "the dangerous consequences of Englishwomen mingling too much in Foreign society. Since the war,[157] there appears to have been a great deal of mischief done."

Andrew enjoyed a pleasant week's holiday. New Year's Eve was spent with Melville at the home of a Mrs Carstairs, while a furious storm with thunder and lightning raged without. On New Year's Day he went to Dysart where he "was kindly received by the ladies", by whom he must have meant Mrs Normand and her sisters. On 2nd January 1829 he took the ferry across the Firth of Forth to Newhaven and stayed a few days with Captain and Mrs Jameson in Dundas Street, Edinburgh. That evening he attended a rout[158] at the home of a family called Patrick, where, arriving a little after 8.00 p.m. he "danced till 1 a.m. There were about 72 people of both sexes among whom were several fine-looking girls." He returned to Cupar on Monday the 6th and walked back to St

---

[157] Presumably the Napoleonic Wars.

[158] He is using this word in its now archaic meaning of "a large evening party or reception". (O. E. D.) There is no mention of his uncle and aunt accompanying him.

Andrews the following day. That evening he wrote in his diary "I must be very strenuous in my studies for some time now."

His labours of the previous term had not gone unrewarded because on the evening of his first day back at university he refers to success in what he describes as his "public and private exercises".[159] These were essays he had composed concerning the use of certain Greek suffixes, and since he has received "very liberal praise" in this area he proposes "to prosecute the subject most vigorously" and "to include in a public essay the result of these investigations and remarks on the nature and use of suffixes in general". One can but admire such dedication to etymological minutiae. His more immediate object, however, is to write upon "The Question of the Authenticity of Livy's Early History of Rome", an issue that had been engaging the attention of German scholars for the past few years.

He continued to work steadily throughout January and February and was pleased that he was making progress in what had been his weakest subject, natural philosophy. His assiduous attention to his studies continued into March when he became ill for over a week with what he refers to as "severe cold, headache and general lassitude" that rendered him totally indifferent to all academic work. He attributed this illness, probably correctly, to the massive intellectual efforts to which he was subjecting his mind, not least having read, in addition to his normal academic work, all eighty chapters of Cicero's *De Oratore* in four days. He made a full recovery, and the diary certainly does not suggest that when he resumed his studies he approached them with any lessening of his accustomed ardour.

On 22nd April 1829 he writes of receiving "the happy intelligence" that his brother James' ship had reached Southampton from China. It is interesting to note that there were no classes on 23rd April because that was the birthday of the king and that he had found time to read Scott's *Rob Roy*, although he feels "such indulgence is half criminal at this time, at least very imprudent" because the excitement of the novel is "inimical to grave study".

---

[159] One may perhaps hazard a guess that "public" essays were related in some way to prizes.

It has now become common practice in universities to hold final examinations for the award of a degree. This was not the case in the first part of the nineteenth century. Provided a student had completed satisfactorily the work that had been required of him over a particular session, he was permitted to advance into the following year of his course. It may be remembered that Robert had been unsuccessful with Greek in 1821–22[160] and, as far as can be judged from correspondence and the Almanack, he did not thereafter return to the university. Andrew Jameson does not refer to any end of session examinations in April 1827 but at the end of the following year he writes that there were class examinations, which, as far as he was concerned, presented no real academic challenge. For his fifth and last year he had no equivalent of today's final degree examinations.

All that we learn from his diary is that on 20th April 1829 the Latin professor appointed a committee of five students, of which Andrew Jameson was foreman, to decide on who should be awarded the class prizes. Their deliberations extended over twelve hours across the next two days and "without any encouragement from me" Andrew was accorded the title of "Facile Princeps".[161] He also won the prize for "English composition in the Greek". He received from the professor of natural philosophy a certificate that was "cautiously worded, but certified attention and exemplary conduct". These prizes and the certificate were distributed in the Parliament Hall[162] on 1st May 1829 in what must have been the equivalent of today's graduation. This ceremony, at which there is no mention of his father being present, marked the end of Andrew Jameson's career at St Andrews University. The previous day had been his eighteenth birthday, an age at which most of today's undergraduates matriculate for the first time.

His summary of his years at St Andrews is worth recording in full. The

---

[160] v. p. 29 supra.

[161] Indisputably foremost.

[162] The largest building available for such ceremonies until the building of the Younger Hall in 1929. It was called the Parliament Hall because the Scottish Parliament met there in 1646 when they tried and condemned the supporters of the Duke of Montrose whose attempt to restore the fortunes of Charles I had been ended by the rout of his army at Philiphaugh.

clarity of the script and the nature of the content make it almost certain that it had been carefully prepared before being entered in the diary.

> Thus ended my academical career at St Andrews. I reviewed the five studious winters, which composed it; and there was nothing either for much exultation or regret in the retrospect. A want of preliminary instruction retarded my advancement in the Mathematical branches. But I prosecuted the study of Classical Literature, of Moral Philosophy, of Logic, of Political Economy, of Philology and of English Composition with unaliated[163] diligence. Considerable proficiency in these departments has been the reward of my labours; and ten prizes, of which seven are of high rank, are the public rewards of my exertions; and five certificates are individual testimonials of success. I cannot reproach myself with indulging in idle dissipation, a vice too common among my fellow students; or with the more dishonourable practices of calumny and intrigue by which too many attempted to procure a paltry prize.
>
> The advantages which I owe to the College of St Salvator are manifold and inestimable. I will ever remember with pride her ancient Halls, which have educated my Father, my Grandfather and my brothers but neither shall I forget the private conduct of Alma Mater, her stepmother prejudices, her Aristocratic partialities, and detestable servility to power, family and wealth. The professors at St Andrews will find it their advantage to become somewhat less exclusive in their attention to wealthy fools and young men of little promise but great prospects. They are men whom patronage or merit has raised from obscurity, and young men of talent and respectability will never endure their studied neglect or paltry notice.

This is a damning indictment of the academic integrity of Scotland's

---

[163] There is no doubt that this is the word written in his diary. It does not appear in the O.E.D.

oldest university. Throughout his diaries Andrew Jameson makes no complaint about the academic staff except, rather oddly in view of his eventual national prominence, Thomas Chalmers. Yet his criticism of Chalmers was neither about neglect nor favours shown to undeserving students but about some lectures in moral philosophy, which, although excellent in themselves, appeared to have had little relationship to the curriculum.[164] Many of the professors invited students to breakfast or entertained them in their homes on other occasions and maintained the academic standards appropriate to their subjects. If they did demonstrate some partiality towards students in more comfortable circumstances than Andrew Jameson, it must be remembered that academic staff were remunerated in part through class fees and for that reason might have been prepared to make exceptions for academic weaknesses so that "wealthy fools" could be retained on their registers.[165] This does not, of course, excuse any willingness to assess academic work more highly than deserved, if that did in fact happen.

In his criticism of his fellow students there is a slight touch of Robert Burns' satire[166] on the self-righteous, who ask God to understand that while their failings are excusable those of others, being more heinous, deserve no compassion. On the other hand, if some students did indulge in deliberate misrepresentation and underhand methods to secure undeserved academic recognition, Andrew Jameson was correct to deplore their conduct. If any success did attend these unworthy stratagems the responsibility must have lain with those members of the university staff whom the author excoriates for their less than even approach to the assessment of their students.

---

[164] v. p. 56 supra.

[165] One is reminded of a case much later in that century, when a professor, unable to attract students to the course of study that he was offering, entered into a financial agreement with a local school to teach their pupils. A student publication subsequently published a witty satire on this curious arrangement:

> There was a professor MD
> Who had neither a class nor a fee
> So the wily old buffer
> He simply said "Suffer
> The little children to come unto me."

[166] "Holy Willie's Prayer".

CHAPTER THREE
Professional Training

The weather of summer 1829 was warm and sunny and Andrew Jameson enjoyed it to the full. He would not be returning to St Andrews and so no longer does his diary contain entries reproaching himself for wasting time that might have been more profitably employed in study. He paid visits to his relations and to neighbours, went for long walks and, above all, spent many happy hours at his favourite pursuit, angling.

He and Melville had walked home together on the afternoon of 1st May after the formal closing of the university session. The following day the family were at Drums, where his aunt and uncle hosted a celebratory dinner in his honour at which the sheriff, Andrew Clephane, was present. Andrew mentions that the "Madeira was excellent", as one would have expected at the table of someone as successful in his career as Captain James Jameson.

It will be appropriate at this point to say something about Sheriff Clephane, since he was to become a considerable figure in the life of Andrew Jameson over the next few years. Not surprisingly in view of his position as Sheriff of Fife and Kinross, he was often a guest at the table of his sheriff-substitute at Cupar and had come to form a very favourable impression of his son, Andrew, who described him as his "chief patron". Clephane was the younger son of an old Fife family, the Clephanes of Carslogie, whose family had owned a large house near Cupar for almost twenty generations.[1] Clephane was also well connected socially. His wife was a Douglas of Strathendrie and his mother's family had owned Kirkness House[2] near Loch Leven. This

---

[1] Memoir p. 157.

[2] It had been used by Oliver Cromwell in 1650 on his march north to defeat the remaining supporters of Charles II after the Battle of Dunbar.

was now the property of his niece, the Marchioness of Northampton,[3] who gave him permission to live there over the summer months. Throughout the four years that Andrew Jameson was to spend in his legal studies at Edinburgh, the sheriff often invited him to dine with his family at his town house. He allowed him the use of his library, introduced him to persons prominent in the law and, in general, did much to further his career.

That year, Sophia Thomson, a cousin of Andrew, had become seriously ill and the doctors gave her no hope of any recovery. At her request Andrew called to see her at Eden Park, her parents' home just outside Cupar and, immediately thereafter, at what appears to have been the suggestion of their father, he and Melville went off to stay with their sister at Perth. Sophia was suffering from what Andrew describes as "Inflammation of the Inner Coat of the Stomach" and she died a few days after his visit. His Thomson cousins were singularly unfortunate. The eldest, David, had already died and another had been severely disabled as a result of an accident aboard an East India company vessel. In November 1829 a third son, James, was shipwrecked in the Arabian Sea and, although taken to Bushire, died there of the privations he had suffered. Sophia also had two sisters, Jane, who married an alcoholic, and Elizabeth, for whom Andrew, as this chapter will show, at one time showed deep affection.

Andrew and Melville took two days on the journey to Perth because the first of these was spent fishing on the River Farg below what he refers to "our ancestral lands at Arngask". Perhaps he was recalling his visit of the previous July to Graycraig, when his grandaunt had told him about the improvidence of her father. It was, however, somewhat of an exaggeration to refer to Arngask as "ancestral". By the marriage of his great-grandfather to Margaret Gib, Arngask had come into the family but had been left in trust to their younger surviving son, John. However, through a stratagem that was legal but reflected no credit upon him, the father deprived his son of his inheritance.[4]

---

[3] In 1820 Sir Henry Raeburn painted her playing a harp.

[4] v. p. 9 supra.

A few days later Andrew crossed over to Dundee to meet his brother James, who must have been returning from London by boat.[5] On 15th June there was a family party where Andrew Jameson (Senior) had with him his sole surviving daughter and all his sons except John. As the diary records, "we did not forget him, who was in distant lands". Andrew Jameson (Junior) records that on the following day "a general dispersion took place" and, as events turned out, such a family gathering would never be repeated.

Andrew left for Edinburgh to spend a week at the home of his friend, Patrick Stirling, who was later to receive frequent mention in the diaries. He paid a visit to the Parliament House and was very impressed with both the building and the activities he witnessed. He also makes reference to a call he paid on a Mrs C. and "was gratified to see my amiable cousin in all appearance as happy as her friends could wish".[6] He then crossed over to Dysart and remained there for nearly a fortnight before returning home on 7th July.

Fly-fishing in this beautiful summer was now his principal pursuit and, possibly feeling a twinge of guilt at his neglect of any preparatory study for his law classes in Edinburgh, the diary enters into an argument expatiating on the benefit of the sport and of walking tours. "The frame is braced for exercise and all its muscular energy developed by repeated and varied exertion. The hand acquires dexterity and the mind, address,[7] at the same time that an acquaintance is gained with those sports, which may beguile many a weary hour of after life. The sporting or touring excursion leads to nature's happiest scenes of sublimity or beauty and insensible must the heart be that has not all

[5] We know from the Almanack that James arrived from London in July 1827 (presumably after a voyage to the east) and left for London in February 1828. The next entry concerning him is that he arrived home on 15th June 1829. The normal length of time an East India Company trading vessel took to reach the east and return was about a year to fifteen months, and this would fit neatly into James Jameson's period of absence from home. This, however, is somewhat at odds with the *Biographical Index of East India Company Maritime Service Officers 1600–1834* published by the British Library in 1999. According to this publication James Jameson served as fourth mate on the *London* 1827/1828 and 1829/1830. Is it possible that 1827/1828 is a mistake for 1828/1829?
[6] From this point on Andrew Jameson, frustratingly for anyone reading his diaries, refers to many people simply by the first letter of their surname.
[7] The word is used in the sense of "skill" or "adroitness".

its finer feelings kindled in the contemplation of fine scenery and the consequential enjoyment and cultivation of taste. It is part of man's immortal constitution and a remnant[8] of his divine origin that he desires little satisfaction from those exertions, which cannot extend their pleasurable influence beyond the day or hour on which it was at first felt; whose happiness cannot be diffused beyond the moment of enjoyment. Yet it would be folly to discard altogether the sources of pleasures even so transient. They leave an effect on the mind, when, oft repeated, which though only a faint emanation of this first excitement, yet lends a freshness to the spirit exhausted by that study, which is a wearying of the flesh."

Angling was also the sport most enjoyed by Sheriff Clephane and, during the dinner at Drums on 2nd May, he had extended to Andrew an open invitation to visit him at Kirkness House. Andrew spent four nights there from 20th August 1829 and was treated with the utmost courtesy throughout his visit. On the second day the sheriff took him fly-fishing on the River Leven, and on Sunday, after church, they climbed Ben Artie, described in the diary as the "Pride of Kinrossshire". Andrew gives a full pen-portrait of his host. "Mr C is the handsomest man one ever has a chance of seeing. His limbs are beautifully symmetrical, his chest in graceful and manly amplitude it would be difficult to match, his bold and rather haughty face and high bearing all unite in forming one of nature's favoured sons." On the day he left Kirkness House the sheriff even conveyed him on the back of his horse halfway to Graycraig, where he was expected by his 92-year-old grandaunt. After a fortnight at Graycraig he walked to Drums where he had a week's fishing during which he "killed in all nine dozen and a half". Today this might be considered slaughter rather than sport.

For the next six weeks, although fishing was not entirely neglected, he returned to his studies, paying particular attention to civil law, which, fortunately, he found very interesting, since it was "necessary to the profession of an Advocate at the Scottish Bar, for which I am destined". This is the first specific reference to his proposed career

---

[8] The word is used in the sense of a "surviving trace".

in the law apart from a comment made three years previously by his father to his sister Sophia.[9] He confides to his diary that he would have preferred to prepare himself for a career in medicine or the church and expresses some doubt about his prospects in the law. He makes it clear that since it is the profession that his father had always intended for him "that circumstance with his sanguine expectations and real influence form at present my only inducement to the choice" and so on 4th November 1829 he began his course of study in the Faculty of Law at the University of Edinburgh.

He had come across to the capital on 30th October to look for suitable accommodation and after some difficulty found satisfactory lodgings, described as a parlour and bedroom, with a family called Macfarlane in South Adam Street.[10] This was a most convenient location, since it was only a few minutes walk from where he would have to attend lectures. His curriculum was widely different from that undertaken by today's postgraduate students of law. Civil law, would, as he writes, "form the great object of my labours and demand most of my time". However, several other subjects would "severally engage my attention". These were French, German, chemistry and what he describes as "general literature". This is an excellent example of the breadth of study that was undertaken by Scottish students of that era and distinguished them from graduates of the only two universities in England, Oxford and Cambridge.[11]

He resolved to dedicate himself to a regular course of study that would mean a very busy winter. Meanwhile, he took the opportunity to reflect on the previous summer and its many days devoted to fishing, with the implication that there would be fewer opportunities in future to indulge in this pleasurable sport. What may be described as his "farewell to fishing" is beautifully written and on that account worth quoting in full.

---

[9] v. p. 54 supra.

[10] His friend, Robert Christie, also lodged with the Macfarlanes. The Memoir, p. 156, describes him as "studying medicine" but it is clear from Andrew Jameson's diary that he was a fellow law student.

[11] Within a few years England was to add London and Durham to the number of its universities.

I will ever remember with pleasure the many happy days I have enjoyed in the amusement of flyfishing, the pure joys of a serene and handsome spirit, of quiet scenery and agreeable excitement and poetic musing.

I shall always look back with grateful reminiscence upon the pleasant Saturdays devoted to that most philosophical recreation. When all vigorous with health and buoyant in the youth I set out for the pleasant streams of Rumgay[12] ... my experienced eye observing the clouds coming over the Lomonds,[13] the Avant Couriers of a convenient obscurity and delighted by the incipient murmurs of the south-west breeze in the woods of Tarvit.[14] When reaching the place appointed, I prepared my slender implements, "the tapering rod and full stretching line"[15] and sauntered along the verdant banks in the very fullness of a happy mind, thinking of old Isaac,[16] of Horace's[17] streams of love, of philosophic mysteries, of the world and its follies, of old times, of my despairing prospects[18] and a thousand phantasies.

When capturing the silvery trout and gradually filling my baskets, I followed the placid Eden[19] by road and brae, stream and pool, admiring the old castle of Dairsie[20] of memorable associations, the leaf-crowned hill of Kemback[21] and the lovely entrance of Dura Den,[22] until, contented with

---

[12] This is an area just outside Cupar.

[13] Two prominent adjacent and similarly sized hills in the middle of Fife.

[14] The Hill of Tarvit (now the property of the National Trust for Scotland) lies about three miles south of Cupar, the former county town of Fife.

[15] Since he uses quotation marks this may be taken from *The Compleat Angler*.

[16] Obviously Isaak Walton (1593–1683), author of *The Compleat Angler*.

[17] Quintus Horatius Flaccus (65–8 BC), Roman satirist and poet.

[18] He was about to prepare himself for the law, a profession wherein he did not believe he would succeed.

[19] A somewhat sluggish river that rises in Kinrossshire and flows past Cupar to reach the sea just north of St Andrews. It gives its name to one of four famous golf courses situated on the north side of St Andrews.

[20] Andrew Jameson and his brothers often fished a pool below the walls of this castle that stands halfway between Cupar and St Andrews but not on the Eden.

[21] A village on the Eden between Cupar and St Andrews.

[22] Still a well-known beauty spot near St Andrews.

my sport I turned homewards through the glades of Madden and the parks of Prestonhall,[23] my beautiful native town[24] in the distance and the green Lomonds beyond. My joyful steps by the Cart Haugh,[25] a brother sportsman greeting and envying the content of my spoil, my arrival at home, the enquiries, the congratulations and the supper of the delicious fry at night. How vividly these pleasing recollections recur to my memory in the midst of this great city.

Or perhaps varying my course I bent my steps another day up the river, wandered along Pitlessie streams, the woods of Crawford Priory, the seat of the last wretched remnant of Scotland's oldest Earldom and by the side of Ballomill[26] of royal memory. And after whiling the serene hours in the quiet exercise of the Art, roaming in the buoyant glee of youthful spirits through the plantations of Springfield.[27] The period of infancy or boyhood, when mellowed by the hand of time and softened by the flattering retrospects of memory, when its little pains and miseries are forgotten and its innocence and pure pastimes and freedom from harassing care alone remembered, is often assigned as the happiest portion of life.[28]

This particular entry in the diary concludes with a lengthy passage in Latin, wherein we learn how smitten he has become with a young woman. He refers to her as Delia but later we learn that she is his first cousin, Elizabeth Thomson, a sister of the recently deceased Sophia.

The last week of October offered me a great acquaintance of the pleasures of love because on the Sunday I became

---

[23] Cupar has now extended its boundaries eastwards to include Prestonhall.

[24] i.e. Cupar.

[25] This is now part of the public park of Cupar through which flows the River Eden.

[26] A small place just north of Cupar.

[27] These lie about three miles south-west of Cupar.

[28] The Flyfisher's Classic Library, Moretonhampstead, Devon, was informed of this enconium on the joys of fly-fishing. The curator sought and received a copy for which she was grateful.

attracted to a girl for the first time. Delia, who had been in my youthful heart for four years, smiled sweetly when acknowledging me, causing my breast to swell and my blood to stir within me. I was torn with desire for my cousin. The day before I had arisen from sleep on a beautiful day and snatching such sweet and beautiful kisses from this loveliest of girls, I had held her close and accepted her loving and tender pledges. That evening I had held her in my arms and I must assert that nothing improper took place because it was more the beautiful game of love than a display of violent passion.

I saw my cousins for the last time about nine o'clock in the evening. On the excuse that we wanted to have music, I managed to separate the girls from the rest of the family and in the company of young people I had a very happy time. It was all innocent fun and we had pleasant and delightful conversation for some hours. For the first time in my life I experienced the attractive power of loving conversation. That night love seemed to hold me within some wonderful place; words, caresses, embraces, kisses, each succeeding the other in joyful order. It all happened in thoughtless abandon. Her hair formed the cause of a sweet struggle between us. Her appearance, her touch, they all affected me. I sought the assurance of her former friendship, holding her hands, her arms and then, clasping her round her waist, laid my head upon her breast with my eyes looking tenderly into hers. Thus were tenderness, sweetness, love, even philosophy all united inseparably. Despite all this however, she refused me a lock of her hair.

Next morning we had the fondest of farewells beside our little family gig; her coral red lips, her neck of purest marble, her handsome figure, those beautiful eyes, her lovely hair. Never before have I taken the road with such happy expressions of love or tenderness.

There are further entries in the diary concerning matters of the heart in Latin. It is possible that this was to protect his private feelings from anyone who should read his diary but at that time there were few educated persons who had not a sound grasp of the language. A more likely explanation is that he felt more at home in the classical language when communing with himself.

His resolution to devote himself to his studies soon came to naught. We learn nothing specific from his diary for the very good reason that there were no further entries until 6th January 1830. There, in language reminiscent of his self-criticism of October 1826,[29] he chides himself for having wasted two whole months in idleness and pleasure. He has taken expensive lessons in German and yet has barely mastered the pronunciation or made much progress in understanding the grammar. The lectures in chemistry have brought him "no accurate acquaintance with any part of that interesting science". He has read almost no French but did find time at the end of November to read the first 600 lines of the *Hecuba* of Euripides. He had attended regularly his lectures in civil law but, even there, had not carried out the "profound and careful study, which it demands". He explains that "the chief cause of this inattention and flagrant inactivity is to be found in the extent to which I have joined in the pleasures of society since I came here. Invitations have poured in upon me since my arrival and as they were the first ones I could not well refuse them." Some weeks he had as many as four invitations to dinner but he realises that "it is really shameful that one advancing to manhood and with so much to do and to learn should waste his time in frivolity and idleness. After losing almost two months of the session, I must make a strenuous endeavour to employ the remaining two thirds in such a way as to compensate for this loss."

James had come over to visit him in Edinburgh on 24th December 1829 and two days later Andrew accompanied him back to Cupar. The following week must have been a cold one because Andrew comments on the fine skating they had enjoyed. Melville and he walked to Perth on 30th December to celebrate the new year with their sister Sophia and

[29] v. p. 50 supra.

her family and returned to Cupar on 2nd January 1830. That evening he paid a visit to the Thomsons at Eden Park and in a short Latin entry regrets that he found Elizabeth somewhat distant and unaffectionate. Perhaps she felt that she had been given less attention than she had expected. For his part Andrew makes no further comment and he was back in Edinburgh on Saturday 4th January 1830, determined to attend to his studies with much greater diligence when his university classes resumed on the following Monday.

Over the remaining months of the session, Andrew Jameson certainly applied himself assiduously to his studies, especially civil law. The weather in January and February was particularly severe and he did indulge himself occasionally with skating on Duddingston Loch. Captain James Jameson and his wife always took a house in Edinburgh (22 Dundas Street) during the winter months and they were generous in the hospitality they gave to their nephew. Occasionally he accompanied them to St Stephen's Church and seldom missed divine service on other Sundays. Occasionally he called upon Sheriff and Mrs Clephane. However, while he continued to receive invitations to dine they were fewer than before and he did not allow them or meetings with his fellow students, Stirling, Ogilvie and Christie, to deflect him from his determined pattern of work. By the end of January he was pleased with his progress in German and while he was finding the lectures in chemistry interesting he had not time to read around this subject. He was thoroughly enjoying the French classes; he and Christie read Molière together but, more importantly, he was doing well in all the different areas of law.

On 22nd February 1830 there was an important examination in law. He and Christie had prepared well for it and felt they deserved to enjoy a night out. They went to "an evening party at M. L. George H.". This was possibly the George Hotel in George Street, where, in 1787, a dancing establishment had been set up in rivalry to the more fashionable one in Buccleuch Place.[30] They danced:

---

[30] Cockburn, H., (1909) *Memorials of his Time*, p. 27. Foulis. Edinburgh. It can be assumed that this was the same building where Andrew Jameson and his friend enjoyed their evening.

five quadrilles – as many country dances – three reels, a
set of the Lancers and one Gallopade.[31] I enjoyed a very
pleasant evening but the varied adventures of the day were
not yet over. In my way home with another young man we
descried the firemen engaged in their useful and laborious
occupation.

It was a fire in some house opposite the High Church;
there was fortunately little wind and the alarm had been
given in time so that in about an hour or so it was subdued.
But one could not but admire the very picturesque effects
of the whole accompaniments of the scene. The red glare of
the flambeaux throwing such varieties of appearance upon
the motley group of bystanders and the old buildings that
stand on each side; the wretched inmates of the adjoining
and attached tenements watching with such intense eager-
ness the effects of the firemen's efforts; and some of the sad
victims of debauchery turned out from their disgusting dens
with all the symptoms of recent dissipation. Add to all this a
thick fall of snow making a curious contrast with the strong
lights and dark shadows of the rest of the scenes.[32]

Melville had arranged to visit him the following weekend. The very
close friendship between the two brothers has been commented upon
earlier and this is further emphasised by the language used by the elder
brother in his account of the visit. Of passing interest is the public transport that was now available. As mentioned in the previous chapter[33]
Andrew had used the steamboat service that plied along the Firth of
Tay when he had visited his sister in Perth. There was now a regular
ferry between Newhaven and Largo, a port only twelve miles from St

---

[31] A Hungarian dance.
[32] Seventeen years later Hans Christian Andersen visited Edinburgh and wrote thus of a visit
to the old town: "The main streets are narrow, filthy and with six storey houses; one has to
think of the great buildings in the dirty towns of Italy; poverty and misery seem to peep out of
the open hatches which normally serve as windows."
[33] v. p. 69 supra.

Andrews. Melville wrote that he would take the one o'clock ferry and arrive in Edinburgh in time to dine with his brother four hours later. Things, however, did not go quite according to plan.

> The morning opened auspiciously, but towards noon the wind, which was westerly, began to blow with great violence and excite unpleasant apprehensions. I with difficulty ascended the Calton Hill and endeavoured to get a sight of some of the passageboats. But I saw none and from the state of the frith there seemed too much reason to suspect that there had been no passage to Largo. After attending the classes I came home to my lodgings and busied myself in active preparations for the expected repast. When all was in readiness I walked to the Dutyhouse to ascertain if the boat had sailed to Largo and whether it was likely to return.
>
> They told me there was no doubt of it and buoyed up with fresh hopes I paraded the front of the Register Office[34] in the expectation of receiving him on his way from Newhaven. As it grew dark I began to think that he might have arrived and found his way to my quarters by another route. I hastened home – looked all along the streets on my way – and on reaching my lodgings ascertained too surely, that he had not yet come. I waited for him till between 7 and 8 p.m. and then sat down solitary and cheerless to the comfortable repast, which I had fondly hoped we would share together. Mortified and fatigued I soon retired to rest, still cherishing the hopes of seeing him next day.
>
> I rose early and studied Heineccius[35] to 10 a.m. I again went and inquired about the Boat and remained on the

---

[34] This building is situated at the eastern extremity of Princes Street and at the top of Leith Walk. It was the obvious place to await people who were expected to cross from Fife to Edinburgh.

[35] Johann Gottlieb Heineccius (1681–1741), a professor of jurisprudence at Halle and other universities. He belonged to the school of philosophical jurists and developed his legal doctrines as a system of philosophy.

outlook till 11. I then returned and destitute of all hope now ordered Breakfast. I had scarcely however sat down, when the bell was rung – the door opened and Melville entered after all.

We were overjoyed to see one another and a few moments explained the cause of his detention, which verified my previous suspicions. The Steamboat had not ventured down to Largo and he was obliged to continue his walk to Dysart. During a hearty breakfast he satisfied all my enquiries about the progress of his studies and my former fellow students at Alma Mater. We subsequently visited the Parliament House, the Advocates' Library, the Exhibition of the Scottish Academy – and the new High School,[36] with all which he was much gratified. We enjoyed an excellent dinner together and had a cheerful and agreeable talk afterwards. At 9 we went to the Theatre, in which we had two hours of very delightful amusement. R. Christie joined us at supper and post duo cantus et unum Poculum (after two songs and a drink) we retired and shared the same couch.

When we had dressed we took a turn to George Square and heard the melodious song of the blackbird for the first time this season. Melville only staid in Edinburgh till noon, when we went down to Newhaven and took the steamboat to Pettycur.[37] The weather was rather calm and pleasant. The sail was not disagreeable and as we perambulated the Deck we held sweet converse together. We afterwards on landing had a bason of soup in the Inn and then proceeded to Dysart on foot.[38] We dined on our arrival with Mrs N.[39] and spent

---

[36] This replaced earlier premises where Sir Walter Scott had been a student. It was built 1825–1829 on the Calton Hill with Greek Doric columns based on the Temple of Theseus, Athens. The school moved to more modern premises in the Barnton district of Edinburgh in 1968.

[37] A small port between Burntisland and Kirkcaldy.

[38] Dysart is six miles from Pettycur. Presumably there was not a suitable boat direct to Dysart or Kirkcaldy.

[39] Presumably the Mrs Normand of the same paragraph. As previously stated she was a granddaughter of Mrs John Jameson by her first husband, John Anderson.

the evening pleasantly. We visited Mrs T's [40] family and I had great pleasure in introducing Melville to their acquaintance and re-newing my own – especially with the younger branches. We slept together at Mrs Normand's.

They parted the following morning, Melville returning to St Andrews by way of Cupar and Andrew to Edinburgh by the Pettycur ferry in time for his afternoon classes.

Six days later he learned that his father was in town and they breakfasted together "in one of the Boxes in the Coffeeroom at the Black Bull". He was brought up to date with domestic news, particularly the progress of George Gray's convalescence from an illness. They spent the forenoon together and after giving his landlord instructions to prepare a supper for both of them in the evening, "I then had a delightful walk by Duddingston to Northfield where I had been yesterday asked to dine. The dinner was excellent and the family Party very agreeable and the afternoon glided away very smoothly in various and interesting conversations. Mrs S. [41] was sorry that my father had not accompanied me. It was moonlight when I came home and the ruins of St Anthony's Chapel, the rocks of Arthurseat [sic] and the ancient Palace of Holyrood looked remarkably picturesque. At 9 p.m. my father and party arrived. I thanked my father for giving me this opportunity, the first in my life of entertaining him; and hoped that it would be the prelude to many such occasions. He left me at 11 p.m. post duo Pocula."

A less sober evening was spent on the following Friday (12th March 1830) at the home of Professor Cheape, [42] who had invited him and some other young men to dinner. They spent a happy evening with the professor at what Andrew Jameson refers to as his first "carousal". They drank claret, champagne and hock and then the youths went

---

[40] It may be Mrs F.

[41] This is another case, already commented above (p. 79), of the diarist's infuriating habit of not giving the full surname of persons whom he visited. This is, however, certainly Mrs Scott.

[42] Douglas Cheape (1797–1861) came from Rossie in Fife and knew Andrew Jameson's father. He held the chair of Civil Law at Edinburgh University.

to the Caledonian Theatre returning later to the Cheape household, where they found the professor highly inebriated. Andrew retired at 1 p.m. (apparently at the professor's house) and awoke at six in the morning feeling very unwell having "experienced all the disagreeable consequences of excess". To recuperate he "walked about all day with J. A. a bottle companion of last night". While on this perambulation of recovery Mr Cameron, his former teacher at Perth Academy, called. Andrew was sorry to have missed him and comments that this was "a sad instance of the effects of dissipation".

On the Sunday morning he went to church with a Mr M.'s family, attended a Catholic chapel in the afternoon and dined with his friend Patrick Stirling. Reflecting on the past week in his diary he writes that he looks "back upon the gaieties of the bygone week with no great self-complacency".

Today it would be most unusual to combine a visit to the theatre with dinner beforehand or to meet friends for supper as well before returning home but in 1830 the time for dinner was much earlier than it is today. The following excerpts from Lord Cockburn's *Memorials of his Time* allow us to understand how Andrew Jameson could accept invitations to dinner and then visit friends later that same day, often with the addition of supper. This also accounts for theatre performances beginning as late as ten o'clock and for the late hour that Andrew Jameson sometimes returned home.

> The prevailing dinner hour was about three o'clock. Two o'clock was quite common, if there was no company. Hence it was no great deviation from their usual custom for a family to dine on Sundays *between sermons*[43] – that is between one and two. The hour, in time, but not without groans and predictions, became four, at which it stuck for several years. Then it got to five, which, however, was thought positively revolutionary; and four was long and gallantly adhered to by the haters of change as "the good old hour". At last even

---

[43] Use of italics is by Lord Cockburn.

they were obliged to give in. But they only yielded inch by inch, and made a desperate stand at half-past four. Even five, however, triumphed and continued the average polite hour from (I think) about 1806 or 1807 till about 1820. Six has at last prevailed, and half an hour later is not unusual. As yet this is the furthest stretch of London imitation, except in country houses devoted to grouse and deer, where the species called sportsmen, disdaining all mankind except themselves, glory in not dining till sensible people have gone to bed. Thus, within my memory,[44] the hour has ranged from two to half-past six o'clock; and a stand has been regularly made at the end of every half-hour against each encroachment and always on the same grounds – dislike of change and jealousy of finery.[45]

A few pages later Cockburn continues thus. "Early dinners begat suppers. But suppers are so delightful that they have survived long after dinners have become late. Indeed this has immemorially been a favourite Edinburgh repast. I have often heard strangers say, that Edinburgh was the only place where people dined twice every day."[46]

Andrew Jameson devoted the Monday and Tuesday following the entertainment at Professor Cheape's house to hard study of the law of contract since there was an examination on the 17th March. He was able to answer all ten questions as did three other students whom he refers to as "competitors whom I am near to". That evening he and R. Christie decided to practise their debating skills in the privacy of each other's company. They chose to debate the French Revolution and Andrew felt that he acquitted himself well with a speech lasting twenty minutes, although he concedes that in the absence of any audience other than his friend his confidence was under no pressure. On Saturday he entertained to dinner his friend Stirling, who was

---

[44] Henry Cockburn (1779–1854), Solicitor-General of Scotland 1830–1834, raised to the bench as Lord Cockburn in 1834.

[45] Cockburn, op cit, pp. 30–31.

[46] Cockburn, op cit, pp. 36–37.

about to leave for the West Riding of Yorkshire.

Professor Cheape's manner of entertainment did not always follow the pattern of the "carousal" of 12th March 1830. Andrew Jameson gives in his memoirs an account of a very different evening that took place during that same winter.[47] That the eighteen-year-old student was present is another example of his good fortune in being connected in various ways with his host and some of the distinguished guests.

> One interesting symposium or rather Dinner Party of that winter deserves to be remembered. It consisted of Professor Wilson then at the zenith of his fame and more like the bronze statue in Princes Street, than he was in later life, Duncan McNeill now Lord Colonsay, lately President of the Court of Session, Patrick Robertson,[48] the facetious and ready advocate, afterwards Lord of Session, Dr. Chalmers, who had been invited to meet some of these leaders of the Tory Party in Parliament House, Campbell-Swinton, who after filled the Civil Law Chair, Lubienski, a Polish Nobleman, son of a Patriot of that unhappy country, and myself youngest of the Party, which met in the house of Professor Cheape in Nelson Street. P. Robertson, who was apt to play the buffoon rather too grossly on such occasions, kept us in a roar with some of his usual performances, such as his Song from the Italian Opera, in which in a sort of recitation he referred by name to each of the guests. The most remarkable thing that occurred was the conduct of Chalmers. Some equivocal sentiments had been expressed by some of the *Wits* – he looked grave, but seemed to doubt whither he might not have misunderstood their meaning. The offence was repeated more grossly, and then the soul of the Christian Orator was stirred, and

[47] No date is given.

[48] Along with McNeill, he had represented William Burke, the "resurrectionist", at his trial for murder in 1828. v. p. 189 infra.

with a burst of virtuous indignation and eloquent rebuke he silenced the foulmouthed buffoon and his thoughtless associates.

The date, purpose and personnel of this dinner party are interesting. There was at this time considerable political turmoil on account of the demand by the Whig party for the abolition of the "rotten" and "pocket" burghs and their replacement by parliamentary constituencies that reflected more accurately the distribution of population throughout the country. The Duke of Wellington, who had been prime minister since 1828, opposed reform. Professor Cheape, Professor Wilson, Duncan McNeill, Alan Campbell-Swinton and presumably Robertson were strong Tories. John Wilson (1785–1854), who held the chair of Moral Philosophy from 1820 to 1857, was a great friend of William Blackwood (1776–1834) who, in 1817, had founded *Blackwood's Magazine*, as a rival to the Whig-supporting *Edinburgh Review*. The purpose of the gathering, as stated by Andrew Jameson, was to introduce Thomas Chalmers to these men, doubtless because Chalmers was already recognized as a national figure able to influence opinion throughout the country. As it happened, George IV died in the summer of 1830 thus precipitating a general election that returned the Whigs to power after almost a quarter of a century in the political wilderness.

On Thursday 25th March 1830 the diary has a curious entry that runs as follows. "A. Murray had a cup of rum with me and we waded into the genealogy of the families with tolerable success. We both agreed that our greatgrandfathers showed a culpable want of attention to their interests in not examining into the rights of their common fatherinlaw." They would have had four great-grandfathers but it is almost certain that they were referring to John Gib, whose elder daughter married a Murray of Couland and younger daughter Andrew Jameson.[49]

Term was now nearing its end and he decided to visit his grandaunt at Graycraig. On the Saturday he caught the Stirling steamboat and after

---

[49] v. p. 5 supra.

sailing for two hours reached Crombie Point,[50] where he disembarked. He took dinner with a Mr G. and set off for Graycraig at five o'clock. It was a long walk to Graycraig but the evening was particularly fine and he comments that "I enjoyed it all the more that my way was a rustic footpath from Torrie grounds. As I approached the Saline and Ochil Hills with the beautiful variety of hill and dale which intervenes, my heart beat high with the recollections of former years and past joys. I arrived at the gloaming[51] and was received by my Cousins with their usual warmth of Politeness. My old aunt was very glad to see me and I sat a long while with her, in which she went thro' the whole circle of relations. She seems still to possess her faculties in much of their usual [indecipherable word], tho' her memory occasionally makes a slip but recovers on reflection".

Next morning he attended church with his cousins[52] and in the afternoon spent three hours in conversation with his grandaunt. On the Monday he set off early for some fishing and breakfasted with a Mr and Mrs Colville of Hillside before resuming his sport that brought two dozen trout back to Graycraig, some of which provided that day's dinner. On the Monday, having risen early enough to catch the 7.00 a.m. steamship, he reached home by noon and attended an evening party "at Miss C. where I had a good deal of dancing and was introduced to some pleasant girls".

His final lecture in civil law was on Thursday, 1st April 1830 after which the students received their marks. At the top was a Robert Horn of Bridge of Allan, who was awarded the class prize. The next competitor, Mackenzie (later Lord Mackenzie) was only two marks below him and Andrew Jameson was third, a mere five marks behind Horn. All the other students were "completely distanced to use the Turf's phrase". He regretted not winning the Civil Law Prize because

---

[50] Crombie Point is on the south coast of Fife, only four miles west of Rosyth and about a mile south of Torryburn. That it took two hours to reach there from Newhaven suggests that the boat must have called at several stops on both sides of the Firth of Forth.

[51] The walk must have been about seven miles, and if he arrived in the gloaming this suggests that he was both a swift walker and that it was much lighter in late March evenings than it would be today, when the clocks are arranged to give more light in the morning.

[52] He does not say who they were.

it was an eminent and honourable distinction that would have been useful professionally. He made the reasonable point in his diary that, as concerned the top three students there could have been "very little difference of merit when we came so close" considering the number of questions that they had been asked to answer over several examinations. In what was almost a throwaway comment he writes that "we have had some very interesting lectures on Electricity and Galvanism for several days in the Chemistry class". He makes no reference to examinations in this subject nor in the classes that he also took in French, German and general literature for which he had enrolled at the start of the session.

The next day he had a "long and satisfactory" interview with Professor Cheape, when they discussed his performance over the past session and the subjects that he would be taking in the second year of his course. The professor approved of his father's decision for him to be attached to a writer's office in the country during the summer. On the Saturday, after a round of farewells to several families who had entertained him during the academic year, he left Edinburgh for Cupar.

He spent the first two weeks of April relaxing at home doing little more than reading and taking days out with his rod. In the third week he went over for a few days to stay with his sister Sophia at Bowersburn in Perth and on returning home on 24th April learned that his cousin James Thomson had died in November 1829 at Bushire in Persia. This was a second bereavement for the Thomson family within a few months since their daughter Sophia had died in May of the same year.[53] On the Sunday Andrew visited the Thomson home to express his sorrow at their loss and the next day took the family pony and went over to St Andrews to convey the sad news to Melville. He was pleased to be recognized by some of the students and by "some honoured Masters". He stayed overnight with Melville and attended the distribution of prizes that marked the end of the session. Melville took the second prizes in Greek and moral philosophy.

At this point in the diary three pages have been neatly cut out, and

---

[53] v. p. 78 supra.

the next entry is that for 10th June from which it is clear that he has now started his attachment to the office of Drummond and Berwick, writers, in Cupar. The term "writer" was used somewhat loosely in the nineteenth century to denote someone in legal practice, and as late as the 1950s some solicitors in Edinburgh were still referring to themselves as writers.[54] The term must not be confused with that of Writers to Her Majesty's Signet, a body that can date its foundation back to the sixteenth century and which will accept as its members only those lawyers who meet its criteria of entrance through further examinations set by the WS Society.

His brother Robert was approaching the end of an apprenticeship there, and Melville was to follow him in May 1831. There is little worth recording from this period until 11th August, other than that when out fishing with a Mr Douglas on 17th July his fellow angler clumsily struck him on the right eyebrow with the brass ferrule of his rod. It drew blood and was painful enough for him to take to his bed on returning home. There were some young people visiting the house that evening and although Andrew was not able to join them he "regretted it somewhat the less that E. favoured my couch with a visit. She came and sat for a few minutes with me at my bedside." Clearly there had been some *rapprochement* between them and perhaps the details had been written in the three pages that were later excised. A few days later, when fully recovered, "I stole away and called on my fair companion of the other evening. I inspected her drawings."

His father had agreed that he could go on a walking tour of the "Land of Scottish Minstrelsy" from 11th August 1830. Two days before that he was invited to dine with Mr Berwick, who gave him a present "for my past exertions". The next day he was "anxious to bid all fair friends a tender adieu before my departure". He describes himself as fortunate that several were not at home because "I descried the wished for object moving by the banks of the river with a companion tant mieux. I walked up to them, saluted and asked them to prolong their walk – they

[54] I am indebted for this information to Professor Angelo Forte of the Faculty of Law, University of Aberdeen.

were all complaisance – we staid out till the shades of twilight were deepening around us. We amused ourselves very pleasantly. I could not help smiling at the success of this my first rencontre. I thanked them for the honour they had done me and expressed my wishes for a better acquaintance." It seems unlikely that "the wished for object" was Elizabeth since he would not have used the term "first rencontre" if it had been her and a friend.

He set off on his journey carrying his fishing rod and basket, "not so much for the sake of fishing as that it is more gentlemanly than carrying a knapsack". One would think that these would be encumbrances on a walking tour, the rod less than the basket because the rod would probably be of the type that came in three or more parts that were fitted together when there was fishing to be done. He must have had some container for his personal effects and clean clothing and surely this was not the fish basket.

He made notes during his journey and these were used for what he calls his "cursory outline of my route" that was written with commendable diligence on 5th September, the day after his return to Cupar. He wrote this account in such clear and lucid prose that it demands reproduction in full.

> I went no further than Dysart[55] on Wednesday 11th August, the day on which I left home. Next morning I crossed the Forth and walked on in the course of the day to Whitburn Inn in Berwickshire between Lauder and Greenlaw – passing thro Edinburgh and Dalkeith and over the Lammermoor Hills at Soutra. Next day I walked to Dunse by Greenlaw and disappointed as I had been with the first view of the Coastal regions of the South in the bleak uplands of Lauderdale – it was highly gratifying to approach and enter the rich plain of the Merse, stretching down to the sea in one beautiful

---

[55] He had written in his diary on 11th August 1830, just as he was about leave, that there had been heavy rain during the morning. We know from his notes that he took a coach from the New Inn to Dysart.

succession of cultivation. I remained at Dunse[56] till Monday 16th Aug. when I proceeded to Kelso by Coldstream and the lovely banks of the Tweed. Pausing for a day to admire the beautiful environs of the former town,[57] I pursued my journey by Dryburgh Abbey to Melrose. With the farfamed ruins of the latter I was much gratified, the elegance of the workmanship as well as the beauty of the design are superior to anything of the kind I ever saw. Next morning I visited Abbotsford and saw the gifted owner sitting in his study. The collection of ancient armour here and the hallowed relics of many a battlefield must interest all Scots men.

At this point it would be appropriate to interrupt Andrew Jameson's brief account of his walking tour and give here in full the account that he wrote of his visit to Abbotsford.

Thursday 19 Aug. As I understood that the morning was the most favourable time for seeing Abbotsford, or rather the time, when the intrusion of a stranger would be less discernable and least offensive I reserved my visit for this morning. About 7 o'clock I left the inn and in less than an hour I descried the turrets of this farfamed mansion. I entered an unassuming gate, and the avenue to which it gave entrance speedily lands you in front of the house. You first have to pass via a Gothic Archway which is in accordance with the castellated style of the whole building. I stepped tensely through and felt a degree of reverential awe as I gazed at the habitation of so much genius. The house is in the Gothic Style and is rather a good specimen of the Modern Antique. I surveyed it for some time with a

---

[56] Although the author of this work was brought up in Dunse (now Duns) and has a natural loyalty to it, he wonders what Andrew Jameson could have found to do over the three nights he spent there. Perhaps he needed a rest and one of the days was a Sunday.

[57] Presumably Floors Castle in particular, the seat of the Dukes of Roxburgh. By "former town" he meant Kelso.

host of complicated feelings and in turning to take a nearer view my eye fell on the figure of the great man sitting in his library seemingly intent on some book or writings before him. He wore a black suit and had a pair of spectacles on. His air was calm and engaged. I felt awestruck at beholding him and the thought of his fame and his works. Perhaps he has been their pathway for posterity and was embodying the Ideas that were to delight his contemporaries and their descendants. I felt that this stolen view was a trespass of the learned seclusion of this gifted writer and tore myself away to another part of the house. A maid servant happened to be sweeping up the threshold, who asked me to step in to the Entrance Hall. I needed no second bidding, and had the pleasure of inspecting its richly covered walls. It is all of oak panelling enriched with beautiful [next word unclear] work of the same material and is hung with full and half suits of ancient armour, swords, battleaxes and a great variety of weapons, valuable for their age or rarity, on the battlefields where they had been found. After surveying this curious collection with much admiration for some time and inwardly regretting that I had no person to point out the most curious objects to me I was thinking of retiring in case the advancing hour should draw any of the numerous inmates and visitors from their apartments when a Genteel boy of about 12 or 13 emerged from a neighbouring ante-chamber and came into the hall. I asked if he could give me any information as to the war relics on the walls. He said he could and would be happy to show me through them. He pointed to the armour of the Polish Cuirassiers as used at Waterloo, the shield of the ancient wild bull or urus[58] of the country and the gigantic horns of an elk. He then led me to an antechamber, the walls of which were hung with minuter

---

[58] The *Concise Oxford Dictionary* gives this as "Kind of wild bull described by Caesar = AUROCHS (L, = Gk ourus)".

specimens of armour and precious relics of antiquity. Rob Roy's [word illegible and it may be in Gaelic] with his name scratched on it, James VI hunting horn, the key and lock of the Tolbooth of Edinburgh, the pistols of Napoleon, the sword of Claverhouse.

Unfortunately the following pages (and surely there must have been more) are either missing or have become attached to some other documents. One can but hope that they will turn up somewhere, sometime. The summary of the tour continues.

I now left the banks of the Tweed and passed over into Teviotdale. On Friday 20th I visited Jedburgh, which is a fine old border town and marched on by Hawick to Mosspaul, where I passed the night. Next morning I descended the pastoral valley of Tevesdale[59] to Langholm – and walked leisurely by the banks of the Esk, the lovely woods of Canonby and over the border into Cumberland. I reached Carlisle by sunset, spent the Sunday there and heard for the first time Divine service performed in its most appropriate temple – an ancient Cathedral. On Monday 23rd I beat my steps to the Lakes of Cumberland. The succession of tame and bleak country all the way to Penrith surprises and disappoints the traveller, who looks for the rich plains of Merry England, when over the border. I turned to the west at Penrith and soon reached the side of Ullswater. I have seldom experienced more enthusiastic delight in viewing fine scenery, than I did as I slowly wound my way along the banks of this romantic lake to Patterdale. The road sometimes courses along the margin of the water and again winds through the beautiful woods, which clothe luxuriantly its sides. The hills and precipices that surround the Lake are picturesquely indented with ravine

---

[59] This is clearly a mistake for Ewesdale.

and hollow and continually vary their aspect at every turn. On Tuesday crossed the hill to Ambleside, in the descent to which I had a fine view of Windermere. I pursued my way to Keswick by Rydal Water to Grasmere. The rich valley in which Keswick lies with Derwent Water at one extremity and Bassenthwaite at another, and the fine chain of hills along the sides is picturesque and lovely beyond description. On the morrow I directed my course to the coast by the Romantic Borodale, Buttermere, Cumnock[60] and Lowes Waters to Whitehaven – where I arrived in the Evening – having thus seen most of these celebrated Lakes in three days, in the course of which I walked upwards of ninety miles. I was vastly delighted with the whole, and congratulated myself on having made this extension of my original plan of my tour. On Thursday 26th I crossed the Solway to Dumfries, where I staid all next day. It here came on to rain very heavily, which continuing all day prevented me seeing the town and country to advantage. On Saturday I walked to Kirkcudbright, 28 miles in nearly seven hours and got drenched most thoroughly. I spent Sunday here and on Monday proceeded to Gatehouse, Creetown and Newton Stewart. I spent the night at a hovel in the Muirs of Galloway[61] – and in the evening of the next day reached Ayr, having got a great deal of rain by the way. On Wednesday night I was at Glasgow, on Thursday at Stirling, on Friday at Edinburgh and having crossed the Frith to Largo yesterday I walked up here to dinner, happy that I have arrived home in safety and have made out my excursion so agreeably.

---

[60] This must be either a spelling mistake by Andrew Jameson or the former name of what is today Crummock Water.

[61] This must have been in the country some miles north of Newton Stewart because even a young man of Andrew Jameson's prodigious walking determination could not have reached Ayr in one day from Newton Stewart.

He was back at his desk on Monday, 6th September 1830 and contrasts the "change from the most active exertion and perpetual variety to my usual solitary and monotonous labours". However, he must have enjoyed the visits to and from his friends and relations who were "eager in their interogatories about my late excursion and the pleasures of travel were renewed in recounting its adventures".

It had now become necessary for all law students who intended to become advocates that they found a situation in the office of an agent[62] during their second year at Edinburgh University. Andrew Jameson had letters of recommendation to a particular agent from Mr Drummond,[63] who had told him that his letter of recommendation backed by the presence of his father meant that he could not fail to succeed in his application. So he and his father made arrangements to cross over to Edinburgh on Friday, 22nd October, about two weeks before classes began.

He spent the previous day on a round of farewells and with Melville attended an evening party with their cousins. When Andrew Jameson uses the term "cousins" it is seldom clear whether they are Thomsons or Ogilvies. Andrew Jameson (Senior) had two sisters, Sophia and Rachael. Sophia married James Thomson and lived at Eden Park, Cupar, while Rachael married James Ogilvie and lived in Dundee.[64] The term may perhaps have been used to include second cousins. There were cousins who were staying at Graycraig when he visited his grandaunt[65] and it is possible that they may have been descendants of her sister, Janet Bethune.[66] On this occasion the diary tells of a delightful evening spent by the young people and it is so very different from a similar gathering today that it is worth giving the whole passage.

---

[62] This was the term used for the solicitor of today.

[63] Described in the diary as "my late master".

[64] v. p. 14 supra.

[65] v. p. 95 supra

[66] v. p. 12 supra.

Melville and I joined our Cousins in the evening. When I entered, they were searching the Old Testament for the text "Is not her sister fairer than she?", which formed an interesting quotation in a late letter from the insidious madman, whose malignant passions and great baseness has occasioned them so much uneasiness.[67] I assisted them but the attempt was fruitless. The time flew swiftly by in music, dancing and conversation. I waltzed for the first time and with E. She gave me some excellent lessons on Tuesday – under such instruction I would speedily have made a tolerable proficient. It is a captivating dance – a fascinating experience of excitement. We talked long and doucement. Tender regrets oft repeated but never tiring gave the conversazione a pensive and doucereux[68] rather than a sprightly air. We all sat round the fire and sung that beautiful little ballad The Mistletoe Bough – so full of simplicity and pathos. At Supper I sat next E. and afterwards we removed to the sopha where our tête-à-tête was renewed. I rose to depart – I stayed a short moment behind and at the top of the Staircase whispered a tender fare-well and matched its delightful yet sad token. Vale Vale est memoro nostri.

As soon as he and his father arrived in Edinburgh they called at the agent's office but received an instant refusal. This was a disappointment, but as he wrote in his diary "he had no very sanguine hopes", which suggests that he had a more realistic judgment of his sponsor's influence with the lawyer concerned. He had no option other than to call on as many other agents as time allowed but, although always greeted in a courteous manner, he failed to secure a post. A Mr Boyd, whose family had entertained him on several occasions during his first session

[67] One can but hazard a guess that the writer may have been an unwelcome admirer.
[68] This is a curious conjunction of two adjectives having contrary meanings. "Pensive" can mean "melancholy" or "plunged in thought" (Concise Oxford English Dictionary) while the French word doucereux suggests the interchange of what are today referred to as "sweet nothings".

at Edinburgh, introduced him to Daniel Fisher, SSC,[69] who had a very large practice but all that emerged from the meeting was a request from the lawyer that Andrew call on him the following week.

He had managed to find good lodgings with a Mrs Park at 17 Dundas Street. On 30th October Robert came across to stay with him for a week and on his departure took a letter for Elizabeth together with some "braid to weave her long promised chain for me". He called on Daniel Fisher, as requested, but the lawyer told him that he had not yet decided. He therefore continued on the weary round of calls at lawyers' offices and when classes resumed on 9th November 1831 he was still without a place.

There was some solace for him when his Cupar friends, R. Christie and his brother George, arrived to take up rooms in the same house in Dundas Street. Christie brought with him a letter from Elizabeth and a small parcel containing the braided chain. Andrew confides to his diary that he "felt very much pleased at this instance of her regard and will long be proud to wear it for her sake".

On 12th November 1830 the Court of Session met and was opened by a speech from the Lord President. There was a great crowd in the Parliament House and he met Robert Horn, who had won the Civil Law prize in the previous session, and Mackenzie, who had come second. Mackenzie advised Andrew to join the "Select Literary Society" or, at least, take a look at it next Thursday evening. He also met there a Mr Alexander, who said that he had spoken to Daniel Fisher in his favour. The following Thursday he walked down to Princes Street from the Parliament House with Sheriff Clephane, who told him that he had just spoken to Fisher, "who seemed favourably disposed". That evening he dined with Professor Cheape, who informed him that he had approached Fisher on his behalf. There was an interesting second guest, Leon Lubienski, who was joining the professor's class in Civil Law and whom Andrew had first met at the dinner held at Professor Cheape's the previous winter.

---

[69] Solicitor to the Supreme Court. Despite its grandiose title, it was and remains a very common qualification among Scottish solicitors.

Since he was supported by a sheriff and his professor and by others who all held him in high regard, it does seem odd that while many of his fellow students were successful in their applications to lawyers, Andrew Jameson was still searching for a placement. It must have been very frustrating for him but he did not, at first, allow it to deflect him from his studies nor to disturb his social life, which occupied a surprising amount of his time. Indeed, his diary for November and December contains far more information about meeting friends, dinners and parties than about his classes. The three days 17th to 20th November provide a good example of this.

On the night of the 17th, after a soirée at the home in Regent Terrace of a family called Johnstone, where he was a regular visitor and where there had been music, dancing and recitation, he met on his way home Spalding, another colleague. They had supper at the Café[70] and then "we joined some of his companions, who were regaling themselves in an adjoining box and adjourned with them to the Turkish Divan. Après tout cela illi me spectante puellas visunt, sed nil impure fit." (After all that they, with me watching, looked at the girls but nothing shameful occurred.) Earlier that day he had been walking along Princes Street and recognised Peter Russel of Aden and one of his brothers, whose home in Aberdeenshire he had visited at the start of his walking tour in August 1826. He and Peter arranged to breakfast in the Star Hotel on the morning of the 18th, during which Peter pressed his friend to make another visit. Before he had bid adieu to Peter Russel, another friend, G. Moncrieff, entered the room and they arranged to have supper together later that day. After dinner he attended the debating society that Mackenzie had recommended to him. "I have been looking out for a fit Institution of this kind to attach myself to, as public speaking is so indispensable a part of an advocate's profession. I think from what I saw of this Society that it will form a very good preparation for some of these more advanced clubs, which I may afterwards join." Next morning he

---

[70] This place is often mentioned and appears to have been a favourite place for young men to forgather.

breakfasted with Moncrieff, dined with Telfer, another colleague, and had supper with Moncrieff and Patrick Stirling, yet another name that crops up frequently in the diaries. The next day, a Saturday, he and the two Christies attended the first of a series of lessons in dancing and "the Master[71] has already given me some useful hints as to postures and to carriage of the person".

On 22nd November he again called at Daniel Fisher's office, and once more the lawyer told him that he would see him eight days later. As he writes in his diary, "It is cruel and ungentlemanly to keep a person on in this state of suspense, if he does not intend taking me into his office." His pursuit of a situation continued and since all these visits were made on foot he began to experience some physical stress. On 25th November he joined the Select Literary Society and that same day met a Mr Baxter to whose practice he had applied earlier but unsuccessfully. Mr Baxter said that there was a situation available with Mr Heriot of Ramornie,[72] but after a visit to Mr Heriot he decided not to pursue the matter since, in any case, there was still the possibility of a place in the office of Daniel Fisher. However, he decided that he could not continue to accept the prevarication of Daniel Fisher and determined that at the appointment arranged for 30th November he would insist on being given a straight rather than an evasive answer. Again the reply was inconclusive and, although not a downright refusal, he accepted it as such. He resumed what he calls "the unremitting and ineffectual search for a situation" and as these words indicate he was beginning to despair of any success. Moreover, his constant peregrinations around the city were making inroads on the time he needed for a proper application to his studies.

His brother-in-law, George Gray, had business in Edinburgh and came to the city on Saturday, 11th December. He stayed until Wednesday evening with Andrew and dined with him every evening.

---

[71] Such instruction was common at the period. Charles Dickens introduces into Bleak House the dancing academy run by the Turveydrops, senior and junior, who appeared to make a comfortable enough living from their establishment.

[72] Ramornie is a village near Ladybank in Fife. Mr Heriot appears to have been a member of the minor aristocracy of Scotland, who include a place name after their surname.

Since they took coffee on the Sunday in the Turkish Divan, one must assume that it was not quite the establishment of doubtful probity as suggested earlier.[73] On the following Monday both were guests for dinner at the home of a Mr Dickson W.S., to whom George Gray had been apprenticed when training for his profession, and thereafter they attended the theatre. It is not clear of what the entertainment consisted since the diary records that "We had a very extraordinary exhibition of Ducrow's[74] astonishing powers in Raphael's dream. I never beheld and could scarcely have conceived such a power over the muscles and such a command of attitude." During his stay in Edinburgh, Gray called on Daniel Fisher to plead his brother-in-law's suitability for a placement in the lawyer's office but even he received the same indeterminate response that had been the experience of Andrew Jameson.

The next evening at the Select Literary Society that was more a general debating club than a literary association, he gave his maiden speech, arguing against the proposition that the lower animals are guided solely by instinct. Nervous at first, he had warmed to his theme and before he reached the conclusion of his argument he felt that he "had crossed the Rubicon." He believed that he would no longer be nervous before speaking in public.

He made further unsuccessful attempts to find a solicitor who would accept him into his office. "Considerably mortified with the failure of all the various applications for a period of two months" he decided on 18th December that he would that day approach Mr Heriot to see if the situation in his office was still open. Fortunately it was and he writes "Mr Heriot received me politely – said that I was welcome

[73] In The Warden, the first of his Chronicles of Barchester, Anthony Trollope has the delightful but naive Rev. Septimus Harding visiting London. At 5.00 p.m. he is directed for coffee to what Trollope calls "a cigar divan", where there are long rows of sofas. The elderly clergyman falls asleep on one of the divans and awakens over four hours later to find the room full of people, probably not unlike the customers who attended the equivalent in Edinburgh. (Chapter XVI of the novel.)

[74] Almost certainly Andrew Ducrow, "The Pocket Hercules", 1793-1842. He was trained from infancy in tumbling, rope dancing and riding and later developed a horsemanship act that has been handed down to today's circus performers. He also appeared on the stage in tableaux and Raphael's Dream must have been one of them. In Milton's Paradise Lost Eve tells Adam of a troublesome dream (Book 5) and in Book 8 Adam and Raphael have a discussion.

to a desk in his office and see any business that was going. I thanked him for his kindness and agreed to come on Monday. Notwithstanding the discouraging accounts I have heard from different quarters of this situation and which prevented me from accepting it sooner, I do not regret the step I have taken. I will be in the way of reaping some instruction, however little, and I can remove to a more eligible office, as soon as I have the opportunity of doing so. At all events it is a respectable chamber – Mr Heriot's station, character and connections are highly respectable."

Since, despite having had his original offer spurned, Mr Heriot had been kind enough to accept Andrew Jameson, it does seem a little uncharitable of the young man to write that he would move to a better situation as soon as one presented itself. On the other hand, Mr Heriot's clerk "corroborated the unfavourable accounts I had heard of the office." He was given nothing to do until late in the afternoon when he got a legal document to copy, a task that would take him a few days.

Christmas Day was a very cold one and he writes in his diary that the temperature was 22 degrees. He knew that Duddingston Loch would be bearing and after a visit to Sheriff Clephane, with whom he had a long conversation, he went to Duddingston where he found "the Loch crowded with skaters and ladies." The Loch, when frozen, must have been a place where young people knew that they could enjoy the company of others of their own age. Among the latter were the Johnstone girls, who must have been the attraction behind the many visits that he paid to their home in Regent Terrace. He returned home "just in time to dress for Mrs Chrystie's dinner party at ½ past." How interesting it would have been to learn half past what hour in order to compare it with what Lord Cockburn wrote about Edinburgh's times of dinner.[75] He left the party at nine o'clock and, collecting George Christie on the way, went to the Johnstones, where they "spent the rest of the evening in singing, waltzing and conversation."

The next day saw the start of a considerable change in his manner of life. His cousin, John Ogilvie, called to say that his grandmother and

---

[75] v. p. 91 supra.

grandaunt had succeeded to some property in Newington[76] following the death of a Dr Duncan and that they had requested him to occupy the house of the deceased relative until a final decision was made about its disposal. Up till now Ogilvie had appeared occasionally in the diaries, first as a contemporary at St Andrews, who at times accompanied him when he walked from Cupar to St Andrews, and later, just as infrequently, when both attended Edinburgh University. There is no reference even to the courses of study upon which Ogilvie was engaged, but we know that they must have been in law because Ogilvie was later to join his father's legal practice in Dundee.

Ogilvie had called to inform him of his change in circumstances and to invite Andrew to join him at the house in Newington. After service in St Stephen's they went out to Newington and found the house in excellent condition, having just been painted that summer and the furniture entirely new. It would appear that Dr Duncan had died suddenly and unexpectedly for his hat and greatcoat were still hanging in their usual place in the entrance hall along with other signs of recent occupation. The house was being cared for by a "moaning domestic." Ogilvie agreed to hold his offer open until after the New Year.

On the Monday there was no work for him at Mr Heriot's office nor had there been since Wednesday evening and so he decided to have a few days at Cupar. He arose very early on Tuesday, 28th December, a day that was to have more than its usual share of physical exertion and local events. Along with G. Christie he took the six o'clock boat from Newhaven to Pettycur, breakfasted with his aunts in Dysart, walked on to the New Inn, whence he took the coach to Cupar, arriving there at two o'clock. It is interesting to note that it was possible for Christie and him to send their luggage in advance by coach and that they could request the nightwatchman to ring their doorbell at 5.00 a.m. The rest of the day is narrated in full detail in his diary.

---

[76] Now a suburb of South Edinburgh, it would then have lain just outside the city boundaries. Dr Duncan was the brother of Susan Ogilvie, who was grandmother of John Ogilvie and mother-in law of Rachael Ogilvie, a sister of Andrew Jameson (senior).

My father was looking out of the window and I met Robert in the street. Our meeting was very happy after a separation of two months. R. & I went to Tarvit Pond before dinner, where I had a little skating and afterwards we dined together at home and exchanged our news. It being the evening before the day of the Election for the Delegate[77] preparatory to the choosing of a representative for the Burghs in parliament, the town was in a state of great excitement. The great body of the Inhabitants and the mob are strongly in favour of the Lord Advocate Jeffrey,[78] who is one of the Candidates, while a party and the more influential party of the Town Council were pledged to his opponent Capt. Ogilvie of the family of Airly before the Lord Advocate made his appearance. While sitting talking with my father Robert dispatched a messenger to inform me that Jeffrey was about to harangue a meeting in the Church. I went there immediately and heard his Lordship's speech on the occasion. It was received with great applause and after the dismissal of the meeting he was carried off amid immense cheering on the shoulders of some of the mob and deposited in a carriage, which was immediately drawn through the town. The mob rapidly encreased in numbers & their enthusiasm grew in proportion. They burned some of the obnoxious party in effigy and

---

[77] In 1830 Scotland had a population of 2,600,000 of whom only 4,500 had the right to vote (0.6% of the population). A total of 45 members were returned to the House of Commons, 30 representing counties and 15 representing groups of neighbouring burghs. Cupar was included among the five Perth Burghs along with Dundee, Forfar, Perth and St Andrews. The town councillors of each burgh appointed one of their number as their delegate in the election of the member of parliament to represent Perth Burghs. Thus, while the appellation of the terms "rotten" and "pocket" were used in reference to English constituencies that were either tiny in population or virtually in the gift of prominent personages (and they could be both "rotten" and "pocket"), members elected for Scottish constituencies were even less reflective of the mood of the population.

[78] Francis Jeffrey (1773-1850) was one of the founders of the Edinburgh Review, a periodical that set the tone for similar publications throughout the nineteenth century. He was its editor from its inception in 1803 to 1829 and was responsible for its promotion of the principles of the Whig party that was then out of power. He married as his second wife a niece of the radical politician John Wilkes. The by-election of January 1831 saw him returned as the member for Perth Burghs but he was replaced in March by Captain Ogilvie, following a petition alleging malpractice. In the general election a few months later he regained the seat, which was abolished under the 1832 Reform Act. In the general election of 1832 he was elected member for Edinburgh but two years later surrendered that position on his appointment as a judge, taking the title Lord Jeffrey.

paraded the Streets in great masses. The scene was quite unusual in Cupar, a quiet country town on ordinary occasions, and as a specimen of popular ferment and agitation was very interesting. It was a beautiful night, fine moonlight and hard frost and the views of the mob and the buildings were often exceedingly picturesque.

The political agitation continued on the next day. Captain Ogilvie was chosen by a majority of one "but the opposite party with the Ld Advocate and the Crown Counsel had previously left the Council and those who remained were not sufficient for a Quorum, which may be a ground for annulling the Election." A few days later, when the delegates of the five burghs met, the Lord Advocate was elected.

That afternoon Andrew visited his aunt and cousins at Eden Park. Once he had spent such time as politeness required with his aunt and cousins, he and Elizabeth went out to Tarvit Pond. Whether they were chaperoned by her elder sister, Jane, is unclear but Jane came to dinner with Andrew and his father and Robert. He then escorted her home where they "had a great deal of delightful waltzing, singing and conversation." On bidding them goodnight at 11 p.m. he went to Tarvit Pond where he skated alone for an hour. "The moon was shining brightly and the stars reflected in the chrystals of ice resembled an ocean of gems. This brilliancy was relieved by the dark fringe of wood, which encircles the winding sheet of water. I was quite solitary and the loneliness of the place & the hour had something striking to it. On my return home my expedition was denounced Quixotical."

The frost remained hard on the Thursday and for the first time he "played at the very agreeable game of curling" along with Robert Christie. The early afternoon saw him back with Elizabeth at Eden Park with whose family he took dinner. There was a dancing party at a Mrs D.'s from 7 p.m. which Elizabeth did not attend but he enjoyed many waltzes with Jane.

He and Robert had arranged to give a Hogmanay party at their house with both tea and supper. Unfortunately they were in competition with some other parties and a shortage of girls which reduced the opportunities for dancing. Elizabeth, however, was present and he claimed that she was "the Cynosure of all eyes". At supper Elizabeth was sitting between him and a young doctor and flirted with both of them. "We had a great deal of fun in the trio. I sung the Boys of Kilkenny about 5 minutes of 12 o'clock and as the striking of that hour ushered in a new year we arose and enjoyed its privileges and wished each other many happy years." As stated earlier, when he wishes to record something of an intimate nature, he uses French or Latin and for an account of what followed on this particular evening he uses first one and then the other. "Elizabeth seemed very interessante as she received my devoirs. By and by the visitors departed, but as it had been previously arranged, E. remained and her mother. After all the guests had said good-bye I led my cousin to another part of the house, where we sat side by side in front of a small fire and conversed pleasantly together. The time fled quickly with caresses and embraces. She was delightful and loving and conducted herself amiably and affectionately. She sat talking and smiling so sweetly.[79] Passion and temperament were gently united with the remembrance of all that was dear. At last the beloved retired to her room and I threw myself onto my couch."

Captain and Mrs Jameson were holding a family dinner party to celebrate New Year's Day, but Andrew had time to spend the morning with Elizabeth. His father, who now owned a gig, drove to Drums with Robert while Melville came with George Gray from Perth. Andrew records that he "had a ride so far with a young lady." The Grays took their turn to entertain the family on 3rd January at Bowerswell. Back in Cupar on 5th January, the day before he had to return to Edinburgh, he made a hurried visit to Elizabeth before dinner and then was back again in the evening, which "passed away pleasantly at E's side and in the same style as on similar occasions." He now continues in Latin. "As the night drew on and the time for farewell approached, I began to feel gloomy. However, our conversation had set racing the pulse of my beloved and I enjoyed the caresses to which we were now accustomed.

---

[79] A classical scholar, he was adapting a quotation from Horace: dulce ridentem Lalage amabo dulce loquentem. (I love Lalage when she is smiling and conversing so sweetly.) Lalage is either a pseudonym for a real woman or simply an imaginary lover.

She then sang beautifully followed by some other songs most pleasing to me – a Greek song and a song of Liber."[80] He was clearly smitten with his cousin but he was about to return to his studies in a city where he was a popular guest at many homes. Although his association with the young women of these households did not reach the passionate intensity of his relationship with Elizabeth, the capital offered him a much wider social circle than was available in the little town of Cupar.

Presumably he had discussed with his father the offer made by John Ogilvie and on the 7th January 1831 he told Ogilvie that he would join him at Newington. He gave his landlady a week's notice. At the late hour of 8 p.m. that same night, they drove out to 10 Salisbury Place, Newington, in Ogilvie's noddy[81] and spent two or three hours inspecting the premises. He decided to take a bedroom on the ground floor that looked out on to the garden. The house was spacious with a fine drawing room and was fully equipped with all that was required for comfortable living. There was presumably a stable or some outhouse for the horse that drew the noddy. Ogilvie drove him back to Dundas Street in the noddy and as the diary states "without it indeed, the distances we should be obliged to walk backwards and forwards would counterbalance all the other advantages of the plan." There is no mention of the "moaning domestic" but since there is reference later in the diary to their "servant" it is at least possible that she remained in employment at the house.

The following Monday he gave a supper for several friends to celebrate his good fortune. On the Thursday John Ogilvie called with the noddy to take away half his luggage. Mrs Park was not at all pleased at losing a tenant and sent him what he describes as "an impertinent note" claiming compensation for not fulfilling his agreement with her. He decided to ignore "this piece of impertinence" because there had been a mutual understanding that one week was all that was required to terminate the engagement. The landlady was made of sterner stuff

---

[80] Liber was an Italian deity associated with Bacchus. We can safely assume that this was a love song.

[81] A noddy was a small two-wheeled conveyance. The term was in use only in Edinburgh and central Scotland in the 19th century.

than he realised because on the next day she would not accept his payment for one week's rent and claimed £3 15s. to compensate her for what she alleged was a breach of his contract to occupy the room until the end of term in April. She refused to listen to his understanding of their agreement and eventually all that he could do was ask two fellow residents to witness that he "had tendered payment of what I owed her."

The next day, Friday, having sent his trunk with all his remaining belongings out to Newington, he attended lectures and met Ogilvie by agreement at the college at 4 p.m. They walked out to Newington where he settled himself in his new quarters. Later that evening they drove to a party hosted by Mr and Mrs Murray of Couland.[82] "There was a great deal of nice dancing and no want of fair and agreeable partners. A Miss Balfour, Gayfield Square, was the beauty of the party. I had the pleasure of dancing four times with her and was glad to find her personal well supported by her mental and conversational qualities. 'Simplex Munditus'[83] she was a striking contrast to the enormous sleeves etc of the other young ladies. Her waltzing was excellent. J. O. says he never met with better. I certainly never did. I hope this will not be our last meeting as it has been the first." His social life continued to flourish because on the following evening he was a guest at the home of a Mr Pearson, whom he describes as an old friend of his father's. "We had after a sufficiency of excellent port, capital music and waltzing." At 10 p.m. that same evening he met Patrick Stirling who was in Edinburgh on business and they had "a dozen or two oysters."

Sunday worship at St Stephen's followed by a quiet day at home reading *Paradise Lost* was a great contrast to the activities of the previous seven days and doubtless provided sufficient relaxation for the busy week that was ahead of him. On the Monday he attended a jury trial, on the Tuesday he collected some title deeds for George Gray

[82] Presumably the parents of the young man, whom he had met on 25th March 1830. v. p. 94 supra.
[83] The term may be translated as "Dressed simply and neatly".

115

and despatched them to him at Perth, on the Wednesday he entertained Patrick Stirling to dinner and had a melancholy time recalling mutual friends who had died, on the Thursday he sent to Melville a copy of Donnegan's *Lexicon*[84] and on the Friday sat an examination set by one of his lecturers, Professor Bell. On the Saturday he decided to visit the Christie brothers and was handed a note from Mrs Park, informing him that since she had now let his room to two young women she had withdrawn her claim on him for payment in lieu of proper notice. It is interesting to note that since his return to Edinburgh there is no mention in his diary of any attendance at the office of Mr Heriot, although he had been much troubled the previous term about his failure to be accepted by the many writers to whom he had made application.

At the end of January 1831 he, Ogilvie, the two Christies and his friend Murray agreed to form a private debating society in order that they could develop their skills in debating and other forms of public speaking. This had long been his wish, and back in March 1830 he and Robert Christie had decided to practise these skills together but there is no evidence that they had continued this method of self-improvement. This was a more formal agreement because they elected a chairman, not surprisingly Andrew Jameson, and agreed to meet each Monday at 17 Dundas Street. They appear to have kept to this timetable.

He was examined on 27th January on servitude in Scots Law and then for the whole of February 1831 he was in almost constant receipt of invitations to dinners that were often followed by dancing, at one of which he was happy to find that the delectable Miss Balfour was also a guest. His enjoyment of his social life was, however, marred, on occasion, by severe toothache that turned out to result from the growing of his wisdom teeth. Towards the end of the month the pain was sufficiently severe to prevent him attending either his classes or the office and to seek medical assistance. A Dr Spence scarified the gum and the toothache gradually abated. The brief mention of the office may imply that he did attend Mr Heriot's premises more regularly than the diary suggests. Perhaps Elizabeth had learned of his suffering for

---

[84] A Greek dictionary and a precursor of the later and more famous Liddell and Scott dictionary.

she wrote to him and enclosed with her letter a Greek air, which he describes as "written in her own hand".

By Friday 25th February he was well enough to go into town and this was a preface to an extremely busy weekend. That evening, on his return to Salisbury Place, he found his father waiting in the drawing room. They dined and exchanged news. Thereafter Andrew drove his father to the Crown Hotel "and the novelty of the chaise amused my father not a little." He returned to dress for a rout given by a Mrs Cook, and when he arrived at half past ten dancing had just begun. However, he felt "rather flat from the effect of my late indisposition" and left the party at half past two when, apparently, it was still in full flow. His father was over on business concerning a Mrs Falconer's Trust and both John Ogilvie and Andrew were invited on the Saturday evening to join his father and the other trustees for dinner at 5.00 p.m. where they "had as much Champagne and Claret as we wished." The evening was far from over because after dinner his father took him and John Ogilvie to the theatre where they heard "a new masterpiece of some merit." The young men did not reach home until 2.00 a.m. On Sunday father and son dined with the Clephanes and spent the rest of the evening in the Crown Hotel. The next morning he and John Ogilvie walked to his father's hotel, where they breakfasted before seeing the sheriff-substitute off in the Fife Coach at ten o'clock. As the diary records, "Of course I have enjoyed this paternal visit very much. I must study hard this week and make up for the total loss of last."

The month of March was spent in serious study interspersed with an almost constant round of parties, in one week alone five invitations having been accepted. His aunt, John Ogilvie's mother, together with a brother and sister came across from Dundee on 4th March to stay in their property at 10 Salisbury Place. They remained until the 24th but Andrew did not allow their visit to distract him from either his studies or his attendance at parties, one of which did not break up until half past five in the morning.

At the end of the month he determined to honour a promise to Melville that he would visit his brother in St Andrews before the end of the academic session that would be Melville's last at the university. Friday 25th was a very stormy day and no ferry was available until the afternoon, when the Burntisland ferry decided it was safe enough to make the crossing. This was far less convenient than Kirkcaldy or Earlsferry and required him to set out on foot in pouring rain to Cupar, more than twenty miles away. Not long after leaving Burntisland a horseman leading another horse, which had been bought at a sale, allowed him to ride bareback on the led horse as far as Kirkcaldy.

This gave some rest to his legs but no shelter from the rain and it was not until nine o'clock, six hours after landing at Burntisland and thoroughly drenched, that he reached home. There he was refused admittance because Robert was ill with smallpox and infection was feared. He dashed into the house, presumably to divest himself of his sodden clothing, and went to Eden Park, the home of Elizabeth.

"As I entered the lobby there I discerned a figure stealing along the side of the wall; I felt, I touched and found Elizabeth." Since his father was staying at the George Inn it may be assumed that his son found accommodation there also. The next day was still too stormy to allow him to travel to St Andrews and the day was spent with Elizabeth. "Poor girl; I was quite sorry to find that she had been so solitary and dull all winter 'losing her sweetness on the desert air' instead of mingling in that society she is so well-fitted to adorn".

On the Sunday he walked over to St Andrews and spent the day with Melville, returning to Cupar the following morning. He spent the evening with Elizabeth and, as now had become common, the diary continues in Latin when he wishes to describe their mutual endearments. "There were loving caresses, gentle laughter and sweet singing the whole evening until one in the morning. E. is as beautiful and charming as ever. She sat smiling in a large chair, speaking sweetly as I lay before her feet in the manner of a lover." Next morning they walked along the banks of the River Eden before saying their last farewells and the diary merely adds that he reached 10 Salisbury Place at 6.00 p.m. "much the better of my trip".

Somewhat surprisingly in view of his recent illness, Robert arrived on 5th April to stay for a few days and was well enough to accompany his brother to a performance of Hamlet. The acting of Young who played the part of Hamlet was much admired but the supporting members of the cast were weak. Two days later they saw Young in Macbeth and were equally impressed. By contrast, there was no encomium for Professor Bell, whose course of lectures ended on 8th April. "My opinion of the course is that of all his hearers; that his method of instruction was meagre and unacademical, his observations uninstructive and his manner absurd and finical. The conclusion of Mr Cheape's interesting lectures was a more impressing scene. Count Leon Lubienski of Poland by the result of two separate competitions, showed a decisive superiority to his classfellows and received the Gold Medal amidst the deafening plaudits of a numerous assemblage of students. This young man is possessed of remarkable talents. Six months ago he came to this country a stranger to its language and already has he carried two of the highest honours of the university. Mr Cheape introduced me to him early in the winter and I have been on very intimate terms with him since. His father commands the right wing of the Polish Army in this present eventful contest."[85]

The next week he made farewell calls on the many families that had given him hospitality. The establishment at 10 Salisbury Place, Newington, was broken up in preparation for a sale of all its furniture and the private debating society was adjourned for the summer. Whether he had been attending with any regularity the office of Mr Heriot is unclear because there is no mention of it apart from the one entry when he wrote that toothache had prevented him attending both classes and the office. He must have made some appearances at the office because he seems to have been present when Mr Heriot told his clerks on 13th April that he was giving up business immediately since "his affairs have got into a state of embarrassment and he is going under Trust."

He returned home to Cupar on Tuesday, 19th April, Robert following on Thursday. Elizabeth came to supper but "I was in a curious humour at parting and ranted à la Théatre to a great extent." He spent the

[85] An account of this young man and his background is given in an appendix to this chapter.

Wednesday and Thursday with his rod, paid calls on the Friday and spent the weekend at Drums with his uncle and aunt. He saw Elizabeth on the Monday evening but confined himself to reading and fishing over the next two days. On Thursday the 29th he with John and James Ogilvie attended the Assembly Rooms in Cupar, where they enjoyed dancing with many "very agreeable partners" and on the Friday he called on some of these partners of the previous evening. It is possible that Elizabeth's star was on the wane since he writes that he called at her house simply because it was on his way. He was now moving in Edinburgh society, and meeting many other girls, such as the attractive and sophisticated Miss Balfour, had made him aware of a wider field of female acquaintances than Cupar could offer. For her part, Elizabeth may have been feeling neglected because he writes that he "prevailed upon her to go [to] the Ball that night." This suggests that she was initially reluctant but, while it may have been no more than a lover's tiff, later events were to prove that Elizabeth was not the only pebble on Andrew Jameson's beach.

Saturday, 30th April 1831 was his twentieth birthday, and he writes in his diary that he is 5 feet 7¾ inches and in the best of health. Perhaps any indications that his ardour for Elizabeth was cooling were misplaced because he spent time alone with her "from 11 to 4 very delightfully." He gave her some attar of roses as a present. There was a dinner that evening in his honour attended by Sheriff Clephane and others after which Melville and he "went to the Park". This must have been Eden Park, the home of Elizabeth, and he writes nothing in his diary other than the Latin for "This is a place upon which I do not look back upon with any great pleasure," a curious comment in view of the several hours of dalliance spent there with Elizabeth.

He had now completed successfully two years of study in law at Edinburgh University and he decided on 1st May 1831 that he should take the examination in civil law that was a necessary preliminary for admission to the Faculty of Advocates. As he writes in his diary, "There was a report of a contemplated addition to the fees, already so expensive, which precipitated my intentions. My father agreed entirely with me and thought that I should pay my Grandaunt a visit to request fulfilment of her promise to him and me." This promise, presumably, had been an offer to pay the substantial fee required by the Faculty of Advocates, a small portion of which went to a fund that gave support to widows of lawyers.

Andrew visited his ninety-two-year-old aunt four days later but found her conversation to be "the drivelling of dotage." He remained at Graycraig over the weekend and on the Monday he found her "much more collected." The minister of Culross, the Reverend A. B. Duncan, who was also a grandnephew of Miss Jameson, came to make a pastoral call and he advised Andrew to approach his aunt again. She pleaded poverty and added that "thro time she might do something for me." This was virtually a refusal and Andrew returned to Cupar.

The only other method whereby he could raise money was through a loan. Wisely he approached his brother-in-law, George Gray, whose legal practice in Perth was flourishing. Gray had previously shown interest in Andrew's career and had even paid him a small commission for some work carried out on his behalf. As Andrew writes in his diary, Gray "promised to stand by me, as long as I continued worthy of support and made some animadversions on my Father's mismanagement[86] of his affairs, which I endeavoured to meet the best way I could. He at last arranged a plan for raising the necessary funds by a bill, in which my Father, Uncle, he and myself should join." The necessary financial arrangements were agreed by 14th May and it was left to Gray to draw up the formal documents required.

Andrew immediately set himself to the task of preparing for his examination or "trial" as it was then described. He determined to concentrate upon the *Institutes* of Justinian, reading them in their original Latin. Unfortunately, on the evening of that very day (16th May), he tripped over some lumber in the attic and fell against a piece of iron, damaging his shin bone. The wound seemed inconsiderable

---

[86] Had it not been for the benevolence of his wealthy brother, Captain Jameson of the East India Company's Maritime Service, Andrew Jameson (Senior) could not have survived the morass of debt into which he had earlier fallen. v. p. 23 supra.

at the time and his father bound it with balsamic ointment. It did not respond to this treatment but he was not incapacitated enough to prevent him from travelling to Edinburgh with his father on Friday the 20th by private gig and coach, staying the night with George Christie who was still at 17 Dundas Street. On Saturday morning they made the necessary arrangements with the Faculty of Advocates for him to take his examination and returned to Cupar.

The exertions of the journey to and from Edinburgh exacerbated the pain and on reaching home his leg was examined and found to be heavily inflamed and suppurating under the plaster bandage. Succour came in the form of Elizabeth, who came at ten o'clock, and he enjoyed, as the Latin prose reports, "two of the happiest hours, full of kisses, her lips delightful, our mouths together, heads leaning against each other, our tongues touching, the closest of embraces and caresses." With bathos that is barely credible he completed this paragraph with the mundane comment that "Melville entered Berwick's office on 16th."

On the following Monday he returned "with redoubled vigour" to his study of the "Institutes" of Justinian. He had a brief visit from Elizabeth on the evening of the 24th, had a short walk with her the next night and dined with her and Melville on the Saturday. He wrote nothing in his diary for two weeks, when the following entry was made on 12th June 1831.

> The same routine of study, anxiety and confinement. I was engaged from 8 to 10 hours each day at Civil Law and the wound on my shinbone now became very troublesome and prevented me enjoying any of that relaxation out of doors, which is so necessary and so agreeable.
>
> At first I was permitted to be carried to the garden and sit at the foot of the Iargonelle tree[87] or by the side of Melville's Laburnum with my grandfather's Corpus Juris in my hand – and the umbrageous privacy was as favourable and certainly far more pleasant place for study than the

---

[87] An early-ripening variety of pear.

Drawing room Sopha. But latterly the surgeon has ordered constant use of the limb and day after day passes over me, each more bright and glorious than its predecessor and I can only hear of but cannot enjoy the Season's pleasures.

On 10th June his brother James, who had now served for thirteen years with the East India Company's Maritime Service, arrived by sea at Dundee. He was in the poorest health, suffering from the effects of dysentery that had affected almost all the crew, of whom eighteen had died before reaching England. He was too unwell to be allowed to come home and was put in the care of a Dr Davidson, who owned some form of private clinic in Dundee.

Andrew, himself, needed treatment for his leg but obviously it did little more than restrict his movements. A doctor came regularly to dress the wound and over the next fortnight there was some improvement. His injury did not interrupt his studies and possibly allowed him more time for them than would have been the case had he been fully fit. On Sunday, 12th June Robert, Melville and their father went to Drums and Andrew wrote a letter[88] in French to Elizabeth inviting her to visit him. She came after church and they dined happily together followed by much caressing and kissing.

On the Friday Robert and their father went to Perth to share in the anniversary of the marriage of Sophia to George Gray and Elizabeth paid a visit with her mother. It seems probable that there was another reason for his father going to Perth, the completion of formalities concerning the loan that George Gray had arranged so that the fee could be paid for Andrew's examination before the Faculty of Advocates. They returned from Perth on the 20th with better news of James and a promissory note[89] that Andrew as well as his father had to sign.

He was due to travel to Edinburgh on the following Thursday, and on the Tuesday Dr Grace drove him out to Crawford Priory thus allowing

[88] Why he should use French can only be guessed. Perhaps he did not want a servant or someone else to read it.
[89] A signed document containing a written promise to pay a stated sum to a specified person at a specified date.

him his first sight of the countryside for a month. Elizabeth came to wish him farewell and good fortune but there was some premonition of his declining ardour because he describes her behaviour that evening as extremely childish.

He left for Edinburgh on 23rd June and, although his diary records that "I was put into the inside of the coach and conveyed to Edinburgh still in a helpless state," he was the next day able to prepare and sign his petition to the Court of Session for examination. The Clephanes had invited him to stay with them during the days leading up to his examination and the sheriff had even arranged with the Lord President for the date and time of Andrew's trial to be held over until Tuesday 5th July, the last day available, so that there was time for the wound in his leg to heal. On the Saturday before his examination Sheriff Clephane introduced Andrew to Andrew Skene, who was President of Examinators in Civil Law. Then on the Sunday evening the sheriff put questions on civil law to Andrew and "thought me fully prepared to undergo the ordeal." It is not too much to suggest that the sheriff regarded the young man as his protégé and, as stated earlier,[90] Andrew Jameson was very fortunate to have secured the support of so prominent a person at the very outset of his career.

The diary entry for Monday, 4th July 1831 consists of two words: "Revision general." The description of Andrew's activities on 5th July cannot be better expressed than that given in his diary for that important day.

> I woke early & walked up to the Parl House at 8 a.m. in a fine Summer morning. I had more confidence than at any time previously.
>
> After waiting for some time in the apartments of the lower Library the Secretary informed me the Examinators[91]

---

[90] v. p. 77 supra.

[91] I am grateful to Dr David Parratt, Advocate, of the Advocates Library in Parliament House, for supplying me with the names of the examinators in Civil Law in 1831. They were Andrew Skene (Preses), John Shaw Stewart, Charles Neaves, Adam Paterson, William Penney, James John Reid and John F. Stoddart.

were ready and proceeding thro a dark antechamber I was speedily ushered in to their presence. Bowing as I entered I walked up to the foot of a long table, at the head of which sat the President with his colleagues along the sides, in their wigs and gowns and old massive folios of the Civil Law before them. The President commenced by putting a variety of questions on the Civil Law in general – the Divisions of things, obligations and actions. Mr Neaves followed on Usufruct, Paterson on Legacies, Penney on Sale, Stoddart on Marriage and Mr Reid concluded.

After answering all their questions with little difficulty the President told me to turn to Pandects 26:1:1 on Tutors – a passage of easy translation.[92] This being finished I was motioned to retire & withdrawing to the lighted antechamber with its old portraits, who seemed to smile grimly on the anxious candidate, I waited patiently for the issue of the Ballot. In a little time I was called in, when the President rose & said he was happy to announce to me that I had been unanimously found qualified in Civil Law and was certified as such & ready to proceed to my other trials. He then left the chair and shook hands with me, which the rest followed in succession. I at the same time received my Petition signed accordingly and the receipt for the fees & widows fund, which I paid on Saturday. They amounted to about £265.

On ascending to the Outer House I met Mr Clephane, who enquired in his facetious[93] manner "Well – is it all over with you?" It is all over I am glad to say I replied. I walked about for some time & received the usual congratulations from acquaintances, some of whom would have been as well pleased that I had been rejected. In the course of the day I wrote to my father, Capt Jameson and Mr Gray.

---

[92] Pandects: a digest of Roman civil law, compiled for the emperor Justinian in the sixth century AD and part of the Corpus Juris Civilis. Also called "Digest".

[93] In 1831 the word meant "jocular", a slightly different meaning from today.

The following Friday he took his leave of the Clephanes and crossed over to Dysart, where he stayed with relations until Monday. Part of the hospitality that he had received from the Clephanes was treatment for his injured leg by a Dr Johnstone, who had recommended bathing as treatment for the wound. Accordingly, while at Dysart, he took the opportunity for some sea bathing. He also records during this weekend that he "hoped to throw all the information I have collected into a connected history of the family. It would be interesting to its members." This intention was carried out several years later and, described simply as the Memoir, remains, apart from Andrew Jameson's diaries and correspondence that has survived, the primary and virtually sole source of the Jameson family history from 1680 to 1846.[94]

On reaching home he discovered that James had been removed from the clinic in Dundee "to Bell Brae Cottage situated to the S. of Cupar below the Garlie bank on the E. of the Nursery ground." He went there immediately and was distressed to see his brother so unwell. He was to visit James every day thereafter. While at Bell Brae that first afternoon he met Elizabeth and, whether this was by chance or design, there were the warmest of embraces. Next day there were more amorous exchanges in the garden of Eden Park, and again on Wednesday night there were further intimacies that Andrew refers to as "Columbationes." Elizabeth had to play second fiddle to fishing on Thursday until ten o'clock, when there was much passion between them up to midnight. Nothing is recorded on Friday but on Saturday, 16th July he writes "Presented 'Songs of the Affections' to Miss E. Thomson."

The affectionate relationship between Andrew Jameson and his

---

[94] The Memoir provided the history of the Jameson family that appears in the chapter entitled "Captain Jameson's Ancestry" in the author's book *Captain Jameson 1773–1834* published by The Robert Gordon University in May 2002. A slightly amended version appears as the first chapter to this work on Captain Jameson's nephew, Andrew Jameson. A copy of the Memoir is currently held by Andrew Jameson's great-grandson, J. N. St. C. Jameson, WS. It is possible that another copy may be in the possession of another descendant, Mr J. McCulloch. Certain slight mistakes concerning names of places in and around Cupar, which were probably made when the Memoirs were transferred from manuscript to typescript, are dealt with in *Captain Jameson 1773–1834*. The same book disposes of the totally erroneous belief that a Jameson collateral ancestor fought at Culloden.

cousin Elizabeth Thomson was soon to cool, at least on Andrew's part, and descend into indifference. Some slight indications of this have already been mentioned and his amorous dalliance with her during the past week can be criticised as giving the girl a misleading impression of constancy whereas he was simply enjoying the heavy flirtation. He composed the following two stanzas about this time.[95]

I

Lady! I'll not chide thee more
Tho'methinks t'was cruel and strange
Such cold and chilling slights to throw
On one, who never dream't of change.
   – Yet t'was folly to have deemed
Thou wer't ever all thou seemed.

II

– T'is past – and I'll not repine
Tho' regret may cast a shade
Over a spirit not made to whine
For the loss of flowers that fade.
Fit emblems of that fragile thing
The heart of a female changeling.

It is interesting that the verses were written during a week, when, to Elizabeth at least, his actions can only have been interpreted as an expression of his true feelings for her. Apart from the final line that does not scan it is an acceptable piece of verse – one can hardly call it a poem – about unrequited love. It reflects, however, the anguish of a rejected lover. Although the diary is our only source of the relation-ship between the two young people, Elizabeth comes over as an ever

---

[95] They are written in his diary for 16th July 1831 but with the comment "I scribbled these two stanzas about this time."

willing recipient of Andrew's attention and, even at times, appears to make some of the running herself. It is, therefore, unlikely that these two stanzas arose out of some sudden change of mind on the part of Elizabeth.

There is no further mention of Elizabeth until 10th August and the words in the diary for that day say all that is necessary. Andrew was setting off on another walking tour of the Highlands and Elizabeth accompanied him as far as Balgarvie toll.

"Last night I went up and shewed my accoutrements for my journey and gave her a long lecture, which has lifted the veil and will probably cloud our mutual good understanding. Few intimacies can stand a full exposure of the faults & follies of any of the parties from the lips of the other. It was well meant on my side, tho' tinged with bitterness & seemed to be received with displeasure and disappointment." What was said can only be guessed but at least Elizabeth was prepared to walk a short way with him the next morning.

This excursion into the Highlands had been planned for early August between Andrew and one of his student friends in Edinburgh, a Macrae from Skye. However, Robert had become severely ill again and this had made it necessary for him to postpone his departure from the date originally determined.

We learn from the diary entry for Saturday, 16th July 1831 that Robert, having completed his apprenticeship with Drummond and Berwick, was now concerned about his future. It is clear that he was not nearly as intellectually accomplished as his two younger brothers and, as Andrew writes, "Poor fellow: he asked me to write out a list of books for him and we went down to the public library together and selected some for his perusal." From what happened later it is clear that Robert was in the early stages of severe depression. On Monday the 26th Andrew went over to Dundee, to stay with his aunt, and returned on the Friday to find Robert had been in a despondent mood for some days. Next day their father encouraged Robert to accompany Andrew and him to Drums but he refused. The diary gives a graphic account of what happened late on the Sunday night.

On this night Robert's disease came to a climax. I'll never forget the terrors of that night: our fears, when he was first missed, my father's agitation and our unavailing search. The horrors of the first discovery were unspeakable. My feelings were worked up to a dreadful pitch. I seized him in my arms and thank God he was in life.

Monday 1st August to Monday 8th. For this week I have tended very constantly on poor Bob. I have seen the duties of an attendant upon the sick and experienced their sadness. My father and Melville went to Graycraig on Saturday 6th to meet Major Montgomery and see Old Aunt and returned today.

The medical attendant thinks that now the fever, which seems to be a Typhus, has considerably abated and that he will gradually get the better of it. James, who found the cottage dull after we required to give Robert so much attendance, went out to Drums on Thursday 4th August and is already better of the change.

As events were to turn out the optimism expressed concerning these two young men was sadly misplaced.

The tour of the Highlands lasted seven weeks and the diary records little more than the route and the time spent at various places. He reached Inverinate on Loch Duich on 17th August via Loch Earn, Crianlarich, Glen Orchy, Glen Coe, Fort William, Loch Oich, Glen Garry and Glen Shiel. He appears to have spent a week there before crossing to Skye on August 24th. Since it took him only two days to reach Talisker on the far west of the island, a distance of over forty miles, he must have walked with great determination. He began his return journey immediately, staying at Dunan for one night before reaching Camasunary at the foot of the Cuillins on August 28th. He spent three days on the Strathaird Peninsula that lies immediately to the south of Camasunary, and it is possible that he was exploring the remains of Viking farms and Bronze and Iron Age sites that are currently attracting the attention of archaeologists.[96] There followed three days at Corry on Broadford Bay. There is no mention of any meeting with his friend Macrae when he was on the island, and he returned to Inverinate on September 7th. He then walked north up the Great Glen in slow stages to Beauly, where he passed three days. Dingwall on August 15th was his furthest point north before he started on his return journey through Inverness, Culloden, Granton-on-Spey to Tomintoul. After descending the Ladder Hills on August 24th he took a detour up Glen Buchat, no doubt recalling that his collateral ancestor Captain Leith had received a commission in Gordon of Glenbuchat's regiment that was raised there and in neighbouring Strathdon to support the Young Pretender in 1745. On the 25th he stayed overnight at Skene, near Aberdeen, and turned here north-east to visit his friends the Russels at Aden, where he had hospitality for three days. Since he came to Aberdeen on September 30th and reached Cupar the following day it must be presumed that he did not cover these last ninety miles entirely on foot. With a curious lapse of concentration for one so meticulous in his habits Andrew Jameson writes that he came home on September 31st.

His health that had suffered from his confinement in the summer on account of his injured leg was now fully restored. It was very different for his two ailing brothers, who, he had understood on leaving for his excursion, had been on the way to recovery. Moreover, when he had reached Inverness, he had received a letter from his father saying that James was much better and able to come down each day for meals while Robert's fever had gone and "his dreadful sores from being bedrid are healing every day and his appetite is good." Now on returning home he found that James had had a relapse and that Robert was still suffering from dreadful ulcers. Andrew writes that "the first time I saw them I felt as if I was to faint and a more harrowing sight I have seldom witnessed. Poor fellow, he is dejected and in sore distress, unable to move himself in bed, pained when he is moved by others. He seldom speaks and seems little interested when spoken to."

[96] The peninsula is now owned by the John Muir Trust.

Unsurprisingly, in view of his words with Elizabeth on 10th August, he received a frosty reception from the Thomson family when next day he paid a call at Eden Park. The rest of the month was spent mainly in fishing and paying calls. He notes that Elizabeth and her mother left for Graycraig on 10th October, and it may be that old Miss Jameson's relations thought it wise to show their concern for a relation now past her ninetieth year. Many other relations had been visiting Miss Jameson over the last twenty years or so and Andrew had himself paid visits in May 1827 and July 1828 before his abortive stay in May 1831. Then on 9th November 1831, just as he was making preparations to return to Edinburgh, news came that his old grandaunt had died the previous morning.

The funeral of Miss Jameson was arranged for Monday the 14th. Mrs Thomson and Elizabeth returned from Graycraig on 11th November and since he would be leaving for Edinburgh immediately after the funeral he went to Eden Park to say his farewells on the Saturday evening. Six simple Latin words record the resumption of amorous relationships with Elizabeth. This was certainly a case of true love never running smoothly, but how true was the love of Andrew Jameson?

There was a "respectable assemblage" at the funeral, where Sheriff-Substitute Jameson took the role of chief mourner. The only other persons mentioned by name were Captain Jameson, Mr Ogilvie (father of the young man with whom Andrew had stayed at 10 Salisbury Place, Newington), a Dr Craig from Edinburgh and a Major and Mrs Montgomery from Kilmarnock.[97] After the interment at Saline churchyard the family members returned to Graycraig, where the will was read. It must have been a considerable blow to the sheriff-substitute, who had never managed his financial affairs satisfactorily, that his share was a mere £300. Apart from a few trifling legacies the whole property, together with about £6,000, was bequeathed to the

---

[97] These last must have been some connection of the Jameson family, although the first appearance of the name is in the diary for 8th August 1831, when it states that Melville and their father had been to Graycraig to meet Major Montgomery. It may have been through this Montgomery connection that Andrew Jameson many years later met Margaret Hotchkis, his second wife.

Rev. A. B. Duncan, the minister at Culross. Perhaps the visit of Mr Duncan to Graycraig on 9th May had been less than wholly pastoral.[98]

At 5 a.m. on the following morning Andrew left Graycraig for Edinburgh with Dr Craig and at the invitation of the Clephanes stayed two nights with them while he sought suitable lodgings. These he found at 11 Scotland Street, where a large consignment of wines and spirits arrived from the Clephanes on the Saturday. The sheriff also offered him the use of his library, a considerable advantage for any student of law, and thus yet another favour that assisted him towards qualification in his chosen profession.

From this time until the end of December the pattern of his life was attendance at classes, principally the course in conveyancing delivered by Professor Napier, and acceptance of the many invitations to dinner that he continued to receive. Two of these dinners are of interest.

One was a farewell dinner with Captain Jameson and his wife. His uncle was about to depart for Calcutta to take up the post of Master Attendant, the most senior post abroad of the East India Company Maritime Service.[99] The other was an invitation from the Murrays on the 22nd December and, although he had agreed to open a debate at the Select Literary Society that evening, the early time of dinner then common in Edinburgh allowed him to accept the invitation. If he had known that the delectable Miss Balfour had also been invited he would certainly have made arrangements to withdraw from this commitment. He remained by her side as long as he could before running all the way to present his paper at the Society.

A few days earlier his father had written to him with news that James and Robert were now seriously ill again. He came home on Christmas Eve to find his brothers in a sorry state. "Poor James in the parlour distressed and emaciated and evidently getting worse. Robert in the next room unable to move from dreadful sores in his back and the two brothers – formerly so intimate – unable to see or speak to one

---

[98] v. p. 121 supra.

[99] Captain Jameson died only two years after reaching Calcutta. His widow, who had not accompanied him to India, survived until 1851.

another. It was a saddening sight."[100] It was not a joyous Christmas and doubtless he was glad to return to Edinburgh after the New Year, but on Friday, 13th January 1832 he received a note from Melville to say that James was very ill indeed. He returned the next day to Cupar, where he found that his brother had died on the previous evening.

James had been attended by three doctors during his last months and each had given a different diagnosis: consumption, liver failure and bowel disease. The family decided that they would like to know the real cause of his death and a gruesome scene was enacted in their dining room on the Monday evening. Watched by the father, his two youngest sons and his son-in-law, three doctors lifted the body of James onto the table and cut it open at the parts where they needed to examine it. They found that the liver was perfectly sound but that the left lung was severely congested and the bowels inflamed.[101] Having said nothing could have saved him, they replaced the parts that they had examined, sewed up the skin and replaced him in his coffin.

The funeral took place on the Tuesday and followed the traditional pattern of the times. Family members and close friends assembled in the drawing room, where the minister, Mr Birrell,[102] pronounced a blessing and gave a prayer. There followed refreshments and wine, and when the coffin was brought downstairs they followed it out onto the street, where the other mourners were waiting. The procession passed through the town to the cemetery and James was laid to rest in a deep grave by the side of his mother and two sisters.

Andrew went back to Edinburgh on 24th January and resumed his attendance at classes. Partly because he felt very much the death of his brother and partly because he had to pay increasing attention to his

---

[100] Memoir, p. 175.

[101] The author detailed this description of the bowels to a doctor, who said it was almost certainly carcinoma.

[102] The career of the Rev. John Birrell (1788–1842) was extraordinary. After graduation he taught at George Watson's Hospital (now College), was appointed tutor to the family of James Home of Cowdenknowes near Earlston in Berwickshire, became Professor of Materia Medica at Edinburgh University, took holy orders and was licensed by the Presbytery of Edinburgh in 1819, was ordained and appointed minister to the rural parish of Westruther in Berwickshire that same year and was presented by George IV to the living at Cupar in 1825, where he served until his death.

legal studies, his social life, although not dormant, was considerably less active than it had been when first he came to Edinburgh. He enjoyed a visit from Melville (24th–29th February) and in March determined to seek a position in the chambers of a writer in order that he could have some practical experience of the profession he was intending to follow. He was as unsuccessful in this regard as he had been in the autumn of 1830. He visited his father and brothers in Cupar for a long weekend in mid-March and found Robert apparently much better.

This first return home after the passing of his brother rekindled his memory of the sad Christmas and New Year that had culminated in the death of James. This had a profound effect upon him and on 27th March there is a very long entry in the diary that is again reminiscent of his self-criticism in October 1826. At that time he had considered that he had fallen into the grip of the deadly sin of sloth and that, as a good Christian, he must show greater endeavour in his studies; in other words he had to contend the sin of sloth with the virtue of zeal.[103] This entry of 27th March 1832 is similar in its self-criticism with the words "shameful negligence" appearing in the first sentence. The seven pages of closely written but beautifully formed script suggest that this was not an extempore entry but a piece over which he had pondered deeply and had first rendered in draft before committing the final approved version to his diary.

The first part of what is a statement of intent deals with his duty to God. In particular this means that he must use the talents that he has been given by his Maker with constant diligence. "I am imperatively called upon, as I value the love of God and my own peace, to pay a constant and unremitting attention to my professional studies in so far as they interfere not with that portion of time, which must be sacred to the worship of God and religious meditation." He observes that hitherto he has been supported in all the comforts of life by his father but now he must impose upon himself the obligation of self-reliance and, as soon as possible, maintain himself by his own exertions and begin to make some contribution towards the provision of those comforts that

---

[103] v. p. 50 supra.

the approaching old age of his father will demand. He is brought to this conclusion by his remembrance of the Fifth Commandment that enjoins believers to honour their fathers and mothers.

This is followed by a short paragraph wherein he realises that, having irrevocably chosen law as his profession, this necessity to exert himself is "encreased by the state of the profession, over stocked as it is with members to such a degree that the only prospect of success to me is by greater diligence and more strenuous industry."

Thirdly, he writes that all his family credit him with the studious habits and consequent sound progress that justify the expense of his being kept by his father. He considers that he has been deceiving their just expectations because it is only upon his first session at Edinburgh that he can look back with satisfaction.

He continues in this strain, writing that he still has very little acquaintance with the profession of the law though he has "been pretending to study it so long." He believes that his fellow students are all now more successful than he and that he is losing valuable opportunities to demonstrate his abilities. "In every point of view my past conduct and present state with regard to my professional studies are in a very great degree sinful, immoral and contrary to my urgent duties and interests."

To amend his behaviour and drag himself back to the paths of righteousness that include more energetic application to his studies, he lays down what he calls "a proper division of the day" and resolves to adhere to it with reasonable constancy. First of all there is religion. After accepting that "we have certain duties assigned by God to do in this world and a proper discharge of them necessarily requires a considerable portion of our time," he argues against the requirement that the "greater portion of our time should be devoted to actual praise and prayer." For this reason he makes his own interpretation of the fourth commandment that the sabbath be kept holy, whereby he will devote one seventh of each day to religious thought and contemplation, so that Sundays can remain a day for other pursuits, including study. He then moves to a consideration of his professional studies and compares

135

himself with "artisans and hired workmen paid day wages," who have fixed hours of the day as the time for their daily labour. He assigns ten hours for each weekday (and he includes time for preparation for debates here) and law reading six hours. Finally he comes to sleep, food and exercise and he decides that he needs two and a half hours for exercise and calls, one hour for meals and seven hours for sleep.

This was a rigorous schedule indeed and one must presume that he made a genuine attempt to observe it. One indication of his early resolve may be seen in his diary, if one can now call it that. Whereas it had previously provided a lot of information about his classes, his friends and his social activities, it now becomes little more than a catalogue of the briefest kind, such as that for 29th March where the entry is simply "Dined with Professor Cheape."

He left Edinburgh for Cupar on 14th April, visited relations in Dundee, went fishing and caught a severe cold that kept him in bed for a week. His twenty-first birthday was on 30th April but all that happened was that Robert was able to come down to the parlour for, presumably, some form of celebratory meal with his father and brothers. There is no mention of Elizabeth or even of any calls at her home.

There is a long entry in the diary on 2nd May 1832. He has returned to Edinburgh "principally for the purpose of endeavouring to procure a situation in a Writer's office." He sees it as a step of the utmost importance, and although his many applications have been unsuccessful he is determined to put disappointment behind him and redouble his efforts to secure a position. If he is not successful he will return home and spend the summer concentrating on his legal studies. He also reminds himself that he "must use greater diligence and by strict attention to the rules formerly laid down, I hope to pass my time profitably and agreeably – so help me God."

He was as good as his word and at last, on 21st May, he received a note from a Mr Bertram that there was a vacancy in the offices of Messrs Nairne. He called there immediately and, being found satisfactory, "was installed in a desk where I continued very busy all week." It was fortunate for him that the offer came when it did because on the Friday (25th) he received two letters, one from Robert virtually commanding him to come next day and one from Melville urging him, in less imperious language, to come to Cupar because "Robert was in rather an excited state." Andrew crossed over on the Saturday, and there is a long entry in the diary that would be tedious to comment upon other than to say that Robert was now exhibiting all the symptoms of extreme dementia and during this weekend had even attacked one of the servants. There is no mention of any medical attention being summoned and the family must have resolved to look after him as best they could. Andrew decided that, having just secured a position in a writer's office after so many disappointments, it was necessary for him to return to Edinburgh but felt it was his duty to come again to Cupar on the following four weekends to give his support to the family.

The diary does not tell if Robert became quieter, if not better, but Andrew did not feel any reason for him to continue these weekend visits. Life resumed its normal pattern with the added bonus of not having to seek for an appointment to a lawyer's office. There seems to have been some relaxation of the severe pattern of religious devotion and rigorous study that he had promised to impose upon himself at the end of March because he accepted invitations to dinner and attended the theatre to hear Kemble[104] in *The Hunchback*.[105] His classes had now ceased for the session and he attended regularly at the office, where much of his time was passed in copying documents. In an age when there was no method of copying documents other than manuscript, delegation of this task to apprentices was not the least effective way of training them.

On Saturday, 11th August 1832 a letter came from Melville[106] urging him to come over as soon as possible, since Robert was much worse. He left immediately but as he approached the house he saw that

[104] Possibly Henry Kemble (1789–1836), a member of the Kemble-Siddons acting dynasty.
[105] Probably a play derived from some earlier work, where the Hunchback of Nôtre Dame was featured. Alexandre Dumas, author of the famous book of that name, was only a child in 1832.
[106] A letter from Melville dated 10th August 1832 was found by the author among some 1843/44 correspondence and Andrew Jameson has written on it: "This letter was not delivered and I did not again see my brother in life." Did Melville write a second one that day?

all the blinds were drawn, a clear indication that Robert had died.[107] The sad but necessary preparations were made for the funeral on the 14th August, when the service and interment were similar to that so recently carried out at the death of James. Andrew notes that his father was disconsolate, having lost two sons within seven months in addition to two of his daughters some years previously.

He returned to Edinburgh the day after the funeral and although the entries in the diary are scanty in the extreme, it seems that he went to seek leave to be with his family for a few days and to take a short walking holiday thereafter. Sophia had her father and two brothers to stay with her at Perth after the funeral and, following a few more days at Cupar, he set off on 31st August for another Highland tour. His route was along Loch Tay to Loch Awe, south to Inverary and back through the Trossachs to Dunblane, Perth and Cupar. Even though Melville had taken him to Newburgh in the family gig, whence he took the steamboat to Perth at the start of his journey, and had met him there on his return on 6th September, he covered a remarkable number of miles in those seven days.

It must be mentioned here that the diary from the middle of March to 6th September 1832 consists of four small separate notebooks. From the time he was an undergraduate at St Andrews the entries had been made into strong hard-backed notebooks consisting of about 100 to 120 pages each. The last of these had its first entry in December 1831 but after thirty pages the entries cease and the tale is continued in the four small, somewhat fragile, notebooks. Had he mislaid his hardback diary? If he had, he found it again later and, after leaving about fifty pages blank, resumed entries at 23rd December 1832. These peter out after twelve pages that take us only to 24th February 1833. There follow a few blank pages and then entries are resumed from November 1834, when he had returned from an extended European tour. Separate diaries for this tour begin at the end of April 1833. Failing the discovery of any documents for the period

---

[107] The custom of drawing the blinds to indicate a death continued in Scotland into the second half of the twentieth century. On occasion, the custom continues.

early September 1832 to mid-December 1832 and late February to early March 1833, the only guidance concerning Andrew Jameson's third year at Edinburgh University are the few entries made in the diary from mid-December 1832 until late February 1833.

We learn very little from these twelve pages. He was still living at 11 Scotland Street, the lodgings that he had first taken back in November 1831. Melville visited him from 24th to 28th December, when they returned home and left immediately with their father to stay at Perth with the Grays. Sophia's fourth child and third son was christened next day and, since the infant had been given the name Robert, their father was in tears throughout the ceremony. Back at Cupar for New Year 1833, he sprained his ankle skating on Tarvit Pond. This attracted a visit in the evening from Elizabeth and her mother, and next day he trotted over on the family pony to Eden Park to reciprocate their call but did no more than converse with members of the family.

Monday, 8th January 1833 saw him back in Edinburgh at Messrs Nairne. There is no mention of any classes at the university but we can safely assume that he was attending at least some instruction there because on 31st January Professor Cheape "tried hard to persuade me to undertake his Prize Essay for this year on the subject of "Written and Unwritten Law". His social life was as active as it had been during his first two and a half years in Edinburgh and it is obvious that he no longer followed the strict personal regime that he had laid down for himself in March 1832. There is even a slight hint of romance with a Miss Marion Scott.

From the time he first came to Edinburgh there are frequent entries in the diary about visits to the Scott family at Northfield,[108] which is described in the Memoir as a "hospitable farmhouse" near Duddingston. Since it was "graced by the presence of four charming sisters"[109] it is not surprising that Andrew Jameson became a frequent visitor. The father of these sisters was David Scott,[110] whose sister was married

[108] Northfield is now a suburb of Edinburgh.
[109] Memoir p.160.
[110] David Scott is described in the Memoir as "a fine old gentleman" and this accounts for an apparent generation gap.

to a brother of Mary Spittal, second wife of John Jameson, Andrew's grandfather. On 16th January he arrived there, drenched from a sudden heavy downpour, and thought it would be better for him to return home to dry himself. Marion, however, made him divest himself of sodden shoes and stockings, fetched some replacements from her brother's wardrobe and invited him to dinner. He writes that he "could not resist this and spent one of the happiest evenings it has ever been or ever may be my lot to spend here." Six days later he went to skate on Duddingston Loch and, as noted earlier,[111] this was where young people would go with the strong presumption that they would meet there some of their contemporaries. Marion was of their number that day. She allowed him to escort her home, invited him to dinner and there was another happy evening there for Andrew Jameson. The heavy frost continued into the next day, when Duddingston Loch repeated its attractions for both young people and again it was dining with the Scotts at Northfield. Saturday, 26th January saw a busy day at the office and although he did not dine at Northfield, he attended an evening party there along with some other young men and women and enjoyed the dancing.

He was finding his work in the office of Messrs Nairne both interesting and useful because, unlike his attachment of the previous year to the office of Mr Heriot, there was much less hanging about with nothing to do. Saturday afternoons were then part of the working week where work would continue until, in the winter months at any rate, candles became necessary for illumination. It is a reasonable deduction from what we know of Andrew Jameson that he would always act in a courteous and responsible manner and thus earn growing confidence from his superiors in the firm, who would delegate work to him in accordance with his abilities. Professor Cheape thought highly of him and told him that "he was pleased to say I was the only one in the class who could write a credible Essay on it" (the topic of the prize essay that the Professor was anxious that he should attempt).

February 1833 was spent in attendance at the office and in his usual social round, including visits to Northfield. He presumably attended

[111] v. p. 109 supra.

some university classes because on 22nd February Professor Cheape again suggested he attempt the prize essay competition. Although only a fortnight was left before the final submission date, Professor Cheape said that he would allow him a further week and again commented upon his excellent qualifications for writing on the topic that had been set. The diary does not tell us if he did submit an essay.

The entry for 23rd February consists of four pages about the criticism of his character made to him by a young lady, whom he had escorted to some exhibition, and his responses to the accusations. His three main faults, he was told, were "sometimes very absent in conversation", "not endeavouring to please those whom I do not like" and "self-conceited". He makes good answers to both the first and second charge and since the young lady said that although she did not find him self-conceited, others did, he did not feel it necessary to debate this alleged fault in his character.

The last entry is that for Sunday, 24th February 1833. It starts with the words "My Cough having increased and a cold wind blowing I kept the house all day." He carried out some hard study before attending church in the evening. As stated above, the diary comes to an abrupt end at this point. There follows a gap of a few weeks until April 1833 when he leaves for a European tour, but for this we must follow the life of Andrew Jameson through surviving correspondence and in a series of many but much shorter notebooks.

We can safely assume that Andrew Jameson did not take any final examinations followed by graduation as has been the pattern in Scottish universities for the last century and more. In 1833 formal graduation was not considered to be necessary because the certificates that students received from their professors were perfectly adequate for employment purposes.[112] Moreover, in July 1831, he had been successful in the Civil Law examination, or trial as it was then officially known. This qualified him to go forward at a later date for his trial in Scots Law that in its turn, provided he was successful, allowed him

---

[112] I am grateful to Mrs Irene Ferguson, Assistant to University Archives, University of Edinburgh, for this information.

entry into the Faculty of Advocates.

Now, at 22, he had completed a long and continued period of study at school, undergraduate and postgraduate levels. Despite occasional private doubts concerning his character and, at times, even his academic progress, he had acquitted himself well and had constructed a very firm foundation upon which to build a successful career. He was not a student of the mole-like variety, emerging from his accommodation to attend classes and returning immediately thereafter, disdaining all other forms of contact with fellow students and staff. He was popular with fellow students and staff and maintained a proper balance between the requirement for diligent application to his studies and the pursuit of those pleasures that young people normally enjoy. The many invitations that he received to dine at the homes of established Edinburgh society demonstrate how far his presence on these occasions was valued. It is also unlikely in the extreme that Sheriff Clephane would have sustained his interest in Andrew Jameson had the young man not reciprocated this valuable connection in an appropriate manner. The valuable contribution that the sheriff made to his career was to be vindicated over the succeeding decades.

APPENDIX TO CHAPTER THREE
Napoleon Leon Lubienski

Napoleon Leon Lubienski was born in 1812, the son of Count Tomasz Lubienski, who, in common with many of his compatriots, joined the Polish Legion that gave military support to Napoleon. Their objective was the restoration of their country's independence. He fought in many battles, distinguishing himself at Wagram in 1809 and in the campaign following Napoleon's retreat from Moscow. After 1815 Russia retained control of most of Poland and Lubienski retired into private life.

The subordinate position of the Russian-controlled Grand Duchy of Warsaw was unsatisfactory to many Poles. Students in particular resented the political constitution imposed on them by the Congress of Vienna in 1815 and one of the foremost agitators was Napoleon Leon Lubienski. He joined an organization called the Patriotic Youth and took such a prominent part in their activities that in 1830 he was expelled from Warsaw University, where he had been studying law. He came to Edinburgh where, as we learn from Andrew Jameson's diaries, the two young men became acquaintances.

In November 1830 an armed uprising took place against Russian rule in what is sometimes called the Cadet Revolution on account of its origins with the Patriotic Youth agitation. By this time Napoleon Leon Lubienski was in Edinburgh and so was unable to participate in the revolt. His father, rather against his will but succumbing to an appeal to his patriotic spirit, accepted command of one of the armies that had been hastily recruited. The Poles fought bravely but sheer numbers of the Russian armed forces saw their defeat by the end of 1831. Count Lubienski was deported to Russia but after a private interview with the Tsar was pardoned and returned to live on his estate. Born in 1784 he lived until 1870. His connection with Napoleon saw him awarded a

Commander of the Legion of Honour in 1858 by Napoleon's nephew, the Emperor Napoleon III.

Napoleon Leon Lubienski returned to Poland in 1833. He became a director of the Polish Bank in Warsaw but his main interest lay in supporting Polish literature and culture. He was one of the founders of the Warsaw Library (1841). For twenty years he organized at his home in Warsaw tutorials on literary and artistic subjects. These were held every Sunday morning and were well attended, although participants knew that the only refreshment provided was bread and water. Whether this was an idiosyncrasy or a realistic acceptance that his finances were not limitless must be left to conjecture. These weekly meetings attracted suspicion from the authorities because principal among his guests were poets, whose published work and political activities promoted democratic objectives. As a result of this Lubienski was arrested in both 1846 and 1847 but does not appear to have suffered any severe sentence. His tutorials may have contributed to the 1863 revolt but he died in 1860.

CHAPTER FOUR

A Continental Interlude

Concerning documentation; there are two main sources that supply information on Andrew Jameson's absence in Europe during the summers of 1833 and 1834. One of these is the series of small notebooks wherein he writes about the places he has visited and his activities there; for convenience, these notebooks will be referred to as his diaries. The other source is the voluminous and detailed correspondence that he undertook with his father and brother. Unfortunately most of these letters were written on poor paper and consequently the script in many of them has deteriorated to the point of illegibility. Moreover, in many cases where the writing paper has survived, the author has followed the habit, common at that period, of saving paper by writing across the pages that have already been used. After the passage of over 180 years, script that was once perfectly legible has become increasingly difficult to decipher. For these reasons this chapter will rely heavily on the shorter but more legible diaries up to mid-July 1833 at the end of his first journey into Spain. Thereafter he either ceased to keep a diary or it has been lost. Thus from mid-July until his return home in 1834 the correspondence remains the sole source of his activities with one exception: these are the 25 pages that he wrote between 30th November 1833 and 14th January 1834, when he was in Rome.

Before he left Cupar on Saturday, 27th April 1833 for Glasgow, to take a passage for Bordeaux, there is not a single entry in Andrew Jameson's diaries indicating any intention to take an extended holiday abroad at the conclusion of his years of study. Indeed, his diary comes to an abrupt stop on 24th February 1833 with the comment that he has studied hard that Sunday before going to evening service. However, that entry had begun with the comment that his cough had worsened.

There had been no earlier indications that he had been troubled in this way but the reason for this decision to travel to the south of France can have been no other than a sudden deterioration in his health.

Reference has already been made to the Almanack kept by Sheriff-Substitute Jameson, wherein he recorded in the briefest terms national and family occurrences.[1] The entries for 1833 are among the scantiest in the Almanack, commenting solely that in March Andrew had become ill and had returned home, that in April he had gone to Perth (possibly to consult a doctor) and had been advised to go abroad and that in May he had left for Dublin en route for Bordeaux. (These entries were probably made some time after Andrew had left for Bordeaux because it was still April before he had left Cupar.)

He would be away for twelve months. Unless other written evidence emerges, it is certain that his father had to finance him while he was in Europe. His father had maintained him throughout his years at St Andrews and Edinburgh, and Andrew had already acknowledged this debt to him in his diary entry of 27th March 1832.[2] Although sheriff-substitutes had been awarded an increase in their salaries from 1825, their remuneration remained modest in comparison with most other professional men. Melville was still to be supported until he qualified as a lawyer and it is possible that some, perhaps most, of the payments on the £265 loan, which George Gray had arranged for Andrew's trial before the Faculty of Advocates in July 1831, remained outstanding. However, Sheriff-Substitute Jameson had already lost four of his eight children, two within recent memory, and the loss of a fifth would have been hard to bear.

An extremely fragile[3] document, entitled "expenses to Pau May 1833" has survived. It begins with the information that he received £60 on 25th April and he has listed thereafter, in meticulous detail, his subsequent daily expenses for each day to 30th May. There is one

---

[1] v. p. 440 infra.

[2] v. p. 134 supra.

[3] A small part of this document is missing on the left hand margin but fortunately these are mainly a few dates between departure from Glasgow and arrival at Bordeaux. It is not difficult to discover what the expenditure was during these days from the text that survives.

curious omission. In an undated document that was written later and is headed both "My Letters from the Continent 1833–34" and "Note of first part of Journey to Pau",[4] he writes that on 29th April, when in Edinburgh, he had lost £10. There is no question of this being misread because the script is clear. This would have been an enormous loss, one sixth of what he had been given four days earlier and yet it does not appear in his daily account of his expenses. Perhaps his memory was at fault when he mentioned this loss. At all events, by the end of May he had spent £29 13s. 8d. The reverse page contains some complicated arithmetic where French currency is introduced. There is reference to a bill for 600 francs, together with a calculation that since his remaining Bank of England £5 note is worth 127.5 francs and he has 42.5 francs in loose change, his available capital amounts to 770 francs. He then, at the conclusion of these calculations, reveals that he has what he terms a "reserve" of nine sovereigns. This converts to 229.5 francs, which added to the 770 francs gives a total of 999.5 francs or £41 12s. If we ignore the "reserve" he had spent half of his initial subvention by the time he reached Pau.

His route to Glasgow is an interesting illustration of travel in the era that immediately preceded the establishment of railway communication. Accompanied by Melville he first rode to Largo, where the young men stayed overnight before crossing the Firth of Forth by steamer to Edinburgh, where they enjoyed the hospitality of the Scotts at Northfield. Perhaps Miss Marion Scott still held charms for him.[5] On the evening of Monday 29th April he said farewell to Melville by Slateford Aquaduct, where he took a canal boat to Glasgow, not reaching there until 7.30 a.m. the following morning.

This excerpt from a letter written on 30th April to his father from the Exchange Room, Glasgow, makes it abundantly clear that he has become ill and that he is going abroad in the hope of a recovery.

---

[4] This is a three-page résumé of his journey from Cupar to Bordeaux, highly legible since it is written on good paper.
[5] v. p. 140 supra.

I arrived here about 8 o'clock and have reason to congratulate myself upon choosing the Canal boat conveyance in
preference to travelling by Coach. It is rather tedious –
being a 14 hours passage – but the motion is gentle and
pleasant, which I feel to be a matter of great consequence
to my comfort. I had a little sleep between 3 and 5 but I did
not feel much the want of it.

I embark on the Scotia for Dublin in an hour – or at least
in a steamer which conveys the passengers to that vessel –
lying at Greenock. The weather has been very unfavourable
for me as could be but I think I have been better than I have
been since last Thursday, the last genial day we had.

Melville would inform you that I had a very satisfactory
interview with Mr Wood,[6] who was extremely kind. He
intended to have written you some of these days, recommended the step I have taken and from what I have experienced for some days, notwithstanding great caution I am
more convinced of the propriety of the step and somewhat
undecided as to the total removal of my complaint, which
the kindness of my friends led me to believe along with my
own feelings.[7] But this may look somewhat like repining
– when I have so much to be thankful for – particularly for
your most affectionate kindness.

This is my 22nd birthday and I cannot help being melancholy when I think the day after tomorrow would have been
Robert's 24th as well as the way he celebrated mine last
year.

I hope my dear father that I will return to my native

---

[6] This man could have been a doctor, but in a document giving a brief account of the events
between 27th April and 10th May Andrew Jameson states that on the morning of 29th April,
having borrowed a pony from the Scotts of Northfield, who had provided Melville and him
with hospitality for the night, he "called at Woods and Chrysties". This sounds more like a
social than a professional call but when Andrew consulted him again in March 1835 the diary
records that "he prescribed for me".

[7] This would seem to imply that Andrew Jameson's friends had assured him that his sojourn
abroad would restore him to health but that he himself was not entirely convinced of this.

land with this unfortunate complaint completely removed and cease by the blessing of God to occasion you any more anxiety.

The *Scotia* ran into a violent storm a few hours after leaving port and rolled about the Irish Sea for two days before ultimately taking refuge near Downpatrick in Strangford Lough off the coast of Ulster. The captain was reluctant to proceed on the Friday and so Andrew and some other travellers hired a coach that brought them the eighty miles to Dublin by seven o'clock on the Saturday morning. He felt very tired and his breast was painful. He consulted a Dr Stokes, who prescribed a purgative and he then went to The Gresham Hotel[8] where he took his medicine, had a bath and lay down on a bed to sleep for two hours. Before this he had been able to reserve a passage on the *Leeds*, a steamboat for Bordeaux that left that evening.

Almost immediately it ran into fog but by Monday, 6th May, after a brief call at Plymouth, they had passed the coast of Cornwall and begun their crossing of the Bay of Biscay in beautiful weather. As he writes, "This dreaded bay was calm as a Lake, except a long majestic rolling wave, from which, I suppose, it is never free and that made our Sail the more agreeable. After the miseries of the previous part of my voyage, which had been a suite of disasters, this change was indescribably grateful to my feelings." On the afternoon of Wednesday, 8th May 1833 the boat entered the wide estuary of the Gironde and at four o'clock docked at the Lazaret[9] de Trompeloupe, thirty miles from Bordeaux. There, all passengers and crew were required to remain on board because the captain had omitted to bring a certificate of health from Plymouth. This was at that time an international requirement when a vessel's previous port of call had been in a foreign country.

As he records, their detention was "vexatious" rather than disagreeable. They were treated politely and, after a deputation to the authorities of which Andrew was a member, allowed to walk

---

[8] Ireland's oldest and most famous hotel, founded 1817.
[9] A building used for quarantine.

in the gardens. The weather was congenial and they enjoyed their perambulations around the pleasant gardens of the Lazaret. He was highly amused to see that any coins handed over for coffee or wine were immediately put in vinegar and that the gendarmes kept themselves a safe distance from the passengers. They diverted themselves one evening by dancing to the music of a flageolet. On Saturday, 11th May the passengers and crew were inspected by the physicians of the Lazaret, found clear of any disease and the vessel was fumigated. It then sailed down the thirty miles of the Gironde and, as it approached the quayside, the boat's resident musicians gave a spirited rendering of "Rule Britannia" and the "God Save the King". There were no immigration procedures that inconvenience travellers of today and along with a young man from Manchester called Collins and the son of the President of Colombia, with both of whom Andrew had struck up a friendship, he found accommodation at the Hôtel de Richelieu at a cost of thirty sous per day. Collins, in common with several of the other passengers on the boat, had, like Andrew Jameson, come to Bordeaux to seek some improvement in his health.

Awakening on the Sunday morning, Andrew Jameson comments that he found "my French bed quite a luxury after being nearly a fortnight in the confined berths of steamships." After breakfast they called on some of their fellow passengers, including a Lieutenant Leckie and his sister, who had taken rooms at the more prestigious Hôtel de France. In his diary that evening (12th May 1833), Andrew Jameson gave an account of their visit to the Leckies.

"The young officer, poor fellow, had passed a bad night and seemed too ill to be much concerned about anything else but his own melancholy complaints. Alas! That national malady is a ruthless destroyer. Its victims are so often the younger and fairest flowers. The approach is often so little striking, the progress so lingering and delusive but the end how sure. The Doctor[10] urged me much to go to Bayonne and drink the waters in order to restore the tone of the digestive organs and accelerate the re-establishment of my health." The symptoms of

---

[10] v. p. 153 infra.

the illness as stated by Andrew Jameson are those of consumption that well merited the description "national malady."

It is unclear what particular medical disorder was affecting Andrew Jameson. While he did appear to have some of the symptoms of consumption, the fact that he had periods of recovery and relapse over the next fifteen years suggests that he was suffering from dysphonia, an impairment of the ability to produce sounds using the vocal organs.

Like most travellers today, he and Collins set out on a walk around the place, observing the more prominent buildings and remarking upon them. Principal among them was the Église de St Domenique that he describes as "a fine venerable building in the Gothic style", but he had a poor opinion of the religious art that decorated its walls. He reserved his most favourable comments for the city's trees. In the "Jardin Public" the foliage of the trees was lovelier than he had seen anywhere before and the view of the streets leading from the Place de Tournai "with long rows of trees before the houses is striking and to me was entirely new."

He was to remain a week in Bordeaux and made no separate entries in his diary for each day but on 18th May wrote several pages containing his observations on what he had seen in the city and on the differences between it and his home country. He began by making the sensible comment that British visitors to France tended to dwell upon differences between them and the French that were of small importance such as dress, while ignoring the many aspects where there were similarities. In so doing they widened instead of diminished the separation between the two nations. As an example of this he refutes the generalisation that the French exhibit a gaiety of character stretching almost to frivolity. "We are accustomed to have strange ideas of the gaiety of the French. I was much surprised to observe the quiet demeanour of the citizens of Bordeaux, who to a stranger appeared as laudably engaged in business and as little devoted to idleness as the inhabitants of any of our towns."

There were, naturally, differences but, as already stated, they were not fundamental. He found it odd that in the crypt of La Cathédrale de

St Michel it was possible to view corpses that were preserved by some curious property of the ambient atmosphere. "You are conducted into this subterranean dungeon and may examine by torchlight the bodies of its dismal inmates. The bodies are ranged along the wall of the vault and are very strange to look at. The skin is hard and thick as leather but the features are not discernible." By contrast, when he visited the Palais de Justice he found it not dissimilar to the Parliament House in Edinburgh. There were about fifty advocates walking about wearing gowns and what he called "black bonnets" instead of grey wigs. He attended a case concerning an appeal about the price of a ship and noticed that when addressing the court the advocates removed their bonnets. On another day he watched a criminal case and discovered that the procedure was very much the same as that of the Scottish courts.

He comments on two other issues that have an uncanny resonance today. The first is the contrasting attitudes to the consumption of alcohol. "I have seen no instance of intoxication nor open profligacy such as hourly meet the eye in our own towns. One evening I went to see a Ball of the Tradespeople to which the price of admission was a few sous. Everything was conducted with propriety and from the absence of intoxication none of those reprehensible scenes were visible, which are said to be so frequent in similar meetings in England."[11]

The other matter is what he calls "the catalogue of folly and disaster, which have risen from the Mercantile Policy" of the government of France. Although the prosperity and growth of Bordeaux was entirely due to the development of its wine industry in which half the population was engaged directly or indirectly, this was not sufficiently recognised by the government. At this time Bordeaux was exporting only slightly more than half the tonnage of wine that it had exported in 1788. This was because of government policy that not only protected the linen and iron trades from any foreign competition but prohibited any inward investment from foreign manufacturing companies. There

---

[11] It is impossible to know whether he meant England as distinct from Scotland or whether he was using the word loosely to cover the whole of the United Kingdom.

was thus not the full and free exchange of capital that would have enhanced further development of Bordeaux and its wine industry.

On the 16th May he wrote[12] to his father and, after commenting on what he has seen in Bordeaux, refers to his health. "My health has already considerably improved and my strength is gradually returning. I have nearly recovered from the effects of the violent inflammatory attack in the Irish Channel, which I suppose was Influenza. The cough and spit had disappeared within a day or two. The original complaint[13] is also better but I must be longer in France and further South before I can expect it to be removed. This is not a place for chest complaints." One day it had rained and "my breathing became affected as at home but I must have patience as the Doctor says and a dry climate. When I speak of the Doctor I must introduce to your acquaintance a Dr Charles Bell[14] lately a Physician in London, I believe of some eminence, who joined us at Plymouth with his daughter who is = £10,000[15] but not good looking. He would have gladly got me for a Patient and a beau for Mademoiselle but I would not like the hunt."[16] Dr Bell was a physician of considerable (rather that "some") eminence. "In France, Bell's name was so venerated that a professor of anatomy, when Bell visited his lecture room, dismissed his class of students with the words: c'est assez, messieurs, vous avez vu Charles Bell."[17]

His letter continued with the information that Dr Bell had advised a dry climate and consequently he had declined the invitation of

[12] If all his other letters had remained as legible as this one, the details of his European travels would have made easy reading.

[13] The illness was never specified but appears to have had some symptoms of consumption, which was the reason for his having come to Bordeaux.

[14] Charles Bell (1774–1842) was a Scottish surgeon-anatomist, who first established that the nerves of the special senses could be traced from specific areas of the brain to their end organs. Bell's palsy, a paralysis of the facial muscles, perpetuates his name.

[15] This must mean that Miss Bell had £10,000 in her own right, a very large sum in those days. Her appearance must have been sufficiently unattractive to deter so far the attentions of acceptable suitors.

[16] There is no doubt that this is the word, and it must have been used in the amatory sense of men pursuing their suit on women whom they wished to win as wives. Unfortunately the *Dictionary of National Biography* makes no mention of the unfortunate Miss Bell and so we do not know if she found a husband.

[17] Ashby, E., (1963) *Technology and the Academics*, p. 20. Macmillan, London. Ashby does not give the name of the college.

Collins to accompany him on a walking tour towards the Basque country and thence into Spain. "My plan is to be quickly at Pau or Toulouse for 9 weeks or so and if it please Providence to get quit of my chest complaint." He learned from several of the passengers who had come over on the boat with him from Dublin that they were returning to England by the first available passage. They included Lieutenant Leckie, who, he wrote, appeared to be dying.[18] He tried to dissuade them from their purpose but they were deaf to his advice. One can only assume that their expectations of some immediate cure had been disappointed or they were the kind of people, unlike Andrew Jameson, who saw only the differences between themselves and the native French and felt, on that account, uncomfortable in a strange land. Moreover, none of them had a word of French.

By contrast, Andrew Jameson was well read in French literature but had experienced no opportunity to converse in the language with native speakers. He was determined to improve his communication skills and soon found that "I can ask questions, make bargains and so forth but it will be a long time before I can carry on a conversation. I have been two or three times to the theatre but I could not make much of what was said." Although he does not comment upon any progress in the language, it would be inevitable that continual use together with his sound foundation in the language would soon lead to ease in conversation with native speakers.

He concludes by telling his father that he has now got his money affairs satisfactorily arranged although "Mr Johnston does not think that I shall have enough but I think I shall." It would have been interesting to know how his financial matters were organized but no details are supplied. There had been no previous mention of Mr Johnston but since he was one of the chief wine merchants of Bordeaux it is highly probable that George Gray, whose family had a flourishing wine and spirit business in Perth, had given Andrew a letter of introduction. In a second letter to his father from Bordeaux dated 18th May Andrew repeats much of what he had said about the city in his letter of two days

---

[18] His supposition was correct since the lieutenant died on the return journey.

previously but writes "I now have my money matters satisfactorily arranged. Mr Johnston has been very kind." It is possible that George Gray had been in communication with Mr Johnston and through him had arranged for money to be made available for his brother-in-law. This, however, is mere speculation.

Early on the morning of 18th May Collins set off on his walking tour to Spain by way of Bayonne and both hoped that they would come across one another again in the course of their travels. Later that day, as previously arranged, Andrew met Mr Johnston and was driven out to his house in what he describes as "a sort of double Phaeton drawn by a pair of Mecklenburg horses."[19] His host was clearly a man of considerable means because his home, called Belsito and newly built in the Italian style, was large, beautifully proportioned and exquisitely furnished and decorated. To his surprise Andrew was supplied with a valet who came originally from South Queensferry.[20] An excellent dinner was provided and the wines were superb, the claret being "the most agreeable and delicious I ever tasted." The next day, Sunday, they attended a service in the British consulate. He left Belsito[21] after breakfast on the Monday and spent two days at Langon, a few miles south-west of Bordeaux. He returned to the city on the morning of Thursday and made preparations to travel to Pau by coach.[22]

He left Bordeaux at seven o'clock on the morning of Friday the 24th.[23] The route was first south-east to Langon and then south for Roquefort[24] and Mont de Marsan, travelling through the sandy Landes area, where he found the dust disagreeable. After a halt at Mont de Marsan to change horses they continued their journey to the south.

---

[19] A breed originally developed in the East German Duchy (later Grand Duchy) of Mecklenburg.

[20] The man told him that France had a delightful climate "and would be a fine country if it was under British Government". The reason for reporting this unimportant comment is that Andrew Jameson had first used the term "English" and then scored the word out and superimposed "British".

[21] An appendix to this chapter gives the full account, as recorded in his diary, of his visit to Belsito.

[22] His fare in what he refers to as a diligence was £1 13s. 4d.

[23] The diary says "23rd" but this is obviously a mistake.

[24] This is not the place of the same name where the famous Roquefort blue-veined cheese is matured in caves.

It was now dark but he managed to get some sleep during the night and awoke to see in the distance the Pyrenees. On arriving at Pau, where he was to stay two months, he took a room at the Hôtel de la Poste. That evening a Mr Hay, who lived with his family in the town, called and it is a reasonable presumption that he had heard from some mutual acquaintance of the young man's intention to come to Pau. It was exactly eight weeks since Andrew Jameson had left home.

He lived quietly at Pau for almost five weeks. He moved out of the hotel on 29th May and took lodgings in la Rue de la Préfecture. Rather to his surprise, Collins arrived that evening and they enjoyed each others' company until 2nd June, when Collins left for Toulouse. Apart from a two day visit to nearby Eaux Bonnes and Eaux Chaudes,[25] spas renowned over the centuries for the healing powers of their waters, he spent the entire time in daily walks around the countryside that reminded him of his native Scotland.

There is no doubt that Andrew Jameson had the happy faculty of making himself immediately agreeable to people on their first acquaintance of him, and a particularly good example of this occurred one day. He stopped outside one of the better houses in the district to listen to some familiar airs being played on the piano and as he did so a man came out and asked if he would care to see the house. On entering, "another gentleman came forward and saluted me in English and was followed by a pretty girl, who returned my obeisance gracefully". The man also introduced his wife. The girl was their daughter and it was her playing that had arrested Andrew in his walk. There followed an invitation to join them for lunch, after which, while his host was showing him some beautiful views of the countryside, the daughter "presented me with flowers and gathered strawberries for me and all with a trace of modesty that was very delightful." Afternoon tea followed and this suggests that the family must have been British. The young lady, who was doubtless very pleased to have the company of such a presentable young man, entertained her parents and their guest with more music. He was prevailed upon to stay for dinner and

---

[25] About twelve miles south of Pau and just outside the larger town of Larens.

was "not allowed to depart without an invitation to return to see them and with any of my friends that I thought proper." There is no record of any return but it is not surprising that Andrew wrote that he had been "highly delighted with the day's adventure, which brought to my recollection some of the incidents of my early excursions in Scotland."

During these five weeks he had made the acquaintance of other young men who were in Pau for the same reason as himself. In a letter to Melville of 25th June 1833 he gives an interesting account of the British community there. "I have been very much pleased with my residence in Pau. The society is very agreeable and though, it may, of course, be a great deal broken up by daily departures to country quarters I found quite enough visiting. Things are on such an easy pleasant footing that you can have just as much or as little as you choose. Today, Manning and two other young men and I have been dining together previous to our separation and after having been much in one another's society for some time. One of them, Watson, is a Scotsman and has an estate in Berwickshire, where he is a ward of Sir Alexander Hope. Another is Lushington, a Fellow of Christ Church and a nephew of the Judge.[26] They intend going to Saragossa and Madrid and intend passing the winter in Malaga."

In this letter he tells his brother that he has been contemplating "an excursion thro' the Pays-Basque and the adjoining Spanish frontier and I shall return here only for a day or so on my way to some of the Pyrenean watering places.[27] I have been contemplating this excursion for some time and have only waited till I was sufficiently strong to undertake the journey." This was the "separation" referred to above. Manning, who was a few years older than he, suggested that he might join him on this venture and Andrew was delighted to have his company, especially since Manning owned a gig.

They left Pau on Wednesday, 26th June, reaching Navarrenx by evening and travelling on next day to Saint Palais. There they turned

[26] Stephen Lushington (1782–1873). An ardent reformer and member of the Anti-Slavery Society.
[27] He was later advised not to go there. v. p. 161 infra.

south to reach Saint Jean Pied de Port by the 28th before turning north-west to Cambo les Bains, where the axle of the gig broke. They stayed there for the night of the 29th and, somehow, possibly by walking alongside it, brought the gig next day over the ten miles to Bayonne, where it was repaired. Here and in neighbouring Biarritz they spent the next two days, and on Tuesday 3rd July they travelled a few miles along the coast to Saint Jean de Luz. This town certainly drew the admiration of Andrew Jameson, and he filled several pages of his diary with descriptions of what he had seen there and where he had been. Next day, having left the gig behind, he and Manning rode to the Spanish frontier "en cacelot",[28] a method then common in the Basque regions of France and Spain. Instead of sitting astride a horse in a saddle, either one or two passengers sat on a wooden seat with a backrest lashed across a horse, a mode of travelling that they found "very social and convenient".[29] They hired a boatman to take them across the estuary of the Bidassoa to Fuenterrabia in Spain. This was the area where only twenty years before British troops under Wellington, having stormed the fortress of San Sebastian on the Spanish coast, had crossed the Bidassoa and entered France. The Peninsular War battles were therefore of recent memory and the diary gives some details of the fighting that preceded the capture of Bayonne.

In a long[30] letter to his father of 18th July, three days after his return to Pau, he begins by saying how much he had enjoyed his recent excursion and railed against the French for "the lies which they are fond of inventing against the Spaniards". He and Manning had found nothing but "kindness and attention" wherever they went. They were received with great cordiality by Capuchin friars at a monastery near Fuenterrabia and having no Spanish he conversed in Latin with his hosts, something he had recourse to throughout the rest of their time in Spain. Then, on their way to San Sebastian, they called at a Jesuit college. In both establishments Andrew found their libraries

---

[28] The word is of Basque origin.

[29] He suggests that this would be a very suitable way to travel in the highlands of Scotland and in general for women and invalids.

[30] Fortunately, he made a copy of this letter on good paper and in a legible hand.

most interesting, and from later correspondence[31] one suspects that Manning was slightly aggrieved at the time his companion spent "kicking up" dust in them.

They came to San Sebastian on 4th July. The town had been practically razed to the ground during the siege of 1813 but had been rebuilt "and a cleaner and more beautiful fortified town it is impossible to see". By 7th July they had reached "the city of the great Pompey, the capital of Navarre, Pampelona" and remained there until the 11th July, "and I was never more gratified with my stay in any place than with these short five days."

He was not able to enjoy his stay here as much as he would have wished because he was running out of money and Manning had become ill, hardly stirring from his room. On three successive days he attended the "corrida de toros or bullfights, 21 bulls killed, 8 horses and two men wounded." He described the spectacle as "magnificent", reminding him of the "games of the Romans or the Tournaments of Chivalry and not nearly so horrible as I expected; in fact, they do not appear so cruel as our boxing matches and cockfighting." He did, however, find himself astonished "at the sangfroid of the ladies, who could applaud the killing of a horse or the death of a bull."

Manning and he decided to return to France over the Pyrenees by a road that took them through Roncevalles, scene of the famous defence of the pass of that name by Roland and his band of knights on behalf of Charlemagne in 778, later (c.1100) mythologised as "Chanson de Roland". They would know the story of Roncevalles and perhaps this was one reason for choosing to go that way. Another reason was that it was the most direct route back to Pau. After a night near Roncevalles they crossed over the Pyrenees into France at Arnéguy. Their decision not to return by the coastal plain was a mistake, as he explains to his father. In contrast to Manning, he had been feeling better than he had "since the commencement of my illness – during the whole time I had not one attack of short breathing – so perfectly well was I that I had resolved on returning to Pau to take the route to Paris after seeing

---

[31] Letter of 1st August 1833 from Manning in Pau to Andrew Jameson at St Jean de Luz.

Bagnères[32] and Toulouse and was about writing to Melville when he would be required to set off to meet me and see the sites [sic] of Paris so that I expected to return to you an altered person by the end of the month. Conceive then my disappointment and sorrow when repassing the Pyrenees and returning to France, we encountered thick heavy fogs with Scotch mist and rain during the two days we took to drive here. We did not get much wet but the change from the fine dry pure air of Spain gave us both the cold and I was seized with severe pain in the chest and great obstruction."

On 13th July they reached St Jean Pied de Port and went back to Pau by way of Mauléon, Tardets and Oloron, driving into the town on the evening of 14th July. They had been away for just under three weeks.

Sensibly, he consulted a doctor and was advised that it would be "utter folly" to return home and that he must winter in the south. He asks his father for advice but, at the same time, suggests that his education will not suffer from a longer stay on the Continent, comments that most young men with his affliction stay for at least one year and that "I believe it is a better time for making the stay now than immediately after passing Advocate as is often the custom with young (men) of the same prospects as myself." He concedes, nevertheless, that this will be "an additional expense to an already expensive education, which you may not be able to afford. Otherwise, as to my health, tho' I think with a shudder of the horrors of an Edin winter, yet I might be able to stand them and probably this affection of the chest resulting from some adhesion or congestion of the lungs, which can never be remedied, may be equally the same whether I winter in a bad or a mild climate. I certainly feel perfectly different in damp and in fine weather and from my experience of my health in Spain, where I was a few days without feeling or thinking of any obstruction, I think that further residence in a Southern climate may effectually restore me."

He strengthens his argument by saying that the doctors have advised him that he must avoid damp weather and for that reason he must not

---

[32] Another spa town in the French Pyrenees. It lies on the main road from Pau to Toulouse.

even visit spas up in the mountains where any benefit provided by the waters will be counteracted by the damp mornings.

He tells his father that £40 will be enough to support himself over the coming winter but that if he were to go to Italy, as some have advised him, he will need "a good deal more – Rome is very much recommended for winter quarters but that is beyond any hopes."

In this long letter of 18th July 1833 he made the irrefutable case that a return to Scotland would adversely affect his health, although he does accept that it is for his father to decide whether he can still afford to support him. The arguments he advanced and the way in which they were addressed demonstrate how well he was suited to his chosen profession. Only a father who was totally devoid of affection for his son or one without income or friends could have demanded his return to Scotland. The suggestion that a visit to Rome would be advantageous, despite requiring support beyond the £40 necessary to see him through a winter in southern France, may, however, justifiably be criticised as putting pressure on a father who was already supporting him to the limit of his financial ability.

Two days later he wrote to Melville regretting that he had "found it necessary to write such a letter to my father, when instead of that I expected to have been giving you directions for setting off to meet me." He mentions a possibility of a meeting in Paris at the end of September but that "if I should stay here all winter it will be still better next spring, when you will have finished your apprenticeship". He concludes by asking his brother if he "would like to enter into a little bit of trade." He would buy one or two casks of Navarre wine, each costing "£10 or 9d a bottle", ship them from San Sebastian to Dundee by way of Liverpool or London and, if Melville could dispose of it among their friends, "we could make a little money."

The weather was now almost oppressively hot, and his doctor agreed that he would do himself no harm if he spent a few weeks at the coast where the sea breezes alleviated the summer heat. He left for St Jean de Luz on 22nd July and, arriving the next day, remained there until 27th August. One of the letters he received during this time was from

Manning,[33] and it provides an interesting insight into the character of Andrew Jameson. Manning writes that he believes "romantic adventure and learned research" have enticed his friend back to the Basque area. Recalling their visits to the Capuchin monastery and the Jesuit college, he is certain that he will enjoy "kicking up" centuries of dust in old libraries. He then adds "Must I say how easy it were for me to imagine you romantically employed basking in the rays that beam from under a mantilla and inhaling the ambrosial breezes that breathe from a fan."

From a long letter to Melville, written 20th August, in reply to one he had received from home, we learn how he had occupied his time since coming to St Jean de Luz. After the usual thanks for inquiries after his health, he writes "I am very much obliged to my Father for the promised supply of pecuniary assistance. I shall endeavour to make it good as far as possible in effecting the objects for which it is destined. I certainly have constantly to regret that my health has not been sufficiently established to permit me to return home this month as I had intended." He asks him to assure their father that the money made available for staying abroad will not be wasted. Manning had suggested that they make another journey together but Andrew declined because he wanted complete rest in his search for improved health.

His lodging was a large apartment in a house in the centre of the town within which, in 1660, Louis XIV had married his cousin, the Infanta Maria Theresa. The apartment above was occupied by the "principal family of the place, where I go occasionally and spend the evening." That his rent was a mere shilling a week, less than he had been paying at Pau, explains why £40 was sufficient to last him over the winter. On the other side of the square there was a large house which had been occupied by both Napoleon and Wellington as they passed through St Jean de Luz and was now rented by an Irish baronet, Sir Simon Bradstreet. As Manning had suggested, he soon found attractive female company. "There are four daughters like the Northfield[34] beauties, all

---

[33] Written from Pau on 1st August 1833.

[34] The Scotts, from whom Andrew Jameson had received much hospitality in Edinburgh. v. 139 supra.

very pretty and accomplished. I generally see them every day and often walk with them in the evening. They had an aunt and his cousins whom I knew at Pau, visiting them lately and in consequence there was a round of parties, perfectly astonishing in a small place like this. I am happy to say that I could join in the danses [sic] with more freedom than at Bordeaux. Indeed, I feel myself so strong that I should think my farther stay in France unnecessary were it not for an occasional pain in the right side of the chest and some difficulty in breathing which every day becomes less. I am certainly better at present than I have ever been since the commencement of my illness and I have great reason to be thankful to a kind and gracious providence for my speedy recovery." On three occasions he accepted invitations from the Bradstreets to join them on brief visits across the Spanish frontier.

In this letter he also mentions debts. "I have several debts in Edinburgh for clothes as you know, which I would thank you to get arranged for me. There is something owing to Craig, the man who made the shooting coat." Another clothier is owed for "a black coat and black trousers." He does not suggest how Melville might have these debts "arranged".

The letter concludes with the information that he has now been long enough at St Jean de Luz and that he intends to go to Bagnères and, thereafter, Toulouse. The letter concludes: "My departure will disappoint the good folks here, who had it that I was to marry one of the Miss Bradstreets, tho' I am sure I gave them no reason to suppose so." He makes the usual requests for his brother to convey his regards to their father, to the Grays and other friends, and since these include Elizabeth, we gather that she has not been completely forgotten.

On 27th August he left St Jean de Luz, not for Bagnères, but on a yacht for Bilbao on the Basque coast of Spain. Sir Thomas Dyke Acland[35] "had been cruising along the coasts of England and France for some weeks, accompanied by Lady Acland, his daughter, four sons

---

[35] Sir Thomas, the tenth baronet, was a member of a distinguished Devon family and had represented his county in Parliament from 1812 until 1831, apart from 1818 to 1820. He was to be returned for North Devon from 1837 to 1857.

and a captain in the navy." They had come ashore at St Jean de Luz where they met Andrew Jameson and learned how interested he was in the Basque country. It is another illustration of the attractive manner of Andrew Jameson that after what can have been but the briefest of acquaintanceships the English baronet invited the young man to join him and his family aboard his yacht. They called at towns on the Basque coast, and Sir Thomas must have had excellent connections in Spain because a government minister had provided him with documentation excusing his vessel from the usual quarantine requirements and allowing it free entry into all Spanish ports. At one of these, Montrico, "our arrival excited an extraordinary sensation. The whole town and neighbourhood seemed to have turned out to see us. The harbour and rocks were literally covered with spectators and all the balconies filled with ladies. The Alcalde[36] received us with the greatest respect and conducted us thro' the crowd with official formality to his house where we were regaled in the most hospitable manner with various refreshments. Some of the fair sex appeared to pay their respects to the English Lady and I was of some little service as an interpreter from having picked up a little Spanish in my former excursions."

When Sir Thomas and his family departed Bilbao, he presented Andrew Jameson with a copy of *Gil Blas*[37] and the New Testament in Spanish. He had thoroughly enjoyed his several days with the Aclands "after being so much among foreigners. So many of the English families one meets in France are so frenchified that one is more inclined to pity them than respect them."

The information about his cruise in Sir Thomas Acland's yacht comes partly from a short diary but mainly from a letter written in Bilbao on 7th September to George Gray. He begins by thanking Gray profusely for what he describes as "its unexpected enclosure" from which we can safely conclude that his brother-in-law had sent him some money. Gray had written to Andrew because he had been

---

[36] The mayor.

[37] *Gil Blas* was written in French between 1700 and 1730 by Alain-René Le Sage (1668–1747). Although set in Spain it is very French in its characterisation and theme.

consulted by Melville about Andrew's suggestion that the brothers attempt to enter the wine business by importing to Scotland casks of Navarre wine.[38] Andrew now explains to Gray that he has looked further into the matter and "on making most careful inquiries I found it to be next to impractable [sic], unless I had been residing on the spot and had larger funds at my command."

A letter written from Pau on 29th September 1833 to his father gives an account of his time in Bilbao after the Aclands had left. He took a room in a boarding house and remained for a week in Bilbao. "I lived completely in the Spanish style. The eating part of it commenced on the morning about 7 o'clock by a small cup of chocolate, a piece of bread and a glass of cold water, which scarcely suited a Scotsman's taste in the way of breakfast. At 2 p.m. the dinner was served composed always of some soup, the Puchero,[39] a regular Spanish dish, consisting of boiled beef garnished with cabbage and beans with slices of ham and tomato sauce and then roast fowl or mutton and the repast was crowned by a splendid desert – muscatel grapes, very far superior to anything I have tasted in France – peaches, delicious melons and a glass of Malaga.[40] All these fruits were selling in the market of Bilbao for a mere nothing. After this substantial meal came the Siesta. At 9 p.m. we had a supper, which was a second edition of the dinner."

He also provided an item of rather unusual information. "I forgot to mention before that I found a certain accomplishment I have learned from you very serviceable in Spain. Cracking the fingers or Scottish castanets. The natives were always astonished with it and on one occasion at Pamplona they forced me to come and dine with them because I had amused myself accompanying some of their music in that way." This throws an interesting light upon Sheriff-Substitute Jameson, who must have been a rather jollier person than surviving records suggest.

---

[38] v. p. 161 supra.

[39] Andrew Jameson gives an accurate description of this dish, sometimes claimed to be the world's most versatile stew. The only addition that need be made is to say that the meats and vegetables are served to diners from separate large plates with sauce poured over the vegetables.

[40] A white or red fortified Spanish wine.

While in Bilbao he met six fellow countrymen, who were going to college in Valladolid,[41] and they asked him to accompany them on their journey. He would have liked to go to Valladolid because he had letters to the Rector of the college,[42] where "I strongly suspect that there may be some records preserved there connected with Scottish history and it was for that reason I wished to go." This bears out the comment of Manning that "learned research" was as great an attraction to Andrew Jameson as "romantic adventure." However, "the state of my purse would not permit a further journey in Spain." He returned to Pau on 11th September.

The earlier part of this letter to his father comments on family and financial matters. His father had been on holiday in the west of Scotland and had met his old friend, Alexander Campbell, Sheriff-Substitute of Renfrewshire. "You don't say anything about any of the young ladies getting married, which I think rather surprising." The only reason for quoting this excerpt from the letter is that eleven years later one of these daughters would become Mrs Andrew Jameson.

He goes on to tell his father how he had received a letter from George Gray that had enclosed some money. We learn from the greater detail given in this letter that the money had been advanced to assist him in his projected venture into the wine exporting business, which he had very wisely decided to abandon. He had asked his brother-in-law to allow him to retain the money "as a loan to me to be repaid as soon as I had it in my power, as you were unable to advance so much to enable me to take so long a journey as to Rome, where I am anxious to spend the winter. This letter which contained some lines to Sophia, I hope has arrived. Otherwise you must be astonished at

---

[41] This must have been The Royal Scots College (Real Colegio de Escoceses), originally founded in Madrid in 1627 but transferred to Valladolid in 1771. In 1988 it was moved again, this time to Salamanca. Its deed of foundation states that its purpose is to train young men "of superior character" who, "when they are well versed in [several subjects are listed] may proceed to the Kingdom of Scotland to preach the gospel and convert heretics".

[42] How he obtained these letters is not known. Possibly he had received them from the Capuchin monks at Fuentarrabia or from the Jesuit priests at the college near San Sebastian, establishments that he and Manning had visited on their tour of the Basque country in July of that year. This, however, is no more than conjecture.

my silence. I was expecting that it would reach Perth about the time you were at the Circuit and I would have had an answer about this time and that it would have been in my power to set out immediately before the season gets too advanced. In the meantime I propose setting off in that direction, as having seen almost everything that is interesting in this part of the country and a great deal more than 99 out of the 100 take the trouble to visit, there is nothing to detain me here." He had the day before returned from a tour of some of the local watering places to the south-east of the town. These had included Lestelle, Argelès-Gazost and Cauterets, towns at the foothills of the Pyrenees and not susceptible to the morning dampness that he had been advised to avoid. "Notwithstanding, I shall leave Pau with some regret as well, on account of the many agreeable friends I shall see no more as of its general advantages as a continental residence and the charming country with which it is surrounded. My friend Manning is very anxious to keep me. He has sold his horse and gig in which we had such a delightful excursion and intends to bury himself in some country place away from the dissipation of Pau." The nature of the dissipation is not stated and perhaps he wanted to assure his father that he was always careful with what funds he had.

Thus, on the last day of September 1833, in anticipation of receiving confirmation from Scotland that he could treat as a loan the money sent to him by George Gray for another purpose, he set off by coach for Toulouse on the first stage of his journey to Rome. He was in Toulouse for four days before travelling on to Montpellier by the Canal du Midi.[43] There are no documents that give any information about what he saw or did in Toulouse or Montpellier because although he wrote a long letter to Melville from Montpellier on 7th October it consisted entirely of descriptions of the towns and countryside that he had visited south-east of Pau immediately before he had left that town. However, on October

[43] This canal connects the River Garonne at Toulouse with Sète, a few miles south of Montpellier. Built to avoid a long sea voyage round the coast of Spain lasting one month, it offered a much quicker and safer passage for goods and travellers between the Atlantic and Mediterranean coasts of France. It was a remarkable feat of engineering for its time and was opened officially by Louis XIV on 24th May 1681.

25th/26th he wrote another long letter to Melville from Florence after he had been a week in the capital of Tuscany.

The first part of this letter is a detailed account of the towns that he has visited on his way to Florence. He was enthusiastic about the Roman remains at Nîmes. "They were in a wonderful state of preservation. The Amphitheatre, which is supposed to have been built by Agrippa is a magnificent edifice calculated to hold 20,000 spectators." The most interesting of all the buildings was the Temple of the Forum. "This beautiful edifice is the most perfect Roman remains now existing. It is small but exquisitely proportioned combining great elegance of workmanship with the utmost symmetry of parts."

While sitting alone among these magnificent ruins and far from his own country the feeling of solitude made him "rather forlorn. That longing for home, with which Scotsmen and the inhabitants of all mountainous countries are often attacked, when solitary wanderers in foreign lands may be a weakness but I am sure it is allied to some of our best feelings. This 'Maladie du pays' as the French call it has troubled me a good deal since the alteration of my plans and the arrangement to spend the winter on the Continent. I have great reason to be thankful that I have no other species of sickness. I had a great mind to come home this winter after all when in the south of France, so completely well have I felt for the last month that I felt pretty confident that I was quite able to take my chance of an Edinburgh winter and avoid the expense to my father of more travelling abroad – but all the medical people and my other friends spoke so strongly against my project that I abandoned it and resolved to go on to Italy. What they said was probably very true that should I return this winter and catch another cold before my chest was any more strengthened by some good climate against similar attacks, I might repent of my precipitancy. So I believe it is all arranged for the best and particularly as it meets with the approval of Papa and you and all my other friends. You may be surprised that I do not speak with more enthusiasm of the opportunities, which my father's kindness affords me of visiting much that is highly interesting – a good fortune that formerly I could not have dared to hope for – but the fact is that unfortunately in travelling as in every other source of pleasure there are boundaries to enjoyment and what with disappointed expectations and absence from home, want of friends the relish becomes blunted and one is surprised at their own indifference. Washington Irving has expressed this very beautifully in (as nearly as I can remember[44]) the following words. 'The smooth place roughens as he approaches; the wild place becomes tame and barren; the fairy tints that beguiled him on, still fly to the distant hill or gather on the lands he has left behind him and every part of the landscape seems greener than the spot he stands on.'"

On the 26th October he continued his chronological and descriptive account of his travels after he had reached Marseilles on 12th October. Most importantly, he had found "to my inexpressible delight" a letter from Melville waiting at the post office. This had been sent to his address at Pau and Manning had forwarded it to Marseilles. There was also a letter from Mr Johnston, the Bordeaux wine merchant, saying that he expected to meet him in Italy, but there is no reference to such a meeting in any of the subsequent correspondence.

He thought little of Marseilles and on 16th October, having left a message for the postmaster to forward any mail to Rome, took a steerage passage for Leghorn.[45] They sailed along the French coast past Toulon and Nice as far as Genoa in a manner that reminded him of his voyage along the north coast of Spain with Sir Thomas Acland. He had an opportunity to look round Genoa before the boat departed in the evening for Leghorn. It was a rough passage, and for the two days after they docked at Leghorn it rained incessantly. He and a young American, visiting Europe for the same reason as himself, found accommodation at a "comfortable inn kept by Mrs Thomson, a sister to Mrs Smith the manufacturer's wife and originally from Perth. I was very sorry to learn the news of Mr Laing's death, who has been so long our neighbour." Was it just coincidence that he found himself at this inn or was he aware that a fellow countrywoman owned the establishment?

---

[44] Apart from one punctuation error this was an accurate quotation.
[45] Now almost always referred to by its Italian name of Livorno.

The rain relented to allow a visit to nearby Pisa, where he admired the cathedral and "the falling Tower". His journey from Pisa to Florence was marred by more heavy rain but the weather on the day after his arrival was delightful and continued so, thus allowing him to savour to the full the magnificent architecture, sculptures and paintings of the city of the Medicis, of Dante and of Michelangelo.

He would gladly have spent the winter in Florence "were it not that the winter months are very cold here, while the climate in Rome in winter is celebrated for mildness and salubrity. The English are now flocking there like bands of locusts, only that instead of sterility and devastation they fill the land with gold. Things are said to be very dear at Rome on that account. I am now anxious to get there as I find my money fast melting away in this continual moving from place to place for in travelling it is difficult to practise much economy. With all that I can do and taking many a dinner of grapes and bread (which is not bad fare) I shall find myself at Rome with little more than £25. However, I shall make this go as far as possible."

He concludes by saying that since it is possible that some letters sent on to Marseilles, presumably through the good offices of Manning, may not reach him, he would like his brother to write again immediately. Until he finds accommodation, all communications are to be sent "to the care of Messrs Torlonia, Banquiers, Rome, Italy."

His next communication is a letter to his father written on 16th November 1833 from Rome. Since he uses the phrase "during this fortnight" he must have reached the city on or around 2nd November. Obviously he could not afford a private coach from Florence and so had taken the only available public transport, a "vetturina". This would have been little more than a cart drawn by an ox or a horse, with room for travellers and what luggage they had. The travellers would walk by the cart for most of the way, especially if the gradient were steep, and had to make their own arrangements for food and accommodation. Individuals made private contracts with a vetterino,[46] who was prepared to go to Rome or any other town in central Italy.

---

[46] Coachman, although his status was nearer that of owner/driver.

Andrew made a bargain for nine dollars (which he says was c. £2 15s.). A British officer and a Yorkshire man agreed to fourteen dollars (probably because they could not speak Italian) while a Franciscan friar and two students from Genoa paid similar amounts as Andrew.

Their route was via Arezzo and Perugia and then across the Appenines. Fortunately the weather remained dry because he slept in the open each night. For the greater part of the way they followed the route taken by Hannibal and one night he slept on the banks of Lake Trasimene. He was thoroughly familiar with Livy's history of the Punic Wars, and the surrounding fields and countryside still allowed him to comprehend the manoeuvres adopted by Hannibal to gain there one of his greatest victories. Passing on through Terni, he recalled this town as the birthplace of another famous Roman historian, Tacitus. As they approached Rome he recognized the Campagna and described it as a twenty-mile stretch of country around Rome notorious for the "noxious malaria that broods over it from June to October."

He was disappointed with his first few days in Rome because it was a very different city from the Rome that had entered his mind through his classical education. He complained that "from the moment of his arrival I am a victim of rapacity and extortion." He put up at an inn for three days before finding accommodation at twelve shillings a week, the cheapest that he could obtain. No. 71, Piano[47] 2, Piazza di Spagna was no more than a small, poorly furnished single room. Moreover, the weather was unpleasant and he had received no communication from his family since Melville's letter of 25th September that Manning had forwarded to the Marseilles post office. Perhaps he had begun to doubt the wisdom of coming to Rome.

However, after visiting the Coliseum, the Forum and other remains of Rome's imperial heritage, where he felt he was standing on "sacred ground", and having made friends with an American, an Englishman called Spalding,[48] two Swedes, an Italian and a German,

---

[47] Flat.

[48] Spalding was a fellow student at Edinburgh. Oddly, Andrew Jameson does not mention this Edinburgh connection, just referring to him as an Englishman.

he became more cheerful. On 30th November he began to keep a diary of his stay in Rome and these 24 pages together with long letter to Melville, written over the period 28th December 1833/2nd January 1834, give a very full account of what he saw and did in Rome. By a happy chance, he had seen in the "Travellers' book" at the inn where he had first stayed the name of Charles Lees,[49] a rising artist from his own town of Cupar. He must have made himself known to the artist and his wife because he refers to their kindness towards him, although the only specific occasion mentioned in the diary is his acceptance of their invitation to dine with him on New Year's Day 1834. From an entry in his diary in November 1834 after he had resumed his studies at Edinburgh, we learn that Mr and Mrs Lees had also visited Naples at the same time as Andrew Jameson and had entertained him there.

At last, sometime in early December 1833, he received a letter from home. It was from Melville written on 16th November and contained the sad news of the death of Captain James Jameson in Calcutta. Andrew wrote a beautifully composed letter to his father, consoling him on the loss of his only brother. Very appropriately he did not use the occasion to describe what he had been doing in Rome. He did, however, say that an earlier letter mentioned by Melville as having been written to him at Marseilles had not been forwarded and he hoped that with a more permanent address he would not be so long again without news from home.[50] He also thought it appropriate to assure his father that his health was now completely restored.

He and Spalding, whom he describes as "already an author", visited the ruins of the Baths of Caracalla that he describes as "large, clumsy but imposing." Together, on 16th and 17th December, they made an

---

[49] Charles Lees (1800–1880) was born in Cupar and trained as a painter under Sir Henry Raeburn. Elected a Royal Scottish Academician as early as his thirtieth year, he had a successful career as an artist, building a reputation in sporting subjects from 1840. His most famous painting is *The Golfers* (1847), copies of which hang in many Scottish golf clubhouses to this day. He was spending six months in Rome at the time when Andrew Jameson visited the city. Lees was a near contemporary of Andrew's two elder brothers and the families probably knew each other.

[50] A letter from his father did arrive a few days later.

excursion into the Campagna, staying two nights at Tivoli.[51] This town with its five cascades particularly pleased him, and since it was eighteen miles from Rome it is evident that his ability to walk many miles in one day had not deserted him. Indeed, they spent the following day traversing the Sabine Hills that lay north of Rome and paid a visit to Horace's[52] farm. Not surprisingly, he wrote that he "returned to Rome late on the third day, a good deal fatigued."

On Christmas Day he went to St Peter's to view the religious celebrations, but "I can speak with more pleasure of my daily walks among the ruins." He attended a place of worship every Sunday and enjoyed the singing of their choirs. One of these was the Sistine Chapel, but he was disappointed to be refused entrance to hear Mass there on Christmas Eve because he had "a surtout[53] on instead of a coat. I felt more for a gentlemen with two ladies – one of them young and very pretty – who was repulsed in the same way. His fair companions of course could not enter without him and were forced to retire." He had to make do with the church of San Luigi dei Francesi where he experienced "nothing striking".

His expenses were now troubling him again. He acknowledged that the purpose of his visit to Europe had been to recover his health and that since this had now been achieved it was "my duty to undertake no further journey of mere pleasure even tho' it might have the plea of 'instruction'[54] which would add to the unavoidable expenses of my maintenance here and of as yet a long journey homewards." He had been unable to economise at Rome, and although he had been living more frugally than any of his acquaintances he had not thought that it would be possible to accompany them to Naples until he had read "the few words at the end of my Father's letter." What his father had written is not stated but it is clear that further financial subvention had been promised. Since "I can procure a trifle from my friends to

---

[51] The Emperor Hadrian built a palace there and for centuries it became the site of country villas built by Roman families anxious for relief from the bustle of the city.
[52] Quintus Horatius Flaccus (65 BC–27 BC), Roman satirist and poet.
[53] A frock coat.
[54] The inverted commas were his.

keep me afloat until the remittance arrives", Andrew believed that he could now join his friends on their visit to Naples. He asked that the remittance be sent to him at Florence care of Messrs Torlonia,[55] who were correspondents of Sir William Forbes and Company. This, he suggested, would be the safest route since he would be returning to Scotland through Florence, Bologna and then over the Alps.

Before leaving for Naples he and an acquaintance visited the studios of both David Scott (1806–1849) and Bertel Thorvaldsen (1770–1844). Scott, an artist, a member of the Royal Scottish Academy, was at that time living in Rome[56] and not then widely known. By contrast, the fame of the Danish sculptor was already European-wide. He lived mainly in Rome from 1797 to 1838 and now, towards the end of his career, found himself visited by almost every European visitor to the city. Although they had called to see what he refers to as "Thorvaldsen's collection", Andrew Jameson entered the following account in his diary. "I confess that I thought himself the most interesting object and I had more curiosity to see the master than the gallery. He was walking about the room when we entered and received us with great politeness. He is a man of about 6 feet considerably advanced in years, of a calm benevolent aspect and a fine high brow. He wore a fur cap below which streamed a quantity of lank grey hair. His appearance was altogether peculiar but perfectly unaffected." Thorvaldsen even gave the two young visitors a tour of his private apartments and, discovering that one of them was Scottish, showed them a bust of Sir Walter Scott upon which he was currently working.

He set out for Naples on the 20th January 1834, unaccompanied because two fellow Scots, after agreeing to accompany him on foot, changed their plans because they were afraid of bandits. Their fears did not dissuade Andrew Jameson, who reached the city without the

---

[55] Sir William Forbes, James Hunter and Company was a banking company that had its origins in the middle of the eighteenth century. It was successful enough to begin to issue its own banknotes in 1782 and in the next century became the Union Bank of Scotland. It had agents in large European cities. Those in Rome and Florence were Banco Torlonia founded by Giovanni Torlonia, who was extremely successful in the murky field of Papal bonds.

[56] Scott lived about 18 months in Rome between 1832 and 1834 and his studio and appartments are now Hotel Scott House in Via Giobarti.

slightest trouble in five days. In a letter to Melville of 29th January he gives very full details of the scenery through which he traversed but little else.

His next letter, written to his father, was begun on 22nd February but not completed until 2nd March. His first few days in Naples had been difficult because he had come under suspicion for no other reason than that "officious emissaries of the Police" could not conceive of any normal British subject reaching their city from Rome on foot. He was followed wherever he went for a few days until he went to the police headquarters to demand an explanation, and there he received a full apology together with the assurance that he would be troubled no further in this manner.

These early days were spent mainly in the Museum of Antiquities, where there were displayed discoveries made among the ruins of Pompeii and Herculaneum. This had prompted him to join two Russians on an expedition to Vesuvius that had begun, for no apparent reason, at 4.00 p.m. No gig had been available for hire, and so they had to walk through a night that was dark, cold and rainy. At times he had repented at having joined the expedition but had soon felt that the state of the weather made the scene more awesome because the "burning lava which streamed down the side of Vesuvius borrowed additional grandeur from the surrounding obscurity and like a pillar of fire seemed to guide us on our way." They reached the town of Resina, where, after refreshing themselves with some bread and wine, they had procured horses and two guides carrying lighted torches. Halfway up the mountain there was a house called the Hermitage, where they had refreshment and waited, in vain, for the weather to moderate. They continued and thirty minutes later they had to dismount and set off on foot. It had taken them another hour to reach the crater because, the torches having been long blown out by the wind, they had to grope their way in the dark up the steep and precipitous path walking on ashes and scree[57] that had made

---

[57] The *Concise Oxford Dictionary* defines scree as "small stones (on a mountain slope) that slide down when trodden on" and this fully explains the difficulty Andrew Jameson and his two companions experienced in the final stages of their climb to the summit of Vesuvius.

it difficult to keep a foothold. As the dawn broke he had seen the molten lava that flowed slowly down on one side and the smoke rising out of the crater, and in his letter he gave a long description of all that he had seen from the summit including the Bay of Naples and its city. Now completely worn out they had wrapped themselves in their cloaks and slept among the ashes, the warmth of the lava nearby giving them some relief from the intense cold.

He had, however, scraped his left ankle on some protruding rock and though it seemed immaterial at the time, since it did not impede his descent and return to his hotel in Naples, by the next day the wound had become inflamed. This meant that, although he had been ready to start his return journey, he had been forced to remain another week in Naples bathing his ankle with milk until the inflammation died down. This added to his expenses and, in addition, he writes that although he had exercised the greatest possible economy his expenses would have been "still less were it not that being a good deal in the society of young men of some fortune, one requires occasionally to spend somewhat more for the sake of fellowship." He stressed his economy by comparing the cost of his trip from Rome to Naples, three dollars,[58] with the fifteen they had paid.

Despite saying that he had been ready to begin his return journey, he decided that he should visit Pompeii. He gave a very long description of what he saw there, interspersing it with comments related to his classical education. He then concluded this long letter by saying that since he could not yet trust his ankle to stand up to a lot of walking he would sail from Naples to Leghorn, although he regretted that the fare of £3 10s. was considerably in excess of what he would have expended were he to travel on foot. He ended "I hope to receive letters at Florence with money and also to hear from you at Venice."

His next letter was written to Melville, dated 17th March at Rome and 28th March at Bologna. His ankle had improved sufficiently for him to abandon his original idea of a passage by sea to Leghorn, and he had walked to Rome without any recurrence of the inflammation.

---

[58] This was 13s. 6d. in British money.

He went to see some parts of the city that he had not visited during his previous stay. Depending on the weather he would leave for Florence the next day, and since he would have to cross the Apennines he expected the journey to take five or six days. Instead he chose a route through Viterbo and Siena, and when he arrived at Florence he was delighted to find letters from both his father and his brother waiting for him at Messrs Torlonia's bank. More importantly, although he was too courteous to even suggest it, there was money of which his purse was in desperate need. The source of this finance was not his father but his oldest brother John, who had been serving with the East India Company's army in the Bombay Presidency since 1820. In this letter from Bologna it appears that his brother had been saving to allow himself some leave in Scotland but had decided to make some of it available to assist his family. Andrew wrote that he "felt the liveliest gratitude" and asked Melville to write to John on his behalf because there was no chance of a letter reaching India from Tuscany.

Travelling by "*vetturina*" (as he had done from Florence to Rome the previous autumn), he reached Venice on 2nd April 1834, where he found waiting a letter from his father to which he replied on 15th April 1834. This letter consists mainly of expressions of gratitude to his father for making it possible for him to travel so widely and, as he rightly claims, so advantageously. His father's letter has not survived nor has a second, which must have arrived just after he had posted his letter of 15th April. One can only judge from the tenor of his son's reply to this second letter, written only three days later, that Sheriff-Substitute Jameson had been questioning his delay in returning home from Europe and raising doubts about the appropriateness of Melville and Andrew meeting in Paris. Andrew had raised this possibility the previous year, when he had expected to return to Scotland after spending the summer in Pau but this had become impossible when he had been advised not to return to Scotland until winter had passed.[59] When writing from Italy he had resurrected the idea.

He begins by saying how grateful he has been for his father's

---

[59] v. p. 160 supra.

support and the recent financial support from John. He agrees that the principal reason for his going abroad was to recover his health and that this object has been attained. He goes on, however, to justify his travels in Italy on the grounds that it is an excellent thing for a young man to broaden his experience of the world through entering "the Society of Nations without which he can neither learn their language nor observe their manners and practices." As part of his justification he mentions how he had recently met "some young men of Family in Ferrara" when he had passed through this town and that they had prevailed upon him to stay with them a few days. He even went to the length of saying how valuable it had been for him to have visited Rome, where the civil law of Scotland had its origins. He used these and other arguments to encourage his father to allow Melville to benefit from the experience that would be afforded to him of a short visit to the Continent. The letter then described, at great length, the buildings of Venice that he found very impressive.

Six days after he had written this letter he was in Verona, about 75 miles to the west of Venice. He wrote to Melville from there on 24th April, and it is clear that he believes that his arguments in favour of their meeting in Paris will have convinced their father. The letter is so interesting, especially concerning the developments in Melville's career and the advice on the arrangements for the visit to Paris, that it is given here in full.

> I wrote my Father on the 18th current a long letter in which I urged what appears to me to be strong and good reasons for your coming to meet me at Paris, as we both have so long contemplated. I have no doubt, that by the time this reaches you, all objections have been removed, and that you only wait to know when it is likely that I may be in Paris to set off on your journey. If it is otherwise, I shall be indeed very sorry, not only because I shall not have the enjoyment of your society and the happiness of such a meeting after this long separation but also that you are denied a short

space of rational relaxation after your laborious service as Apprentice and the opportunity of getting much interesting and useful knowledge. Just now you will receive more advantage from travel than you can ever afterwards. Your impressions would be stronger, your gratification much more vivid and after my lengthened stay among foreigners, I have an idea that I could smooth your way a good deal & make your trip to the French Metropolis more interesting as well as more instructive. After you have fulfilled your period of service I cannot see that your masters have any further claims upon you. If they have or you might reap greater benefit from a longer probation at their office, you might give them to understand that in a few weeks you will have pleasure in resuming your station or at least giving a considerable portion of your time to their service. But as I said before, I cannot doubt that all is nearly arranged for your departure. I have therefore to inform you of my intended motions.

I mean to leave for Munich in Bavaria today or tomorrow. I suppose I shall arrive there on Monday evening, passing by Trent and Innsbruck. The higher Alps are completely covered with snow but the road is quite open. I must spend a few days in Munich to examine the Gallery and the public buildings which are celebrated. From thence I will go straight to Paris by Stuttgart, the Capital of Wurtemberg and Strasburg. And I hope to arrive there about 14th or 15th May. I trust therefore that you are nearly ready to depart. Your funds you will require to economise and also bring the remaining £15 to pay my expenses in Paris and carry me home. The best way you can bring money is in Bank of England notes or British sovereigns, at least if the exchange is not unfavorable [sic], which it seldom is. You must allow two days for getting your passport in London from the French Ambassador. You might get it from the Consul there or at Edinburgh but then you must pay 10/– whereas the other is gratis.

I recommend you to take the Steamboat from London to Calais or Boulogne according as you find it cheaper but this you will be able to judge of better than I can. When you arrive at a French inn, where you mean to sleep, always ask the price of your Room. There are Rooms of all prices in the best Hotels, but you should not pay more than a franc a night for bed. In the cafés you can generally breakfast cheaper than in the Inns and you can dine á la carte in the Restaurateurs.

Read Polonius' advice to his son in Hamlet before you set off – that and your prudence will be your best guides. Take care of the Sharpers who lie in wait for young Englishmen and pretend to be good friends.

Fortify yourself with good letters for London, which I hope we will deliver together. Mr Wilkie the Painter[60] and Papa will give you a paper of Instructions about London. Do you remember Mr Stoddard, one of the members of a society that met in my room – Geo Chrystie can give you his address? You might write him to ask him in my name a letter to his friend Dr Robinson[61] in Paris, whose Lady I have often met with. Write me to Paris Poste Restante when you receive this with all your plans and also from London. I will leave a letter addressed to you in the Post Office of Paris telling you where I am to be found: but perhaps you may hear of the Hotel I stay in before your arrival.

---

[60] This was David Wilkie (1785–1841), one of Scotland's most prominent artists in the first half of the nineteenth century. He was born at Cults, near Cupar, where his father was the parish minister and the family must have been known to the Jamesons. In 1823 he succeeded Raeburn as Royal Limner for Scotland. He was appointed Painter in Ordinary to the king in 1830 and six years later was knighted. He lived mainly in London from 1805. He was the godfather of Wilkie Collins, the novelist.

[61] There is no reference in his diaries or correspondence of a Dr and Mrs Robinson.

I am on the point of setting off for Trent[62] so excuse me being briefer than usual. I refer you to my letter to Sophia, which goes by the same post for my impressions of Venice. I spent three delightful weeks there and, as I have always done, where I have been happiest, I wished more of your company here than in any other Italian city. The little German that I once knew I have long since forgot so this is another unknown tongue to me.

My kindest compliments to my dear Father.
Your most affectionate Brother,
And. Jameson

He made very good time from Verona to Stuttgart, reaching the Würtemberg[63] capital about ten days earlier than he expected. He wrote to Melville from there on 6th May 1834, giving an account of his journey from Italy. He had travelled by "*vetturina*" to Innsbruck through Trent, Bozen,[64] Sterzing and over the Brenner Pass into Bavaria. He had found the journey no more difficult than walking in the Scottish Highlands, and there was the added pleasure that he and his travelling companions had discovered Austria and Bavaria to be much more attractive than Italy. "Instead of disgusting filth was seen scrupulous cleanliness and instead of sulkiness or servility, we had ready civility and a constant willingness to oblige. We could at last enjoy 'tired nature's sweet restorer'[65] without nocturnal molestation. It was evident we were among a different race, not only in language & manners but in character and disposition." After a day in Innsbruck he and one of his companions had set off for Munich and had arrived there on his birthday, 30th April, exactly one year since he had sailed from Glasgow.

[62] Trent is in the South Tyrol, which was Austrian (and therefore German speaking) until the whole province was transferred to Italy in 1919 as a reward for support of the allies against Gemany and Austria-Hungary in the Great War. This is why Andrew Jameson refers to his poor command of the language.
[63] At this time Würtemberg, like Bavaria, was an independent kingdom.
[64] Now more commonly known in its Italian form of Bolzano.
[65] This is a quotation from the minor poet Edward Young (1683–1765).

He had much admired Munich's public buildings and the landscape gardening that was superior to any other capital cities that he had visited but felt he had to press on towards Paris. By 3rd May he had departed, spending that evening at Augsburg and the next at Ulm before coming into Stuttgart on 5th May. He had travelled by stagecoach and recorded in his letter that "The Ride from Ulm is almost a continual Orchard." He concluded his letter to Melville with the information that he would soon be leaving for Paris by way of Karlsruhe and Strasbourg and that he looked forward to meeting him in Paris.

This letter from Stuttgart was the last that he sent to Cupar from Europe before his return home. His notes on his journey from Venice to France conclude with a comment on his pleasant journey to Strasbourg. His father records in the Almanack that Melville left for Paris on 21st May, and there is a letter dated 26th May 1834 wherein Andrew tells his brother that he expects him within two days at the most and that he has taken rooms at 31 Rue de Provence.[66] He was also in possession of two letters from a M. Edouard Odier, whom he had met in Venice. One was to this man's brother Auguste Odier, the Conseilleur Référendaire à la Cour des Comptes[67] and the other to Professeur Audouin, Bibliothécaire de l'Institut au Palais.[68] M. Odier commended Andrew Jameson to them as a fit and proper person to be allowed access to the Revenue Court and the libraries of the French Institute.

Whether Melville received Andrew's letter of 26th May is doubtful because we learn from Andrew Jameson's account of the three days 27th to 30th May that the two brothers were united on the evening of the 27th at the Paris Bureau des Diligences. They dined in a cafe in the Palais Royal, where "we had many a story to tell to each other and in answering and asking questions the greater part of the night passed away rapidly and pleasantly."

---

[66] Presumably he left this letter for collection at the Boulogne Bureau des Diligences (coach office).

[67] Public Auditor at the Revenue Court.

[68] Librarian at l'Institut de France, which is the equivalent of the Royal Society. L'Institut comprises five academies including arts and sciences.

The following day they went to see the Exposition d'Industrie Nationale in the Place Louis XV, and Andrew gives a long description of what they saw together with the comment that as regards machinery the French were still far behind the British. The place was crowded "chiefly of the Bourgeois of Tours and Provence. 20,000 persons are said to have been attracted to Paris from the Provinces by this national spectacle." Later that day they went to what he refers to as the Depot of Sèvres Porcelain in the Rue de Rivoli.

Unfortunately the information on what they did on the next two days is restricted to the names of the places they visited. On Wednesday, 29th May it was Jardin de Luxembourg,[69] the Ecole des Médecins[70] and Hôtel des Mines.[71] On the 30th they went to the Jardin des Plantes[72] and the Hôtel des Monnaies. This last named was the French Mint and today still contains a museum of coinage. Andrew made copious notes about the coinage that he observed there. One can only assume that they made use of the letters of introduction Andrew had received from M. Odier in Venice, especially that to the Librarian of the Institut au Palais. This would be just the sort of place Andrew Jameson loved to see round because he never tired of any fresh intellectual stimulus.

No further letters or documents have survived, if, indeed, any were written, about the visit of the brothers to Paris and their return home. Perhaps they visited the artist, David Wilkie, when they passed through London because there is a document date-stamped 23rd June 1834 addressed to Andrew Jameson at 8 Burr Street, St Katherine's Docks. It simply reads "Mr Wilkie has obtained a ticket for Mr Andrew Jameson admitting a party of 5 to see the King's Pictures on Wednesday week which he hopes they will be able to make use of."

---

[69] This is a public park in the Latin Quarter that remains very popular with Parisians.

[70] This was then either a medical school or the equivalent of the Royal College of Physicians, of which membership was awarded to deserving practitioners.

[71] This is now one of the Grandes Écoles for the study of science and, in particular, civil engineering. Its origins go back to 1783.

[72] This is now part of the Natural History Museum of Paris. As when the Jameson brothers visited, it consists of gardens open to the public and laboratories – rather like Kew or Edinburgh Botanics – but on a smaller scale.

The Almanack shows that they "arrived[73] from London at ½ past 10" on 8th July 1834.

The prime object of Andrew Jameson's sudden departure from Scotland for the south of France had been to recover his health and this had been achieved through the sensible care he had taken of himself. He had also taken the opportunity to travel widely and consequently had added considerably to the maturity that had already been developing during his years in Edinburgh. He was now ready to take his final examinations in law with the confidence that he could thereafter launch into his chosen career in the belief that it would not be impeded by ill health. In this matter he would soon be disappointed.

---

[73] At Cupar.

APPENDIX TO CHAPTER FOUR
Excerpt from the Diary of Andrew Jameson on his Visit to Belsito
Saturday, 18th May 1833

At 3 p.m. I joined Mr Johnston at the coaching house and soon afterwards we set off along with Mr Lawton, a young Englishman, who has been for a short time in the country and is a relative of Mr Johnston. The vehicle was well suited to the climate, being airy, shaded and open. It was a sort of double phaeton drawn by a pair of Mecklenburg horses and had originally been ordered in Paris by one of Charles X' courtiers and thrown, of course, on the maker's hands, when the intended purchaser had been compelled to fly.

We proceeded along the Quai de Bourgogne and across the bridge and then about a mile and a half to Libourne, which I had taken in my walk of Wednesday morning. We then turned to the south along une route départementale, a country road which was in excellent order and runs by the foot of the chain of little eminences, which follow so far the course of the river.

Mr Johnston's country house – Belsito – is situated upon this rising ground with the ground sloping down to the plans,[74] which stretch along between the hills and the river.

The situation is very fine commanding as it does a view of the river and the surrounding country, the spires and streets of Bordeaux and the arches of the noble bridge in the distance on the other side; the eye wanders over the range of cultivated knolls with the beautiful little valleys in front well planted with woods and hedgerows and the sides

---

[74] He uses here the French word *plans* meaning level ground.

covered with vines.

The house which is new and is in the Italian style. The front is comprised of a beautiful range of Corinthian pillars with a broad portico underneath. The door opens with an entrance hall at the other extremity of which is the entrance to the public rooms which occupy the whole north frontage of the house. This door opens into a beautiful drawing room, large and airy with windows opening onto the lawn. It was a delightfully cool and pleasant house even during the noonday heat. At one end of the drawing room was a library round the walls of which were alternally[75] book cases and mirrors. The latter reflected in a variety of images the beautiful scenery – the river and the parterre. At the other end of the drawing room there were two doors, one of which led to the suite of sleeping apartments and the other into the dining room, which is painted in imitation of marble and done so admirably that it was difficult to distinguish the real marble of the mantelpiece from the painted pillars and walls. The walls of this room were also hung with mirrors. All the floors were, of course, bare in the style of the country but this even was beautifully painted.

The winter apartments are all on the south side of the house and furnished in a different style. I was very much struck with the beautiful verdure of the lawn and called to mind what I had often read in English travellers' accounts that there was nowhere anything like an English lawn. On mentioning this Mr Johnston told that it was very uncommon here and expected this one and another at his nephew's place, Lescure near Bordeaux, were the only ones in the whole country. Some peasants were mowing the grass and haymaking on the lawn in English style.

I was not a little surprised to find the manservant, who showed me to my room and brushed my clothes, a fellow countryman from South Queensferry in West Lothian. He was a very creditable specimen – intelligent, civil and good looking. He had been sixteen years with Mr Johnston, having entered his service very young. I afterwards heard that he had money but that it was not likely he would ever leave his master to whom he was invaluable, until death terminated their

---

[75] Today we would use the word "alternately".

connection. To my inquiry what he thought of France he answered that it was a delightful climate and would be a fine country if it was under British government.

Our dinner was excellent combining the advantages of English and French style like everything about the place and the benevolent owner. I need say nothing of the wines at the table of one of the chief merchants of Bordeaux. They were excellent and of great variety, Bordeaux wines of different kinds and first quality, most excellent [word illegible] graves, Sauternes-Frontineaux and Leoville[76] and a delightful claret made of the first pressing or dropping of the grapes when gathered together without any pressure but that of their own fullness. This nectar is called vin des gouttes[77] and is the most agreeable and delicious I ever tasted. On being drawn it diffused a fine aroma thro' the room. The flavour is ethereal – as if the essence of claret – the sublimated juice of the grape. Of course it is seldom if ever exported and from the way in which the trade is conducted could never be made an article of commerce. So it is not probable that I may ever meet with it again, which makes me the more particular in mentioning it. In the evening, which was lovely, Mr Lawton and I sauntered thro' the grounds, which are very tastefully laid out, a combination of lawns and gardens, a perfect blush of roses, which have a more ethereal smell than in England, acacias and a beautiful specimen of horse chestnut with a purple flower, which has but lately been discovered. The views from the walks were beautiful, especially when lighted by such a sunset as they have been in this favored region.

Before dinner I had been introduced to Mrs Guestier, a niece of my host, whose husband is a successful merchant in Bordeaux and a Proprietor in Médoc. Their country house, Fleurac, is immediately adjoining to Belsito, the villas being within five minutes walk of each other. Madame Guestier was very agreeable and asked me to accompany her and see her place. I found it much in the same style as its neighbour with a finer view up the river but not such a fine house.

---

[76] Probably a local wine.
[77] Translated into literal English it is "wine from drops" (i.e. from dropped grapes).

Everything looked beautiful. The flowers were so lovely, the trees so green. Among the beauties of Fleurac I must not forget a very pretty young lady, Mlle Guestier, the eldest of the family. We came upon her by surprise as she was drawing at a window which opened upon the lawn and she was so much engaged with the head that she was copying we had time to admire the finer picture, before she was aware of our presence. Her appearance was very engaging and her manner easy and agreeable. I was very much surprised to find that I had been egregnantly[78] mistaken as to a small but important point of manners. In England it is the privilege of the Lady to take notice of the Gentleman first and in France where "Place aux Dames" is so much the way of all things one would have thought that they could not be behind us in this. But here it is here the Gentleman who first takes notice of the Lady. Of course, from a different idea of politeness but I scarcely think so correct an idea. In this instance it was my duty to have taken off my hat and made a profound bow to Mad'lle at the window and asked her how she did – instead of waiting most respectfully till the mother should introduce me.

I was telling Madame Guestier of the melancholy state in which some of my fellow passengers were – who had come here for their health and in one little week tired of the country, where they could get none of their usual comforts and intended returning by the vessel in which they had come. She mentioned that she had known too many cases of the same kind.

Addendum

The entry in the diary concerning his visit to Belsito as a guest of Mr Johnston ends, rather abruptly, at this point. He went to church with Mr Johnston at the British consulate next day and on Monday, 20th May 1833, after a walk before breakfast, he returned to Bordeaux, presumably with Mr Johnston in the phaeton.

---

[78] Either Andrew Jameson made up this word or, if it ever existed, it no longer appears in even the best English dictionaries. Its nearest approach today would be "egregiously" and this would fit the context.

CHAPTER FIVE

The Young Advocate

As stated at the end of the previous chapter, no documents have yet been found (assuming any were written) to let us know what Melville and Andrew did when they were in Paris during the summer of 1834, other than that they attended an exhibition and visited some public places. At present, therefore, the story of Andrew Jameson's life must contain a gap of five months from his comments on Melville's arrival in Paris to the start of the diary of his last session at Edinburgh University on 3rd November 1834.

He and Melville travelled to Edinburgh on 3rd November 1834 and over the next four days attended what his diary refers to as "Introductory Lectures". These included Dr Knox's[1] first lecture of the session on "textures of the body." Andrew also renewed his acquaintanceship with the many families who had given him hospitality in the years 1829–33, such as the Clephanes, Scotts and Johnstones. The hospitality of the Clephanes was very quickly resumed with the following invitation, addressed to "Andrew Jameson Esq. Student of Law and Melville Jameson Esq. Writer conjunctly and severally" to dine on 21st November.

> A porker with his throat cut has arrived at No 5 West Circus
> Place and Dr Knox lectures tomorrow on its dry bones.

---

[1] Dr Robert Knox was a key figure in the trial of William Burke and Helen McDougal in 1828. (William Hare, equally culpable, escaped prosecution for lack of evidence.) Knox and other lecturers in anatomy needed a steady supply of corpses and the normal providers were the "resurrectionists" or grave robbers. Burke and Hare, instead of disinterring bodies from graves, chose the easier but less legitimate method of murdering people and supplying fresh corpses to Dr Knox and his colleagues. The notoriety of the case meant that for some years afterwards Dr Knox's lectures were attended as much for their entertainment as their instruction in basic anatomy, sometimes by several hundred students.

Moreover, in these days of chops and changes 'tis meet that good Christians should combine and stand by Church & State. So, if you will abjure Judaism, take no oath agt suicide and drink damnation to the Whigs, Mrs Clephane will be glad to see you and Melville at 5 on said day to hear and see as use is according to the laws and practice of this realm. If so – good – If not – well.

A bag arrived last night filled with the brains of Andrew Jameson, Esq, S. S. of the County of Fife – to be inspected and lectured upon at said meeting.

After a few days' temporary lodgings at Andrew's previous accommodation in Scotland Street, the brothers settled into comfortable quarters at 33 Dublin Street. Andrew realised that having been absent from his studies for over a year he had to make up for lost time. Fortunately, as he wrote on 22nd November, he was experiencing "a growing attachment to my legal studies. It is a noble field of reasoning and must now command almost exclusive attention. I feel that I am far behind and nothing but determined persevering study with due economy of time can enable me to make any considerable progress." He was pleased to be invited to dinner on 29th November by Mr Nairne, in whose Writer's practice he had served from May 1832 until his sudden departure for Europe and to find that his "old deskmates" were also present.

Early in December he met Spalding, who had accompanied him on his journeys around Rome and whom he had last seen at Naples. Spalding had returned by way of Ancona on the Adriatic coast and had then spent the summer at Leipzig. He also met by chance Dr Chalmers and "was shocked with the alteration of his appearance." He resumed his membership of the Juridical Society and by December was participating in its debates.

The days before and after Christmas were spent back at Cupar and with the weather favourable for skating this was the main social activity. On 29th December "Mr Thomson of Leghorn dined with us", and this must have been the husband of the Mrs Thomson, at whose inn Andrew had stayed during his brief stay there in October 1833.² He and his father drove in a gig to Perth on 31st December to spend New Year with the Grays at Bowerswell. They were back in Cupar early on 2nd January 1835, and the following evening his father hosted a dinner party for the Thomsons of Eden Park. Elizabeth was present with her parents, sister Jane and two brothers but there was no dalliance with her as there had been at Hogmanay in 1830.³

By 5th January he was back in Edinburgh, where he resumed his studies and his considerable social life. The weather was cold and his entry into his diary of 25th January states that three days of skating had interrupted the routine of his studies that he had laid down for himself. Nor had he prepared himself for contributions to the debates of the Juridical Society, and he resolved that he would endeavour "to speak on all occasions as it is only by long practice that I can hope to arrive at ease and fluency." Although the continuing cold weather still attracted him to Duddingston Loch for skating, he wrote on 1st February 1835 that he was satisfied with his week's work. On the other hand, although he had contributed in a debate at the Juridical Society, he had been "ill at ease" in his delivery.

Mrs Scott of Northfield, who had been most generous in the hospitality that she had offered Andrew Jameson from the time of his first arrival in Edinburgh, died on 20th February after a very short illness. As recently as the 1st February she had entertained him to a meal, and her death affected him deeply. "She has performed the part of an excellent mother and I never received anything but kindness from her." Was the term "mother" used simply in the general sense that she had been a good mother to her children or was he implying that she had acted, to some extent, as a substitute mother to him?

There is a curious entry in his diary for 25th February. "I witnessed the dangerous operation of tying the carotid artery for aneurism by [name illegible]. I afterwards walked through the wards and saw some fearful pictures of disease." Does this suggest that he had attended not

² v. p. 169 supra.
³ v. p. 113 supra.

just the first of the lectures of Dr Knox on anatomy but subsequent ones? He had been suffering from a cough for three weeks and, on Friday 27th, deciding that a change of air might do him good, "took the Steamboat up the Forth and walked from Stirling to Dunblane, where I staid till Monday". He was accompanied by his friend Stirling and they returned late on Monday 2nd March. Whether the weekend visit got rid of his cough is not stated but by the end of the week it was now severe toothache that incapacitated him to the degree that he had to keep to his lodgings.

If he did seek treatment for his ailment, it is not recorded, and indeed there are only a few brief entries for the month of March 1835. The briefest among them is for 12th March where only two words appear: "Miss Campbell." He was to marry a Miss Campbell in 1844 but it is unlikely that he had begun his courtship as early as this and it is probable that this was someone quite different. His father came over for a few days to attend a trial, possibly a case that he had referred to the Supreme Court from the sheriff court in Fife on account of its seriousness. He dined on two occasions with his sons and accompanied Andrew to Northfield to express in person their sorrow at the death of Mrs Scott.

As the university term gradually wound down during the last days of March he began to feel pain in his chest and "I consulted Wood who told me to be cautious and prescribed for me."[4] This, together with the coughs to which he refers on a few occasions, is an indication that he was not yet fully recovered from the illness that had prompted his sudden departure for France two years earlier. The diary from November 1834 onward makes frequent reference to cold, unpleasant weather. This bears out his good sense in heeding the advice of the doctors in Pau that by autumn 1833 he had not yet recuperated sufficiently to survive an Edinburgh winter.

As the weather improved so, apparently, did his health because there are no further references to colds, coughs or pains in the chest. He spent the brief vacation between the university's second and third

---

[4] v. 148 supra.

terms studying hard at home, and on his return to Edinburgh on 5th April set for himself a most rigorous programme of study in preparation for his trial[5] before representatives of the Faculty of Advocates. He applied himself with praiseworthy diligence to the task. Apart from attending the seven meetings of the specially convened Summer Club of the Juridical Society,[6] at all of which he spoke, he virtually ceased all other social activities and, returning to Cupar at the end of the university session in May, he continued in similar vein, allowing only a few family occasions to interrupt his preparation. He was offered and accepted 23rd June 1835 as the date when he should appear before his examiners. While in Cupar he obtained a copy of his birth certificate from the session clerk of the church where his birth and baptism had been recorded and which he had to provide for the Secretary of the Advocates' Widows Fund, were he to be successful in his trial.

No better account of his trial can be provided than what he wrote in his diary and it is here rendered in full.

19th and 20th June. Wrote my thesis.

Sat 20th June. Mr Clephane introduced me to Mr Maconochie, Sheriff of Orkney, President of the Scots Law Examinators. Dined with Horne.[7]

Mon 22nd June. Mr Clephane examined[8] me for an hour. I dined with J. Hill[9] and went out to a party at Northfield at 9 p.m.

Tuesday 23rd June. I dressed and went up to the Parliament House in a full suit of black with white neck-cloth. There were four candidates. I was called in first and

---

[5] As stated in Chapter Three, this term has now been replaced by "examination".
[6] The official Juridical Society of Edinburgh University had closed its 1834–1835 session in March 1835, when it made Andrew Jameson an honorary member.
[7] This man had been a fellow student of law at Edinburgh University.
[8] This was probably a practice run for the real oral examination that took place on the next day rather than part of the actual examination process. It is another example of the kindness shown to Andrew Jameson by Sheriff Clephane.
[9] Presumably another former student aquaintance.

answered all the questions easily, which is not saying much as they were very simple. My fellows were Mr Glasgow and two Gordons.[10]

Wednesday 24th June. We distributed our Theses at the top of the library stairs to all the advocates that passed. Mine was dedicated to Mr Clephane and I was more troubled about the Dedication than anything else. The subject was a good one – The Action of Recovery of the Roman Law. De Rei Vindicatione D.VI-T1. I studied the Pandects and Code carefully upon the Title with the commentaries of Peregius, Donellus and Heinecius and then wrote it up at once without composing it at all in English. Melville revised it for me and I wrote a clean copy for the printer. The latter, who pretends to be a judge, commended the Latin thereof. The Theses of my colleagues were bought and sold being composed[11] by that erudite gentleman, Mr Lyon – Grinder[12] to the Faculty.

Thusday 25th June. I was introduced to the Dean, J. Hope[13] by Mr Clephane. We defended our Theses before Mr L'Amy, Sheriff of Forfar[14] and a larger audience than is usually congregated. Blackie[15] shared a bottle of Claret with us. I went down to Northfield in the evening.

Friday 26th June. Mr Clephane introduced me to the Lord President Hope in the Robing Room. My Lord Justice Clerk was sitting and asked how my father did. We took the oath

---

[10] v. Appendix to this chapter.

[11] Though not quite the empty formality that it later became until its abolition early in the twentieth century, the preparation and presentation of Latin theses was still part of the examination process. Quite clearly Andrew Jameson had no difficulty in composing his own, being more concerned with the dedication to Sheriff Clephane than the content. It is clear from what he enters in his diary that some candidates did purchase theses from Mr Lyon and it is probable that the examinators would be aware of the practice. Presumably candidates who purchased their theses took the precaution of studying them in order that they could defend them in the oral examination, such as Andrew Jameson had before Sheriff L'Amy.

[12] A coach or crammer of students for an examination. (*Chambers Encyclopaedia*)

[13] It could just as easily be read as I. Hope.

[14] Normally the Dean of the Faculty of Advocates would have taken the chair but for some reason did not do so, although earlier that day Andrew Jameson had been introduced to him.

[15] v. Appendix to this chapter.

de fideli before the 1st Division, the Oaths of Allegiance and etc before Lord Moncrieff and thereafter put on our gowns and began to walk about like the other lawyers. I received the congratulations of our friends.

I paid the fees amounting to £71-4-6 which added to the former fees paid at passing the Civil Law Trials are £350.

Mr Gray and my father arrived on business.

Sat 27th June. I got my first fee, £22 and moved two petitions in the 1st Division and also a motion before Lord Cockburn in the Second.

We all dined with Mr Clephane when my health was drunk in good claret. The Sheriffs of Argyle and Linlithgow were of the party.

At the conclusion of his examination in civil law, he had been congratulated on his success by his examiners.[16] There is no mention of any similar action after his appearance before Sheriff L'Amy, but one must presume he was told that his candidature had been successful. The record of the Faculty of Advocates states the following:

Edinburgh 25th June 1835

In the absence of the Dean, Mr L'Amy took the Chair.

Mr Andrew Jameson, fourth son of Andrew Jameson, Esq., Cupar, Fifeshire, – upon LibVI, Tit. I Digest De rei vindicatione ... publicly Examined and found sufficiently qualified.

The two petitions and the motion before Lord Cockburn were merely formal and did not require any exercise of judgment. The same can be said of the petition he moved a week later in the Second Division and of the "motions before all the Lords, but Jeffrey." For the next two weeks he attended law courts and after the Session closed on 17th July, he

---

[16] v. p. 125 supra.

returned to Cupar.

He had studied hard over several months in preparation for his trial and was due a holiday. He often went fishing, and there was a continuous round of entertainment, mainly dinners at the homes of family friends in Cupar and the surrounding neighbourhood. On 31st July he attended a ball, where dancing continued until 4.00 a.m.

Mr Nairne and a party of friends visited Fife in the first fortnight of August 1835, and Andrew and his father dined with them at the New Inn on the 6th. The next day he was with his father at Bridge of Earn where they were surprised to meet Mr Scott of Northfield and two of his daughters. They had just arrived from Edinburgh and were on their way to Scone. Andrew and his father stayed the night at Bowerswell with the Grays, and the following day the two Miss Scotts broke their return journey from Scone to call on Sophia. They then dined with Andrew at the "Ordinary"[17] in Bridge of Earn and set out to climb the adjacent Moncreiffe[18] Hill. They failed to reach the summit but found great amusement in descending by a difficult footpath arriving "en Chantant at the Inn. I came home at 12." Next day was Sunday and the Scott girls with their father joined the Jamesons for church and dinner, thus allowing Andrew to repay some of the hospitality he had received over the years at Northfield.

He returned to Edinburgh by the evening of the 13th August. He spent the next few weeks reading legal publications to increase his understanding and knowledge of Scots law and attending a series of dinners with various acquaintances. He had not been feeling well for a few days and, since the 31st was a glorious day, he took a bathe at Granton. It certainly did him no good because he writes "I awoke sick and felt muddy all day." His stomach had been upset, and he states that "I have not felt in good trim for working hard." Nevertheless, he could not refuse an invitation from the Dean of the Faculty to dine at his home on 4th September along with three others – Mackenzie, Patton

---

[17] An establishment, usually an inn, where the meal was a fixed price.

[18] This is the spelling given in a modern atlas of a hill about 700 feet high lying just to the north of Bridge of Earn. The diary gives the spelling Moncrieff and this is certainly the more normal spelling of the name.

and Turnbull – who may well have been, like him, recently admitted to the Faculty.

He spent the rest of September until the 27th doing very little apart from making two separate visits to Cupar. On the 28th Sheriff Clephane introduced him to Lord Moncreiff and on that afternoon he dined with the judges. He had an appeal case offered him but it was withdrawn. Indeed, there is no reference to any gainful legal work until 21st October when he was counsel to two men accused of theft with aggravation. After ninety minutes of conversation he decided that their case was hopeless and he advised them to plead guilty. He describes this as "my first professional conference."

On 30th October he received a Sheriff Court Process to provide answers to a petition written by an advocate called Mar. He wrote a paper that was "necessarily long and argumentative" and comments with pleasure that this was "the first time I exercised my profession, for the motions and papers signed before, soon after passing in July, were merely formal. I found the occupation extremely agreeable and was glad to find that it had proved satisfactory afterwards."

A few days later, 12th November 1835, he wrote in his diary that he "had made motions and prepared with small expectations for what business Providence should throw in my way." This suggests that he was not sanguine about his prospects of attracting clients, but he was utterly mistaken because work came to him to such a degree that he had no time to continue with his diary. He did not return to it until 8th February 1836, where he gave a long account of what he called his "first professional winter."

He had written seven opinions and petitions concerning cases before the courts and had "found the labour exceedingly agreeable though I was generally pressed for time." On 25th January 1836 he had appeared for the first time in the High Court of Judiciary, before the Lord Justice Clerk, Lord Moncreiff, and addressed a jury. He was representing a John Hunter, accused of several thefts. "The court was crowded and many of my acquaintances were present. I was more than once interrupted by the Justice but did not falter and found the exercise agreeable." He does not say if his arguments convinced the jury but it is clear that he had spoken with confidence and this would not have gone unnoticed by more senior members of his profession.

He also managed to carry out a prodigious amount of reading, both general and relating to the law. Invitations to dinners and parties flooded in but he had to decline some of them on account of the demands of his work. He had enjoyed a quiet ten days' break over Christmas and New Year at Cupar. Melville was continuing to share accommodation with him and was working hard to win the Civil Law prize. This involved him rising as early as five in the morning and we learn later in the diary that his endeavours met with success. The only time they had to themselves was on Sundays.

More regular but not daily entries to his diary were now made, and while it is clear that his career was prospering it was not accompanied by good health. In the middle of February he suffered from what he called "a stupifying cold" that he was unable to throw off, and as late as 11th March he was writing "This catarrh has dulled my sense and faculties for a whole month. I cannot rise in the morning with alacrity, eat with appetite or think or write with spirit." Nevertheless, his work must have continued to give satisfaction because he was retained as junior counsel with a George Bell for a case to be heard in the Outer House of the Court of Session.

Thursday 17th March. Anderson and Moon was called at 11 a.m. I stated our objections to the competency of the action. F. Maitland replied. My Senior, G. Bell, was engaged in the Jury Court. I resumed the debate when the brother T. Maitland concluded. The Ordinary, Lord Cockburn, repelled our Pleas and we gave notice that we were to go to the Inner House.[19] This was my first actual debate and it was a tolerably tough one. It was luckily a very fine point to argue and although a little flurried at first, I found it very agreeable and spoke with ease and forcibly. The Agent and

[19] i.e. he intended to appeal against the decision of Lord Cockburn.

opposite counsel gave me the credit of having stated the case fully.

I was very glad when it was over and I had thought of it till my heart was sick. A few more such contests and I trust I may become hardened.

Friday 18th. Again prepared to plead the merits of this case and put off as we reclaim on the Ordinary's interlocutor.

The Law Session finished a few days later. He made a brief visit to Cupar, spent an evening (5th April) with Melville at the home of Sir William Allan, President of the Royal Scottish Academy,[20] and writes of a pleasant walk on 11th April to Ravelston. The diary now peters out, and no following diary giving a personal account of his activities has, so far, been found. The entries in the final pages of the diary that ended in April 1836 are spasmodic and, as stated above, there was a gap of three months from November 1835 until February 1836. He did then give an account of his activities over the three winter months but thereafter ceased to make entries on a daily or even, on occasion, weekly basis.

Since he was now actively engaged upon his profession it is perfectly understandable if he no longer kept a diary, because, as he had written on 8th February, "I was generally pressed for time." He was successfully launched upon his career but, as a young man, had to work hard to maintain the early progress that he had made. He was, however, a regular correspondent with his family, and it was from the letters that he wrote and received that his story can be continued.

[20] Sir William Allan (1782–1850). Allan travelled in Russia from 1805 until 1814 but when his paintings did not sell well he returned to Scotland where he found a patron in Sir Walter Scott. His painting turned now to Scottish historical events, one of the best known being the *Death of Rizzio*. There is no previous mention of this painter in the diaries and while it is understandable that the Jameson family knew Sir David Wilkie, because his father had been the minister of the parish of Cults near Cupar, any connection with Allan can only be conjecture. It is, perhaps, possible that Andrew and Melville Jameson had met him at one of the many houses to which they had been invited and had received an invitation from the painter to call upon him.

APPENDIX TO CHAPTER FIVE

The three other candidates who were examined with Andrew Jameson on 25th June 1835

Nothing has been discovered about the candidate called Glasgow but the two Gordons had distinguished careers.

Edward Strathearn Gordon (10th April 1814–21st August 1879)

Solicitor General 1866–1867
Lord Advocate 1867–1868 and 1874–1876
MP for Thetford 1867–1868
MP for Glasgow University 1869–1876
Dean of the Faculty of Advocates
Lord Gordon of Drumearn 1876–1879

John Thomson Gordon (19th March 1813–22nd September 1865)

Rector of Marischal College, Aberdeen 1849–1850
Sheriff of Aberdeen 1847–1848
Sheriff of Midlothian 1848–1865

His wife, Mary, was the daughter of Professor John Wilson (1785–1854), a founder of *Blackwood's Magazine* and for over thirty years Professor of Moral Philosophy, Edinburgh University. He had been one of the guests at the special dinner convened by Professor Cheape on 12th March 1830.[21]

---

[21] v. p. 94 supra.

The Blackie with whom they shared a bottle of claret would, almost certainly, have been John Stuart Blackie (28th July 1809 – 2nd March 1895), the son of an Aberdeen banker. He was admitted to the Faculty of Advocates in 1834 and became Professor of Humanity, Aberdeen University 1839–1852 and Professor of Greek, Edinburgh University 1852–1882. A distinguished classical scholar and in politics a radical and Scottish nationalist, he was responsible for the foundation of the Chair of Celtic at Edinburgh University.

CHAPTER SIX

Illness Inhibits Career Progression

Although Andrew Jameson ceased to keep a diary after the spring of 1836, a lot of family correspondence has survived. These letters provide a useful account of his relationships with other members of his family and of the development of his career as an advocate.

Much of the family correspondence for the three years after April 1836 revolved around Andrew's eldest brother, Captain John St Clair Jameson, who arrived home in May 1836 for an extended period of leave.[1] Through the influence of his uncle, Captain James Jameson, John had received a cadetship with the Honourable East India Company's Bombay Native Infantry at the age of 16. He had left home in December 1819 and sailed for Bombay in the *Earl of Balcarres* that was under his uncle's command. He had kept a very full diary of this voyage that lasted over five months, and its 205 pages of highly legible script make most interesting reading. He had soon been promoted to a lieutenancy but, in common with other officers of the time, had to wait for over ten years before reaching the rank of captain. He was a good correspondent, and the letters that he sent home gave an account of what military matters took place in that part of India between 1820 and 1835.

John Jameson was reunited with his father on 3rd May 1836, having first been met by Andrew, possibly at Leith. There is no other reference to Andrew in this year although he would have been delighted that Melville had indeed been awarded in March the Civil Law Prize for which he had studied all winter.[2] It is also a fair assumption that, his

---

[1] In page 51 of the author's *Captain James Jameson* (Robert Gordon University, 2002) it is stated that John St Clair Jameson did not return for leave at any time. Further documents have now come to light and we know that he was back in Scotland for three years, 1836–1839.
[2] v. p. 198 supra.

father's sister Sophia Thomson having died at Dundee[3] on 27th July, he attended her funeral. Mentions of Andrew in the Almanack are as sparse in 1837 as they are in 1836, but perhaps the information that in April John was attending classes at Edinburgh University "for amusement" allows for the possibility that the two brothers saw quite a lot of each other at this time and that perhaps John stayed with Andrew at 33 Dublin Street. Andrew visited Cupar in July and October and attended a meeting of sheriff-substitutes in St Andrews on 17th November, presumably as a guest of his father. All the family, including the Grays, were together in Cupar on 31st December to attend the formal opening of new St Michael's Church. Since an entry in the Almanack for 20th March 1837 specifically refers to the laying of the foundation of "new St Michael's" it is probable that it was a replacement for a previous building that had fallen into disrepair.

By 1838 Sheriff-Substitute Jameson was again in financial difficulties. He had become jointly liable with a James Webster for the latter's debts, and on 27th March Melville writes in a letter to John: "I may mention that I have induced my father at last to agree to a proposed arrangement with Webster by which he would be at once and for ever quit of that man." That arrangement, whatever it was, did not settle his affairs with Webster, and we learn in Melville's letter to John of 19th November, that Sheriff-Substitute Jameson's financial affairs remained in a troubled state. By contrast the career of his son Andrew was prospering. Andrew was able to finance himself on a visit to France in the spring of the year and, moreover, following the death of Sheriff Clephane in August, he was appointed Interim Depute Sheriff of Fife. This was a singularly appropriate appointment because Sheriff Clephane had done much to support Andrew when he was a student at Edinburgh University, but no matter how close had been the relationship between him and the late sheriff, the appointment would not have come to one so young unless he had already proven himself worthy of the office, no matter how temporary. In a letter to John of 1st October Andrew expresses considerable amusement that for a few

---

[3] She was the mother of Elizabeth and her home was Eden Park in Cupar.

weeks he has been able to count his father as a subordinate.[4]

The visit to France was occasioned by ill health. The old trouble with his breathing had returned, and there is an entry in the Almanack for 2nd March that Andrew had met his father at Kirkcaldy court where he had told him that he had been advised to go abroad. He made the necessary arrangements to cover his professional responsibilities and in mid-March he took a steamer from Leith to London, where, during his brief stay there, he was "very unwell" as he wrote to John from Tours on 28th March. Accordingly he had consulted an "eminent physician"[5] and finding that his advice coincided with that of a Dr Hood, who appears to have been the medical practitioner whom he consulted in Edinburgh, he left immediately for France. His letter states that he had "a pleasant passage to Calais of 10 hours" and had travelled all night to the French capital by diligence.

Arriving there on a Saturday evening, it was typical of Andrew Jameson that the following morning he attended one of the reformed churches where he felt familiar with the order of service and the hymns. The journey, however, must have taken more out of him than he realised because by the afternoon he felt a severe pain in his chest and returned to his accommodation with difficulty. He must have recovered quickly because on the Monday he was able to visit the Court of Cassation[6] where he "heard some good pleading." That night he took a coach to Orléans, where he admired the city's cathedral on the Wednesday, and then on the Friday travelled by steamer down the River Loire to Tours. He spent two days in search of suitable lodgings and eventually found some "in poor enough quarters in Rue des Acacias with M. et Mme

---

[4] Later that month an advocate called Menteith was appointed Sheriff of Fife.

[5] In a letter – possibly only a draft – of autumn 1840, Andrew Jameson said two winters previously he had consulted Sir James Clark on his health. This must have been the "eminent physician" whom he mentions in this letter. Sir James (1788–1870) came from Fordyce in Aberdeenshire and after graduating at the Universities of Aberdeen and Edinburgh served six years in the army before travelling in Europe and investigating the mineral waters and the climate of various health resorts. He was appointed Physician in Ordinary to Queen Victoria in 1837 and in 1835 had published a treatise on pulmonary consumption. He was, therefore, a highly appropriate doctor for Andrew Jameson to consult.

[6] The Court de Cassation is the main court of last resort in France and has its seat in the Paris Hall of Justice. The Court judges final appeals with respect to the system of justice, excluding cases of administrative justice, which go before the Conseil d'État.

Porchien, quiet and respectable people."

His letter of 28th March 1838 from Tours to John is the source of information about his journey from Leith to Tours. It includes the following words that suggest that initially he was worried about leaving his responsibilities to clients and others so precipitately but had now put these fears behind him. "I thank God, that notwithstanding a good deal of suffering of late and a very solitary state, it is one by no means unblessed. I have been able to cast off the fears about my professional duties, which distressed me before my departure. I dare say I will not be much missed."

In a letter to his father written on the same sheet of paper he expresses himself in more gloomy terms. He had not been at all well over the last six weeks and his breathing had been difficult, "keeping me in a great state of feebleness." He had not felt like walking about Tours and could not even summon up any energy for reading. France had experienced a severe winter, and the flowers and foliage of the area were no further on than in Scotland. There was a large British colony in Tours but he did not feel physically fit enough to make the acquaintance of any of them, feared that it would take him a long time to recover his health and "it might be long before I see dear Scotland."

His mood changed remarkably within seven days. He wrote to John on 7th April that he intended to be back in Edinburgh by 7th May, and since he would be returning by way of Paris, suggested that they meet there. He was still unwell but hoped to be better after another fortnight. He had not attended church although he had heard good reports of the young Protestant minister and regretted that "on account of my illhealth I have not yet been able to make his acquaintance but will, I hope, before I depart." His father had written to suggest that he stay longer "here or further south till I am quite well", but he believed his health was not as bad as to require this. "I may be able to do my business during the session – and may get through with the warmer weather." He was disappointed that the weather in Tours had not been "much in my favour but the air is dry and healthy. It may have done more good than I suppose – but as yet I am much the same as when I left you."

The Almanack makes no mention at all of Andrew's return to Scotland nor of any tour of Europe undertaken by John, although the absence of any family correspondence with John between the end of May and October suggests that he did visit Europe that summer.[7] Andrew's resumption of his professional life did allow him the opportunity to accept the interim appointment of sheriff[8] but his return may have been premature. He visited Arran for a holiday in August and was unwell again. When he wrote to John on 1st October he tells him that he has been having difficulty with his breathing, and Melville mentions in his letter of 19th November 1838 to John that Andrew has been complaining about the early arrival in Edinburgh of cold and snowy weather. Not surprisingly Andrew was affected by the inclement weather and wrote to John that "I have found it necessary to take to the couch again."

The year 1839 began well. Sheriff-Substitute Jameson wrote to Andrew on 2nd January that he was looking forward to having all three of his sons under his roof over the coming weekend. We learn from Sophia Gray in January that Andrew was well. He had written to John earlier that month that pressure of work made it impossible for him to accompany his brother to visit their Dundee relations after the Cupar weekend and from this it is clear that, whatever the state of his health, his professional life was flourishing. Ineffectual though he was in the handling of his private financial affairs, Sheriff-Substitute Jameson was highly respected by the legal profession and Andrew was invited to attend a dinner on 1st March that its Kirkcaldy members were giving to honour his father.

1839, however, was dominated by the wedding of John St Clair

---

[7] There is a delightful letter, dated 19th May 1838, from Effie Gray to her uncle John thanking him for her tenth birthday present of some essays. They appear to have been written by John because his niece says, "I hope I shall soon be able to write similar ones." Effie goes on to say how her birthday was celebrated by "a fête champetre on the green 5 and 20 young Ladies eating curds and cream".

[8] v. p. 203 supra.

Jameson to Marion Buchanan, sometimes referred to as Marion
Snodgrass Buchanan. Of the 35 letters that have survived from this
year, the majority were written to John by members of his family. It
would be appropriate to divert from this narrative of the life of Andrew
Jameson in order to comment briefly on his eldest surviving brother,
John St Clair, the first of the family to bear the name of St Clair
within his name, a tradition that has been continued into the twenty-
first century. Although he had been serving with the Bombay Native
Infantry since 1820, there had been very little military activity during
the sixteen years that followed and, perhaps as some antidote to what
must have been a very monotonous existence, he began to take an
interest in a society that had been established to promote the education
of Indian women. There is no reason to doubt the sincerity of his
involvement because John Jameson was possessed of the same deep
Christian conscience that imbued all members of his family. During
his leave he addressed many meetings to encourage the foundation of
local branches to support the cause.[9]

Now nearer forty than thirty years of age, John was still a bachelor
when 1839 began. Whether he had been looking for a wife or was content
with his single status must be a matter of surmise but sometime early
in 1839 he met Marion Buchanan. It is possible that she had attended
one of the meetings he addressed on the need to educate Indian women
but there is no documentation to confirm that. When the engagement
was made public in April, Melville wrote to congratulate his brother
and told him the Buchanans were known to Sheriff Menteith[10] and that
he approved of them.

From the financial point of view it was not a good match for either
party. This was made clear to John in the acerbic response from the
widow of his uncle Captain James Jameson to whom he must have
applied for funds. His aunt pleads that she has little to give to her

[9] Sometime after the establishment of the Free Church of Scotland in 1843 the name "Missions
to the Zenana" was applied either to this society or one analogous to it and the Jameson
family gave it financial support. The author's late father-in-law, Mr A. St Clair Jameson, was
informed by the Free Church of Scotland when it decided to wind up the society.
[10] v. note 4, p. 204 supra.

relations, who often approach her for financial assistance. She upbraids him for his lack of care over money and says that it had always been her intention to give him £50 on his departure for India. "You were casting away a blessing, when you refused a home (possibly her Dundas Street residence) that might have been the means of enabling you to keep a wife." Then, later, "But I really think John that it is a sad prospect to marry a wife who brings nothing for her keep; women who have nothing are generally extravagant when they get money in their spouse." Then, again, "Hopping [sic] you have got your leave lengthened and that every thing good will attend you in this world and that your wife will be a good one – all depends on the choice – a needy woman takes the first offer."

His father, too, was in no position to assist financially. He wrote to his son reminding him that John had nothing to offer his bride but his rank and "his character as a gentleman." He did make some rather imprudent suggestions for raising money that were thankfully ignored by John. Miss Snodgrass Buchanan, as he calls her, appears to have written to her prospective father-in-law and he told John: "I am much obliged by her kind and polite attention in asking my consent and I beg you will embrace the earliest opportunity of informing her, with my best respects, how heartily I approve of her choice." He authorised John to spend £10 to £12 on a breakfast and tea set as his present to the couple.

The wedding took place in a Scottish Episcopal Church in Edinburgh on 28th July and the honeymoon was spent at Innerleithen. There is little more that we hear about the couple apart from a letter from the sheriff-substitute to his son Andrew informing him that he was trying to raise financial support from friends to enable John to leave the East India Company Army. The poor reputation of his father in the realm of private finance would be well known in the Cupar district and it is not surprising that we hear no more about the matter. Either in late December 1839 or in early January 1840 the couple sailed for Bombay. A brief account of the remaining few years of the life of Captain John St Clair Jameson is given in an appendix to this chapter.

While the arrangements for the wedding were in train Sheriff-Substitute Jameson wrote to John asking him to warn Andrew about his conduct towards women. To put it bluntly, he told him that his brother's reputation in Cupar was that of a philanderer. This relevant passage in this letter of 19th June 1839 is as follows:

> Private. When a convenient opportunity arises I wish you would mention to Andrew to be cautious of his attentions to his cousin E. T. (This must be Elizabeth Thomson with whom Andrew had been affectionate when he had been a student.) I saw nothing particular in his last visits [to] her – but it is curious how storys [sic] go. Old Sol (or Lol) gives it one for a match and others have remembered the intimacy. I do not want to interfere in love concerns but when there is no intention of serious courtship, which, I presume, is the case with Andrew, he should be cautious to avoid every thing which may lead the Lady to suppose the Gentleman serious. Many women are very susceptible of any attentions. If E. T. has any notice of Andrew – I am sure she does not show any mark of it, when in company of other young men and altho her behaviour is perfectly correct and modest, it is evident that she has no objection to be admired by others and to admire others. I think Andrew should just be a little more prudent particularly when the eyes of some people are upon him. It is much against the steadiness of both parties and I can assure him he is not far from being condemned like his brother Melville as a faithless lover – and yet continuing as one.

John either did not find a "convenient opportunity" to speak to Andrew or, not surprisingly, did not wish to confront his brother directly and instead wrote to him. Andrew sent a furious reply on 19th July. After some conventional comments he continues: "Many thanks for your kind letter. With regard to what you said at the end of it, the matter appears to me to be too absurd and ludicrous to require a serious refutation. At the same time as it seems that some take up the <u>evil report</u> against me, from whom I would have expected more justice and charity, I have to state that it is totally without foundation – or as one would express it in the Perth house, false and calumnious. I should suppose that you thought as surely, else you would have spoken to me on the subject." What particularly annoyed Andrew was that he had recently been paying a visit to Barnhill, Dumbarton,[11] staying at the home of his father's friend, Sheriff-Substitute Alexander Campbell. He was later to marry the sheriff-substitute's daughter Alexa, and it is just possible that she had already caught his eye. They were not to marry until 1844, but this delay was in all probability on account of another severe attack of his illness that required him to go abroad for several months in 1840–1841.

As an advocate Andrew Jameson was required to address judges and juries and this contributed to the continuing problem with his throat and lungs. His recurrent bouts of ill health were impeding progress in his profession, and as early as 1839 he realised that he should seek an appointment as a sheriff-substitute since this would make considerably fewer demands on his physical strength and at the same time allow him to exercise his profession. He discussed this with his closest friends, and in August of that year Patrick Stirling, himself now a sheriff-substitute at Stirling, let him know that there would soon be a vacancy for a sheriff-substitute at Dunblane. Later correspondence lets us know that he did not pursue the matter because he believed that his health was on the mend.

He certainly continued to practise his profession. Neil Campbell, later to become his brother-in-law, wrote to him in early January 1840, to say that he had opened an office in Glasgow. He had yet to attract a client but "I am glad to hear of your increasing success. I trust it may be the preamble to still greater things and if Mrs Fortune be pleased in pouring out a libation upon you, I have no objections that she should extend a small sprinkling to your friend here." The eleven-year-old Euphemia Gray wrote to her uncle to say that the most recent

---

[11] He and Melville had been guests there in August 1827. v. p. 65 supra.

addition to the family had been born on 4th January and would be called Andrew[12] after his grandfather and uncle but more interesting was the final sentence: "Tell Elisabeth Thomson mamma was quite delighted to hear of her visit to Drums." Andrew Jameson must have been staying with his father because the letter was addressed to him at Cupar and the Grays assumed Andrew would be seeing his cousin.

Sophia Gray was a remarkable woman. She was still in her teens when she took over from Miss Baird the running of her father's household in Cupar and acted as mother to her two much younger brothers Andrew and Melville. She bore her husband fifteen children, of whom seven died before reaching their seventh birthdays, a not uncommon misfortune at that time. Her brothers continued to seek her counsel for many years after she had married and as late as January 1840 Andrew sought her advice about his future. She replied that his letter had "vexed me not a little. I really can give you no other advice than to attend to your health." He should find work more suitable for his constitution than "the arduous duty of an Advocate."

At the end of that month his father wrote to him, expressing anxiety about his health. Andrew had not felt up to attending the christening of his new nephew and, in a letter of 2nd February describing the occasion, his father suggested that he move his bed into the dining room to take advantage of the fire. The Edinburgh winter was affecting him adversely, and he submitted to treatment in the form of leeches and blistering. In yet another letter his father says that he is glad to learn that there is a fire in his room and writes "Do not expose yourself in any way until this unfortunate complaint is completely eradicated." Further letters from his father in February suggest sponging with water, chewing horseradish (a remedy, the sheriff-substitute said, advised by Elisabeth) and blistering and bleeding.

From these and other letters it is clear that he had been continuously unwell since the start of the year and probably had been unable to accept much work. Melville wrote on 26th February to say how sorry

---

[12] An earlier child of the same name had been born in 1831 but did not survive the year. This second Andrew died shortly before his fifth birthday.

he was that his brother seemed to make no progress towards better health and told him that he had, at last, managed to settle the affairs of his father with James Webster, which now allowed him to look at other money troubles of their father. On 2nd March 1840 his father writes again, this time to say that, although Andrew has written to tell him that he is feeling better, he should take a period of convalescence before returning to work. This advice was superfluous because the illness did not abate, and Patrick Stirling promised to come into Edinburgh to visit him. Despite the arrival of warmer weather he was no better, and his father suggested that he come to Cupar, live very quietly and seek a sheriff-substituteship.

From the surviving correspondence of the summer of 1840 it appears that Andrew Jameson did not accept his father's invitation but remained in Edinburgh. He did, however, set out seriously in search of a post as sheriff-substitute. The emoluments of this post were now more attractive since the annual salary had just been raised to £500 per annum. He must have written to someone called J. Macfarlane because this man sent him the names of a few persons who might be influential with Henry Bell, who had been a successful advocate in the city before securing, in 1839, the post of Sheriff-Substitute of Glasgow.

Although not completely recovered he felt well enough to accept an invitation to stay a few days at the end of June and beginning of July first at Barnhill with the Campbell family and then at Arochar[13] on Loch Long. Neil Campbell wrote to him saying that he had heard from his sisters that Andrew had not been able to speak during his visit to Barnhill but that he was apparently well enough to undertake a visit to Loch Long where Campbell hoped to join him. Andrew and Patrick Stirling were staying there in the Arochar Hotel and must have been invited to nearby Ardmay House,[14] the home of Duncan Macfarlane, Principal of Glasgow University. The Principal may have been the father or other family connection of the man of the same name who

---

[13] It must have been on this holiday that Andrew Jameson composed "Lines at Arrochar, 1840" that are reproduced as Appendix C to this chapter.

[14] Ardmay House is now an activity centre for outdoor pursuits such as sailing and climbing.

supplied Andrew with the names of people who might be influential in his quest for a sheriff-substituteship. Principal Macfarlane was described by Queen Victoria, when she visited Glasgow in 1849, as "very old". Whatever the connection, this is yet another example of the remarkable ability of Andrew Jameson, still not yet 30, to be found a congenial companion by persons of all ages and conditions of life.

Unfortunately, his ill health continued and there is a suggestion that his complaint was bringing with it some symptoms of lethargy. In normal circumstances Andrew was a most dutiful correspondent as far as his family was concerned and particularly in the case of his father, but the sheriff-substitute wrote on 11th July to chide his son for not having congratulated him on the increase recently applied to the stipends of sheriff-substitutes. He promised, nevertheless, to keep making inquiries about any vacancies for sheriff-substituteships that were likely to arise. By contrast Melville and their sister Sophia were in the best of health. George and Sophia Gray were about to leave for a tour down the Rhine followed by a visit to Geneva and a return journey via Paris, leaving their four younger children at home with domestic servants under the supervision of Melville. At the beginning of August 1840 Andrew was a guest of the family friend Dr Craig at Ratho, just outside Edinburgh, and Melville wrote to him there suggesting that he should come to Perth to join a farewell party that was being given for Rachael Ogilvie (daughter of their aunt) and her husband, who were bound for India. Melville uses curious phraseology when he writes that "Elizabeth Thomson of bitter memory" will be there. There remains no documentation to let us know whether or not he crossed over to Perth for this occasion.

Sophia Gray wrote to him from Geneva on 26th August to say that she and her husband would be back in Perth by 20th September and that "Mr Gray is to make every inquiry about Madeira at Mr Ruskin's." She would doubtless consider that, through his now wide connections within the wine trade, John James Ruskin[15] could provide knowledgeable advice on the suitability of that island for someone

---

[15] How the Gray and Ruskin families first became connected is explained later. v. p. 235 infra.

with her brother's illness. Spain, however, was Andrew Jameson's preferred choice, perhaps because he had twice visited that country, albeit only in its Basque region. He wrote to a Dr Cormack for advice about Spain. Dr Cormack not only approved of the choice, presumably mainly on medical grounds, but also advised him not to go by fruitship. This would take too long and it would be much preferable to go by steamer to Cadiz, which would be £20 more expensive but would enable him to reach Cadiz within eight days. He should then transfer to a boat that would take him up the Guadalquiver to Seville, and after wintering there he should go across country to see Granada.

Andrew Jameson finally decided around 20th September to return to the southern parts of Europe in search of relief from his affliction. He had not been able to practise for about six months and needed to avoid the distress that another Edinburgh winter would bring upon him. He seems to have made this decision suddenly because there is a flurry of letters just after that date. Already in London staying with the Miss Rutherfords in Pall Mall, he received a letter from his father, dated 25th September, advising him that the political instability current in Spain made that country an unwise choice and that a Mr Crichton had recommended Madeira. This was followed immediately by another letter hoping that the steamer passage to London had been comfortable and telling him that his brother sheriff-substitutes were recommending a present to him of 200 guineas "for my trouble".[16] His friend Robert Horn wrote that he had heard from Spalding of his decision to go abroad, sympathised with him and advised him to do no work but concentrate on improving his health. What financial arrangements he was able to make are not recorded, but the J. Macfarlane mentioned above was prepared to offer him a loan and was arranging for the sale of his subscription to the Edinburgh Library. Perhaps his father was suggesting that some assistance might come from him when he referred to the possible gift of 200 guineas from his brother sheriff-

---

[16] As stated earlier in this work, Andrew Jameson (Senior) had long been prominent in the struggle by sheriff-substitutes to obtain salaries that reflected their responsibilities. The recent increase to £500 per annum had, in all probability, been due to further exertions by Sheriff-Substitute Jameson. Whether he received the 200 guineas is not recorded.

substitutes. Dr Cormack wrote again, on 27th September, this time with information about where he should stay in Spain. Andrew Jameson paid his passage to Cadiz on the steamer *Montrose* and left London for Cadiz on 1st October 1840.

He answered his father's letters while his ship was anchored at Falmouth on 3rd October, waiting for mails for Spain and Portugal to arrive from London. From this we learn that he had made the acquaintance of a fellow passenger, a Mr Gordon, who turned out to be a partner and brother-in-law of a Mr Cranstoun to whom he had already a letter of introduction, possibly from Dr Cormack. Mr Gordon must have let him know that he had been in Perth earlier in the year and it is possible that he had met the Grays.[17] More relevant, in view of its subsequent importance in his career, was the advice from the captain that for someone with his complaint there was no place better than Malta to spend January and February during the winter months.

---

[17] We learn of this Perth connection from a letter of 12th December 1840 to Andrew Jameson from his sister Sophia. Mr Gordon had dined with a Mr and Mrs Reddie, acquaintances of the Grays.

APPENDIX A TO CHAPTER SIX

Andrew Jameson on Roman Catholicism
as observed at Tours

Andrew Jameson's character was strongly moulded by his firm belief in Christianity as practised by the Church of Scotland. He and his family were soon to be involved in the Disruption, when they associated themselves with their friend Dr Chalmers in the foundation of the Free Church of Scotland. He was no fanatic and as shown in previous chapters was perfectly happy to worship in a Roman Catholic church.

When he wrote to his brother from Tours on 7th April 1838, a large part of his letter concerned the religious aspects of the French that he had observed in that city. To have included such a lengthy comment within the narrative of his stay would have been an unnecessary interruption, and it is given here as an appendix.

> I had occasion, since I came here, to see how sad is the lot
> of those who look not beyond this present scene – and how
> inexplicable the Divine government is to them, who will not
> receive the light of the Gospel. Alas – in what a state this
> county[18] is between a wretched bigotry on the one hand and
> a blighting fidelity on the other. The popish priests are very
> active at present. I do not say that the light of Christianity
> does not sometimes penetrate the vile mass of corruption
> and error with which they obscure it. We know that it does.
> They are strict and austere enough, many of them condemn-
> ing music, dancing – the common innocent amusements

---

[18] He does not write "country" and presumably he is referring to Touraine, the French province of which Tours is the main city.

of life – in order to gain influence or from a mistaken and monastic point of view of religion. Others of them violate the Commandments which they preach and corrupt by their example and insidious counsels. The Protestants are but a handful and too often shelter themselves in the reformed religion as a cover for indifference.

APPENDIX B TO CHAPTER SIX
The Remaining Years of John St Clair Jameson

At the end of 1844 John's regiment had been operational in a campaign under Sir Charles Napier against the Baluchi hill tribes to the north and west of Sind, which had been recently annexed by the government of India. John was commended by the Commander-in-Chief, Sir Charles Napier, for the manner in which he had carried out his duties and promoted major. Napier then made his base at Sukkur on the Indus at the end of 1844, where many of his soldiers went down with fever. Almost all the 78th Highlanders succumbed to disease, but Napier surprised the Baluchis by marching with his much reduced but well-equipped army into their tribal territory and capturing Shahpur. Major Jameson was left as part of the garrison and the campaign was brought to a satisfactory end on 9th March 1845.

It was at Shahpur that John learned of the marriage of his brother Andrew to Alexa Campbell. On 10th February 1845 he commenced a letter of congratulation that was not completed until 9th May when he was in Hyderabad, much lower down the Indus and just north of Karachi. The reason for this is given in a letter of 10th June 1845 from Marion Jameson (now in London) to her father-in-law, brothers-in-law and sister-in-law, wherein she informs them that John had gone down with what she calls "intermittant fever" at Shahpur. He would not have survived had his devoted servants not carried him in a palanquin to Sukkur, where he was treated with the greatest kindness by Lady Hunter, the wife of the general commanding his regiment. When General Napier learned that he had recovered he ordered Major Jameson to Hyderabad, where he charged him with forming a "Camel Baggage Corps", to assist with the transport of all food, tents and general supplies necessary for an army on the march. It is in that part of the letter that is dated 9th May that John informs Andrew that he has almost completed the formation of the "Scinde Baggage Corps" of which he has been given command and that Marion hoped to visit Scotland later in the year. We know from correspondence in mid-1844 that she was already back in Britain to seek relief from some illness that the Bombay climate was not assisting to cure. Melville Jameson visited her in May 1845 at Epsom, while on a visit to London, and in a letter to his father of 28th August 1845 Andrew Jameson wrote "Mrs Buchanan writes that she has been visiting Marion and has found that her doctor has misunderstood her case: it is very sad."

More than a year later, in September 1846, John Jameson was still at Hyderabad and must have heard there of the death of his father. His letter to Andrew Jameson dwells mainly on the loss of a good father, but it also reveals the financial quagmire in which the sheriff-substitute had lived. The following excerpt from his letter is appropriate since it demonstrates the incompetent manner in which this otherwise estimable public servant had organized his personal affairs.

Both dear Melville and kind Mr Duncan wrote me. I did not know very well how to act with the printed writ he sent me. I sent it to Melville to fill up. Take care for me of all the articles our dear Father bequeathed to me. It is sad to think he was in debt even to the extent of a few hundreds after the sacrifice made at Drums, but I trust the effects will cover all and keep us clear of getting into the hands of James Webster or anyone else. You speak of Melville getting nothing and that you give up your interest in the garden, now as far as I am concerned I do not wish you to give up one farthing, and Melville may get something else – do as you like about it. I never had any hopes of having money left me by our dear father and all I wish is I may not be called upon to defray that which I am [letter torn here and word incomplete] for."

He concludes his letter by saying that there is now a Free Church of Scotland in Bombay that is currently small in numbers but with prospects of growth.

Major Jameson must have remained at Hyderabad throughout 1846 until on 9th March 1847 when he became very unwell. There is a detailed and graphic account of his illness, which appears to have been dysentery, written by an Assistant Surgeon called Gibbon. John's condition had soon deteriorated to the extent that he was sent by riverboat down to Karachi and thence to Bombay by steamer. The vessel docked on 21st March, but he was too ill to be taken ashore. Friends from his church took it in turns to be with him, and he was able to join with them in prayers. He died the following day, and two clergymen, Webb and Nesbitt (probably of the Free Church of Scotland in Bombay), who had been among those at his bedside, wrote beautiful letters of condolence to Marion, who was in England. One interesting sentence in Webb's letter is as follows: "Dear Major G. Jameson was also here and deeply afflicted for he loved him as a brother." Was this man some distant relative?

APPENDIX C TO CHAPTER SIX

Lines written at Arrochar 1840

I came a stranger to your gate
With shattered health, and weary breast.
Speechless, lonely, desolate
Thy kind welcome gave me rest.
Bade hope arise, where sorrow sate,
In gloomy dulness drest.

O'er the water of your ancestral lake
When we sailed at Eventide
Along the still shore beneath the brake[19]
That clothes the steep mountain side
How softly thy gentleness did make
All on my charmed senses glide.

To dark Glencroe[20] we often bent
Our longing eyes, and in silence gazed
Upon the frowning battlement
Where the "Cobler" with head upraised
Mid storms of clouds has reared his tent
Now clothed with mists – now with lightning rent.

---

[19] An old Scottish word for "bracken".

[20] Not to be confused with Glencoe, which would not have been visible from Loch Awe. Glencroe is the pass in the mountains between Arrochar and Glen Kinglas that leads on on to Cairndow at the head of Loch Fyne. At the Glen Kinglas end is the famous "Rest and Be Thankful", where vehicles and pedestrians have a very steep ascent if they are travelling to Arrochar from Cairndow. The Cobbler, or to give it its official name, Ben Arthur, is a mountain almost 3,000 feet high, just to the north of Glencroe. Its summit is shaped like a shoemaker's last from which derives its popular name.

And the sound of the distant waterfall
Came fitfully o'er the placid sea
Like music in some old Gothic hall
With a wild yet gentle melody
Whose notes Eolian sometimes recall
The memories of the dead; & lull to reverie.

O'er the glad waters we roamed at will
Till Fancy chose some lonelier scene
Whereon pleasures cup to fill.
And Thou didst sit our banquet Queen
At Dal upon the shore – at Dhuin beside the rill
And last, upon the Seagirt fairy green.

Our happy circle with wit refined
Charmed all weariness away.
Good sense with mirth combined
Feeling, fancy, the graces of the mind
Brightened conversation's play
From blithe morn to the sweet close of day.

And then was heard the Evening prayer
And each bowed the head & bent the knee
Before the great Supreme, who there
Was worshipped reverently.
Thy silvery voice did bear
Our orisons on high
Embodying hopes, that never die.

CHAPTER SEVEN
A Second Continental Interlude

After a rough crossing of the Bay of Biscay the *Montrose* reached Cadiz, where correspondence from home was awaiting him. His father and Melville had both written giving a lot of family news, principally the engagement of Melville to Miss Jessie Duncan, the daughter of the Procurator Fiscal of Perthshire. Having learned that Andrew had met Mr Gordon, his father suggested that he arrange to send a barrel of sherry to Cupar, apparently to initiate a wine-importing business.

Mr Gordon, or Don Jacobo Pedro Gordon as he called himself in Spain, was clearly someone in prosperous circumstances because he had aboard his own horses and carriage. His Aberdeenshire grandfather had founded what was now a successful wine business that was located at Jerez de la Frontera, about twenty miles north of Cadiz.[1] Andrew was not feeling at all well, and Gordon invited him to stay at his home until he recovered. At first the genial climate assisted a return of health and in a letter of 15th October to his father he said that he thought that he would continue for some time in this part of Spain. He remained with Mr and Mrs Gordon until mid-November, when, as Dr Cormack had advised, he took a river steamer up the Guadalquiver to visit Seville, where he stayed about twelve days. He appears to have introduced himself to some lawyers and comments that there was much corruption and economic disarray in Andalucia. Towards the end of November the weather became colder, and almost continuous rain rendered the atmosphere so damp that it affected his breathing. He then recalled the advice of the captain of the *Montrose* and changed his original plans by deciding to go to Malta. He returned to pay his respects to the Gordons, went down to Cadiz and then on to

---

[1] See appendix A, which gives an account of this interesting Aberdeenshire connection.

Gibraltar by a coastal steamer.

It was now 1st December 1840 and he must have informed his family and friends that he would be in Gibraltar around this time because there were letters waiting for him from Melville, Dr Chalmers[2] and his niece Euphemia Gray. Melville had joined his father in the suggestion that Andrew should assist in opening a family business venture in the importation of sherry, but Andrew wrote to explain why this was not practical. The letter from twelve-year-old Euphemia, now a pupil at Avon Bank School near Warwick, is a delightful description of her visit with fellow pupils to Warwick Castle.

He was still unwell during his short time in Gibraltar and left there for Malta on 7th December on the SS *Great Liverpool*.[3] The passage took four days and on reaching Malta he found lodgings at Strada Brittanica No 53. He wrote to his father that the weather was "like our finest summer", and perhaps this was why he found the island "bare and burnt up beyond description." Slowly his health began to improve, but for some time he could not take even gentle exercise because "the streets and stairs are too trying for me." Instead, he took a boat and rowed himself around the harbour. He took in the sights and sounds of the island and on one day saw on parade, pipes playing and banners waving, the 92nd Highlanders, who were serving as the garrison. They marched to "There's Nae Luck aboot the Hoose" and "it thrilled through every vein and nerve of my body." He set out to follow them "till my windpipe stopped me."

Once he felt well enough he went about the business of introducing himself. He left his card with the Governor, Lieutenant-General Sir Henry Bouverie, but unfortunately he did not add his address to the card. It was some days before he found in the post office a letter from Sir Hector Greig, Chief Secretary of Malta, informing him that they had tried

---

[2] Unfortunately, this letter has not survived.

[3] This vessel belonged to the Peninsular and Orient Steam Navigation Company that had just secured a government contract to deliver and collect mail at Gibraltar, Valletta and Alexandria. This was its first voyage. The P & O had such continuing success with this venture in attracting passengers, mainly for India, as well as mail that it was a contributory factor in the decision about 25 years later to construct the Suez Canal.

to locate him in all the hotels and had been left with no option but to use the local poste restante. The Governor said that he would be delighted to help in any way, and even if this reply would not have been very different from that to any other British subject visiting Malta, it demonstrated that Andrew Jameson had been recognized at the highest social level. He must have sent his address immediately because the following day, Christmas Eve, he was invited to dine with Sir Hector. As has been already stated in this account of his life, Andrew Jameson always made a most favourable impression on persons older and senior to him, and Sir Hector proved to be no different in this respect for he invited him to dine again on 31st December in order to meet Lord Lynedoch.

This was a significant honour for the young Scots lawyer, who, it must be remembered, was not yet 30. Thomas Graham, Lord Lynedoch, was now 92 and had a remarkable career behind him. He had lived the life of a country gentleman until 1792, when his wife, whose portrait[4] by Gainsborough is in the National Gallery of Scotland, died aboard ship off the south coast of France. Crossing France to Bordeaux to take ship for Scotland, he and his party were surrounded by French soldiers, who opened the coffin of Lady Graham and molested the body. Graham was so incensed at the treatment of his wife's corpse that almost as soon as her obsequies had been completed he joined the army to fight the French. Through his bravery and ability he soon rose to the rank of Colonel, and with the local rank of Brigadier-General he was sent to assist the Maltese in the successful blockade and capture of Malta from the French occupying force. He later served with equal distinction in the Peninsular War, first under Sir John Moore on the retreat to Corunna and then under Wellington, who appointed him his second-in-command. He retained his remarkable vigour well into his old age and in his nineties rode his horses on the Campagna outside Rome. It was on this last visit to Italy that he decided to visit Malta, the scene of his early military success.

Unfortunately, no account of this dinner survives nor that of a dinner given by the Governor the following day at which Andrew Jameson

---

[4] Known as "The Gainsborough Lady".

was among the guests. There followed another invitation to dine with Sir Hector on 9th January 1841, and on the morning of Sunday, 10th January he received an invitation from Lord Lynedoch to see him that morning. Lord Lynedoch's hand was very shaky and his script is difficult to decipher. The first sentence reads "Dear Jameson, If this day holds up I shall be down at my old Quarters at La Gudja[5] which we talked about the other day." The rest of the letter is illegible. It says much for the character of Andrew Jameson that he had to decline this offer because he had already accepted an invitation from a clergyman, to lunch with him and his family after attending church that morning.[6] A lesser person might have sent his apologies to the clergyman and gone out to La Gudja but Andrew Jameson would have deemed this dishonourable. His reply to Lord Lynedoch has not survived but what was clearly a draft was written on the reverse of the invitation that he had received from Sir Hector Greig. It reads:

> My dear Lord,
>
> I am extremely sorry that I have an engagement with a clergyman's family for today, which will prevent me having the pleasure of availing myself of your Ld's great kindness. It is the greater disappointment that I have been looking forward to the visit to your Ld's old quarters, which have so much interest in the history of the British possession of Malta.

We can infer from this letter that Lord Lynedoch had told Andrew Jameson at the dinner on 31st December that he would invite him one day to La Gudja. There is no record of any subsequent invitation from the old general, although the possibility cannot be discounted.

He was again the guest of Sir Hector Greig on the evening of 11th January 1841. Four invitations within three weeks to dine with the Chief Secretary as well as one dinner as a guest of the Governor suggest

---

[5] This is a village outside Valletta from where he had directed the siege of the fortress occupied by the French. It is now known simply as Gudja.

[6] This must have been the Methodist minister to whom reference is made at p. 257 infra.

something more than recognition of Andrew Jameson as a congenial companion at the dinner table. A few years later he was to carry out a commission for Lieutenant-General Sir Patrick Stuart, who succeeded Sir Henry Bouverie in 1843, and it may be that the state of the law in the island was raised by the Chief Secretary with Andrew Jameson at one or more of these dinners. Malta had been ruled since 1530 by the Knights of St John until it fell briefly into French hands between 1798 and 1800. At the request of the Maltese it became a British Crown Colony in 1813, but the administration of justice was difficult because the legal system was an unwieldy amalgam of Neapolitan, French and indigenous Maltese law.

He may have been dining in fine company on Malta but his money was beginning to run out. On the 28th December 1840 he wrote to his father requesting him to send £30 to £40 to the office of James Close and Company[7] in Naples. The weather was deteriorating with an east wind that was affecting his breathing, and he would be leaving soon for Sicily. Sir James Clark[8] had advised that he should not spend more than about three weeks in any one place but the cost of so many short stays was an expense that he could not afford. Nevertheless, he always made attempts to move elsewhere when his finances and health made this possible. He remained in Malta until 23rd January 1841 leaving it "with little regret" despite his initial satisfaction with the climate. Sicily, he told his father, was "a land of Eden compared with the African desert of Malta."

In a letter of 22nd February 1841 written at Messina in Sicily, Andrew Jameson told his father that a Glasgow man called Ker had brought a letter to him "from Sir Hector Greig at Malta conveying his own and Sir Henry Bouverie's regards with the hope that I might return next winter, which I trust may never be fulfilled. Mr Ker heard

---

[7] James Close went to Sicily in 1819 where he established an investment and banking business with a branch at Naples, which later became his headquarters. He was financial adviser to King Ferdinand II of Naples. A son, William Brookes Close (1853–1923), with two of his brothers, expanded the business which became known as Close Brothers and was very successful in the USA as well as in Britain. It financed the White Pass and Yukon Railway from Skagway to the Yukon at the time of the Gold Rush in the late 1890s. Of purely salacious interest, W. B. Close died at the home of his mistress Florence Desmond, who went on to have a successful career on the stage.

[8] He had consulted Sir James in 1838. v. p. 204 supra.

that there had been some thoughts of getting me onto the bench but I asked the Chief Secretary before I left most particularly on the subject and his answers were decided." One can only guess what was implied by Sir Hector Greig, but the context of the letter leaves us in little doubt that there was to be no appointment in that quarter.

However, in view of Andrew Jameson's later direct involvement in the revision of the Criminal Code of Malta, it will be appropriate to give in full Sir Hector's letter, dated 19th February 1841. From the content of the letter it is clear that Andrew had written from Sicily thanking Sir Hector for his hospitality and mentioning an improvement in his health.

> My dear Jameson,
>
> The Governor and I are both delighted to hear of your improved health as we both feared that Italy was not to prove very favourable. We have a better opinion of Sir James Clark in consequence.
>
> We have no very late hours – all is going on quietly in the East and nothing is yet known as to the thoughts of Ministers – all accounts seem to say that they will not stand out this session.[9] If you should be what I hope you will not be, something of an invalid next winter, I hope you will think of Malta. I will be most truly happy to see you again.
>
> [Name illegible] is still with me and desires his best regards. So does the Governor – we are still without rain and water is becoming very scarce. Our position gets very alarming but we must not despair of rain, until March is over.
>
> > Believe me, my dear Jameson,
> >
> > Yours very truly
> >
> > H. Greig

---

[9] Melbourne's government did indeed fall that year, to be succeeded by that of Sir Robert Peel.

Much of Andrew Jameson's letter of 22nd February 1841 was concerned with religious comment, but in addition to mentioning the letter from Sir Hector Greig he wrote that before going to Italy he would visit some of the Greek remains in Sicily. He was still in Sicily on 1st March because he wrote to his father on that day, and we do not know when he crossed over to the mainland and came to Naples. We do learn from a letter written later from Florence to Giuseppe Laurea[10] that he must have spent a few weeks there. Moreover, he was receiving letters written as late as mid-March at the office of James Close and Company. Patrick Stirling told him how wise he was to have "avoided those melancholy Isles of the Atlantic, Madeira and Teneriffe" and recalled their holiday in Arochar the previous July. Stirling had been to the wedding in Glasgow of "our Ardmay friend, Miss Macfarlane", presumably a close relation, possibly a daughter or granddaughter, of Professor Macfarlane. Neil Campbell sent news about friends and John Blackie,[11] despite his current embroilment with Aberdeen Presbytery[12] concerning his appointment to the newly created Regius Chair of Humanity at Marischal College, Aberdeen, found time to write about national politics and about the seven ministers deposed by the Presbytery of Strathbogie.[13] In addition, he gave his friend some sensible advice: "Hang loose on principle, nothing oftener brings disease and death than being in too great a hurry to get well." He concluded his letter thus: "Horn is writing also, I believe, and will likely give you a good screed. You know I love you – love yourself and don't eat yourself up with cares either now or when you come back to us. 'Sufficient for the day &.' By far the most difficult text in the bible, for you and me. God be with you."

Horn did, indeed, write to him with news of friends, including the

[10] v. p. 230 infra.

[11] v. appendix to Chapter Five

[12] The Presbytery of Aberdeen was seeking to block his appointment on account of his cynical attitude towards the Westminster Confession. The Presbytery was eventually overruled by the Court of Session.

[13] This case brought to a head the question of intrusion – the imposition of a minister upon a congregation at the behest of the patron, usually a local laird, without the consent of the congregation – one of the principal reasons for the Disruption in 1843, when the Church of Scotland lost about one third of its ministers and congregations who founded the Free Church of Scotland.

appointment of Spalding to a professorship in law at the University of Edinburgh. Sophia wrote two letters giving distressing news about their Thomson relations at Cupar. Elizabeth's sister Jane, who had married a man called Scales, was being advised to leave him on account of his drunken habits and associated bouts of delirium tremens, while their father, now old and chair-bound, was becoming increasingly difficult and totally reliant upon the constant attention of Elizabeth. To make matters worse, the Thomsons were now impoverished.

The warm weather of spring brought some temporary alleviation of Andrew's throat complaint. As was his custom, he introduced himself to some lawyers in the city and immediately struck up a friendship with an advocate, Giuseppe Laurea. This man provided him with a route for a short walking tour of the Amalfi coast from Sorrento to Salerno, including visits to the interesting ruin of Pestune and the monuments of La Cana. Laurea had also suggested a tour of Apulia but this had to be abandoned. On 4th April, just after his return to Naples from his visit to the Amalfi coast, his old enemy, inflammation of the larynx, returned to the attack. He was confined to his hotel for a week, and a doctor advised him to leave Naples with a small party of fellow Scots because the air was "too exciting for me." They agreed to have him along with them and were very helpful and considerate of their compatriot. They rested one whole day at Nola but by the time they reached Rome he was exhausted.

As soon as he felt able, he continued his journey northwards from Rome to Florence, and in a letter from there of 7th May 1841 he gave his father a full account of his current state of health and of his journey from Rome:

> I had the high satisfaction of receiving your last two letters
> – and one from Melville and Sophia – eight days ago at
> Rome, whither they were forwarded from Naples. I beg to
> give you my warmest thanks for your kind solicitude about
> my health and other worldly interests, which, for your sake,
> I wish were in a more thriving condition. But Our Heavenly

Father gives us what is best fitted to prepare our characters for that other scene, which is to be our home, to which the present is only the passage and entrance hall. Such four delightful letters were the more acceptable perhaps because I was confined to bed at the time and they appeared like the voice of affection to the forlorn and languishing invalid at the same time that your advice about staying abroad rather disheartened me. That I was not very ill you may be assured from my attempting next morning the journey to Florence, which I was induced to do from a party being made up to go, which rendered it less expensive and more agreeable. Another matter was to get away from the intolerable heat which, acting upon a weak frame produced a sort of Roman fever. On the second evening, however, when we landed at Terni – the birthplace of Tacitus – I was quite knocked up. The next day was happily the Sabbath so there was no travelling. In the morning, a Mr Campbell – one of Sir A. C. of Garscube's sons – who happened to be in the Inn with his sister Mrs Grant of Congalton[14] was kind enough to search out Dr Badham, son of the Glasgow Professor,[15] who came and prescribed. After being drugged and sweated two nights he advised me to proceed and I thank God I have arrived here pretty well and without any remains of fever except debility. You see, I can neither bear heat nor cold. I suspect Sir J. Clark saw that when he said Demerara would soon put an end to all my maladies.

I enjoyed the remainder of the journey very much, there was nothing new to me but it was all in a new dress and made more lovely by the beauty of Spring. I am here waiting your remittance, which I hope will reach me next week, as the heat here is oppressive and prevents free exercise in the

[14] The Grants were lairds of Congalton, a burgh of barony near Dirleton, East Lothian. v. footnote 19 p. 6 supra.
[15] Appointed in 1827 Regius Professor of Medicine and Therapeutics, University of Glasgow.

open air, which appears after all to be the best medicine for my complaint.

From this I mean to proceed to Turin and from thence to Geneva. All travellers, including invalids, are flying from the perils of coups de soleil and malaria fever. Italy, perhaps, has only two summer residences, Castellammare at Naples and the Baths of Lucca near this. Persons who mean to remain another winter and avoid the fatigue and expense of crossing the Alps, resort to either of these, which are both gay, dissipated places, most uncongenial to persons of rational habits and slender purses. If I thought another winter absolutely necessary, I would endeavour to find out some summer retreat of such a kind and not proceed further north at present – but I have great hopes of recovering the ground I have lost since the 4th April by travel during the next two months and that I may have the satisfaction, God willing, to join you before all the gooseberries are over. I often think of you all and of the domestic happiness our Almighty Father has blest us with, though poor in the world's wealth, which might have made us more proud and foolish he has made us rich in the family affections that sweeten existence.

I do not conceal from you that all the medical men who have seen me abroad, especially those who have attended me are of your opinion[16] and I will not make any rash determination to get home at all events. Alas, unless to see you & Sophia & Mel I have little inducement – business gone – prospects blighted – and a sentence of perpetual banishment from the scene of honorable toil and professional advancement. I do not despond. The Lord will provide for the life he has for the present spared. My prayer is that some honest employment may be opened up to me, that I may be

---

[16] In a letter to his son of 6th May, Sheriff-Substitute Jameson expressed anxiety that Andrew might decide to return home before he was in good health. He advised him to remain abroad.

preserved from shame and contempt. If not, I fear, I must try a foreign land, though I think my education, habits and constitution fit me to be more useful in my own country. I will pause at Geneva, where I expect to meet some more promising society than I have lately experienced and yet my illnesses have prevented me seeing such as I had. Young Swinton[17] formed a pleasant companion. He is a brother in misfortune. He says Mrs John Melville is a cousin of his. He thinks it a [word illegible] to be away another winter from the P.[18] house. He was very kind when I turned ill at Rome.

I am very glad to hear such a good account of your health and occupations. None of the newspapers has reached me for a long time – send them regularly now to Geneva. I expect to be in Geneva, God willing, the first week of June – if you don't keep me here longer. If your remittance arrives in course of post as I hope it may, I will be sooner. I prepare to go to Leghorn and Genoa. Most of my fellow travellers are far before me – some by this time in Scotland. I envy them. Mr[19] and Miss Ker, who are not at all what you supposed, are still here but leave in a few days. Recollect to pay Mr James Gordon of Jerez £2.

We must assume that no remittance arrived immediately since he was still in Florence on 20th May, for it was on that day that he wrote to Giuseppe Laurea to explain his departure from Naples without the courtesy of taking leave of him in a proper manner.[20] From a subsequent letter to his father we learn that a remittance did arrive at Florence, and this must have been almost the next day because by 25th May 1841 he was in Leghorn. There he found accommodation at the Hotel Leghorn, where he had stayed in October 1833. It was still run by the Thomson

---

[17] This is the nearest approach possible from the script.

[18] Probably Parliament.

[19] v. p. 227 supra.

[20] It is from this letter that we have details of his time in Naples.

family,[21] and on 25th May he arranged with a David Thomson, either the husband or son of the Mrs Thomson, who ran the establishment, to have forwarded to his father a considerable number of packages. The bill of lading, dated 25th May 1841, lists Etruscan vases, jugs and other ancient artefacts that today would not be allowed to leave Italy. In view of Andrew Jameson's precarious financial position one must assume that he had bought these for a few pence in Florence and Leghorn. Since he reached Turin by 28th May it is highly probable that he took a boat from Leghorn or Pisa to Genoa and came thence to Turin. He took a room at the Hotel d'Europe, read in the hotel register that Mr John James Ruskin and family were also staying there, sent up his card and thus entered history as a minor player in the life of the great Victorian art critic, John Ruskin.

There have been many books written about the life of John Ruskin, not least about his disastrous marriage to Euphemia Gray, Andrew Jameson's niece. Ruskin will be mentioned in this work only when he and Andrew Jameson met or corresponded or where any matter concerning their relationship becomes relevant. It will, however, be necessary, to give some brief background to show how the Ruskins and the Grays became acquainted.

Andrew Jameson's elder sister, Sophia (1808–1894), had married in 1827 a prominent Perth lawyer and business man, George Gray. Gray had bought a large house called Bowerswell on the north side of the River Tay that some fifteen years earlier had been rented by John Thomas Ruskin, who would be described today as a commercial traveller. He had previously been a grocer in Edinburgh, but the business failed and he moved with his family first to Dysart and then to Perth. Dysart[22] was a very small burgh, and it is possible the Ruskins were acquainted with the town clerk, John Jameson, the grandfather of Sophia and Andrew Jameson, but there is no record of this. By his wife Catherine, Ruskin had two children, Jessie and John James. His daughter married a Perth merchant, Patrick Richardson, and his

---

[21] v. p. 169 supra.

[22] It is now incorporated within the town of Kirkcaldy.

son was sent to London, where he carved out an ultimately highly successful career in the importation and distribution of wine. Since John Thomas was away for long periods, his niece, Margaret Cock, was brought from London to live with his family as a companion to his wife. In October 1817 first Catherine Ruskin died and then her husband, now of unsound mind, committed suicide. In February of the following year Margaret Cock married her first cousin, John James Ruskin. Their son John was born in 1819.

It was merely a coincidence that the Ruskins had lived at Bowerswell. Perth was not a large town and the Grays were acquainted through social and business connections with other families, which included the Richardsons. Sometimes John James Ruskin and his wife came north to visit his sister and occasionally met George and Sophia Gray. When Jessie Richardson, now a widow, died in 1828 her brother made himself responsible for the education of her three sons through money left in a trust administered by George Gray. John James also decided to adopt their sister Mary, but before going to join his family in London Mary stayed for several weeks with the Grays in Bowerswell. This close business and family relationship strengthened the earlier existing ties between the Ruskins and the Grays, and the latter were guests of the Ruskins on the occasions when they visited London. In 1840 their daughter Euphemia began her boarding school education in Warwickshire, and she, with her younger brother George, when he attended Charterhouse, stayed with the Ruskins when breaking their journeys to and from Perth.

It is improbable that Andrew Jameson had met John Ruskin before May 1841, but he would certainly have been aware of the connection between his sister's family and the Ruskins. He must have met Mary Richardson during the time she was staying at Bowerswell, because it was to her that he sent up his card when he found that he was staying at the same hotel in Turin as the Ruskins. Andrew was invited by John James and his wife to dine with them on the 29th and 30th May. They had been in Switzerland and then Italy since October of the previous year because John had not been well and his doctors feared that he might be consumptive. A full account of this meeting is given by Mary Lutyens in her *The Ruskins and the Grays*.[23]

John Ruskin and Andrew Jameson, despite the eight years of difference between them, immediately got on very well together and spent two days walking around Turin. Clearly, Ruskin formed a most favourable impression of Andrew Jameson and this was the foundation for the correspondence that took place between them over the next decade, an intimacy that was enhanced when in 1848 Ruskin married Andrew's niece, Euphemia Gray.

It seems likely that he remained a few more days in Turin, building up his strength for the journey to Geneva over the Mont Cenis Pass. He reached Geneva on 12th June, where he was to remain for about four weeks. He had found the journey trying and had vomited much. His first letter was written on the 16th to Melville, saying that he would like to spend another year south of the Alps but that he just could not afford it. He would consult Sir James Clark again as he passed through London. He was delighted to hear that Melville would come over to Europe and join him at Basle in the middle of July. His own itinerary would be to travel there through Interlaken and Berne.

When he told Melville that he could not afford to remain in Europe it was in all probability that he knew his father could not support him any longer. Moreover, news had come to him of some minor scandal in the domestic affairs of his father. After thanking his father and a Mr M. for the remittance that he had received at Florence he continues, "I am sorry to find that you found it necessary to have recourse to the old system of raising funds, having fully understood you to say that you would have been able to have supplied it yourself, when I left home."

There then follows what is virtually a rebuke to his father. He refers to "A calamity and stain upon the respectability of your household. I am very sorry for the poor women themselves, who have been thus led into the path of debasing vice and it adds greatly to the misfortune

---

[23] Lutyens, M. *The Ruskins and the Grays*, p.15. John Murray 1972. Lutyens is incorrect to state that Andrew Jameson was a barrister, a term not used in Scottish law, but an advocate. Moreover, he was certainly not older than Sophia Gray because he had been born in 1811 and she in 1808.

Sketch, never previously published, in letter from Ruskin to Andrew Jameson 1845.

that it cannot be doubted that it was your own mistaken kindness that administered the temptation to which they have fallen victim. I hope you have put a final stop to this ruinous system and that your house is again in some state of respectability and comfort." We can but speculate on what had been happening at his father's home.

Several letters were waiting for him at Geneva or came after his arrival. Horn had written on 21st May to say that he agreed with Andrew's father that he should not return home this year and advised him to "lead a quiet unexcited life until you entirely recover tone and vigor." He went on to suggest that Andrew write a book to be entitled *Journey of an Invalid in Search of Health*. He knew that his friend was anxious to find a sheriff-substituteship and told him it would not disadvantage his chances if he remained abroad because "any opening that may occur in the way of a Sub-ship can be applied for in your absence almost as well as in your presence here."

Spalding, too, had written but over two weeks later. He said that he had discussed with Horn the possibility of an appointment as a sheriff-substitute post but there was no vacancy at present. Early in the year Spalding had spoken with Bell, the Sheriff of Ayrshire, about the prospect of Andrew being appointed a sheriff-substitute, and it would appear that Andrew, before he had left Scotland in September 1840, had written something about his wish to be considered for such a post. It is all very vague because all we know is what Spalding wrote in this letter: "Your note, written hurriedly and unsigned, had been sent to him[24] by one of your Snodgrass-Buchanan friends without any additional information and old Bell did not for some time know who the applicant was." Spalding had explained to Bell the reason for his friend's sudden departure, but Bell had said "he was not pledged for a new Substitute."

There was also a long letter from Sophia, who was on holiday with her children at Ferry Port on Craig by Tayport, and though it does not add anything to the history of her brother's time in Europe it is worth quoting at some length since it gives an account of what had become of Elizabeth with whom he had been very close in his youth.

[24] i.e. Bell

Poor Mr Thomson is gone at last he had been very ill. Mrs Scales went over to see him. He asked to be taken out of bed in the morning at 2 o'clock and being placed in Dr Adamson's old chair expired almost immediately and without a struggle. It is now three weeks on Saturday; he spoke a great deal to the girls for the last two or three days of his life and told Jane he thought much on some things but could not speak of them, expressed great thankfulness that his sons were all well-behaved and able to do for themselves, also spoke of everyone's kindness to him, especially Mr Ogilvie.

Elizabeth goes to Mrs Ogilvie.[25] I was anxious that papa should take her to be housekeeper but he would not hear of it. The Drummonds behaved with great kindness after the funeral. Mr D. waited upon Elizabeth and offered her a home to be a companion to Mrs D she is to pay them a visit before leaving Cupar. Mrs Jameson[26] had come into Cupar to attend Mary Adamson's marriage with a missionary going out to the Colonies and whence [sic] she heard of the death she went down and wept with the girls and gave Elizabeth a £5 note for mournings at the same time telling her when she was at a loss for a home to come to the Drums which was very kind.

At this point Sophia appears to have had an unexpected call from Mr and Mrs Scales.

I have been interrupted by Mr and Mrs Scales coming in to dinner and to spend the day. We have had a nice walk along the beach with the children writing their names in the sand and gathering shells. Scales looked quite steady and sober but he has been behaving very ill while Jane was in Cupar. He was off his duty three days delirious with drink. No-one would believe the life she sometimes leads to see

[25] Her Aunt Rachael, sister of Andrew Jameson (Senior).
[26] The widow of Captain James Jameson.

them together if he does not soon reform she will not be able to live with him. Capt Buchan, who lives immediately before us drank tea with them and escorted them part of the way to Newport to catch the last boat.

Phemy[27] pays her visit to the Ruskins after the 30th and Melville and George will see her there which will be delightful. Melville proposes leaving Perth the first week in July. I feel very sad at parting with George. It will be a solace to my mind that you and Melville see him settled and will be able to judge of the person whom he is to be under. Wiesbaden is a very healthy place and it would be to your advantage to make a short stay there. I mean to leave the children at Cupar and be with George the week before he goes. With kind love to you from all your little nieces, who send a kiss to Uncle Andrew.

A large part of this letter had given an account of the tour taken by George and Sophia Gray down the Rhine to Switzerland [28] and back home by way of Paris. They must have been impressed by some educational establishment that they came across in Wiesbaden because they made arrangements for their oldest son, George, who would be 12 in October 1841, to go there. Melville, who was now a partner in Gray's business, was deputed to conduct George to London, where they would stay a few days with the Ruskins before Melville continued to Wiesbaden with George. It was in this manner that Andrew and Melville Jameson were able to make arrangements to meet in Switzerland.

There was also a letter from Sir David Brewster[29] enclosing a letter of introduction to three academics of his acquaintance in Geneva. It must be assumed that Andrew Jameson had written to the Principal

---

[27] She was at school at Avonbank in Warwickshire and the end of the summer term would be approaching.

[28] v. p. 213 supra.

[29] Sir David Brewster (1781–1868). An outstanding scholar of natural philosophy, who was Principal of the United Colleges of St Salvator and St Leonard (1838–1859), St Andrews University and Principal of Edinburgh University (1859–1867).

of St Andrews University to request such a letter, and considering the difference in age and status of the two men it is remarkable that not only did Sir David do what Andrew Jameson asked but also, as he comments in the accompanying letter, had written it having "only this minute returned from a fortnight's toil in the General Assembly." Yet again one must make the comment that Andrew Jameson had this wonderful facility of making himself immediately acceptable without any fawning or obsequiousness to everyone whom he met. There is no record of him having met Sir David Brewster but in a testimonial written in August 1842 Sir David begins "Having been for some years personally acquainted with Mr Andrew Jameson and having had many opportunities of judging his talents and acquirements ....".

One of the three scholars mentioned by Sir David was Professor Neckar,[30] a relation of the more famous Jacques Necker, the Swiss banker and statesman, who was the Finance Minister of Louis XVI. He held or had held the chair of Geology and Mineralogy at the University of Geneva. Andrew Jameson makes no mention of having met him, and it is possible that he had already left to take up residence in Scotland. Whereas the young Scot was in Geneva to avoid the rigours of an Edinburgh winter, Neckar spent the last twenty or so years of his life first in Edinburgh and latterly in Portree, because the Scottish climate suited him better than that of his native Switzerland.[31]

Meanwhile Sheriff-Substitute Jameson, in a letter of 26th June 1841, continued to fear for his son's health and told him that while he would rejoice to see him he felt that remaining in Europe represented "his last chance of permanent cure." The next communication from home was from Melville who had to report the death from scarlet fever of one of Sophia's daughters, also called Sophia, who was just under 7. This would not alter his arrangements for accompanying George to Wiesbaden and joining his brother in Switzerland but Euphemia

---

[30] This is the spelling given by Sir David Brewster and in the *Gentleman's Magazine* that published his obituary in 1862.
[31] According to the obituary, Neckar had settled in Portree as early as 1839 but it does seem improbable that Sir David Brewster was unaware of this. It is, of course, possible that Sir David knew Neckar paid visits back to Geneva after settling in Scotland.

would come home without delay.

Sophia's letter from Ferry Port on Craig had been written on 13th June 1841, just under three weeks before her daughter died. Tragedy was to strike her family with even greater force because Mary, 5, and Jane, 3, followed their sister in August, and Andrew Jameson would never see his little nieces again. Sophia now had only Euphemia, George and baby Andrew left of the eight children to whom she had given birth, and Andrew along with his younger brother Robert were to die at the ages of 4 and 6 respectively. To have lost seven children, none of them reaching the age of 7, might have been an almost inconsolable loss but remarkably six more children were born to the Grays. Moreover, all reached adult life and Melville Jameson Gray, the twelfth of the Grays' fifteen children, attained his ninety-ninth year.[32]

By mid July 1841 Andrew Jameson had moved from Geneva to Interlaken. In a letter to his father of 17th July he writes that he is "in a great dilemma." His health has improved but it can easily be affected "by unfavourable circumstances". He dreads another Scottish winter but dislikes "eating bread of idleness and living on borrowed money." Doctors he had consulted advised Messina in Sicily but this would be unaffordable. He then passes over to his father the decision about whether he should return or remain in Europe, but can his father afford a small sum without borrowing? At some point in July Melville arrived at Interlaken, where they stayed for a few days.

The brothers must then have travelled north to Berne and then on to Basel, where they took a boat up the Rhine. Andrew wrote to his father from Mainz on 3rd August to say that he had decided against remaining in Europe and that he was returning home "in the hope of succeeding in the quarter you have been making exertions in and being ready to try something else if that does not succeed." After a description of walks around Interlaken with Melville he returns to the main theme of his letter – his future.

---

[32] He married when he was 91.

I am anxious to hear what reply you have had from the Sheriff of Lanark. Geo Lyon W.S. has some influence with him and would recommend me. D. Cheape would give a good letter and Pat. Robertson also. Has Mr Reddie any interest or Lord Pitmilly? It would be good to interest him. Write to me to London at Miss Rutherfords'.[33] We expect to be there in a week.

Although as late as 26th June Sheriff-Substitute Jameson had been urging his son to remain abroad,[34] he had been simultaneously making what his son in his letter referred to as "exertions" towards securing for him a sheriff-substituteship. In particular he had gathered testimonials from colleagues to promote Andrew's candidature for the position of Sheriff-Substitute of Glasgow and had painstakingly made copies of them which he despatched to Andrew at Interlaken. As Horn had said in his letter,[35] it was perfectly possible to apply for such a post while one was abroad. Although the appointment at Glasgow was not to come to Andrew, he was not yet to know this and the possibility would have urged him to return to Scotland as soon as possible.

The brothers took a direct route to London by Frankfurt, Brussels and Ostend, reaching the Miss Rutherfords on 12th August. Waiting for them there were two letters from their father of 7th and 9th August informing them of the deaths of their little nieces Jane and Mary Gray and that Euphemia, in order to avoid possible infection, had been sent to stay with friends outside Perth. After a visit by Andrew to consult Sir James Clark they immediately left for home, presumably by boat to Dundee.

The purpose of Andrew Jameson's departure from Scotland in September 1840 had been to seek improvement in his health. To what extent his travels in Europe during these eleven months had served their purpose may be judged from the opinion of one of the foremost physicians of the day.

---

[33] This was where he had stayed in September 1840 prior to sailing for Spain.

[34] v. p. 241 supra.

[35] v. p. 238 supra.

London
13th August 1841

My Dear Father,

I am at present in Sir James Clark's parlour, waiting my turn to be called and cannot better employ my time, than in writing you.

On our arrival from Ostend on the evening before last, we lodged at the Customhouse Hotel, it being very late before our trunks could be examined. Yesterday morning we drove straight to Miss Rutherfords' and you may conceive our grief, when we read your letters and Mr Gray's.[36]

There follow some well-chosen words expressing his sorrow at the deaths of his nieces, and then he reports on his consultation with Sir James Clark.[37]

Sir James, I am sorry to say, did not find me so well as I told him. He took great pains in examining me and the result was that though considerably improved in general health there is yet a good deal of irritation in the membrane of the respiratory organs. He thinks that I ought by all means to endeavour to get a country situation, where I would not be fagged and have plenty of open air and exercise with a regular quiet life – the bar out of the question this winter – and if I don't get such a situation he recommends me to go abroad again. In the mean time I am to commence a course of small blisters upon the neck. He advises me to make good use of the remaining season and be a good deal on horseback.

---

[36] George Gray had written to his father-in-law, and Sheriff-Substitute Jameson had enclosed it in one of his letters. This is transcribed in full as Appendix A to this chapter.

[37] He had consulted Sir James Clark in March 1840 (v. p. 204 supra), and while he may have consulted him again in September 1840 just prior to his departure for Spain, he does not mention it in his correspondence.

APPENDIX A TO CHAPTER SEVEN

The Gordons of Jerez de la Frontera and Andrew Jameson

In September 1840 Andrew Jameson sailed from London to Cadiz in the *Montrose*. He was in poor health because he had been suffering another attack of the dysphonia that had required him to live in southern France and Italy from May 1833 to July 1834. During the voyage he made the acquaintance of a Mr and Mrs Gordon, who, recognizing that he was unwell, invited him to stay at their home in Jerez de la Frontera, about twenty miles north of Cadiz. At first the genial climate assisted a return to health, but in November the weather became cold and damp with almost continuous rain. Accordingly Andrew Jameson, who had been visiting Seville, returned to Jerez de la Frontera, paid his respects to the Gordons and left for Gibraltar whence he sailed for Malta on 7th December 1840.

Mr and Mrs Gordon were Spanish citizens with the names of Don Jacobo Pedro Gordon and Carlota Villaverde de Gordon. That they had their own carriage and horses aboard the *Montrose* indicates that they were in most comfortable circumstances, and it may be that they had taken their equipage all the way to Aberdeenshire in Scotland, where they had close family relationships.

The connection of Don Jacobo Pedro Gordon with Aberdeenshire is both complicated and interesting. Jacobo Pedro Gordon was the fifth child (and only son) of James Arthur Gordon (1759–1824) and his wife Rosa Archimbaud. One sister had died young and another had married a Spaniard. The elder of the two other sisters married a Gordon Cranstoun of Gordonhall (the name then used for Wardhouse that was built over the period 1773–1815), and the other to a Prendergast from

Banffshire. It is probable that both sisters were already related to their husbands. These marriages demonstrate the close and continuing connection of the Spanish-based Gordons with the north-east of Scotland, even in their third generation.

This Spanish connection had begun with Arthur Gordon (1729[38]– 1815), who went out to Spain (no date is known). He was one of twelve children of James Gordon, 8th Laird of Beldorney, who died in 1740. Through the marriage of James to Mary Gordon, daughter of John Gordon, 3rd Laird of Law in Kennethmont, who had purchased Wardhouse and Kildrummy, the later Gordons inherited Wardhouse. The family were Roman Catholic but the 10th Laird and 11th Laird, nephews of Arthur Gordon, became Protestants, Alexander[39] (1748– 1769) in order to join the British army and his brother Charles-Edward (1750–1832) to secure the inheritance of the three estates of Beldorney, Wardhouse and Kildrummy. It is unclear from the text of *The Spanish Gordons and Huntly,* by Dean and Morrison, if this main branch of the family ever returned to their original faith.

It was not unusual for the younger sons of Scottish families in the eighteenth century to seek their fortune abroad, mainly because their families, if not impoverished, could promise them little inheritance. As it was, Charles-Edward, Arthur's nephew and 11th Laird, had to sell Beldorney in 1777 and live at Wardhouse. Employment with the Honourable East India Company, whether in its civilian ranks or with its army or maritime service was common. Charles-Edward, not thinking that he was likely to succeed his elder brother Alexander, served for a time with the East India Company Maritime Service. Arthur Gordon and his younger brother Cosmo (dates unknown) went abroad, Arthur to Cadiz and Cosmo to Jamaica (possibly to the sugar plantations). Cosmo married a Campbell, and Arthur married a

---

[38] In their privately published book *The Spanish Gordons and Huntly*, Anne Dean and Mike Morrison give 1731 in the text but 1729 in the genealogical table.

[39] In Ireland in 1767 Alexander became involved in a brawl that made it advisable for him to go to France. There he was introduced to the British ambassador, Lord Harcourt, who suggested that he should visit French dockyards but gave him no letters of credit to enable him to do so. He was arrested in Brest, tried as a spy and hanged on 24th November 1769, Lord Harcourt making no effort to save him.

Spanish woman called Maria.

Arthur had joined a small British community in Cadiz and founded a sherry business. He had a close friendship with John Geddes, Principal of the Scots College at Valladolid from 1771 to 1780, and with help from Geddes became a Spanish citizen. By 1784 Cosmo's son Robert (1763–1805) and James Arthur (1759–1824), youngest son of Arthur and Cosmo's brother, John, the 9th Laird of Beldorney, had come to Cadiz, and in that year Arthur and his two nephews formed a company. It was soon trading most successfully, James Arthur living at Jerez de la Frontera, which lay at the heart of the sherry-making area, and Arthur remaining in Cadiz, looking after the business and exporting end of the company. Robert was able to attend the funeral of an aunt[40] at Banff in April 1787 because he was in Edinburgh establishing business connections there on behalf of his company.

In 1788 Arthur's grandnephew, John David (1774–1850), eldest son of Charles-Edward, 11th Laird of Beldorney, was welcomed into the company. By the time he succeeded his father in 1832 he was already 58 and well settled in Spain with a Spanish wife. Since his father had sold Beldorney the family dropped that name from their title and thereafter styled themselves Lairds of Wardhouse. Since the unfortunate Alexander, 10th Laird of Beldorney, had inherited Wardhouse as its 4th Laird, John David was the 6th Laird.[41] From this time Wardhouse was used as the summer home of the Spanish Gordons until it was sold in 1952 to James Cordiner of Aberdeen, who stripped it of everything valuable, leaving it the empty shell it now is. According to the genealogical table provided by Dean and Morrison, the last Spaniard to include Wardhouse in his title was Alfonso, Count of Mirasol (1900–1991), son of Rafael, the 10th Laird.

Unlike his brothers Alexander (4th Laird) and Charles-Edward (5th Laird), James Arthur retained his adherence to the Roman Catholic faith. As the company became ever more prosperous, he came frequently

---

[40] Possibly a daughter of James Gordon, 8th Laird of Baldorney but almost certainly a Prendergast.

[41] This generation had returned to the Roman Catholic faith.

to Britain on business and took holidays at Wardhouse. This close relationship with Aberdeenshire was continued by his son, Jacobo Pedro Gordon,[42] who, as stated above, invited Andrew Jameson to his home in Jerez de la Frontera after they had become acquainted on the *Montrose* in 1840.

For the continuing history of the Gordons of Jerez, reference must be made to Dean and Morrison's publication that is available in Huntly Library, but it does contain some inaccuracies. The fullest and best account is the 19-page "The Spanish Gordons and Huntly" obtainable through the internet.[43] The company founded in 1784 is now the largest producer of sherry in the world. Don Jacobo Pedro Gordon's granddaughter, Maria Gordon, married a Pedro Gonzalez Soto in 1877, and the firm is now known as Gonzalez-Byass.

The lairds of Wardhouse made annual visits to their home in Aberdeenshire. Andrew Jameson served as Sheriff of Aberdeenshire from 1865 until his sudden death in 1870, and it would be interesting to know if he ever met any of Don Jacobo Gordon's relations.

---

[42] The author omitted to take down the dates of birth and death of Jacobo Pedro Gordon from the genealogical table provided by Dean and Morrison.

[43] www.scalan.co.uk/Spanishgordontext.htm

APPENDIX B TO CHAPTER SEVEN
George Gray's Letter to His Father-in-Law

Although this work is an account of the life of Sheriff Andrew Jameson, the author considers that he should provide a transcription of the letter George Gray wrote to Sheriff-Substitute Jameson a few hours before his daughter Mary died. It is beautifully expressed, and what makes it even more acutely painful to read is our knowledge that within six days another daughter was to catch the same infection and die. It conveys the anguish of a father, who is seeing his daughter hovering between life and death and who is trying to see some elements of hope in the smallest gestures and physical movements that his child is still capable of making. It is composed in a manner very typical of its age and time, and it seems wrong to ignore it and return it to the documents which may not be consulted for a long time or perhaps ever again.

Bowerswell Friday
7 o'c a.m.

My dear Sir,

I did not expect at this hour I could have told you Mary is still in the land of the living & consequently still in the hands of an almighty power who may see meet to restore her. When I say this I have said all for really there has nothing occurred since you left upon which to build our hopes. She spent a restless night with great difficulty of breathing but thro' the day she has got no worse & her eye has assumed a livelier and brighter appearance. In the course of the day she ate or rather sucked two oranges & her bowels have moved without medicine in a remarkably healthy way after an interval of two days. Sophia has been able to be with her the whole day and I am sure this has soothed her as she occasionally puts her little hands round mamma's [sic] neck and evinces her gratitude with an endearing hug. Oh that I could say I have still hope. I really cannot but Sophia says she has. May the almighty grant our fervent prayers for we have no hope in man.

Yours very sincerely

Geo. Gray

CHAPTER EIGHT
The Maltese Breeze

The future for Andrew Jameson did not look promising when he returned to Cupar in August 1841. His year abroad had certainly caused an abatement of his chronic throat illness, but Sir James Clark had warned him that he was far from fully recovered.

He was realistic enough to accept[1] that a career at the bar was now out of the question and that he might have to seek employment in another field, but if he was to remain in the law an appointment as sheriff-substitute was the most attractive proposition. He had been actively seeking support for such a post from various people prior to his sudden departure from Scotland in September 1840, but this had come to nothing and letters from friends such as Horn, who had written to him while he was abroad, had not provided him with much hope. However, over the next eighteen months the dark clouds hovering over both his health and his career gradually dispersed until by 1843 his future was secured, success having come from not one but two directions.

The first letters he received once he was back at Cupar were from his friends Patrick Stirling and Robert Horn. Stirling invited him to stay for a few days at his home near Dunblane, and Horn advised him that his health should be his first priority. There was also a letter from Neil Campbell, son of his father's friend, Alexander Campbell, Sheriff-Substitute of Renfrewshire. Andrew Jameson (Senior) had been invited by his colleague to visit him at his home at Barnhill[2] that lay just outside Dumbarton and Neil Campbell proposed that Andrew should accompany his father. This suggestion had the added inducement that

---

[1] v. p. 232 supra.
[2] Andrew and Melville had been guests there in August 1827. v. p. 65 supra.

his sisters would be there. As it happened, Andrew went first on a short visit to Bute before going on to Barnhill a few days before his father could leave Cupar, and this was fortunate because his father was able to send him the following letter dated 4th September.

> I lose no time in forwarding to you a copy of Lord Rosslyn's letter received this morning. What he mentions is worth attending to and I have no doubt that the duty alluded to will form the foundation of a Government appointment, the emoluments of which, whatever it may be, would enable you to remain abroad until your health was re-established and should afford an opportunity, God willing, of returning to your profession.
>
> I have in the meantime written to Lord Rosslyn and given him your address to be communicated to Sir Henry Bouverie.
>
> I expected to have heard from you today. If you see Neil Campbell you may mention my intention of being at Paisley on Friday next. I have directions to Barnhill.

He then adds a postscript on the next page of his letter: "You will, of course, keep the communication of Ld Rosslyn as private – I have enclosed the principal letter." By this he presumably meant the following letter.

> My dear Jameson,
>
> Sir Henry Bouverie who is at present on Leave of Absence and returns to Malta in the course of a month has requested me to ask you where your son whom he saw in Malta last year *now* is and *where he is likely to be during the ensuing winter*. I apprehended from what fell from Sir H. Bouverie that it is not unlikely that your son might be of some use and assistance to him in considering the Project of some new Code of Laws about to be promulgated in Malta and,

if so it is *possible* that that might lead to some appointment but you must consider this as confidential and in fact *only a conjecture* on his part as I *am not authorized* to make any communication of this sort and you must [paper torn here where wax seal had been] where your son is to be found.

Had Lord Rosslyn and Sir Henry Bouverie met by chance and had the latter, discovering or even perhaps already knowing Lord Rosslyn owned extensive property around Dysart, then mentioned the visit to Malta of a young Scottish lawyer from Fife? Lord Rosslyn would immediately have known who this was and agreed to write to Sheriff-Substitute Jameson. On the other hand Sir Henry may have deliberately sought out Lord Rosslyn. Whatever the reason, Sir Henry learned immediately from Sheriff-Substitute Jameson that Andrew would be at Barnhill and wrote to him from 2 Curzon Street, London, on 7th September.

Understanding that it is your intention to pass the coming winter in a warmer climate for the more perfect re-establishment of your health, which I am happy to hear is much amended, I venture to propose to you to pay a visit at Malta, where I shall be happy to receive you, should it be convenient to you to come. I am aware that you are conversant with the various Codes of Criminal Law in use on the continent & as well as with that in use in Malta and you know that our judges have been employed in the revision of a new code and which will, I understand, be completed by the end of the year. Happy as I should be at all times to see you, I do not pretend that I am now endeavouring to entice you to Malta from purely disinterested motives and will tell you fairly that in talking over the matter with Sir Hector Greig we have come to the conclusion that if we could persuade you to come to Malta and to employ yourself in reading over for us the new Codes and giving us such hints as may appear to you necessary it would facilitate the publication of them in no ordinary degree. You are aware, I am sure, that the poverty of all local Govt is such that we can offer you no pecuniary remuneration for your trouble, but should you be induced to try again the climate of our Island and would come there as my guest the employment which I have mentioned might be interesting and amusing to you. Beyond that I can hold out no inducement. I shall be in Malta by the end of October & the Codes will, I understand, be ready for consideration before the end of the year.

It is appropriate at this point to make a comment about the postal service at this time. The replacement of the handstamp by the adhesive stamp and a reduction in the cost of letter postage to one penny had taken place in 1840. This did not make much difference to the time taken for letters to reach their destination because under the previous system delivery time had been just as expeditious. Much depended, of course, on the location of places and letters to and from remote areas took much longer than between towns on main routes. On the other hand communication by post was better and more reliable in 1840 than it has become in the twenty-first century and it is for this reason that surprise should not be expressed at the ease and rapidity upon which Andrew Jameson was able to rely for the receipt and delivery of his correspondence.[3]

An example of this is demonstrated in Andrew Jameson's answer to Sir Henry Bouverie. It was written on 13th September 1841, and he felt it necessary to preface his comments with an apology for so dilatory a reply, the reason having been his "some days absence at a distance". Naturally, the original letter is not among the Jameson family papers but fortunately he wrote and retained a draft of the document. It is far from easy to decipher because there are insertions and erasures (in the sense that a pen has been drawn through some words) but the message is clear.

---

[3] I am grateful to Mr Alexander Stables, an Aberdeen philatelist, for this information. Mr Stables has made a special study of British postal services prior to the introduction of the adhesive stamp.

He thanked Sir Henry for the compliment that the proposal paid to his legal abilities and he recollected the kindness that had made his stay in Malta so pleasant. He felt so much better as a result of his tour of Italy and Switzerland, and although he had entertained hope of returning to the bar, his medical adviser had told him this would just resuscitate the problem with his larynx.

> The most suitable occupation for me and indeed the only that remained to me in Scotland [was to] apply for the first vacancy in any of the county sheriffships. [However,] I can see no *immediate* prospects of any vacancy such as I have alluded to and I can assure you that if I find I can leave without serious detriment to any such application, it will afford me the greatest pleasure to avail myself of your invitation & come to Malta in the course of six weeks or two months at the farthest. No plan or venture of travelling abroad could have equal inducements with me as the occupation you suggest & I shall certainly allow nothing of that kind to interfere with it. I appreciate highly the mark of your confidence and that of my friend Sir H. Greig. I only fear that I do not deserve it and that my aid in revising the New Code could be but of little advantage to your Governorship. If, however, any exertions on my part could be of service to you I would consider my time well and truly employed.
>
> Your Supreme Court meets on the first of November. Before that time it is likely that I will be able to see more clearly what is likely to occur in any of the Judicial vacancies I have referred to. If agreeable to you I will write to you as soon as I am in possession of any definite information. In the meantime I do not apprehend that there will be anything to prevent me being in Malta before the end of November and in good time for the object you propose.

Wisely, Andrew Jameson did not commit himself irrevocably to visiting Malta because he was soon to find that the tide appeared to be turning in relation to both his employment prospects and his health. The following letter to Sir Henry Bouverie, written on 24th November 1841, demonstrates this and although it is a draft the original cannot have differed in any major way.

Since I had the pleasure of answering your favor of the [11th][4] September I am glad to say my health has greatly improved – and I am now gaining ground daily notwithstanding the severity of the season which indeed seems to be in my favor. Notwithstanding that my medical advisers do not therefore recommend any change of climate I would have made every exertion to have come to Malta this month, in order to have assisted you in the object proposed – but having made serious applications for permanent appointments here in which vacancies are likely to occur my absence would incur great risk of disappointment as I experienced last session. My circumstances unfortunately do not allow me to run any risk of this kind, and I have not been so fortunate as to secure any employment prospectively in such a way as would permit me to absent myself during the winter. It is therefore with great regret that I must give up all hope of visiting your Command at present and using my humble endeavours to be of service in the preparation of the New Code. It is with much reluctance that I have found myself obliged to come to this conclusion, although[5] for some time I flattered myself that things might have turned out as to have enabled me to have accepted the appointment you were so kind as to propose. I need scarcely add, that

---

[4] The actual date is missing from this draft, presumably because Andrew Jameson did not have Sir Henry's letter before him at the time and he would add it when he came to write the actual letter.

[5] This was not the word used by Andrew Jameson but what he wrote is indecipherable and this substitution is in line with what he was intending to convey.

this result does in no degree diminish the grateful sense I entertain of your goodness and hospitable intentions for which and this mark of your confidence I will always feel greatly obliged.

I fear it is unnecessary for me to offer my services at such a distance but could I be of any use in considering any part of the projected Code or in facilitating its preparation I would gladly exert myself in that way, under your written direction.

As events turned out, he was to become heavily involved with the revision of the criminal code of Malta, but it is now necessary to return to his domestic life during the autumn of 1841 and the winter months of 1841/1842.

He visited the Stirlings at the beginning of October and there received a letter from Melville inviting him and Patrick Stirling to a dinner that he was hosting for an Advocate in Aberdeen,[6] John Blaikie of Craigiebuckler,[7] who was about to marry Eliza Duncan, sister of his fiancée, Jessie. The other guests at this all male gathering were to be Mr Duncan and George Gray. Melville refers to their nephew, George Gray, whom he had accompanied to Wiesbaden,[8] and writes "May the Lord preserve him from the wicked one." The invitation appears to have been initiated by Jessie Duncan because she was anxious for Andrew to provide for her friend, a Miss Miller, an introduction to the Methodist clergyman and his wife in Malta "with whom you had so much agreeable and profitable intercourse." There is a strong possibility that this was the family whose invitation to lunch had required Andrew Jameson to tell Lord Lynedoch that he was unable to see him that Sunday at La Gudja.[9] Melville adds the cryptic comment

---

[6] By a curious anomaly solicitors in Aberdeen are called advocates. Originally the correct terminology was "Advocate in Aberdeen" but the "in" came to be omitted.

[7] Then outside the boundaries of Aberdeen, it is now a prosperous suburb on the west of the city. Craigiebuckler House, where John Blaikie lived, has been converted into flats.

[8] v. p. 240 supra.

[9] v. p. 226 supra.

that Miss Miller and her brother were "again under the necessity of going to Malta." There is no reference in surviving correspondence to let us know if Andrew did attend this dinner.

The Methodist Church had established itself in Valletta in 1824, and during his six weeks in Malta it is probable that Andrew Jameson worshipped at their small chapel on the corner of Old Bakery Street and Strada Britannica, in which street he had found lodgings. In May 1842 he attended the General Assembly of the Church of Scotland, dined at Holyrood House and was presented to the Lord High Commissioner. He used the opportunity to inform the General Assembly that, despite the presence of the 92nd Highlanders as part of the garrison, there was no Church of Scotland where they could worship. This brought a swift and affirmative response, and by the end of that year the Reverend Doctor James Julius Wood was sent out to Malta.[10]

The next we learn about Andrew Jameson is in November, when he received what was an important communication from Robert Horn. Writing on 12th November 1841, Horn thanked his friend for having introduced him to Neil Campbell, who had informed him that his father was proposing to retire in April 1842. Campbell had already informed Andrew of this and Horn asked Campbell not to mention it to anybody. He advised Andrew "to not lose a moment in bringing your whole artillery to bear upon the man of Fiction.[11] He is a very pleasant looking person and if one can trust to physiognomy will be disposed to do what is right." The obvious person to whom Andrew Jameson would have been wise to approach was the Sheriff of Renfrewshire, and is it possible that this was the person to whom Horn was referring?

This would be one of the reasons why he wrote to Sir Henry Bouverie a few days later explaining why it would be disadvantageous for him to go to Malta, although we know from that letter that he had also been making applications for other positions. On 28th November Sophia

---

[10] In December 1843 the Free Church of Scotland purchased the Methodist chapel. It became too small and a new church, St Andrew's, was built nearby and dedicated in December 1857. This church remains and is well supported.

[11] One can only assume that he was referring to someone prominent in the Scottish legal system who was also an author.

Gray wrote to him at Cupar, where he had been staying since his return from Europe, asking him to arrange for sheets to be sent to her. "I wish 6 yds for each pair of sheets and that will be 24 yds alltogether: the last I had were 5½ and I find them too short, which is a very uncomfortable thing. Tell Jean[12] to get them sent up immediately." There is no doubt that his sister referred to yards and not feet but such sheets, clearly for use on beds, must have been enormous. She took the opportunity of inviting her brother to spend Christmas with her family, especially since he would be able to meet "Miss Blaikie, a 10,000 pounder from Aberdeen, who is to visit the Duncans at Christmas." Perhaps Sophia was implying that one solution for his future would be to marry the heiress from Aberdeen.

Whether Andrew accepted his sister's invitation or not is not recorded but he certainly spent New Year's Day 1842 with his father before going to Perth on 4th January and then to his Ogilvie cousins in Dundee. In February he crossed over to Edinburgh to stay with Neil Campbell at 33 Dublin Street and enjoyed meeting old friends. However, as he wrote to his father on 11th February, "I regret to find that my windpipe is not so strong as I thought & constantly gives way, if I meet many acquaintances." He continued, "The Sheriff[13] has been confined to his house with cold since Sunday. He was in bed when I called yesterday but I saw Mrs M."

This may have been a social visit but perhaps he was calling on Sheriff Menteith to press his claim to a sheriff-substitute post. He had found that he was not the only young advocate seeking preferment in this direction and had decided "it would be for my advantage to take up my residence here for some weeks. I might get a lodging at Morningside or Portobello or Newhaven, where I would avoid the bad air of the town." This, of course, required money and he asked his father for what he called a "supply". He either found nothing suitable in the suburbs or preferred to remain at 33 Dublin Street with Campbell on account of its convenient location.

---

[12] A domestic servant employed by Sheriff-Substitute Jameson.

[13] Menteith, who had succeeded Clephane as Sheriff of Fife: v. footnote 19, p. 6 supra.

On the 15th March Melville married Janet (Jessie) Duncan and Andrew would most certainly have been present. He must have contrasted the success of his younger brother with his own apparently ever bleaker prospects because, despite the hopes expressed in his letter to Sir Henry Bouverie, he was making no headway in his search of employment. Accordingly he decided that he must take up again his practice at the bar, so far as his health would allow him, in order to earn some income. The following excerpts from his letter of 12th April to his father indicate the near despair he felt for his prospects together with his disappointment at his father's apparent reluctance to use any influence on his behalf.

> I came home this forenoon from Paisley having left Caldarvan yesterday morning and breakfasted at Auchintorlie on the way. I was sorry that I could not stay some days with the Sheriff[14] as I intended when I left but I was obliged to come back for the solitary Appeal in the House of Lords.
>
> I fear this will be an uphill work: the law again & the expenses of my small way of living without any *paying* business.
>
> I regret that your delicacy prevents you taking decisive steps to effect the arrangement[15] with the Sheriff. I am very much disappointed that you did not speak out to him. Six months have now elapsed since his request of delay and my health seems to have stood the test tolerably well. It is a very serious thing at the age of 31 to begin the world anew in a profession dangerous to my health and in which I have made so many shipwrecks. I hope you will think of my unfortunate situation seriously and <u>do</u> something where your exertions may be crowned with success.

---

[14] It is possible that he was referring to Sheriff-Substitute Campbell since it is unlikely that he would expect hospitality over several days from another sheriff or sheriff-substitute in the area. In any case it is probable that he had already formed a close attachment to Alexa Campbell, whom he was to marry two years later.

[15] This matter is explained in the first two pages of Chapter Nine.

I believe there is some chance of my meeting you in some proof towards the end of the week. Till then I will be very busy.

NB I am in great want of *clean clothes*. Make Jean despatch my box by the *12 o'clock coach tomorrow*. A couple of bottles of sherry will be very acceptable. Send some of the Cupar papers.

Six weeks later, on 30th May, he was able to write to his father in a less despondent mood. He had resumed practice as an advocate "until something more suitable to my constitution comes up in the country." He would be leaving Dublin Street to live at 20 Abercromby Place, where his plate would be put up on 1st June. He had attracted a brief that required him to speak on a "fine question of International Law. I find the excitement a little too much for me and must try and be as calm as possible." The previous week he had attended a public breakfast, in aid of colonial clergy,[16] and to his surprise the chairman had called upon him to speak. He had felt obliged to do so but had been "severely tried" by his effort.

He had to request his father to send from Cupar all his books in boxes "properly nailed down addressed." He had received the box of clothes that he had asked to be sent[17] but had been required to pay for delivery, although Jean had already paid for this at Cupar. Money was not plentiful and he asked that Jean make certain all parcels (he probably sent his washing home once a week) were clearly handstamped at the coach office.

As stated above, he had attended the General Assembly of the Church of Scotland earlier in May. This was the year before Dr Chalmers and his friend Dr Candlish led one third of the clergy out of the Assembly to found the Free Church of Scotland, and the debates on the question of intrusion were followed with the greatest interest throughout Scotland. As he wrote, "The proceedings in the Assembly never excited so much

---

[16] Presumably missionaries.
[17] There is no mention of receipt of any sherry.

attendance. There are a great many foreigners – German, French, besides English & Irish Clergymen – come to sympathise with the Evangelical Party." He concludes with the information that Sir Andrew Agnew[18] was seeking an interview with him.

Just after writing this letter to his father he received a communication from Sir Hector Greig that was to lead to a resumption of his connection with Malta. There followed throughout that summer of 1842 a considerable amount of correspondence and activity that culminated in his appointment by the Colonial Office to revise and report on the projected Criminal Code of Malta. It would be convenient, however, first to deal briefly with his domestic and professional life during this period and, fortunately, for no other records are extant, his long reply[19] to Sir Hector, dated 9th June 1842, provides some information about this.

As he had informed Sir Henry Bouverie in his letter of 24th November 1841, it had been necessary for him to remain in Scotland to apply for any suitable post that might become available. "Nothing of the kind having occurred, and the exercise and bracing cold of winter having quite restored me to my former health, I returned to the Bar at the end of February last and have been practising regularly in the Courts since that time. As, however, my temporary retirement from practice had of course destroyed a good deal of my business connection and dispersed my old clients and employers, I am not yet entirely occupied with actual practice and am only regaining by degrees the ground I had lost by my unfortunate illness."

Sir Hector had praised Andrew Jameson's expertise in Roman and Civil Law, and we learn from the reply that "several of my brethren requested me to stand Candidate for the Professorship of that department now vacant in the University of Edinburgh but I gave way to a friend, who is older in the profession and who was more anxious for the Chair than myself."

This must have occurred earlier than June 1842 and the friend

---

[18] Sir Andrew Agnew of Lochnaw (1793–1849). He was a strict sabbatarian and when an MP sought annually to introduce a bill for the more strict observance of the sabbath.

[19] He prepared and retained a draft reply that cannot have been in essentials any different from the letter that he sent.

was almost certainly a Douglas Cheape, probably a connection of the Professor Cheape of his student days in Edinburgh. Cheape must have been unsuccessful in his candidature at Edinburgh University but successful in obtaining later that year the chair of Law at the University of Glasgow. This is made clear by the survival of documentation referring to Andrew Jameson's application in October of that same year for the chair of Law at the University of Glasgow.[20] All the pages of this documentation, which consists of 28 testimonials, are professionally printed with the frontispiece stating that they are in support of his candidature for the chair at the University of Glasgow. The testimonials are introduced with the following preface:

> This application to which the annexed Testimonials refer was originally made under reservation of Mr DOUGLAS CHEAPE'S claims, and was accordingly withdrawn when that gentleman became a Candidate. As Mr CHEAPE has resigned the Chair, Mr JAMESON'S application is now renewed, without any qualification.
>
> 20 Abercrombie Place,
> 29th October 1842

Surprise at Cheape's exceedingly brief tenure of the chair is exceeded by surprise that Andrew Jameson was not appointed. He had submitted 28 testimonials, some from persons of such national prominence as James L'Amy, Sheriff of Forfarshire, who had interviewed him in his oral examination for admittance to the Faculty of Advocates, several other sheriffs, Alexander Wood, Dean of the Faculty of Advocates, Dr Chalmers and Sir David Brewster. His friend Spalding, who now held the chair of Rhetoric at Edinburgh University, provided a testimonial and there was also one from Sir Hector Greig drawing attention to his

---

[20] Perhaps there was a slip of the pen in Andrew Jameson's letter of 9th June 1842 and that he wrote "Edinburgh" instead of "Glasgow". It seems possible but unlikely that the chairs of Law in both universities became vacant at the same time.

appointment by the Colonial Office to assist with a revision of the laws of Malta. Whoever was appointed must have been extremely well qualified and suitable for the chair.

It is a reasonable assumption that he made some visits during the summer to Barnhill now that his friendship with Neil Campbell had become very close. He was popular both with old friends and new acquaintances and his visits would surely have been welcomed by the Campbell family, not least by his friend's sister, Alexa.

It will be appropriate to transcribe in full Sir Hector Greig's letter of 25th May 1842 since it sets the scene for the major contribution that Andrew Jameson was to make to the law of Malta. Sir Hector was at Gibraltar en route for London with a manuscript copy of the proposed new Criminal Code for consideration by the Colonial Office.

> It will give me very great pleasure to hear that you are perfectly restored to health and which pleasing event both Sir Henry Bouverie and myself trust has taken place, as we did not hear of you having been abroad this last winter, and indeed, if you had done so, Sir Henry expected that you would have paid him a visit at Malta.
>
> I do not know what your occupations are at this moment, but I am ordered to ask if you would have leisure to look over our new Criminal Code with the view of pointing out what you may consider defects, and chiefly in those parts wherein from its Neapolitan origin, there may be too great a departure from the liberal spirit of English law.
>
> I am now taking the Code home with me in manuscript, and in the event of the Crown lawyers not having time to revise it, or indeed to look narrowly at it, I should like to have your assistance in drawing up a report upon the general features of the Code, so as to bring the subject, in a tangible state, under Lord Stanley's consideration.
>
> I am quite certain that from your knowledge of Roman Law, that you could easily accomplish what I have in view

– and both Sir Henry Bouverie and myself would have great satisfaction if this business is put into your hands. However, our wishes may not be attainable either by your having other more important occupations, or, by the Colonial Office having assistance of their own for the revision that may be required.

My object therefore at present is simply to ask if you would be inclined to undertake this work which I think you would get through in 4 or 5 weeks, as far as a very general report would demand and if I should obtain leave at the Colonial Office to put it into your hands.

I need not say that this communication must be considered strictly confidential, as I have no right to move in the matter without Lord Stanley's express sanction and it may be that His Lordship has now assistance in London to answer all the purposes of a general revision.

I expect to be in London about 5th June and I shall take it in hand if you will write to me, nearly by return of post and address me, care of G. Mayor, Esq, librarian, Colonial Office, Downing Street.

Andrew Jameson was unable to reply until 9th June because Sir Hector had sent his letter to the only address that he knew, namely, Barnhill in Dunbartonshire. In his reply he stated "I will regret this [the absence of full-time work] the less if it will enable me to devote more of my time to the object you propose. I will be very happy to give my best attention to the task of revising your New Criminal Code to the best of my ability and drawing up a report upon its general features & provisions, in the manner which you describe if you should obtain the requisite authority to entrust me with that duty."

He went on to say that had he decided to return to Malta the previous winter the Lord Justice Clerk (Lord Hope) had offered to recommend him to a relation, Henry Hope, the Under-Secretary at the Colonial Office, as someone whom Lord Stanley, the Colonial Secretary, might find useful. "If necessary, I could send you certificates from him – and the Crown Counsel here – upon a day's notice." This was something neither Sir Henry Bouverie nor Sir Hector Greig could have known, when they suggested to Lord Stanley that the revision of the Criminal Code of Malta could be entrusted to a young and, as far as they were aware, almost unknown Edinburgh lawyer. That Andrew Jameson was supported by the Lord Justice Clerk, the most senior legal officer in Scotland apart from the Lord Justice General, must have been of the greatest assistance to Sir Hector in persuading the Colonial Secretary that the Governor of Malta had been wise to put forward the young Scot for the job.

The letter continued: "Our Courts sit till the 20th of July next. After that time I might come to London, if it was thought necessary to have any personal communication on the subject of the Code – and indeed I would do so even during the Session, if deemed advisable or convenient." He ended with the hope that Sir Hector would pay a visit to Edinburgh, adding the interesting information that Alexander Wood, Dean of the Faculty of Advocates, was a friend of Sir Hector.

Not having heard from Andrew Jameson by 8th June, Sir Hector, now at Christie's Hotel, St James' Street, London, wrote again (the address is not shown), repeating the proposal that he should comment on the proposed new Criminal Code for Malta while simultaneously warning him that all correspondence on this matter must be kept confidential until the appointment was approved by the Colonial Secretary. There was, however, a good chance of this because the Colonial Office had no lawyer competent to carry out the task.

On receipt of this communication Andrew Jameson replied immediately to Sir Hector on 11th June,[21] informing him that he had received the original letter, to which he had replied two days previously, addressing his letter, as Sir Hector had requested, to the Colonial Office librarian. He felt that all that needed to be said had already been covered in his earlier letter and that "should you be authorised by Lord Stanley to entrust me with so important a duty, I will gladly devote

---

[21] This is described at the top of the documentation as a copy.

myself to the work in conformity with the views, which you suggest on the subject." He then made a comment which demonstrated full confidence in his ability to revise the code.

> Although the proposed duty should be confided to some better qualified Jurist, I will not take the less interest in the subject. Our studies and pursuits here, being necessarily more connected with the Roman Law and the foreign codes, which are founded upon that great monument of ancient wisdom as well with general Jurisprudence, dispose us to take a greater interest in such improvements as that which you are now engaged in, so that I will be glad to learn what is finally determined in the matter, if you have leisure to write me as well as obtain a copy of the code and relevant documents when printed.

On 13th June Sir Hector acknowledged receipt of Andrew Jameson's letters of 9th and 11th June[22] and told him that he was "now in communication with the Colonial Office." Four days later he was able to write "it is more than probable that Lord Stanley will confide to you the making of a report on the code. In that case I shall come down to Edinburgh with the Code and to communicate the views of the Local Govt of Malta on the subject."

The tone of Sir Hector's letter must have encouraged Andrew Jameson to believe that very soon Lord Stanley would approve his appointment. Sir Hector, however, had been somewhat hasty in this assumption because a fortnight later the matter was still under consideration at the Colonial Office. Sir Hector wrote on 25th June that he had received no answer from Henry Hope, the Under-Secretary.

> I do not know what course they intend to take but in the mean time weeks are passing away, and my stay in England

---

[22] This is an excellent example of the speed and efficiency of the British postal service at that time.

is so very limited, that in the midst of this uncertainty, I am induced to ask if, in the event of Lord Stanley deciding that the task of making this report for the Malta Govt is to be confided to you – what is the earliest day, that it would be possible for you to be in London to receive the Code & papers & explanations connected with it?

I put this hypothetical query so as to save time for my own account when I do receive an answer from Mr Hope.

There follows a postscript which was surprisingly not included in the main body of the letter:

P.S. I shall call at the Col. Office today, & being very anxious to be able to set off for Germany very early in July, I shall press for an answer one way or the other, so that I may be liberated but if they decide that an English Lawyer is to make the report I am certain that the result will not be satisfactory for want of acquaintance with the Roman Law.

In view of Andrew Jameson's later appointment as a sheriff-substitute it is worthwhile including the following part from Sir Hector's letter.

I am really delighted that your health is so well re-established as to permit your returning to the Bar. It would have been a tiresome occupation to have settled in the country as a sheriff depute.

Sir Hector was as good as his word and called at the Colonial Office that day. Naturally, there is no record of what passed between Sir Hector and those whom he met there, but before the month was ended Andrew Jameson received confirmation of his appointment to report on the draft Criminal Code of Malta. He received from Sir Hector the following letter dated 28th June 1842:

I am now authorised to say that Lord Stanley has sanctioned your being employed on account of the Govt. of Malta to make a report on the proposed Criminal Code, with the understanding, as we are a poor Govt., that you will come to London, and having seen the nature of the work to be done, that you will arrange with me, as to the remuneration to be paid to you.

As I mentioned in my previous letters, you are aware that the job will be more honorable than lucrative, but it cannot fail to be ultimately of use to you, by bringing you in contact with the Colonial Office.

I expect an answer from you tomorrow saying when you can come up, but write this today, to let me know how matters stand.

On your arrival, I will introduce you to Mr Stephen[23] and Mr Hope, and from them you will receive instructions on what is to be done. My idea is that after having read out the code with me and having heard all there is to say on the subject, which cannot occupy above 48 hours, that you may return to Edinburgh forthwith with all the papers to work on at your leisure.

It would be an immense convenience to me, if you could start at once for London. I shall promise that you won't be detained here above 4 or 5 days, and I should then be at liberty to quit England.

I do hope that it is not necessary for you to remain to the end of the Session[24] /by the 12 July/ & I do trust that you will be able to come up almost immediately after receiving this.

---

[23] James Stephen (1789–1859) was an outstanding Under-Secretary of State at the Colonial Office. A colleague, Sir Henry Taylor, wrote that "he literally rules the colonial empire" and for this reason was often referred to as "King Stephen".

[24] In his letter of 9th June 1842 Andrew Jameson had mentioned that the Scottish Courts Session did not end until 20th July. v. p. 266 supra.

It is not difficult to sense from Sir Hector's letter that he was anxious to hand over the documents as soon as possible in order that he could take his holiday in Germany before the expiration of his leave from Malta. From Andrew Jameson's point of view this was welcome employment because, although the remuneration would be small, he was still trying to rebuild his law practice that had suffered through his year's absence in Europe. Moreover, as Sir Hector had observed, his appointment by the Colonial Office would bring him to the notice of this department of the state and could lead to further commissions. Looking at the matter from the perspective of the Colonial Office, they were getting a very good deal for a very small financial outlay. Even if a more experienced English lawyer had been available, he would have demanded a remuneration package considerably greater than the young Scottish advocate was prepared to accept.

Andrew Jameson had already replied to Sir Hector's letter of 25th June, saying that he would come to London in a few days. Sir Hector acknowledged this in a brief note on 29th June in which he now said that the time that they would need to spend together would be three days at most. "You will very quickly learn from me all I have to communicate" he wrote.

He must have left Edinburgh "at once", as Sir Hector had urged in his letter of 28th June, because they were at the Colonial Office by Monday, 4th July. This would have allowed him to look at the draft code and discuss it with Sir Hector over the weekend. They were received at the Colonial Office by George Hope,[25] who introduced them to James Stephen, the Under-Secretary of State. Mr Stephen asked him to consider the Code generally and report back to him within two days, stating the time that he would need for the work and the remuneration he would expect.

Two documents are the source of information on what Andrew Jameson did over the next two days. The first can best be described as an

---

[25] In his letter to Sir Hector Greig of 9th June, Andrew Jameson had written that the Lord Justice Clerk, Lord Hope, had offered to recommend him to his relation, Henry Hope, an Under-Secretary at the Colonial Office. The Hope mentioned in Andrew Jameson's account of his visit to the Colonial Office is stated to be George.

outline in general terms of the background to the task that he had agreed to carry out, the principal areas upon which the report would concentrate and a calculation of both the time that he would need and the associated remuneration. From that he had then been able to draw up a second document, the memorandum that he presented to Mr Stephen on 6th June 1842. The first part consists of a statement of his remit from Lord Stanley.

> To receive & examine the new Criminal Code for Malta with the view of pointing out what you may consider defects, and chiefly in those parts, wherever from its Neapolitan origin there may be too great a departure from the liberal spirit of English Law.
> To assist in drawing up a report upon the general features of the Code, so as to bring the subject in a tangible shape, under Lord Stanley's consideration.

He then quotes part of Sir Hector Greig's letter of 28th June 1842. This may have been because it was the only official document that actually offered him the appointment.

> I am now authorised to say that Lord Stanley has sanctioned your being employed on account of the Government of Malta to make a report on the proposed Criminal Code with the understanding, as we are a poor Govt., that you will come to London, and having seen the nature of the work to be done, that you will arrange with me, as to the remuneration to be paid to you.

The second part is his understanding of what the Colonial Office requires of him and his suggested fee.

> I After having done this to the best of his ability it appears to Mr Jameson that it would be necessary in discharging this duty

1 To examine and consider the Code both in its parts and special provisions, and as a whole in reference to the general principles of Penal Law and Procedure.

2 To look on the one hand to the Roman Law & other foreign systems & codes, from which the proposed Code is chiefly derived – and on the other to the principles of English Law & the spirit of the British Constitution in order to see that the provisions and spirit of the Code should be in unison with constitutional principle – or, at least not in collision with their spirit & also that when there was no such collision the regulations of experienced utility, though of foreign origin should be prescribed.

3 To consider at the same time the local ordinances & other laws and the constitution of local government as bearing upon the whole of the proposed Code.

In accomplishing the proposed task of revision and drawing up a report upon the Code and the work of reading and consideration, as sketched above, it seems to Mr Jameson that a period of not less than three months would be necessary.

II It has appeared however to Sir Hector Greig & Mr Jameson that it will be convenient & perhaps indispensable to communicate with the authorities at Malta upon several points, as to which local information is or may be required, especially with regard to the second part of the Code – being the law of Criminal Procedure – and for that purpose that a period of six months might be allowed for the business but upon the understanding that this prolongation is not to be taken into consideration in fixing the remuneration but is only suggested for convenience.

With regard to the remuneration Mr Jameson felt the greatest difficulty and reluctance in making any estimate. But on giving certain data to Sir Hector Greig it was suggested by him, that it should be £200.

In the absence of any documentation to the contrary, Andrew Jameson's interpretation of Lord Stanley's remit must have been accepted by the Colonial Office. He returned to Edinburgh, where he set to work on his commission without delay. However, before commenting further on this, reference must be made to a letter written to him from London on 12th July by a J. Melville.[26]

There had been no previous correspondence from this man – at least none that has survived – and they cannot have been close acquaintances because Melville began his letter with the formal "My Dear Sir". On the other hand the letter closed with a request from Melville that Andrew send his regards to Sheriff-Substitute Jameson.

> I had the pleasure to get the letter you were kind enough to leave for me at the Bank Office in Bishopsgate Street but I regret much that you did not allow me the opportunity of seeing you when in Town. I rejoice that my bringing you and Sir H. Greig acquainted has had the result you inform me of and I think it may lead eventually to some better and more permanent occupation for you. [Sir Hector Greig] told me he meant to be at Carlsbad for a couple of months before returning to his post so I suppose he is now there.

There follows a long and distressing account of the declining health of his sister, who is in a nursing home in the Pyrenees.

It had always been this author's assumption that Andrew Jameson had met Sir Hector Greig simply as a result of having left his card at the office of the Governor of Malta on his arrival at the island in December 1840. If Mr Melville had been in Malta at that time and had effected an introduction to Sir Hector, one would have assumed that Andrew would have mentioned him in his letters home, which were never short of detail. Yet Andrew must have known him because it was he who first contacted the man when he was in London. He was a

---

[26] It was addressed simply to "Andrew Jameson Jnr Esq, Advocate, Edinburgh" and was delivered on 14th July, another example of the excellence of the postal service at that time.

cousin of his maternal grandfather.[27]

Among his papers of this time is an undated document, obviously composed in great haste and headed "Memo. Sir H. Greig." This suggests that before leaving London, possibly on the very afternoon of the day when the Colonial Office had appointed him to carry out the remit of Lord Stanley, he had a discussion with Sir Hector on those points of the Criminal Code of Malta to which he would be required to pay particular attention. The lack of any structure to the document gives the impression that it was written down – scrawled would be a more accurate term – as the discussion took place. Nevertheless, it makes a valuable contribution towards understanding what was being required of Andrew Jameson.

The larger proportion of the items listed are connected with domestic life, using that term very loosely, such as prostitution, clandestine marriage, concealment of pregnancy, abortion and infanticide. Falsifying of passports and plundering of wrecks are other crimes that he has been asked to address. In addition, Malta, having little in the way of pastureland, there appears to have been corruption in the issuing of licences to allow goats to graze.

There are also occasional references to previous attempts at revising the island's criminal code. Under the heading "Jury Trial" appear the words "If objectionable and whether it could be usefully extended" followed by something (illegible) attributed to "Mr Lewis." This was George (later Sir George) Cornewall Lewis, who, along with John Austin,[28] a lawyer with a high reputation in jurisprudence, served as Royal Commissioners to Malta. They produced a report and Andrew Jameson notes it was dated 30th September 1835. He also refers to a report by Sir John Richardson dated 19th August 1826, and it is a reasonable assumption that he had been advised to consult these documents.

In 1913 John Buchan wrote a life of Andrew Jameson's elder son,

---

[27] v. p. 17 supra.

[28] John Austin (1790–1859). Professor of Jurisprudence at University of London 1825–1835 who served briefly as a Royal Commissioner to Malta in 1835.

Lord Ardwall.[29] In the preface to his book Buchan provides a very brief account of Andrew Jameson's career and comments thus on his contribution to the law of Malta. "He made an excellent job of it, and although eminent jurists like John Austin and Sir George Cornwalle[30] Lewis had tried their hands on it, it is the recension[31] of Andrew Jameson, which is in force today." Chapter Ten of this book gives a detailed account of Andrew Jameson's revision of the Criminal Code of Malta and of the political background of the island from 1800 to 1854.

Almost the first step that Andrew Jameson took once he was back at 20 Abercromby Place was to seek an interview with a Mr Blair, who was a Judge of the Ionian Islands.[32] Since the Ionian Islands, like Malta, had been brought under British protection in 1815 and the existing judicial system revised, it was highly appropriate that Andrew Jameson should seek advice from a senior judicial figure of these islands.[33] He also consulted relevant parts of the Code of Law of the Commonwealth of Massachusetts since several other New England states had drawn on this as the prime source for their own codes.

He found that he needed certain documents on Maltese law and wrote to Sir Hector asking that they be sent to him. Sir Hector, still in London, acknowledged receipt of the letter on 18th July and promised to procure all he wanted:

> but it appears that Sir John Richardson's report is not at the C. O. as it cannot be found and the surmise is that it is lost. Therefore I must get a copy made out and sent from Malta.
> I shall also get the procès verbal[34] of Kirkpatrick's time – any assistance from him will be very useful to you, and

[29] *Andrew Jameson, Lord Ardwall*, William Blackwood and Sons, Edinburgh and London, 1913.
[30] This is a misprint for "Cornewall".
[31] A legal term for "revised version".
[32] One must assume that Mr Blair was home on summer leave from his post and that Andrew Jameson knew who he was and his position.
[33] The Ionian Islands were transferred to Greece in 1864.
[34] Written report.

I apprehend, that the present Code is a very different child from what he intended should be produced.

Sir Hector had not yet managed to leave London because he had been detained by other business "but, right or wrong, I start for Leamington[35] on Wednesday [20th] to consult Dr Jephson, whom I am recommended to see. I am glad that your Brethren think that you have undertaken a creditable job. Remember me most kindly to Kirkpatrick[36]." This assumes that John Kirkpatrick had retired, was now living in or near Edinburgh and that Andrew Jameson knew him.

On 4th August 1842 Andrew Jameson wrote to Sir James Graham, the Home Secretary. Although there is no copy of his letter and we know of it only from a brief acknowledgment of its receipt by the private secretary of Sir James, it seems likely from correspondence later in the month that he had asked for an official letter of appointment. He had also written to Sir Hector Greig on 1st August but Sir Hector had been in Paris[37] and was unable to reply until 13th August, the day of his return. He must have enclosed some document because he wrote "if it is not what you require, pray let me know, and I will write whatever will be of service. I hope you received the Italian copy of the Code. I am going to Leamington to consult Dr Jephson and I shall remain a few days there – so you can send me a line addressed to the Post Office. I trust you will get the Chair[38] and if I can be of any use please command me in any way."

---

[35] This must have been his alternative to Carlsbad in Bohemia that had become one of the most popular spa towns in Europe. The town is now known as Karlovy Vary. The first half of the nineteenth century saw a proliferation of "spa" towns throughout Great Britain and one of them was Leamington, still known today as Leamington Spa. Dr Henry Jephson was a leading exponent of hydrotherapy, the treatment of patients by external and internal application of water.

[36] John Kirkpatrick, when Chief Judge of the Ionian Islands, had served briefly (1831–1832) on a Commission to revise the Criminal Code of Malta.

[37] It is difficult to find out from his correspondence where Sir Hector Greig was around this time. It is just possible that he did go to Carlsbad after 6th July and be back in London by 18th July and that he did leave for Leamington on 20th July before crossing over to Paris from which he returned on 13th August. His letter of 13th August informs Andrew Jameson that he is about to go to Leamington "to consult Dr Jephson" but without reference to any recent previous visit.

[38] v. p. 263 supra.

He replied to Sir Hector with a letter of 16th August, as we know from Sir Hector acknowledging it nine days later. Sir Hector makes rather tetchy comments about Dr Jephson, whom most medical practitioners of the day considered a quack. "My stock of patience is nearly exhausted by Dr Jephson & his medicines & his regimen – as yet without much apparent benefit, but he says that I am getting much better & that he will make a good job of me." He also hoped that his testimonial sent in support of Andrew Jameson's application for the Chair of Law at Glasgow University was what he wanted.

He asked him in future to direct all his inquiries and requests for documents straight to Sir Henry Bouverie "now that you are officially appointed under the Secretary of State's direction" and "you must do so at once as the Malta Mail closes on the 31st via Falmouth." After some comments on adultery[39] being more appropriately dealt with under the Civil than under the Criminal Code and stating that there had been an excellent article in the July edition of the *Edinburgh Review* on how the law should deal with duelling, Sir Hector turned to the timescale that had been suggested: "As to the period of 6 months for the giving in of the report – it is really of no consequence whether you take 6 or 9 – & the delay in getting the necessary papers will make 9 months the shortest period in which it can be done."

Andrew Jameson wrote to Sir Henry on 29th August and fortunately kept a copy letter. After thanking Sir Henry for "the kindness and approbation you have shown to me in the matter" he went on to say that for some weeks he had been working "pretty vigorously at the project and find from the extensive system of revision, which I thought necessary, that it will be a work of some time and considerable labour, however inconsiderable the result may be ultimately." He informed the Governor that he had received from Sir Hector various commentaries and reports but asked that the following papers be sent to him in order that his work could be satisfactorily carried out:

---

[39] An inference from the wording of the letter is that adultery was apparently seen in Malta at that time as a crime committed solely by women.

[1] The report of Sir John Richardson.

[2] The procès verbal of the labours of the Law Commission of which Judge Kirkpatrick was a member.

[3] Mr Lewis's observations on the first project.

[4] A copy of the proposed law on adultery.

[5] A report on any criminal trial of importance including the sentence.

[6] Comments of any progress made on the subject of prison discipline and a copy of the regulations on prisons and penitentiaries if there were any such.

[7] The other parts of the Sicilian Code and also that of Corfu.[40]

His letter to Sir Henry presumably caught the Malta Mail because Sir Henry showed no delay in sending the documents in a box addressed to a George Chambers Esq., No. 22 St Dunstan's Hill, London, for onward delivery to Andrew Jameson.[41] Sir Henry's letter may be of some historical interest and so it is given below in full. It is in a beautiful copperplate hand, prepared by one of his clerical staff for his signature. There is no date other than "September 1842".

I have received your letter of the [blank[42]] and I hope that the documents which you wish to have will be sent to you by the "Great Liverpool". They will be sent in a box addressed to you to the care of [blank] Chambers [blank] London, who will have directions to forward them to you in Scotland.

I was very glad to hear that you had been able and

---

[40] These seven requests were made very much in the words that are shown here but were enclosed within the text of the letter as proper sentences.

[41] Andrew Jameson would have given his address in his letter to Sir Henry, and the author can give no explanation why the papers were sent through an intermediary, unless this was some sort of security.

[42] It is probable that the clerk expected Sir Henry to enter the date himself as well as the missing day of September at the top of the letter together with the Christian name of Mr Chambers and his address in London.

willing to undertake the Revision of the Criminal Code; I am well aware of the extreme difficulty of the task and it is on that account chiefly that I am glad that it is in such able hands and that it may be the means of serving you in your Profession to which it gives me sincere pleasure to find you are restored by the amendment of your health.

You mention that you had seen memoranda of mine upon the Code; I am not aware that I have anything more to trouble you with, excepting my objection to the proposed ordinance on Adultery, which consists in the difficulty which I find giving the Civil Court a Criminal Jurisdiction. I do not see why Adultery should be treated Criminally at all, the Civil penalty appearing to me to be a sufficient check, at least as far as there can be a check by Law, and I am very averse to punishing the woman Criminally, unless the accomplice be punished also in the same manner; neither am I in favour of creating a new Prison by Law, for this crime, where the Imprisonment would be bona fide Imprisonment without any obligation of Religious Penance as intended in the old Law; it will be best in my opinion to leave Adultery out of the code altogether but this I give simply as my individual opinion by no means ex Cathedra. I should have no objection to see Duelling dealt with as suggested in the Edinburgh Review.

You are probably aware that our New Prison is built upon the plan as nearly as possible of the New Model Prison in London. From the nature of the Maltese I am convinced that the Imprisonment may be reduced by Two Thirds at least when the New Prison comes into work for the Maltese would die under a long rigorous confinement where they are locked up at Sunset in separate cells and silence enforced throughout the day. They are very easily kept in order & crime is not frequent, nor of a serious nature generally, premeditated Crime very rare, and all Crime has decreased since I came here nearly one half, in consequence of my Endeavours (which have been successful) to give Employment. The Number of Convicted Prisoners seldom exceeds 100 or 120 for Malta.

You will naturally bear in mind that your labours will have to be translated into Italian here before they can be dealt with in any way & that therefore it is very important that Technical terms which cannot be easily & clearly rendered into that Language should be avoided as much as possible. If you should wish to correspond with Sir Ignatius Bonavita,[43] the Chief Compiler of the Codes, I have no doubt that he will be ready to give you any Explanation, which you may require. I have not spoken to him on the subject, but should you wish to write to him, you had better do so thro' Sir H. Greig in the first instance – in this of course you will be guided by your own judgment. I should fear that such a correspondence might rather embarrass than assist you, as he will naturally be jealous, and you should in your first letter to him state that you had been entrusted by Lord Stanley with the task of examining and reporting upon the Code.

I do not expect to remain here long enough to see the Codes brought into action. I shall probably be relieved early in next Summer.

Sir Henry added the following postscript in his own hand: "Enclosed is the list of books and papers and which will be sent by the Oriental, the prison regulations are those now in force & of course will require to be adapted to the New Prison."

By the late summer of 1842 Andrew Jameson had begun work on the Maltese Criminal Code. This was to bring in some remuneration but in the autumn of that same year there was another development in his professional career that brought with it a further upturn in his fortunes.

---

[43] Sir Ignatius Gavin Bonavita was President of the Court of Appeal at Malta.

CHAPTER NINE

Re-establishment of a Professional Career

Knowing that Andrew Jameson was appointed Sheriff-Substitute of Ayrshire in 1843 has made it possible to interpret the few pieces of correspondence that have survived from the autumn of 1842 to the spring of the following year. This is especially so in the case of a letter written by him to his father on 31st October 1842.

> I thank you for your exertions on my behalf – & hope they may be blessed with success. I hear of no candidates yet likely to be of serious consequence but we will have no doubt a crop tomorrow.
>
> Your letter to Lord Dunfermline[1] is very excellent. I hope the rest are equally so. I was trying to get at the Duke of Buccleugh[2] & Sir Geo Clerk[3] today but could not manage it.[4]
>
> My only prospect is the Lord Advocate's good opinion – and the want of powerful competitors. But this may soon take another aspect.

---

[1] James Abercromby, 1st Baron Dunfermline (1776–1858). MP for Midhurst, 1807–1812, MP for Calne, 1812–1830, MP for Edinburgh, 1832–1839, Speaker of the House of Commons, 1835–1839, created Baron Dunfermline 1839, elected Dean of Faculty of Law, University of Glasgow 1841.

[2] Walter Montagu-Douglas-Scott, 5th Duke of Buccleugh. At the time of Andrew Jameson's candidature for the post of Sheriff-Substitute of Ayrshire, he was Lord Privy Seal.

[3] Sir George Clerk of Pennycuick. 6th Baronet (1787–1867). MP for Edinburghshire, 1811–1832 and 1835–1837, MP for Stamford 1838–1847, MP for Dover 1847–1852. At the time of Andrew Jameson's candidature for the post of Sheriff-Substitute of Ayrshire, he was Financial Secretary to the Treasury.

[4] It is difficult to understand what Andrew Jameson meant when he wrote that he was "trying to get at the Duke of Buccleugh & Sir Geo Clerk today". Were these two senior members of the government in Edinburgh that day?

This letter then deteriorated into note form from which emerges a request that his father ask Robert Haldane, Principal of St Mary's College in the University of St Andrews, to write to Principal Macfarlane of Glasgow University, seek support for him from Robert Whigham, Sheriff of Perthshire, and write to the Lord Advocate.

The immediate assumption is that the content of this letter refers to Andrew Jameson's attempts to secure an appointment as a sheriff-substitute and the reference to "other candidates" would seem to confirm that. At the same time, however, there was a curious activity in progress whereby father and son were seeking approval for them to be united as joint sheriff-substitutes of Fife at Cupar. Thirty or so years later this could never have been contemplated let alone considered by the Scottish legal establishment but in 1842 appointments to public office were still conducted in a manner very different from today. After all, Andrew Jameson (Senior) had been appointed Sheriff-Substitute of Fife at Cupar almost solely on the say of Sir James St Clair, for whose property in and around Dysart his father had acted as factor. By the 1840s this manner of appointment had fallen into desuetude but the legal fraternity remained small and closely knit, all well known to each other, and while an arrangement such as the Jamesons sought might have been regarded as unusual, it was nevertheless given serious consideration.

This we know from correspondence during October 1844 between Andrew and his father by which time Andrew had been Sheriff-Substitute for Ayr for more than a year. The rationale behind the application would have been that his father, although now over seventy years of age and finding it increasingly wearisome to continue in his post, was nevertheless reluctant to demit office. In all probability this was because he had never clambered out of the morass of debt that had burdened him for about thirty years. At the same time his son had gained a high reputation during the few years he had been at the bar but was now without full employment and unwilling, because he believed himself physically incapable, of resuming his practice. Thus the proposal had a certain logic to it. The father would continue for a short time as the senior of the two sheriff-substitutes with his son sharing some of the load and having the benefit of his father's experience at the bar. Gradually the son would assume a greater proportion of the work and eventually succeed his father on the latter's retiral or death. A transcription of the greater part of two letters helps to explain what had been going on. The first was of 12th October 1844:

> I cannot let the week close without telling you a piece of news, which had it occurred eighteen months ago, would have given me so much happiness & probably a different color to my lot.
>
> Mr Monteith[5] informed me that the *obstacle* was out of the way and that he wished to know whether I should like to make the proposed arrangement with you. He said that it required consideration, that your comfort and happiness were very dear to me and I felt the great distance from you, that Cupar was much lighter in Criminal & Bankruptcy business than Ayr and that might be an inducement. He remarked that perhaps Mrs Jameson's friends[6] being near might counterbalance this & requested me to let him know.
>
> This was all said in the streets of Ayr, where he had come with Mrs M. & the girls on his way to Wigtownshire but he said had intended writing. He came to catch a steamer which gave up that very day & compelled them to stay the night. I asked them to dinner but it was late and they declined. Let me hear what you think of this business?

Unfortunately the reply of Andrew Jameson (Senior) has not survived, but his son answered it on 21st October.

> I am not sorry to think, that if you have made up your mind to continue in active exercise of your duties for some time

---

[5] Sheriff of Fife.
[6] His wife's family and friends.

longer & though I still regret that circumstances had not happened differently, yet I believe that it will be found, that all has been by the disposal of an all-wise Providence for the best to us all.

I agree with you, that things are altered, and that our scheme of uniting incomes is in the present state of my obligations not a feasible plan. I will write to the Sheriff, as you mention, and think that the longer he staves off the better. It would be a good thing to keep in view till another time.

The narrative must now return to 1842. In his letter of 31st October Andrew also informed his father that he had been to a coach-making firm and seen two carriages costing £50, one of which might suit but that there were no broughams[7] available at present. Sheriff-Substitute Jameson was now nearing his seventy-fourth year and perhaps was feeling the need of some sort of closed carriage to go about the county on his duties. Moreover, we learn from this letter that he had not been well and his son hopes he will "continue to gain strength." Andrew had been "enjoying the frost. Duddingston has never been so fine and I had a skate lesson from Lord Cockburn[8] yesterday. Today he ran off at ½ past 9! It will be a grand scene tomorrow."

The letter continues with the comment that "I am going on with business as if this was my career – some fine new cases, a very important one from John Macrae." It would appear from this comment that although he was very hopeful of the desired appointment to Ayrshire he was wisely continuing to build up his legal practice. He had also been welcomed back into the social life of Edinburgh and was receiving so many invitations to dine that he had restricted them to two in the week. It must be recalled that he was still unmarried and a wonderful conversationalist, two qualities that made him attractive to so many prominent Edinburgh hostesses.

---

[7] A one-horse closed carriage named after Lord Brougham (1778–1868), Lord Chancellor, 1820–1824.

[8] v. p. 91 supra.

Finally, in this letter that is short but full of unconnected pieces of information, Andrew tells his father about the success he has had in raising contributions in India for a particular church objective. "My letter to India, which two big folks here were so cool about has procured £55 from Bombay & £100 from Calcutta for the Mediterranean Churches. So much for a small scroll in the Parliament House. This is very encouraging & has astonished the Colonial Committee."[9]

On 3rd February 1843 his father wrote about the possibility of an appointment to Ayr. "The appointment of s.substitute there [i.e. Ayr] if you are really offered it, requires serious consideration. You know, my dear Andrew, that I have always had a strong wish that you should continue your profession and amass all the honours of the Scots Bar and which I am vain enough to think you are capable and you know I was sanguine enough to enter no tremulous apprehensions of want of business." He was aware that the health of his son was delicate but wondered if it was not now sufficiently robust to allow him to continue as an advocate. "My ambition has, I confess, suffered a [illegible word] for your preferment as a lawyer and therefore, altho' I now say it most reluctantly, I can assure that my sentiments must coincide with yours on accepting the country life." At a later date Andrew Jameson added these words to the letter: "My dear father consents reluctantly to my leaving the law."

In view of his son's history of health problems over the previous ten years the attitude of Sheriff-Substitute Jameson towards his son's probable appointment was slightly odd. Andrew had certainly survived the last two winters and had even mentioned in a recent letter that he was enjoying the frost. On the other hand he had not found it easy to resume his practice as an advocate because he had both to build up a clientele and to ensure that too great a demand was not put on his larynx. It is possible that his father recognized the abilities of his son and in some way was hoping that he would experience through him some of the distinction in the profession that he himself had failed to achieve. Sheriff-substitutes did not enjoy the salaries that successful

---

[9] i.e. of the Church of Scotland.

advocates could attract and he may have regretted that his son was choosing the same pleasant but modestly remunerated position that he himself held. His son's later career demonstrated that had his health permitted he would have risen high in his profession and in all probability been raised to the bench. However, although Andrew Jameson's health was never again to become of serious concern to him, he was not to know this in 1843 and it may well have been that his career move that year was a positive contribution to his ability to sustain a career in the law.

Towards the end of March he received a draft of his appointment to Ayr from Sheriff Bell. He wrote the following letter to his father on 25th March:

> Mr Bell has just sent me the Draft of my Commission to be extended for signature on Friday next.
>
> He has, however, added a clause in these terms "But the appointment and commission to continue only during my pleasure and regulated by the terms and conditions of the Act 1 & 2 Victoria cap 119, section 3."
>
> [Andrew adds in a note:] I consider this to be proper, as containing the exact legal position of the office of Sheriff-Subst. as it now stands, tho' as far as we are concerned, it is probably little more than a form.
>
> 1. In acknowledging receipt of the Draft I made no remark upon this, as Mr B. is said to be particular in minute matters, and it might do more harm than good – especially as the terms of the Commission cannot affect the General Law. But it might be used against me that I accepted such a Commission.
> 2. The reference to the statute perhaps disarms the condition of its obnoxious quality.

> I will be glad to have your advice. The Exchequer people said it was wrong in his first scroll but I observed it and the Orkney Commission, which was the last.

Whether his father sent any further advice or not is unknown, but Andrew Jameson certainly signed the Commission appointing him Sheriff-Substitute of Ayrshire. After he had made his final appearance as an advocate, two judges took their leave of him[10] while Lord Cockburn congratulated him and asked if there were any skating ponds about Ayr. There was a proposal for a dinner in his honour with the Dean of the Faculty of Advocates or the Solicitor General in the chair, but as he wrote to his father,[11] "I entertain a great reluctance to be feted." Accordingly, he persuaded his friends to drop any arrangements for such an event while at the same time "expressing my great gratification for the intended kindness." He found that in turning down this proposal he had won the approbation of many judges who deplored the practice of retiring dinners as a "kind of vulgarity".

He went over to Glasgow to address the Glasgow Committee of the Mediterranean Churches mission, spent a night at Dalmuir with Mr Ker,[12] whom he had met in Sicily, and went on to Barnhill to visit the Campbells. He was very pleased to receive some advice about Ayr from Sheriff-Substitute Campbell and no doubt even more pleased to see Alexa. Glasgow and Ayr were now connected by rail and it is possible that he later went down to Ayr to look for accommodation.

His next letter to his father is dated 20th April. He had found acceptable accommodation at Charlotte Street in a house near the sheriff court and with a fine view of the sea and the hills of Arran, although he was to find it less attractive in the winter. The main interest in the letter is his account of leaving Edinburgh and his installation as Sheriff-Substitute of Ayrshire. He had a long interview with the Lord Advocate on a Friday morning before taking the train

[10] One was Lord Cunningham but the name of the second is illegible.
[11] The letter is undated but the context suggests it was early April 1843.
[12] v. p. 227 supra.

to Glasgow,[13] the first time he has mentioned taking this form of transport. He spent the weekend with the Campbells and on the Monday met Sheriff Bell along with Andrew Rutherford, the Lord Advocate and Mr Traill, member of parliament for Ayrshire. The four of them then set off for Ayr where on the following morning "the ceremony of installation took place. The Procurators[14] appeared in great numbers and seemed very respectable men. I did not think it right to bandy compliments on the Bench & said nothing. Since then I have been taking several declarations and advising processes. The work is very heavy, I see, and I have a great deal to learn. Too much is expected of me, I fear, but in time I may be able to give satisfaction."

Towards the end of this letter he added: "I fear I will have much to do to complete my Code business and must keep clear of visiting in order to finish it." It should be remembered that throughout the period when he had been seeking a sheriff-substitute position and rebuilding his practice at the Scottish bar in case he failed to secure such an appointment, he had been working on his revision of the Criminal Code of Malta. He now had to carry out his duties as Sheriff-Substitute of Ayrshire and in his first few months this would be strenuous, because, as he himself was aware, he had much to learn. He was determined to find time for his work on the Code and declining to accept invitations to dinner or visit friends was one way of doing it.

From a letter to his father of 2nd May we learn that he was about to go on his first circuit to hear cases at Kilmarnock, Beith and Carrick.[15] This letter also gives an interesting insight into his financial position because his father had written to ask which bank he was using. He told his father: "At present I have no money and therefore no banker. I am

---

[13] The Edinburgh–Glasgow railway line was opened in 1842. It ran north to Falkirk and closely parallel to the canals. There were six stops and the journey took two and a half hours. This was at the beginning of a period of wild speculation in railways, leading Lord Cockburn to declare: "The country is an asylum of railway lunatics." Unwise speculation in railway shares by Andrew Jameson's brother-in-law, George Gray, brought him to the verge of bankruptcy in 1848.

[14] They were the members of the Fraternity of Procurators in Ayr, now the Ayr Faculty of Solicitors, whose Minute Books date back to 1710.

[15] Carrick is the southern part of Ayrshire and Maybole was where the sheriff court was held.

getting, fortunately, some bankrupt examinations to pay my landlady." From this it seems probable that sheriff-substitutes were allowed to carry out some private business and so add to their far from generous remuneration. They were probably paid only half-yearly or yearly and Andrew Jameson was yet to receive any payment for his public duties.

He also tells his father of an unusual case that came before him. "I have had some very nice points already. What think you of a claim at the instance of the father of a bastard against the mother for her share of the aliment. The maternity is acknowledged but also she won't nurse or take any charge of the child. What is the mother's share, is it one half? Does it continue 7 years? Put this to your brethren and let me hear the results."

On 22nd May his father replied but since reaching his seventies his writing had become increasingly difficult to decipher and in this particular case virtually impossible. The same can almost be said of a letter of 3rd June apart from the first paragraph and a section later on. In the first paragraph we learn that Andrew had sent him a copy of the Ayrshire paper that had reported on some trials he has taken. His father complains that it gives "a lazy and meagre account of them." The second legible section reports that Dr Chalmers had given a "very unwise and injudicious speech." Only two weeks previously the long dispute within the Church of Scotland over such matters as the right of a patron to appoint a minister, irrespective of the opinion of the congregation, as contrasted with the right of a congregation to refuse to accept a minister so appointed (the "intrusion" principle contrasted with the "non-intrusion" principle) had been resolved by Chalmers leading the non-intrusionists out of the General Assembly of the Church of Scotland. His father hoped that his son would stand by "our Church as by law established", but on this point he was to be disappointed because Andrew, a former student of Chalmers, became a devoted adherent of the newborn Free Church of Scotland.

In a letter to his father of 25th July 1843 that is mainly concerned with arrangements for a visit to Ayrshire, which never took place, he comments that he had "just received some answers from the Maltese

Judges to my queries. Sir Hector Greig was in London two days and wished to come down & see me about different matters but the new Governor requested him to go out with him. I have been doing a very little at my Code – a Saturday once a fortnight. It will now be absolutely necessary to devote time to it, <u>at all hazards</u>. I will therefore be kept busy all next month."

From this date until January 1844 only three other documents have survived. One is a bill dated 29th September from a Henry Gray [16]of Ayr "for writing draft Report and correct copy of Report on the new Code of Criminal Law for Malta and additional trouble connected therewith." Andrew Jameson had thus kept strictly to his intention to get down to serious work on his Maltese commission. The total came to £22 15s. and since the receipt was dated 13th February 1844 Mr Gray had had to wait for over four months to be paid. This was accounted for by tardy remuneration to Andrew Jameson for his work on the Criminal Code of Malta.

Another document is a letter to his father written on 24th October. Mr Heriot of Ramornie, in whose legal office Andrew had served briefly over the period December 1831 to April 1832, paid him a visit and gave him an invitation to dinner that he was unable to accept. A more prestigious visitor was the Lord Justice General. Andrew was feeling somewhat overworked and complained that "the stress of business has set in here and employs my whole time, without any leisure for reading even a book." On his first arrival in Ayr he had taken exercise by running along the beach before dinner but "this perpetual business" had interfered even with that pursuit. He had, however, managed to visit Barnhill one Saturday "to pay my last visit for the season." It must be assumed that he had, at last, received some salary because he says that he had been able to send £30 to his sister-in-law, Marion Jameson, who, for health reasons, had come to live in England. This was a sum that his brother John had "sent me two years ago in case I

---

[16] Henry Gray (1818–1876) was at this time a clerk in the office of the Sheriff-Clerk of Ayrshire. He rose to become Sheriff-Clerk Depute, Dean of Guild and agent of the Ayr branch of the Commercial Bank of Scotland.

should have gone abroad. It was fortunate that it was to the fore as her money had gone."[17]

The third document is from Lord Cunningham, one of the two judges who had taken leave of him when he left the bar. Somehow, Andrew Jameson had in his possession papers that had belonged to a Dr Bell, and he had sent them to Lord Cunningham thinking he might be interested in their contents. The judge returned them with the following comment: "You are right to preserve them carefully as they afford proof of the skill and science of Mr Bell, who seemed to have early anticipated the mode of treating sprains & local injuries to limbs, by the Douche Bath, which has latterly been almost universally adopted both in this country & on the continent." Could this possibly have been the renowned Edinburgh surgeon, Sir Charles Bell, whom Andrew had met on board the *Leeds*, when he sailed in her to Bordeaux in 1833?[18] Sir Charles had died in 1842 and perhaps his papers had recently been sold or otherwise distributed after his death.

Andrew was the guest of the Campbells at Barnhill at New Year and enjoyed a party given there, as he told his father in a letter of 3rd January 1844. He had heard from John "that the Free Church has collected £1,700 in Bombay and that they have effected the separation without any disagreeable feeling. Marion writes that he is not so well but he does not complain himself." That within but a few months of the establishment of the Free Church of Scotland it is little short of astounding that a similar "disruption" had taken place so successfully in Bombay, when communications with the home country were still dependent on sea transport.[19]

That letter was addressed to his father at Edinburgh, who was using

---

[17] There is virtually no documentation that survives about the married life of John and Marion Jameson after they reached Bombay in the early months of 1840. It appears that the climate did not suit her and that she returned to live with friends or relations in England. She may have intended to return to India but her husband died in 1847. v. pp. 218–220 supra.

[18] v. p. 153 supra.

[19] The Rev. Dr Henry Sefton of the University of Aberdeen explained that this "disruption" took place so swiftly because almost all the Church of Scotland missionaries in India at this time were strong supporters of Dr Chalmers and followed him into the Free Church of Scotland.

Neil Campbell's house, 33 Dublin Street, so that he could attend what Andrew refers to as "proceedings". He wrote to him again three days later. His father must have sent him a report on these "proceedings" and it seems likely that it was a committee or gathering of sheriff-substitutes. Things had not gone well, and there was even a motion to dissolve the committee. It will be recalled[20] that it was Sheriff-Substitute Jameson who had been the leading figure among the Scottish sheriff-substitutes in their fifteen-year struggle to obtain an increase in their remuneration so that their salaries represented the degree of their responsibilities. In 1829 the sheriffs held their first joint meeting and these continued until the reorganization of sheriffdoms in 1974.[21] It seems probable that some similar organization existed for sheriff-substitutes but, from what Andrew Jameson (Senior) must have reported to his son, it was poorly supported and therefore ineffectual. His son pointed out that the meeting had been badly arranged and that "on such occasions it should be the first consideration to have the leading substitutes present, who may keep the rest right." He suggested an annual meeting in either spring or autumn "fixed for a certain day, which every person would know." This letter of 6th January 1844 also contains two pieces of information. His father now owns and drives a brougham[22] and that "I have just received a letter from Mr Bell, expressed very cordially and mentioning that he was glad I had not accepted the West Indies appointment." There is no documentation to show if Andrew Jameson had applied for a post there but an unsolicited offer had been made by the Colonial Office, who had remembered the young advocate on his visit with Sir Hector Greig the previous summer.

He gradually became more attuned to the work of a sheriff-substitute but, as he wrote to his father on the 6th February, "I have seen little more of the people here – being so continually occupied

---

[20] v. pp. 21 & 27–28 supra.

[21] v. Nicholson, G., (1991 revised 2000) *The Sheriffs of Scotland 1829 to the Present Day.* This was privately published but copies may be available in the Signet Library, Edinburgh. The author obtained a copy from Sheriff Principal Nicholson, who kindly allowed him to photocopy it before returning it.

[22] v. p. 284 supra.

usually all day in the Court House and all evenings at avizandums.[23] It is a little heavy for me and I feel the solitude & want of exercise and am not so strong as when I came here." This may have been associated with toothache, and his description of a visit at the end of January to a dentist in Glasgow provides a vivid picture of the state of oral medicine at that time. "The tooth broke twice and had to be forced out with a hammer and punch, the most dreadful operation I ever had to encounter. My cheekbone is still sore with the blows. The Dentist said that my teeth were good but spoiled from having got too much mercury when I was an infant: so much for old Dr Grace I suppose."

He was now considerably less enamoured of his lodgings than he had been when he had first taken them. They were "very cold and exposed to the tremendous blasts of winds we get here. If it were not for that Dunfermline Debt, I would look out for a house but I suppose I must wait a little." Here, again, we come across a reference to some financial transaction for which there is no supporting explanatory information.[24]

At the beginning of February 1844 he was hearing cases at Beith, a town in the Cunninghame district, or bailerie, of his sheriffdom near the border of Renfrewshire, of which county Mr Campbell was the sheriff-substitute. There he stayed as guest of an antiquarian, William Dobie, who had written a now totally forgotten book on Lady Crauford of Kilbirnie.[25] Mr Dobie had invited a few local notables to meet the new sheriff-substitute and Mr Campbell was among them. Andrew Jameson must have used the occasion to obtain the permission of Mr Campbell to write the following letter to his father on 15th February:

---

[23] A private consideration of a case by a sheriff before giving judgment.

[24] It is possible, but this is mere conjecture, that there was in Dunfermline some financial house that provided loans to persons of probity and sound background, such as a sheriff-substitute. The Dunfermline Building Society was not founded until 1869 but it may have had origins going back for a few decades before that.

[25] A village about 2 miles west of Beith.

My dear Father,

It was with much pleasure I received your last letter. I will attend to your advise [sic]. The want of exercise I complain of is from want of time, the Court business of one kind & another takes up such long sittings.

I have at present to make a communication to you, which I know will interest you on many accounts. You are aware, I believe, that for several years, I have cherished an attachment to Miss Lexy Campbell, the youngest daughter of your esteemed friend. During my long adversity & sickness I thought it a duty to conceal & restrain these feelings, as I wished to involve no-one – least of all one so dear to me – in my calamity. When it pleased God to restore my health, restraint was no longer a duty and since I came here especially, I have made to her *by my conduct* a plain avowal of my affection and intentions. For some considerable time there has been an entire understanding & reciprocation of regard between us, but it was not until very lately that she expressed a wish that her *father's & your* approbation should be asked before any final arrangement was come to. I did so to Mr Campbell last July, when he expressed his entire consent in a very gratifying manner and I have little doubt that *you*, my dear father, will have as little difficulty. Although this was a proper thing in the circumstances of my frequent visits to Paisley, yet it has been agreed, that the matter should be kept perfectly quiet in the meantime. This is the more necessary, that I am not in a situation to take up house at present, and Lexy's *filial* consideration requires some interval for taking a final leave of her father's house. I hope however, that our union will not be *long* deferred, as having now been a lover for five years I am naturally anxious to conclude that character & take up a more domestic one and instead of my solitary and friendless state, a more comfortable relation. I find the constant pressure of business without any society very heavy upon me and know that my comfort and health would be greatly benefited by the change.

I am sure this intelligence will not be disagreeable to you. It will connect by a closer tie two early companions and attached friends – and although I beg you not to mention the matter to *any one* as it would be sure to get circulated and give annoyance to the young lady, who is rather too sensitive on such things from her extreme modesty of character, it may not be amiss for you to write to Mr Campbell, *if you think proper*. I don't intend to communicate this to Sophia or Melville *just yet* on that account – unless you think I should.

He concludes this communication with some information about his work on the Criminal Code of Malta.

I received a few days since the enclosed letter from the Malta Government. *Please return it safe* unless you would first send it to Melville & Sophia. You see they have given expenses but otherwise stuck to the original estimate. No other notice has been taken as to my statement of the labor [sic] having so far exceeded the rough calculation at the outset. I am very thankful it has been so well received. I will send you the extract from Lord Stanley's despatch. What answer should I give to Sir Hector Greig? [The letter ends abruptly here at the bottom of the page and it is possible that there is a further page that is missing.]

From his next letter (21st February) it is clear that his father had written to Sheriff-Substitute Campbell but had also made the assumption, despite what his son had said in his letter, that the wedding would soon take place. In searching for their first house, Andrew was experiencing the same problems as young people today. "They are dear & few and such as I like, either too small or too large. I have a little place in my eye but it would not give much room for one's friends." He enclosed with this letter, to be returned, a "copy of extract from Lord Stanley's dispatch to the Colonial Government. It is a very statesmanlike production."

In Ayrshire, the Weights and Measures Act of 1824,[26] establishing the imperial weights and measures as standard throughout the country, had fallen into abeyance or may even have been ignored from the outset. This had resulted in many complaints being brought to the sheriff court about suppliers giving short measure and Andrew Jameson found that despite the requirement in the Act, no inspectors had been appointed. From two letters to his father (29th February and 14th March 1844) we learn that he had asked his father to let him know the system operative in Fife and had found it highly appropriate for introduction to Ayrshire. He then called a meeting of the local justices and proceeded to appoint inspectors.

In the second of these letters he also told his father that he had "taken a small house at £42 for 3 years, having unfortunately been unable to get any other. I regret this very much as it will leave me without as much bedroom accommodation for my friends, which I would have wished. I got an estimate of my furniture. It amounts to £330 exclusive of grates, lamps, bed clothes, plate and crockery", an amount that astounded him.

He was continuing to find the duties of a sheriff-substitute onerous. He was working up to fourteen hours each day and "obliged to read my papers en route in the chaises & railway compartments. In fact, there is for 10 months in the year too much business for one sheriff-substitute." He would, therefore, have had little time for family correspondence but this would not have been understood by his niece, Euphemia Gray, who rebuked him delightfully for not having acknowledged an earlier letter of hers. Her first letter of 9th February 1844 reads as follows:

---

[26] 5 Geo IV c. 74.

Avon Bank 9th February

My dearest Uncle Andrew,

The other evening I was sitting by Miss Ainsworth talking about Dr D'Aubigné's[27] history of the Reformation. I mentioned you knew him and Miss Ainsworth said Oh! Is that the writer who used to write you such nice letters from the continent. You should write to him and get him to resume his instructive correspondences and so after writing a long letter to George at Charter House I have about twenty minutes before the bell rings to write to you. I have not heard from you for long before I left home and I think it is rather too bad of you considering I am here alone at school and that a letter is so acceptable and such any easy thing for you to do but on the other hand you have an immense deal of business but I hope you will write me soon. I came here about three weeks ago and I am now fairly settled. We have a great deal to do much more than when I was here before. The garden is very much improved and the school regulations as well but I think we have too much to do but the Miss Ainsworths do everything to make you happy but I don't think the girls are half such as nice as when I was here before and I only particularly like the Parkers whom you know I was staying with in the holidays. Have you seen any of the Campbells lately and how is *dear* Miss Lexie and Neil. I suppose they are all quite well and Neil in Edinburgh. I had a letter from Lizzie Cockburn[28] the other day. She says that both her sister and her Mama are very unwell but I suppose you are now quite out of Edinburgh. How is your ankle? So much for seeing how far you can jump but seriously I hope it is better. I hope if you come again to

[27] Jean Henri Merle d'Aubigné (1794–1872), Swiss protestant divine and historian.
[28] She was a daughter of the judge Lord Cockburn and a particular friend of Effie. They were discouraged at school from talking in their Scottish accent and using Scottish words.

London about the Malta business that you will put down in your remembrance that I would like very much to see you. I think the bell is just going to ring so adieu and with wishes of soon hearing from you

believe me your most affect. niece Effie Gray

Her next letter (of which the final page is missing) runs thus:

Avonbank March 26th

My dearest Uncle Andrew

You really do not deserve to be written to for not having answered my last letter when you know how little time I have. I have not even written yet to Uncle Melville and Aunt Jessie and I told Miss Ainsworth that I thought you very ungrateful and that you were going to be married upon which she did not comfort me at all by hoping you would write to me but said "If he is going to be married you would not expect to hear at all." You cannot think, my dear uncle, how glad I was to hear you were going to follow the good example of your brothers as Uncle Melville says in his letter of yesterday. I always thought it would happen though you declared it was all nonsense. I am sure Grandpapa is delighted at the thought of it as he is so fond of both the Campbells and Neil. I do not think he knows Miss Lexie does he? As I do not know the young lady I do not like to send any message to her but I am sure I will like her very much for your sake, my dear uncle, and she must be amiable (of course you think her perfect) as I know you are very particular. The reason, however, of my writing to you at present is that Miss Ainsworth and a Lancashire[29] family

---

[29] The author William Harrison Ainsworth (1805–1882) came from a Lancashire family. Is it possible that there was any family connection between him and Miss Ainsworth of Avonbank School?

are going into Scotland in summer and this gentleman and
lady wish to leave their family either at Largs or Rothesay,
while they and the Miss Ainsworths go and see the sights
round about and Miss Ainsworth would be much obliged if
you would give me ...

One can but guess the circumstances in which he damaged his ankle but
it was possibly during some merriment over New Year, which he had
celebrated at Barnhill. We cannot know what way he could oblige Miss
Ainsworth but perhaps it was with a recommendation of somewhere to
stay when her party came to Ayrshire. That his niece signed as "Effie"
and neither "Phemy" nor "Euphemia" is interesting. It has always been
assumed that this diminutive was preferred by John Ruskin, and it is
possible that he had already suggested the change during her short visits
to his family home.

Towards the end of May Andrew moved into his house but
occupied only the upper floor, while his landlord made arrangements
for a tradesman to deal with some dampness in the walls downstairs.
Sophia came through to Ayr and gave him "some very handsome
plated articles". His father authorised him to spend £14 as a wedding
gift and he bought something from the local jeweller. Thanking his
father, he wrote that "this kind mark of your interest in our happiness
and the elegance of the ornament will be still more prized for the sake
of the affectionate Giver. I have also to thank you for your kind wishes
for our welfare. The more I see of my bride, the more I admire the
valuable & excellent qualities of her character. I have long felt both in
health & spirits the want of a companion and I am sure I have every
reason to be thankful that I have been so fortunate as to secure one so
gentle, well tempered, affectionate & well principled as she is and that
she should be the daughter of your old friend & the sister of mine is
also a pleasing coincidence."[30]

He wrote two letters to his father on 27th June. The first was from
his courthouse and told his father that he need not worry about any

[30] Letters to his father, 16th and 23rd May 1844.

stewardship duties at his wedding and that there would "only be some dozen toasts in all – proposed by the Elite of the Literary and Oratorial Gentlemen present." He went on to say that he was sorry that "my marriage day does not secure Melville. *Try* & get him to come. Mr Campbell is quite disappointed."

It seems probable that on reaching home, which we learn for the first time was 20 Abercromby Place, that he found a letter waiting for him with news of the death in Dundee of his cousin Duncan Ogilvie. This was a brother of the John Ogilvie with whom he had shared the house at Newington, Edinburgh, in the early months of 1831. The deceased must have been staying at the Miss Rutherfords, where Andrew lodged for a few days prior to leaving for Spain on 1st October 1840, although Ogilvie was not mentioned in the correspondence then. Andrew wrote: "I will never forget his great kindness to myself when so helpless in London on my way to Spain & I little thought he should have been the first of the two to be summoned away for ever." He was unable to attend the funeral in Dundee.

He had also heard from Sir Hector Greig, who bemoaned the delay of the Colonial Office in making any response to Andrew's work on the Criminal Code of Malta and hoped that no English lawyer would be appointed to write the official code for Sir Hector "is sure it will be mangled in this case as they don't know the Civil Law."

Despite the claims on his time Andrew Jameson never forgot his duty to his church. The final paragraph of this letter was as follows: "I had the honor of addressing another assembly of the fair sex last Wednesday as to sending out clergymen to the Scottish people in foreign states."

On 7th July his father wrote that Melville's wife, Jessie, was having a very difficult confinement and for that reason Melville felt that he could not leave her to attend his wedding. Four days later Patrick Stirling wrote a long and verbose letter that can be summed up as congratulations on his forthcoming marriage and an invitation to stay with him and his wife at Dunblane either at the start or the end of the honeymoon that he assumed, correctly, would be in the Highlands.

It is from a letter of 15th July 1844 to Andrew Jameson (Senior) that we first hear that the marriage ceremony was to take place on 9th August. The final page is missing but the context shows that it is from Sheriff-Substitute Campbell. It is far from easy to decipher but fortunately there is clarity at the point where there is a reference to Andrew's health.

> I dare say he has not asked you & may be not written to you but he has been very recently plagued with sore throats & the regimen[31] he has been put upon has made him very weak – so that he has had to confine himself to bed. It will, therefore, I am sure, be extremely agreeable to him if you, or if you can't, that Mrs Gray or Mr Melville should come to see him.
>
> This ailment has no connection with his former throat complaint, but as I mentioned is only the effect of the usual painful & annoying ailment produced by cold or [next two words are illegible].
>
> We shall be delighted to see Mrs Gray or Mr Melville here. Lexy is with me, having come up from Barnhill this morning and found a letter from Mr Andrew, who is now getting [illegible word] and recovering.

Possibly Andrew did write to his father or his father may have written to him following receipt of Sheriff-Substitute Campbell's letter. By 30th July Andrew had come to Barnhill from where he wrote to his father.

> I came here on Tuesday last in the fond hope that a few days may complete my recovery. I became, however, very sick and continued very poorly till Saturday, when I called in Dr Buchanan, who administered a powerful emetic, which did great execution & since then I have been quit of the vomiting. He has also given me some alternative medicine but gives me no hopes of a very speedy recovery.
>
> I am dreadfully weak & quite low. I have lost a great deal of flesh and my appetite & digestion are still very weak. On

---

[31] "A prescribed combination of diet, exercise, drugs etc." (*Chambers Dictionary*).

Sunday, Dr Buchanan, after examining me completely, said that I must make up my mind to put off the marriage for at least a month. I requested him to try a few days longer. He came up this morning and though he thinks I have got the turn, or at least am better, he remains decidedly of the opinion, that I must study health for the next three or four weeks & go to some watering place. He told the Ladies all this and accordingly the wedding is now put off sine die.[32]

This is very unfortunate and I believe it is the best course, which can be followed and that it would be quite improper for me to attempt going through the ceremony in my present state. It is the will of God to which we must bow with quiet and cheerful submission, trusting that he will mercifully turn all to good in the end.

You will, we all hope, come as you intended at the end of the week. I remain here until Monday or Tuesday next and I hope we will see you here on Friday or Saturday.

Neil Campbell is to go down to Ayr tomorrow & I have requested the Sheriff to grant him a commission & he has agreed in the most obliging manner to stay there as long as necessary. The Sheriff is at Leamington[33] upon the same mission as that intended for me & I feel some awkwardness in leaving such a County to go any distance. However, if Neil's commission arrives I will feel little scruple about going.

The Doctor here agrees with the man at Ayr but considers the attack of dyspepsia much more serious. He strongly recommends me to go off to Harrogate next week and we will talk of this when you come.

I do not know if I will go to Ayr at all, but if not the house will be ready for you and a good dinner on Monday for the festival party.

---

[32] From the Latin "without day" i.e. indefinitely.

[33] Obviously consulting Dr Jephson. That there was such swift acceptance by the Sheriff to agree to appointing Neil Campbell as a temporary replacement for Andrew Jameson is yet another example of the speed of postal delivery at that time.

The rest of the letter is of no interest except that as a postscript he mentions that a "Frederick Heriot is to be my best man. I have written to him and Sophia." This name has never cropped up in correspondence before and consequently nothing is known about him or why he was invited to be best man.

The "festival party" consisted of Euphemia Gray, two friends of hers, her mother and Neil Campbell. Andrew Jameson (Senior) wrote from Ayr, where he must have been staying in his son's house, to Andrew at Barnhill on 5th August. "We reached Paisley in good time for the Ayr train but were disappointed in not finding the Young Ladies from Edinburgh. There was a consultation as to the time of attacking[34] your good dinner. I voted for waiting the arrival of the next train and carried my motion without opposition & at ½ past 6 we had the pleasure of being joined by Femy and her two companions, Mr Neil and Mrs Gray[35] having gone to meet and accompany them." The rest of the letter is extremely difficult to decipher, but all that needs to be said is that the party arranged to visit Culzean Castle and that Andrew's father made some comments about the Ayr house, the main one being that there was "a deficiency of light in the dressing room and my opinion is that the Gas in such a room should be rather brilliant than otherwise."

On 8th August Andrew left Barnhill very early to go down to Ayr to pack what he needed for Harrogate and then go on to Edinburgh, where he made arrangements to leave by train for Carlisle on the following day, all seats on the Newcastle train having been already taken. He wrote a brief note to his father, saying that he expected to return on either the 3rd or 10th September. After a night at Carlisle he had to travel across country to Newcastle and then south to York, a journey occupying two more days before he reached Harrogate. He spent time sightseeing in both towns. "The magnificent[36] open streets and public

[34] From what follows it appears that Andrew had expected to be of the party and had arranged for them to have a meal. This they must have taken because in one of the less indecipherable parts of this long letter there is a comment that the "cook did not complain", presumably of their turning up late.
[35] The formality of referring to his daughter by her married name in a letter to his son, her brother, was surely a fashion that by that time was going out of date.
[36] Sadly, some of these streets have not survived the depredations of the 1960s.

buildings of Newcastle quite astonished me", he wrote to his father on 12th August from the Swan Hotel, Harrogate,[37] where he had arrived the previous evening.

He was less complimentary about his fellow guests, who were "not much to my liking, mostly ill-educated English. I have found a Mr Sanderson from Dundee, who has more head than most of them." To his regret a Mr Kennedy, described as "the Ayr banker", had left that morning but he had also made the acquaintance of an English clergyman, "a relation of Mr Charles Orr in Edinburgh." Later in the week a Mr and Mrs Bennet arrived at the Swan from Ireland, and in a letter to his father of 20th August he explains the Orr connection: "Mrs B. is a sister of Mr Charles Orr & cousin of Lexy's mother."

At about the same time he received a letter[38] from Sheriff Bell, who, along with his brother, was at Leamington consulting Dr Jephson. He had already been there for a month but "I feel much *in statu quo*[39] – or rather retrograding. My interieur [sic] as uneasy as ever, my strength decreasing – and, as to appetite for food, I have lost all remembrance of the sensation: and were it not on Dr Darwin's[40] aphorism *"That you must either Eat or be Eaten*, I believe I should give up the practice altogether. Still, I am assured by the *great Doctor* here – and those who have faith in him – that matters are going on well and I endeavour to hope the best."

Sheriff Bell then turned to Andrew Jameson's duties as Sheriff-Substitute of Ayrshire, having first hoped that Andrew would be well enough to attend a meeting at Ayr on 17th September. Andrew had written to him about the heavy demands that the work was making on his time and that the appointment of a second sheriff-substitute was necessary. Sheriff Bell agreed: "I think that the labours of the Sh. Substitute have now grown to such excess, that it is impossible for any man to discharge them with due advantage to the public without such a risque to his own

---

[37] The Swan, now renamed The Old Swan, remains one of the more prestigious hotels in Harrogate.

[38] This letter (19th August 1844) was written in the most beautiful copperplate script. If Andrew Jameson and his father had possessed similar skill with their pens the task of this author would have been reduced by several months.

[39] i.e. as he was before treatment began.

[40] Almost certainly Dr Erasmus Darwin (1731–1802), grandfather of Charles Darwin.

health and life, as it is unjust to impose. Besides, Ayrshire is now the only one of the large Counties, which has not more than a single Subst. and yet (next to Edinburgh and Lanark) it is, I believe, the most laborious of any. We will talk about this at our meeting."

Whatever the effects of Dr Jephson's treatment of the Bell brothers, the sulphurous waters of the Pump Room in Harrogate wrought an almost immediate recovery for Andrew Jameson. By 26th August he was back at Barnhill "quite a different man from the time I saw you last", as he wrote to his father on that day. So well was he, the wedding had now been arranged to take place on Tuesday, 3rd September and he expected to see Mr and Mrs Gray, Melville, Phemy and George (Gray) at Barnhill by noon on that day. He suggested that his father might come to "join me [at Ayr] on Saturday or Monday & we come up together." The only departure from the original plans for the wedding was that "I will lose F. Heriot's assistance by the change of days."

There is no account of the marriage other than this briefest of notes in the Almanack, which his father continued to keep: "1st September. Met Alr[41] and his wife & A at Paisley and arrived at Ayr same day. 3rd September. Barnhill at A's marriage with Miss L. Campbell." No information is available about who were present. The short honeymoon was spent somewhere in the Highlands, and by 9th September the couple were at Cupar. There are entries in the Almanack to show that Andrew and Lexy went next day to St Andrews and then on to Dundee, where his father joined them. Queen Victoria visited Dundee on 11th September and was no doubt seen by them. In the afternoon Andrew and Lexy left for Edinburgh and were in their home at Ayr by 12th September. They had been met at Paisley by Mr Campbell and "Bessie & Miss Jane Orr had come the day before so we had a happy meeting. Lexy was delighted with the house as well as her companions. They think soon to return." Bessie was an elder sister, married to Walter Mackenzie, a Glasgow accountant, and Miss Orr, her cousin.[42]

One of the first letters of congratulation that he received was from

[41] Alexander Campbell.
[42] v. p. 304 supra.

Professor Blackie. Regrettably the second page is missing but what remains is worth quoting in its entirety for the beauty and extravagance of its language.

> All hail! All hail! All hail! *Jacta est alea!*[43] You have passed the Rubicon, you have entered the Sea of Matrimony! Three cheers! Hip! Hip! Hurrah! "Tis a perilous [illegible word] for many – and [illegible word] you a most graceless scamp such as someone that I could name. I should take the liberty of giving you a short prophetic discourse on the duties and dangers of your new career but knowing, as I do, how much better calculated you are than myself for making a wife happy and a family exemplary, I hold my tongue. I hope this note will find you in Ayr, as lawyers cannot afford to have long honeymoons. Mine lasted three months but I was idle: if you get three weeks with your hard law fagging, and your troublesome conscience, you may count yourself very happy.
>
> I am here (Bridge of Allan) with my wife, who is drinking the waters and feeling sensibly better. The fair sex, remember, is also the frail sex. My wife says I hurt her the first month of our marriage by making her take too long walks that she has never recovered since! Take an example "Let your moderation be known to all men."[44] Women should not be spoiled and set on satin shoes – as is so much the case in our times of false refinement – but it is a duty where they are concerned as it is as grace in other matters in all things to use gentleness.
>
> Praying for ...

---

[43] The Romans were inveterate gamblers and *alea* was a dice. The translation is therefore "The die has been cast". The immediate reference to the River Rubicon is occasioned by the belief that that these three words were spoken by Julius Caesar, when he ordered his troops to cross the Rubicon, a decision, which once taken, could not be reversed.

[44] Epistle to the Philippians, Chapter Four, verse 5.

Another letter of congratulation came from a P. Paton of Lasswade that simultaneously acknowledged receipt of an order on the Bank of Scotland for six pounds in payment for two water colours, one of Naples and the other of Clitumnia[45] (an ancient fountain from Roman times near Spello in Umbria).

In October he attended a meeting of the General Prison Board in Edinburgh, where he met Sheriff Bell. He wrote to his father that: "Mr Bell is to speak to the Lord Advocate as soon as he returns to Edinburgh on the subject of a new sheriff. There will be a power of opposition from the Ayr Bar." This letter also reveals the financial position he was in and records his pleasure at the domestic bliss that now blesses his life.

> I am glad you are going to Mr Macdonald's. Do you think you could manage to take any part of the debt – say £50 – just now upon you, making me still liable in repayment to you at more leisure. I would try & send other £50 before the New Year. I have had about £150 to pay I never thought of in my estimation but £45 to the Widows' Fund is dreadful & what I never dreamt off [sic].
>
> Lexy and I are getting on famously but I find the constant uninterrupted pressure of business spoils all enjoyment & society except at meals & on Sunday.

His next letter to his father (6th November 1844) continues with the arrangements to repay Mr Macdonald. The first reference to this man came in the letter quoted immediately above and there had been no previous information about who he was or his position in life. A few years later, when George Gray was in serious financial difficulties, there were many references to a Mr Burns, who managed to guide him towards a restoration of his solvency, and it was only by chance that a letter revealed that he was the manager, or agent as the post was then termed, of the Central Bank in Perth. Was Mr Macdonald a bank agent

---

[45] It is mentioned in correspondence by both Plutarch and Pliny the Younger.

or just an acquaintance of Andrew Jameson (Senior)? Whoever he was, Andrew Jameson was anxious for a swift settlement of the debt due to Mr Macdonald.[46]

> I mean to write to Mr Macdonald immediately apologising for delay and requesting him to let me know the state of the debt, preparatory to my sending an instalment. You kindly spoke of trying to assist me in reducing the debt by a payment for my behoof & I hope it may be convenient for you to do it. Write me whether you can or not. I will be ready to grant my acknowledgement for the amount of your advance, for although I did not consent to the 2nd loan, yet I consider it my debt but I think, considering all circumstances it would be right to make an exertion & have it altogether repaid *at once*. If you agreed to this I would endeavour to raise £150, if you could take the remainder for you. At the same time I have no wish to put you to any inconvenience.

He wrote to his father on the last day of November commiserating on the death of another of Sophia's children, their namesake. He was the sixth of seven Gray children to die in succession before reaching their seventh year and so continued the catalogue of sadness that had begun in the summer of 1841.[47] Right at the end of this letter he tells his father that he has heard nothing from Sheriff Bell about the appointment of a second sheriff-substitute for the county and that "I sent £165 to Mr Macdonald, which leaves me in debt here of £150." From this brief statement it appears that he had raised a loan of £150, presumably in Ayr, so that he would be relieved of the debt owed to Mr Macdonald. He was still in debt but the debt was not one with which, as far as can be judged, his father was involved.

He arranged to be free from business from 24th to 31st December 1844. He and Alexa contemplated visits to both Perth and Cupar but

---

[46] See Appendix A at the end of this chapter.
[47] v. p. 242 supra.

considered that this would be too great a strain on Alexa, who was now pregnant. They decided to go to Edinburgh, where he would leave his wife at Newington with her sister, Margaret, wife of the Rev. Dr James Begg, while he himself would make a quick visit to Perth or Cupar.

The new year saw the first visit of his father to stay with the couple in Ayr. Later that same month Lord Justice Clerk Hope was in the west of Scotland with some other members of the Court of Session, and he and his wife hosted a dinner at which Andrew and Alexa were among the guests. At the end of January Euphemia Gray (now in her seventeenth year) came to stay for a few days, and apparently she made a great hit with their Ayr acquaintances because, as Andrew wrote to his father on 4th February 1845, "Phemy is well & is *perhaps* too much out. The Ayr people seem to have a great liking for her." He had been unable to accompany her on walks because of an injury to his foot.

It will be recalled that, in the previous August, Sheriff Bell had written to Andrew Jameson agreeing that one sheriff-substitute was insufficient for a county as large as Ayrshire. We learn from a letter written in confidence to his father on 25th March 1845 that he had heard from one of the Ayrshire members of parliament that the Lord Advocate had recommended to the Home Office the appointment of a second sheriff-substitute, who would be based at Kilmarnock. It was still confidential because neither Sheriff Bell nor he himself had received any confirmation of this decision. The Procurators in Ayr, however, had also heard of the proposal and were most unhappy about it. "A committee of them desired a conference with me, which passed off pleasantly enough. I have since heard that they are going to memorialise Government against the appointment and that if made, it should be at Ayr. They requested to know what my views were on the subject. I said that I was clearly of opinion that an additional Sheriff-Sub was required – but that I should not interpose as to where he should be placed unless my opinion was asked by the Govt." It must be surmised that the Procurators were considering their own convenience before that of their sheriff-substitute and the people of the county around

Kilmarnock, a growing industrial and commercial centre.

This particular letter also makes reference to the committee of sheriff-substitutes of which his father had been a founder member. In January 1844 Andrew had written that the committee was poorly organized and on that account ineffectual. To remedy this he had suggested an annual meeting in either spring or autumn "fixed for a certain day."[48] He was able to write now that "I am very happy to hear that your active & energetic exertions have been already so far crowned with success. We are much indebted to you for watching our interests & the other matter shews the indispensable necessity of keeping a vigilant eye over public measures affecting us – and that the [illegible word] & Committee should be a *standing precaution*. I still think that we should have a general meeting of the body once a year to consult about our common interests – or at least a meeting of Committee fixed some time in the vacation, which should be open to the general body to attend." His father, now 74, was thus still very active in representing his professional colleagues, a service he had provided for almost forty years.

Andrew's father paid him and Lexy a short visit at the end of April, and in a letter to him of 2nd May Lexy said how much she had enjoyed his visit and that she had heard from a Mrs Boswell that Euphemia Gray had written to her daughter to say that the latest (eleventh) child of her parents had been named Alice.[49] Lexy also mentions that her husband's foot injury was continuing to improve. It did not prevent him from making a weekend visit to the Grays at Perth in the middle of the month but he regretted not being able to see either Melville who had gone to London or his father. There appeared to have been no further progress in the matter of a second sheriff-substitute and, as he told his father, "The Lord Advocate has been a week in Edinburgh & is again off to Parliament, without vouchsafing a word to Mr Bell – with which he has much reason to be annoyed." We also learn from

---

[48] v. p. 292 supra.

[49] Alice Gray (1845–1882), later Mrs Stibbart, became a great beauty and was painted by her brother-in-law, John Millais.

this letter that Marion Jameson, wife and soon to be widow of John Jameson, was at this time living at Epsom[50] and it was hoped that Melville would find time to pay her a visit.

On 4th July Andrew Jameson was in court at Kilmarnock and instead of going home that night came down to Dumfries House,[51] where he spent the night as a guest of the Marquis of Bute. His wife was not alone because her sister, Susan Mackenzie, had come to stay to be of assistance when her baby was born. The following morning he left early and covered the 13 miles to Ayr, where he found his wife had gone into labour. This was earlier than had been expected and, as he wrote to his father that evening, "Lexy had a good deal of suffering, being taken ill at 2:00 in the morning. I am very happy to say that Lexy had a fine boy this afternoon at half past three and both are doing well." He described his son as "plump" and his father-in-law, who came to see him three weeks later, called the child a "stout fellow". From photographs of Lord Ardwall (his title when raised to the bench) he retained this characteristic throughout his life.

Melville was the first to send his congratulations and he followed this up a few weeks later with a case containing a small plated knife, fork and spoon. Although no other letters have survived one may presume that other members of the family wrote as well. The child was given the same name as his father and was baptised on 10th August 1845. Andrew wrote to his father about this sacrament and ended his letter with the simple sentence: "Nothing yet from the Lord Advocate."

The happiness that Andrew and Alexa Jameson experienced in the safe birth of a child was not to be accorded to Alexa's sister, Margaret Begg. She had visited Barnhill with her husband and children in early September and had left there "in the bloom of health", as Andrew wrote to his father on 16th September. Once home she had suffered a miscarriage and died a few days later. Alexa and baby Andrew had

---

[50] v. p. 290 supra.

[51] Despite its name, Dumfries House, built by Robert and John Adam (completed 1758) is about 40 miles from the town of Dumfries and not even in Dumfriesshire. In 2007 the Duke of Rothesay brought together a consortium that included the Scottish Government to purchase this beautiful house and its contents for the nation.

been with them at Barnhill, and Alexa remained greatly distressed at the loss of her sister.

There occurred in mid September 1845 another event that was to have a far greater effect on the career of Andrew Jameson than the possibility of an appointment of a second sheriff-substitute for Ayrshire. This was the sudden and unexpected death of Macdonald, the junior sheriff-substitute of the County of Edinburgh. On 27th September Andrew received a letter from an advocate called John Cowan "asking me to let him know tomorrow if such a change[52] would be agreeable to me." As he told his father in a letter written that same day, Cowan had said that "Mr Speirs' attention had been directed to me among others. Mr Cowan adds that if I liked it, he would write to Mr Speirs[53] 'believing that your appointment would be a very desirable one as well for the public interest as for my friend's private comfort'."

He sought his father's advice because he had just married and had been only two years in his post and although:

> the labour has been to me very oppressive up to this autumn, yet I have much reason to expect relief in the appointment of a new S.Substitute to which the Ld Advocate is favourable.
>
> On the other hand (1) The society of Edinburgh has great attractions to a person of my tastes & here I have none. (2) To a family man Edinburgh has superior advantages for educating & bringing forward in life. (3) It is a position of more usefulness perhaps & Influence.

After further discussion of the advantages and disadvantages of accepting the position he concluded his letter with the following words: "I think I would be inclined to go for after all I may get no relief here & and the society is not to my taste."

Mr Cowan must have been eager to persuade Andrew to allow his

---

[52] i.e. move from Ayr to Edinburgh.

[53] The list of sheriffs for 1838 includes a Graham Speirs for the counties of Elgin and Nairn. (v. Nicholson, G. op cit p. 20 supra) In all probability Speirs by 1845 had become Sheriff of the County of Edinburgh.

name to go forward because he came through to Ayr[54] the next day in order to see him. Andrew had by this time decided to accept, and on 30th September Sheriff Speirs wrote to him formally offering the post. Andrew went through to Edinburgh for an appointment with him at 11.00 a.m. on 3rd October. There he learned the extent of the duties incumbent upon him were he to accept the position and, as he wrote to his father later that day, although they seemed many "I have a good notion that [there] would not be the pressure and weight that I have at present." Thereafter the process of appointing him to Edinburgh was set in motion very quickly because there was urgent need of a swift succession to Macdonald.

The next we hear of this is in a letter to his father of 13th October 1845 from an address in Newington.[55] It is worth quoting this letter in its entirety to help explain what had been happening.

> My dear Father,
>
> I came here on Thursday night and leave tomorrow morning.
>
> I have got my commission signed & it is to be despatched for the Certificate of the Heads of the Court. Mr Speirs intimated the appointment previously & received highly satisfactory answers from both Pred.[56] Boyle and Ld J. C.[57] Hope, who has indeed behaved very handsomely in giving his public testimonial in a way so gratifying to you as well as to me. I have always thought that he had a generosity of feelings at bottom, although he occasionally takes cantrips.[58]

---

[54] It is also possible that Andrew Jameson was in Edinburgh, when he wrote to his father on 27th September 1845, because in a letter of the following day he uses the words "Mr Cowan has been here". Neither letter states where they are being written but it was unusual for Andrew Jameson, when writing from elsewhere than his home, not to give some indication where he was. Whether Mr Cowan went through to Ayr to see Andrew Jameson or visited him at some address in Edinburgh does not alter the fact that this advocate must have been most anxious to secure Andrew's assent to be considered for the vacancy.

[55] He was probably staying with Dr Begg.

[56] "President", i.e. Lord President of the Court of Session.

[57] "Ld J. C.", i.e. Lord Justice Clerk.

[58] The word "cantrip" is defined in *Chamber's Dictionary* as a Scottish term meaning "a

Mr Henderson[59] was very kind. I was obliged to pay £35 for [word illegible] but as you say, I may begin with the £510 – they say the fees will be about £100 more, though the service will [word illegible] reduce them – as the sheriff was hinting.

No word of a successor. *Between ourselves* Mr Bell empowered me to make the offer to Neil, which he has declined after consulting his friends.[60] I was for some time with the Lord Advocate today upon the subject of dividing the county I have left. Tardy justice but I will do what I can for my successors – which it is now clear will be two. The Lord A. was hinting at a reduction of the *Ayr* salary, which I remonstrated against & he appeared to be somewhat moved by my argument. He thanked me for all my suggestions & asked me to give him a memorandum of them.

All my old friends have been congratulating me & almost all approving. Some speak of the fine climate I have lost but I tell them how little I had of the open air in it and in fact instead of getting stronger my stomach has been weakened considerably. I think surely over this winter I will do nicely here – if please God give me my health.

After a great deal of hunting I have taken the house my friend Professor Ferries is leaving on his removal to St Andrews. It is No 14 Carlton Street, Stockbridge – close to St Bernard's Crescent where Dr Paterson is. It is perhaps a little far down the hill but it is within a stonecast of the fields near dry airy walks & pretty well sheltered. I get entry this day 3 weeks. There is an omnibus every half hour to Newington.

It was much the best of the feu I had to choose among & the most moderate. I may perhaps get a better next term.

I am glad to think I will see so much more of you & hope you will come at your first Kirkcaldy circuit or rather as soon

---

wilful piece of trickery".

[59] In his letter to his father of 26th November 1845 Andrew describes this man as "Mr Henderson of the Exchequer".

[60] Later, Neil Campbell became Sheriff-Substitute of Ayrshire.

as we get the house in order, which will be about the term.

I had not time to see Mr Menteith but will call when I return.

Your most affectionate son
Andr Jameson

He left Ayr a few days later before any successor was appointed. During his two and a half years of service as their sheriff-substitute, Andrew must have given considerable satisfaction to the Procurators of Ayr because they presented him with an address which his father described on receiving a copy as "highly flattering & must be very gratifying to you as it must be to all your friends."

While pleased to have secured his post in the County of Edinburgh he was annoyed to find himself subjected to the same injustice as other sheriff-substitutes who transferred from one county to another. This was that their service in the county from which they had transferred was ignored in the calculation of their salary and they were remunerated as if they were in their first appointment. He called upon Mr Henderson and found that Barclay, his fellow sheriff-substitute of Perthshire, had felt very strongly about this treatment and although his request had been turned down he had sent a further letter giving vent to his strong feelings on the matter. In a letter to his father of 26th November 1845 he wrote: "I suppose his new application has arisen from some talk with you at the Circuit. I do not see the justice of excluding services in any case but especially where these have been very laborious. It is plain however that the Treasury don't attend to any thing of that kind – and I fear, that if I cannot get Henderson to go along with me, which before this malapropos shot of our Perthshire brother, he was much inclined to do, I may quietly submit. It is well I have only two years & a half to lose. Tell me what you think."

It will be recalled that his father had fought long and hard for improved salaries for sheriff-substitutes since the early years of the century and although now aged 74 was prepared to continue in this endeavour. From Andrew's letter to him of 10th December it is clear that he had advised his son not to surrender to this unfair practice. Andrew had "prepared a Petition to the Treasury according to the views you suggested & now enclose it for your perusal & correction, if you think it necessary. Mr Speirs has agreed to append any certificate I suggest. I shewed it also to Mr Henderson, who does not think that it will succeed – though he thinks I have stated the proper grounds – but both of them think that it would be of no use sending the Petition *now* until it is seen whether the Cabinet is going out." There followed some comments about the Corn Laws and the probable fall of Sir Robert Peel, the Prime Minister, which did come about. However, hopeful to the last, Andrew then continued "Please return the Petition with your remarks. I have not said much about my services – not so much as Mr Shireff – but I think I have said enough. I mean to get Mr Bell also to certify my services in Ayrshire."

This letter of 10th December also gives some domestic details. Andrew and Lexy were now providing a temporary home for the son of the recently bereaved Dr Begg, who had left to take up a charge in Canada. This nephew of Lexy was now attending the Circus School.[61] Lexy was suffering from an ingrowing toenail and the advice of her father-in-law was sought. One wonders why they did not consult a medical practitioner, but Andrew Jameson (Senior) was often asked to prescribe remedies for complaints and he was even readier to suggest some even when unsolicited. Andrew wrote to him again on 19th December expressing "your kindness in sending prescriptions for my lame foot. I tried them both a little but by that time the foot was getting much better as the suppuration had come to a head. It was very painful for some time before that and the first thing that gave relief after a great deal of poulticing was just cutting the nail out. It is now, I am glad to say, almost quite well." (There was no reference to his wife's toenail.) This may have been the same trouble that prevented him from escorting Euphemia Gray around Ayr when his niece paid her visit in

---

[61] Probably a private school situated in Royal Circus that lies just south-east of the east end of Princes Street.

January of that year.

They had had a visit from Elizabeth Thomson that day. "I was happy to hear that her brother's eyes continue to improve. She talks of being with you on Tuesday so I hope she may get a good day for crossing. She has been rather subject to sore throats of late, I think." Poor Elizabeth. She had lost a sister and two brothers, both parents were gone (her father having died bankrupt), her sister Jane had contracted an unfortunate marriage and her surviving brother was having eyesight problems. Now she was afflicted with symptoms (though how seriously we cannot tell) of the illness that was still, to some extent, troubling Andrew with whom she had once been so close. When Elizabeth's father had died in 1841 Sophia Gray had suggested to her father that he take Elizabeth as his housekeeper but he had refused and she had been given a home by her aunt, Mrs Ogilvie.[62] At some point, however, Sheriff-Substitute Jameson must have changed his mind, because in a letter to his father of 30th December 1845 Andrew concludes: "Many happy returns of the season to you and Elizabeth." One can only guess when his father decided to welcome Elizabeth into his home and his reason for doing so. Perhaps it was out of compassion because she was his niece and had no income of her own, but it is equally possible that since he was now in his seventies he was happy to delegate the running of his house to a younger person.

He concluded this letter by saying that on account of the fall of Sir Robert Peel's ministry there was no point in forwarding the petition concerning the injustice of ignoring previous service in calculating the salaries of sheriff-substitutes who transferred from one county to another.

At the end of 1842 Andrew Jameson's prospects had appeared poor and one can detect at times even a note of despair in his correspondence. Three years later he was settled in Edinburgh as one of that county's sheriff-substitutes together with a wife and child and more than contented with his lot. The letter that he wrote to his father on 30th December 1845 is a suitable way to conclude this chapter.

[62] v. p. 239 supra.

14 Carlton St,
Edinburgh
30 Dec 1845

My dear Father,

Lexy & I are quite happy in the prospect of having an early visit from you in our new abode. I dispatched your note to Mr Campbell & hope to hear from him tomorrow, when I will inform you of his answer. He is spending the holidays at Barnhill with the Mackenzies,[63] who are keeping the house warm for the Winter. The Hayfield people[64] & Neil are also there & we were also expected but thought it best, after our recent transmigration to be stationary this year. If Mr C. cannot come this week, would you not cross over on the Friday at any rate, when you are so near us?

I am liking my new office very well. I have some heavy reading at poor McDonald's processes now and then but am getting them off by degrees. I soon got familiar with the Police courts practise and find it interesting enough though often painfully so.

I have not yet seen anything worse than the Irish blackguardism of the west. In process of time, if I am spared, I hope to effect some improvements in the conducting of the business, for at present it is far from satisfactory, though this is owing in some degree to the want of accommodation.

I have taken the Jury Trials thrice – we always have Counsel – and I feel it a little queer being addressed by my contemporaries.

We have had a great many invitations but Lexy is not going out to parties. She dined *en famille* with her aunt and nieces & another day at Granton. Mr & Mrs Speirs have

---

[63] Susan and Elizabeth, sisters of Alexa Jameson, both married men called Mackenzie.
[64] James and Fanny White.

been very kind to her.

I am engaged to the Solicitor-General on Saty first & invited to Lord Woods on Monday but will not accept if I find tomorrow that Mr Campbell is coming.

Many happy returns of the season to you & Elizabeth. May we become more holier & wiser as we grow older and be enabled to serve Our Heavenly Father more faithfully than we have not heretofore done. Lexy joins in our best wishes.

I am, my dear father,

Your most affectionate son,
And. Jameson

P.S. If the flower pots are ready could you bring the large ones.

APPENDIX A

Short-Term Financing in the Eighteenth and Nineteenth Centuries

The first overdraft granted by a bank was in 1725 but the most common form of short term financing in the eighteenth and nineteenth centuries was the Bill of Exchange, which is still in use today. It is essentially an IOU formally recognised by a debtor and accepted by a creditor as legal evidence of a valid debt repayable on demand or on a specific date. It could have many owners before it was liquidated on repayment. For large capital funding projects such as railway construction Investment Trusts came to the fore in the early nineteenth century and were limited liability companies, which pooled the funds of wealthy individuals, who then invested collectively through the vehicle of the trust in high risk and high value projects both in the UK and abroad.

It was in the early nineteenth century that building or mutual societies were formed in local communities on a temporary basis and were owned by individual members for the express purpose of pooling each member's wealth from which members could draw sums as loans for house purchase. When all the members had borrowed and repaid, the society was dissolved. Later, instead of dissolution, members began adding the word "Permanent" to the organizations they had formed, to indicate that they would continue in existence even after all their members had received and paid loans.

Note: I am grateful to Mr B. C. Scroggie, Lecturer in Financial Management, The Robert Gordon University, Aberdeen, for writing this appendix.

CHAPTER TEN

Revision of the Criminal Code of Malta

The reason for the Colonial Office requiring the revision of the Criminal Code of Malta can be found within the context of the island's history.

Malta had been ruled by the Order of Knights of St John of Jerusalem from 1530 until 1798 when Napoleon Bonaparte occupied it en route for his military expedition to Egypt. He stayed there a few days and during that short time established an administration that was an improvement on that of the Order and replaced the archaic legal system with one based upon French revolutionary principles. At first the Maltese were happy with their new rulers but the French, foolishly failing to recognize the strong affection of the people for their Roman Catholic faith, lost this initial goodwill by their systematic seizure of church property and closure of convents. The populace rose in rebellion and, failing to dislodge the French from their fortifications in Valletta, sought help from the British. In 1800 a force under Brigadier-General Graham[1] captured Valletta.

The Treaty of Amiens in March 1802 ended, for a brief period, the war between Britain and France. Britain agreed to restore the island to the Knights of St John, and one of the reasons for the resumption of hostilities in May 1803 was her failure to do so. In any case, on account of its strategic location and excellent harbours, Britain would never have considered abandoning so valuable a possession as long as there was any possibility of its annexation by some other power.

For the fourteen years from the expulsion of the French, the political status of Malta was indeterminate. "The moment at which the British officials had a legal power to exercise full legislative and executive

---

[1] v. p. 225 supra.

321

power is elusive."[2] Indeed, it was not until 1938 that the Privy Council in considering a legal case[3] "made it a settled proposition of U. K. law that sovereignty of Malta had passed to the British Crown, at least by October 1813." This was the date of the appointment of the first British official with the title of "Governor". However, the Maltese were prepared to acknowledge the British monarch as their sovereign and accepted in 1814 the decision of the Congress of Vienna that Malta should become a British colony.

As early as 1812 a Royal Commission was sent out to look at the existing administrative arrangements and to advise the British government on what form of constitution might be appropriate for the island. This was just the first of many such attempts, and the Royal Commissioners of 1931 wrote: "It would be almost possible to plot a graph of the constitutional history of Malta during the last hundred years showing the rise and fall of constitutions modelled alternately on the principle of benevolent autocracy and that of representative government."[4]

The Royal Commissioners of 1812 suggested an Advisory Council composed of four Maltese and four British members and when, shortly afterwards, Sir Thomas Maitland was appointed Governor he was empowered to form, if he so wished, a Council similar in membership and functions. Sir Thomas, who served as Governor from 1813 to1824, had no intention of doing so and earned the name of "King Tom" because his system of governing was to brook no opposition but "to drive and kick mankind into obedience."[5] Although he made useful improvements to the administrative and judicial systems of Malta, the inhabitants became increasingly resentful at their total exclusion from any part in the running of their island.

The Maltese did not regard themselves as a conquered people, and although the British did not consider them to be so, they nevertheless

[2] v. Davis, H., and Hough, B., *The British Claim to Malta 1800–1813*, Melita Historica 2007 Vol XIV, no. 4: pp. 387–408.
[3] *Sammut v. Strickland* (1938) A.C. 678.
[4] Report (1932) *Malta Royal Commission 1931* p.9. Cmd 3993.
[5] Lewis (1870) *Letters of the Rt Hon George Cornewall Lewis Bart to Various Friends.* London.

saw concentration of power in the hands of the Governor as necessary for stability. The Maltese argued that they had for centuries enjoyed certain rights and privileges under the *consiglio populare*, a form of Parliament whose influence the Order had vainly sought to nullify. Moreover, it was they who had first risen against the French occupation and they asserted that their invitation to the British to assist them was a compact between two nations. Indeed, as early as 1802 their leaders had drawn up the Declaration of Rights of the Inhabitants of the Islands of Malta and Gozo to which the British occupying force had entered no objection.

The demand for participation by the Maltese in the government of their island came to a head during the years 1832–1836. The principal leaders of the islanders had formed "Comitato Generale Maltese", which argued that the absence of any popular assembly was an injustice. One of the more prominent of these leaders was George Mitrovich, whose *The Claims of the Maltese; Founded upon the Principles of Justice* was published in 1835. The agitation was not confined to indigenous sources because the Maltese now had a champion within the House of Commons. This was William Ewart, MP (1798–1869),[6] an active social reformer, who wrote to Lord Glenelg, Secretary of State for the Colonies, asking him to enquire into the affairs of Malta.

By a royal decree of April 1835 instructions were issued for the constitution in Malta of a Council "to advise and assist in the administration of the government thereof". The Commissioners responsible for drafting the constitution were two lawyers, John Austin and George (later Sir George) Cornewall-Lewis. They concentrated mainly on the replacement of ancient trading laws by new regulations that contributed much to the subsequent prosperity of the island, but they paid scant attention to what would be called today the democratic rights of the inhabitants.[7] Published in 1836, the new constitution

---

[6] He was a friend of the Gladstones of Liverpool and the Prime Minister W. E. Gladstone was named after him.

[7] It must be remembered that the Reform Act of 1832 had been passed only four years earlier and, since the majority of British men and all women were not enfranchised, it is understandable why Austin and Cornewall-Lewis did not feel it was a matter of great concern.

came a long way short of what Mitrovich and the other Maltese leaders had sought, mainly on account of the membership of the Council. It was to consist of seven members, four described as "official" and three as "unofficial". The official members were the Commander-in-Chief, the Chief Justice, the Chief Secretary to the Governor and the Bishop of Malta, while the unofficial members were two Maltese citizens and one British merchant, all three to be selected by the Governor of the island.

The Council was nominally legislative, but Maltese politicians treated it with derision because no provision had been made for any elective representation and the Governor retained power to override any decision that it made. Some slight acknowledgment of this dissatisfaction came when the Council was reconstituted in November 1839 with the replacement of the Chief Justice by the Auditor General and the withdrawal of the Bishop on the instructions of the Pope. Although the amended constitution also removed the power of the Governor, except in exceptional circumstances, to oppose the advice of the Council, it still failed to satisfy the aspirations of the Maltese.

Before coming to the contribution that Andrew Jameson made to the Criminal Code of Malta, it is important to understand that in Malta the Roman Catholic Church wielded enormous temporal as well as spiritual power. The Church was highly suspicious towards the new rulers because it feared that they would encourage the activities of Protestant missionary societies, several of whom had established branches on the island. It was sufficiently influential to prohibit these societies from printing anything in Maltese and to require that what they did print was to be for distribution abroad. Indeed, the Anglicans were not allowed any grants from public funds to build a church. They did not have one until 1844, and this was entirely through the generosity of Queen Adelaide, the widow of William IV, who had visited Malta in 1838 and had found no place to worship.

After 1815 the British government was anxious to introduce reforms that would allow Malta to become more integrated within the British Empire, but any suggestions concerning legal, economic or even military reform were opposed by the Church. Help came from the unlikely source of the Pope, with whom the British decided to hold talks on matters relating to Malta rather than with the Maltese ecclesiastical authorities. In 1820 Sir Thomas Maitland visited the Pope and secured his approval for the enactment in 1822 of what was called the Mortmain Law. This prevented the Church from adding to their already considerable amount of property by requiring it to sell any new property it acquired within one year.

A further complication that the British had to face was that the Diocese of Malta fell within the See of the Archbishop of Palermo and the King of the Two Sicilies was anxious to retain some form of authority over the island that his predecessors had ruled until the sixteenth century. The king wanted to influence through his Archbishop of Palermo all clerical appointments within Malta. This issue and the reform of the Ecclesiastical Courts were settled through a visit in 1829 to Rome by Sir Frederick Hankey, the Chief Secretary. He persuaded the Pope to separate the Diocese of Malta from the Metropolitan See of Palermo, although it took nineteen months before the king would accept this decision. In addition, Sir Frederick won papal approval that the Bishop of Malta should not oppose any reforms agreed upon between London and Rome. Where serious difficulties arose between the Church and the Government discussions could now take place direct with the Vatican. Writing to Andrew Jameson on December 1850, Sir Hector Greig, then in retirement in London, said that "it seemed to me a miracle at the time that Rome gave its consent that the Bishop's Court should be so shorn and curtailed & confined to causes purely spiritual." The explanation may be that the Pope, like many who enjoy supreme power within an organization, was determined to keep his subordinates in their place.

The Council was empowered to introduce legislation through Ordinances, and that of 14th March 1839, Ordinance IV, removed all forms of censorship on publications. This caused great anguish to the Church because, as its clergy had always claimed, it would unleash a series of attacks on the Roman Catholic faith. To allay this fear Ordinance

IV was followed by the introduction of a law on libel, which, although general in its application, was in reality to give some protection to the Church. As it turned out, the suspicions of the Roman Catholic clergy were shown to be far from unfounded because before the year was out the editor of a Maltese Protestant newspaper described the Church of Rome as "a system of religion the most detestable the world has ever seen." This earned him a hefty fine and six months of imprisonment in the first case of libel brought under the new legislation.

This had a salutary effect on any other persons who sought to criticise the Church in any form. The influence of the Church remained very powerful with, it must be conceded, the full acquiescence of the Maltese, the vast majority of whom were devout members of their denomination. Ecclesiastical courts continued to function and had jurisdiction over religious matters, although in Malta that term had a much wider connotation than in other countries. In that same letter quoted above Sir Hector Greig advised Andrew Jameson: "I should impress on you the absolute necessity of keeping the jurisdiction of the Bishop's Court within its present limits. No-one not intimately acquainted with Malta can know the harm that was done by that Court."

This, then, was the political background of Malta when Andrew Jameson paid his short visit during December 1840 and January 1841. The constitution had been settled to the satisfaction of the British, if not to the Maltese, and the Council had turned its attention to the question of the island's administration of justice. There were codes of justice for both criminal and civil law but they were outdated and in need of revision. As they stood, the laws were an amalgam of conventions and provisions introduced first by the Neapolitans, who had ruled the island before 1530, then by the Order of Knights of St John of Jerusalem during their rule up to 1798 and then by the French. This was further complicated, as stated immediately above, by the power of the Roman Catholic clergy in Malta.

The appointment of Andrew Jameson to revise the Criminal Code of Malta has been fully covered in Chapter Eight. He started on the revision about the beginning of September 1842 at a period when he had little other professional work to occupy his time, but, as stated earlier,[8] he was soon attempting to resurrect his career as an advocate and did manage to attract some clients. Then in March 1843 he obtained the appointment of Sheriff-Substitute of Ayrshire. The arrangements for moving to Ayr and easing himself into his new role were inevitably time-consuming, and at the end of the following month he wrote to his father that he would have to discipline himself to pay the requisite attention to what he referred to as his "Code business" by reducing his social life.[9] His original estimate that "a period of not less than three months would be necessary"[10] was correct but the inference from this was that it would not take a great deal longer than that.

In early March Sir Henry Bouverie wrote: "We are beginning to look out for your report on the Code", but in this he was to be disappointed. On 30th March Andrew Jameson sent to Sir Hector Greig an interim report and explained that his recent appointment as Sheriff-Substitute would make inroads on the time available for his work on the Criminal Code of Malta. In any case he had some questions to ask, and these were sent out to Malta with his letter to Sir Hector. Sir Hector promised to send answers "by the next packet" but there is no documentation to confirm that this was done.

There is, however, an interesting letter of 8th July 1843 that Sir Hector sent from Gibraltar. From this we learn that Sir Hector had come to London on 29th June hoping to have a fortnight's leave but Lieutenant-General Sir Patrick Stuart, who was about to sail for Malta, where he would take over from Sir Henry Bouverie, "was unwilling to assume his career as Governor of Malta without my being present." Consequently, Sir Hector's time in London was reduced to a mere 36 hours.

In that letter of 8th July Sir Hector informed Andrew Jameson that: "It was my intention to have taken a run down to Ayr to have talked over matters with you & in this way perhaps I could have better

---

[8] v. p. 284 supra.
[9] v. p. 288 supra.
[10] v. p. 272 supra.

answered your queries. On one point, Sir Henry Bouverie and myself were entirely of accord, that no greater protection should or could be afforded to the culture of the Roman Catholic Religion than is to be afforded to the Church of England – & we think also that the Church of Scotland should be included. It would, we think, be an anomaly, that in a British colony we should legislate for greater protection to the Roman Catholick [sic] Religion than to the two established forms of worship of the Mother Country – and there is nothing in Malta, either by law or treaty to call for, or, sanction such a distinction."

In a letter to his father of 25th July[11] Andrew Jameson told him that he had "just received some answers from the Maltese judges to my queries" and this seems unlikely to have come "by the next packet", presumably April or as a result of a request from Sir Hector to the judges once he had reached Malta with the new Governor. Probably Andrew had written directly to the Governor or the judges themselves for information.

Nevertheless, by September 1843, he had completed his work on the revision of the Criminal Code of Malta and, after inquiring of Sir Hector whether he should send it to the Governor or to the Colonial Secretary, was informed that the latter should be the recipient. Accordingly he wrote to James Stephen, the Under-Secretary of State, that his report was now finished and that he proposed to come with it to London in person to provide any explanations that might be required. He added: "When I had the pleasure of seeing you in July last year, I at first thought that the revision of the Code might occupy from six weeks to three months work. It has turned out much more than double that time and labour and this with the necessary correspondence with the Malta Govt must in some measure account for the delay, which has apparently taken place."

Whether Stephen replied to him or not is unknown, but Andrew Jameson presented himself, together with a "memorandum" of his professional fees and expenses, at the Colonial Office on 4th October only to find that Lord Stanley, Secretary of State for the Colonies, was

---

[11] v. p. 289 supra.

at his ancestral home, Knowsley Hall, near Liverpool. He wrote to him that day, saying that he would be returning to Scotland on 6th October by way of Birmingham and Warrington "where your Lp may write me a note to the Post Office and I shall be happy to attend to your wishes."

He possibly thought that this was either an insufficiently informative or somewhat brusque letter to send to a minister of the Crown because he wrote another, longer one the next day. From this we learn that he had deposited the report with the Under-Secretary of State together with the various books and manuscripts that he had received from Sir Hector Greig or had been sent by others from Malta. He told Lord Stanley that he would come to Liverpool the next day and that he would be staying at the Adelphi Hotel until Sunday (8th) and that he would wait upon him if it was convenient. Lord Stanley replied that his engagements made it impossible for him to meet Andrew Jameson and moreover, not having seen the report, any discussion on it would have been difficult. He had, however, "requested Mr Stephen to go through it before forwarding it to me."

On the morning of 9th October before leaving Liverpool he wrote to Stephen that Lord Stanley had been unable to meet him and added that he was having trouble with a sprained foot which his journey to London had aggravated. Andrew Jameson seems to have been prone to injury in various parts of his lower limbs from the time he tripped in the attic and damaged his shin bone in May 1831.[12] In her letter of March 1844 Effie Gray inquired after his ankle[13] and when she visited him and Alexa in January/February 1845 he was unable to accompany his niece around Ayr on account of a foot injury.[14] In December 1845 he thanked his father for sending prescriptions for a lame foot.[15]

On 7th November, G. W. Hope,[16] an Under-Secretary at the Colonial Office, was instructed by Lord Stanley to write that the Colonial Secretary was "impressed with a deep sense of the ability and learning

---

[12] v. p. 121 supra.
[13] v. p. 297 supra.
[14] v. p. 309 supra.
[15] v. p. 316 supra.
[16] v. p. 270 supra, where a footnote deals with the confusion over the Christian names of Hope.

which you have brought to bear on the subject and would convey to you his grateful acknowledgment of the diligence with which that important task has been carried to it's [sic] close. So many however and so considerable are the topics over which the report ranges and the enquiries it suggests that Lord Stanley thinks it due to the great Public interests at stake to afford to the Authors of the Project[17] and to the local Legislature a full opportunity of revising the Code with the aid of your suggestions before he forms any judgment as to the wisdom of adopting them either wholly or in part. His Lordship however anticipates that in many aspects the local authorities will concur with you, and he is convinced that they will bestow upon your Report the mature and respectful attention to which it is so well entitled." The Colonial Secretary's remittance of the Report for its consideration by those in authority on Malta was probably appropriate but this certainly did not meet with the approval of Sir Henry Bouverie.

Now in retirement, Sir Henry wrote to Andrew Jameson on 30th November 1843,[18] saying, "I congratulate you upon the very satisfactory approval of your labours by Lord Stanley. I much fear however that the [word illegible] conceits and policies of the Maltese Code Commission will throw such obstacles in the way as will cause nothing but disappointment. I would have wished that Lord Stanley had taken a more decided part and had sent out your suggestions to be prepared and passed into law without referring them to the original framers but we will see what will come of it. I fear not much."

Sir Hector Greig sent two letters to him on 26th January 1844. One was a stiffly formal one written by a clerk thanking him for his work on the Criminal Code and enclosing a bill on the Lords Commissioners of Her Majesty's Treasury for £265 in payment for his work on the report and associated expenses. The other was a personal one in his own hand:

[17] The term "Authors" must have been used here so that persons such as the Governor and Chief Secretary and possibly some of the Maltese judges whom Andrew Jameson had approached would be recognized as having initiated and to some extent participated in the project.

[18] For some reason Andrew Jameson, when collating his papers on this subject, wrote on the back of the letter that it had been written on 4th December 1843.

I can only say that I am astonished at the extent of your labors, and delighted with the vast amount of information that you have brought to bear on the subject, which cannot fail to be of great utility in correcting the errors of the Code.

It would ill become me to offer my tribute of praise of what you have done – but even as a philosophical essay on Legislation to an enlightened mind, your report is more instructive and interesting.

We are printing the Code & your report and Lord Stanley has directed that the Council of Govt give an opinion whether they approve of the original text or of your alterations. I shall be happy to send you half a dozen copies of the Code & Report if you will let me know how to forward them.

Andrew acknowledged receipt of Sir Hector's letter on 29th February, thanking him for his kind expressions of opinion about him and his Report and it is from this communication that we learn that he had been offered by the Colonial Office "the Attorney-Generalship of Sancta Lucia[19] – said to be worth £2,150 a year but I preferred my £500 here to the dangers of the climate."

Sir Henry had been prescient in his criticism of Lord Stanley's decision to allow the Report to be considered first by the Maltese authorities. He had been Governor of the island from 1836 to 1843 and had experienced the frustrations of opposition to sound administrative proposals from local officials and, to judge from his critical comments on their influence, the Roman Catholic clergy. Incredibly, the consultations about the proposed Criminal Code lasted three years, and there was no more official communication until 22nd January 1846, when the Governor, Sir Patrick Stuart, wrote to Lord Stanley's successor at the Colonial Office, W. E. Gladstone.

After referring briefly to the receipt from Lord Stanley's despatch No. 30 of the 9th November 1843 enclosing the Report of Andrew Jameson, he continued:

[19] v. p. 292 supra.

His Lordship was at the same time pleased to intimate to me that valuable as Mr Jameson's service has proved & extensive as was his acquaintance with the whole subject on which he had written, it was impossible that His Lordship should so far defer to his authority or to his arguments as to adopt his conclusions without being first apprized in what light they may be regarded by the Framers of the Code and by the Legislative Council of Malta.

I was therefore directed to move the Council to enter on a revision of the draft of the code with an especial reference to Mr Jameson's remarks upon it & to narrow the discussion within its proper limits by an enumeration & a statement of the successive questions demanding an authoritative decision.

The Governor then had copies made both of the projected Code and of the Report. Copies were sent to "the 2 surviving learned framers of the Code[20] with a view of my obtaining their opinion whether it would be expedient to adopt in part or in whole the alterations and amendments suggested by Mr Jameson, in order that I might submit that opinion to the Council." These men declined the opportunity to comment, and so the Governor, with the agreement of the Council, referred the projected Code and the Report to Dr Antonio Micallef, the Crown Advocate, for his opinion. He sent his comments to the Governor in September 1844.

This learned gentleman came to the conclusion that the greater part of Mr Jameson's amendments might be freely adopted & approved & that such alterations far from having the effect of destroying the spirit & the basis of the project[21] would render the new Criminal Law useful and salutary & leading as he thought to that improved state of

[20] These were Sir Ignatius Bonavita and Judge Francesco Chapelle.

[21] These were the reasons given by Bonavita and Chapelle for declining to comment on Andrew Jameson's Report.

society at large, which a new Code must always be intended to accomplish.

The Report was then submitted to the Council. As the Governor continued in his letter: "After a very patient, attentive and minute examination of the narrow details adduced to justice, which through adjournments lasted from November 1844 to June 1845, the Council concluded with the adoption of Mr Jameson's alterations and amendments in their full spirit & with but few & slight qualifications in their letter and detail." This had now to be translated into Italian and the greatest care had to be taken to ensure that the Italian and English versions were compatible with each other. Translating had occupied many months and it was only now, January 1846, that the Governor was able to send copies to the Colonial Secretary.

Sir Patrick then went on to compliment Andrew Jameson for his endeavours: "I am bound to say with all deference to the opinion of the learned Commissioners[22] I consider a very great advance has been made towards the improvement of the Maltese Criminal law and procedure by the adoptions of the suggestions of Mr Jameson, who has undoubtedly exhibited in his report a most extensive knowledge of the provisions of the continental Codes as well as an intimate acquaintance with the general principles of Criminal Legislation."[23]

On 24th February Lord Lyttelton, Under-Secretary of State for War and the Colonies, wrote to Andrew Jameson enclosing a copy of Sir Patrick Stuart's letter of 22nd January together with a copy in Italian of the proposed Criminal Code and its English translation. The letter continued as follows:

Mr Gladstone is reluctant, after the great labour which you have already bestowed on the revision of the Code, to give you any additional trouble on the subject, but he considers it so highly important that your suggestions should be rightly

[22] Bonavita and Chapelle.
[23] A full transcript of this letter is given as Appendix A to this chapter.

understood & properly adapted to the Code by the local authorities, that he desires me to express a hope that you will allow the Code in its present shape to be referred to you with a view of ascertaining whether the revisions suggested by you have been made so as to meet your approval."

To this request Andrew agreed, and from Downing Street on the 6th March Lyttelton sent "the revised Code of the Criminal Laws of Malta with a translation of the same & a printed copy of Mr Jameson's Report thereon." In acknowledging this letter and its enclosures Andrew said he would "acquaint his Lordship with the result as soon as his public duties permit."

In two letters to his father of 7th and 18th March Andrew Jameson mentioned his work on the Criminal Code. That of the 7th merely commented that "the Malta papers arrived with my report printed in English. It makes a small pamphlet – not good paper or print – but reads fairly enough". On the 18th March he tells him: "I am very busy with the Malta Code. It is gratifying to find the provision so much ameliorated. They have followed my suggestions to a far greater extent than I could have expected." From a letter in late June we learn that he was still at work on the Code, but it must have been soon afterwards that he submitted his comments to the Colonial Office.

What is more interesting is that in early September Sir Patrick Stuart was on leave in Scotland and staying at Eaglescairnie, near Haddington, only eighteen miles from Edinburgh. He invited Andrew to meet him at the New Club in Edinburgh[24] on 5th September and there offered him the post of Chief Secretary of Malta. Andrew consulted his father-in-law, who advised him to accept provided Lexy was agreeable. On 12th September he wrote to Sir Patrick declining the offer. Four days later he wrote to John Melville[25] to say that he had given the offer a great deal of consideration and that there were three reasons for turning down what would have been a more highly

---

[24] This prestigious club in Princes Street, Edinburgh, is still thriving.
[25] v. p. 273 supra.

remunerated post than that of a sheriff-substitute. The principal reason was that Lexy was unwilling to go but there were two other matters to which he had also given thought. One was that he was always conscious that his health might break down and, if so, he had nothing to fall back upon. The other was that his present position guaranteed him "a retiring allowance" if illness ever made it necessary to resign.

This, nevertheless, was not the end of the matter because about ten days later a more formal offer of the same appointment came from the Lord Advocate. In a letter to Sir Patrick Stuart, Andrew Jameson told him that the Lord Advocate had been totally unaware that he had already been made the same offer. The Lord Advocate, Andrew Rutherford, who was MP for Leith from 1839 to 1851, knew Andrew Jameson well and had accompanied him to Ayr when he was installed as Sheriff-Substitute of that county.[26] We learn from this letter written to Sir Patrick that it was at the request of Lord Grey, who had succeeded Gladstone as Colonial Secretary, that the Lord Advocate had offered the post of Chief Secretary of Malta to Andrew Jameson. The Colonial Office would have been well aware of his recent services to it and would have considered him to be a highly suitable successor to Sir Hector Greig. In answering the Lord Advocate on 5th October Andrew wrote: "I have again had the benefit of consulting some of my nearest relations with the aid of the suggestions you had the kindness to make, and though by no means insensible of the many advantages attached to that office, I have only been confirmed in the conclusion that in the present circumstances it would not be advisable for me to give up my situation here for the appointment, which you have so unexpectedly put again in my power."

On 15th October Sir Patrick Stuart called at the Sheriff Court in Edinburgh to say farewell to Andrew before returning to Malta, but Andrew was away that day in court at Dalkeith. In his letter Sir Patrick said, "I called upon you to express to you my regrets both on public & private grounds that you did not find it would suit you to accept the situation at Malta." Replying the next day, Andrew told the Governor

[26] v. p. 288 supra.

how sorry he was to have missed him and to thank him for his kindness in putting forward his name for the post.[27]

Sir Hector Greig, whose health had been deteriorating and who was on leave in England, wrote to Andrew on 26th October 1846. It was he who had advised Sir Patrick to approach Andrew Jameson on the matter of succeeding him as Chief Secretary of Malta. This letter gives a penetrating insight into the problems of governing the island and is worth transcribing here in full.

> I have not written to you for a long while – partly from poor health and latterly from a desire not to bias you one way or other about going to Malta, but I had certainly impressed Sir Patrick with the conviction that if you accepted the Chief Secretaryship, that your presence there would be a real boon both to himself personally and to the inhabitants of Malta.
>
> I believe, however, that you decided wisely to remain in Scotland, where you have the Bench & your own profession open to you in all its branches and the salary at Malta is in fact too small for a distinguished professional lawyer to think of.
>
> I do not know who is to be my successor, but he will not find the office quite a bed of roses, if I am right in the growing discontent & pretensions of the Maltese.
>
> I have not read your last corrections on the Code – but all & every thing goes out to Malta, by next packet, for enactment.
>
> I am also going to return there, for the winter, & I have this on the 1st[28] – but as I had something to do even with this second reference of the Code, I shall be glad to know from you, *privately*, if anything has been done or said,

---

[27] It is in this letter that Andrew Jameson wrote: "The Lord Advocate informed me that he on being applied to by Earl Grey had recommended me for the appointment, not being aware of your communication to me & my answer."

[28] Presumably this means that he would be leaving for Malta on 1st November 1846.

about a fee, on the occasion, as these things are sometimes forgotten and as you are not the man to talk for yourself on such occasions, I can mention the subject to Sir P. Stuart, as the Govt of Malta quite intended that you should not give valuable labour for nothing.

Pray write me a line.

Andrew obliged him on 28th October with a letter of six pages. After thanking Sir Hector for all the assistance and many kindnesses that he had received from him, he explained to him his reasons for declining the offer to become his successor. "Having now a wife and child and no private fortune I thought that looking to the risks of climate and health, the difficulty of saving anything out of £1,000 a year & the loss of the advantages of education & society at home, it was not advisable in a prudential point of view to leave my present situation even with hard work & small salary." He went on to say that despite what Sir Hector had written "it is extremely unlikely that such judicial promotion should fall in my way. Indeed, I think had no others been depending upon me, I could have run the risk & accepted the appointment and had I done so, your presence in Malta during this winter would have been an invaluable assistance."

There had been no mention of any remuneration for the further work on the revision of the Criminal Code that had been requested by William Gladstone. "In regard to the last reference of the Code as revised, I had little trouble beyond the mere work of going over the whole draft, article by article, & the amendments suggested by me and noting some points worthy of reconstruction, which I embodied in the short report to Mr Gladstone and in regard to which I have had no communication since." On the other hand, in reference to his original work on the Code, "I thought the remuneration fixed upon by us at the request of Mr Stephen on the idea of a revision costing 3 months work was inadequate, when it turned out that the time & labour required even more than double our hasty estimate." After further comment on the nature of the work that he had undertaken, he continued "I state these things with some hesitation and only on account of your kind reference to the subject."

On his return to Malta, Sir Hector took up the question of further remuneration for Andrew Jameson, where time was certainly not of the essence. On 14th April 1847 Sir Hector, who was awaiting the arrival of his successor,[29] wrote to Andrew and after stating that he was about to return to England on account of poor health, added the following:

> Your Code is not born yet owing to the dilatoriness of the local Govt in passing it through the Council, nor from what I see, do I expect that it will come to light for 6 months or more.
>
> The governor has promised me that at the next meeting of Council, that the sum of £100 will be voted to you for your extra trouble. This is far below what you ought to have, but it will at least show the opinion that the Local Govt entertains of your labours. You are quite aware that this proposition was made by me, before I left office, and I am not sure, however, if I ever mentioned it to you. I trust that you will soon hear from Sir P. Stuart on the subject.

After commenting that he was unsure whether he would seek treatment at Cheltenham or Bad Kissingen in Bavaria and that he was retaining his house in Malta for the following winter, he added this postscript: "I understand that the Crown Advocate coincides in opinion with you, in all your late suggestions, therefore they will be adopted."

It was not until August 1847 that he received a letter from Benjamin Hawes, Under-Secretary of State at the Colonial Office, stating that Sir Patrick Stuart had informed the Colonial Secretary that "the Council of his Government, having terminated their consideration of the suggestions contained in your second report on the proposed Code of Criminal Laws

---

[29] Rather curiously Sir Hector refers to his replacement as "your successor", possibly meaning the person who had been offered and accepted the post after it had been declined by Andrew Jameson.

for Malta, unanimously resolved at their meeting of 25th June last, to recommend a further remuneration of £100 being issued to you from the Colonial Revenues in acknowledgment of your services on this occasion." Hawes added that Mr Barnard, the Colonial Agent-General, had been instructed to make the payment to him but when, after five weeks, nothing had arrived Andrew had to write to this man, referring to the Under-Secretary of State's letter and requesting "that you will have the goodness to remit to me the above sum as soon as convenient."

One must assume that this small sum was eventually sent. The niggardly attitude of the Colonial Office towards payment for Andrew Jameson's services can be excused solely on the ground that Mr Stephen, the Under-Secretary with whom the original contract was discussed, was totally unaware of the nature of the work required and consequently of the time and intellectual effort that had to be expended. On the other hand, through his work on its behalf he had certainly earned a high reputation in the Colonial Office and it is not surprising that in 1851 he was invited to carry out a similar revision of the island's Civil Code. What is surprising is that he agreed to do so.

One would have thought that since the Council of the Government of Malta had terminated their discussions on the proposed Code of Criminal Laws for Malta in June 1847 there would have been few if any further impediments to the implementation of the provisions of the Code. This was to be far from the case as Sir Henry Bouverie had forecast. The Roman Catholic clergy remained uncertain at best about some of the provisions and the Maltese remained dissatisfied with the 1836 Constitution that had been imposed on them. There was sufficient agitation among the populace to persuade the Government to consider and then grant in 1849 a new Constitution, whereby the Council of Government would consist of 18 members, ten of whom would be nominated and eight elected.

On the agenda for the first meeting of the Council on 8th January 1850 was a proposal to implement the Criminal Code as revised by Andrew Jameson. Three clergymen had been returned in the election and they immediately sought to introduce a clause stating that although other religions were tolerated in Malta, Roman Catholicism was dominant and that consequently the penalties against those who offended that religion should be greater than those relating to other religions. This naturally caused uproar among the Protestant adherents, the Anglican Bishop of Gibraltar and Malta was outraged and the issue was even discussed in the House of Commons. It will be recalled that in his letter to Andrew Jameson of 8th July 1843 Sir Hector Greig had written: "On one point, Sir Henry Bouverie and myself were entirely of accord, that no greater protection should or could be afforded to the culture of the Roman Catholic Religion than is to be afforded to the Church of England – & we think also that the Church of Scotland should be included. It would, we think, be an anomaly, that in a British colony we should legislate for greater protection to the Roman Catholick [sic] Religion than to the two established forms of worship of the Mother Country – and there is nothing in Malta, either by law or treaty to call for, or, sanction such a distinction."

There seemed no solution to this problem since the British Government was not prepared to allow penalties to be varied in accordance with the religion of persons convicted of a crime and the Roman Catholic authorities were adamant in their refusal to withdraw from their position. Accordingly the implementation of the proposed Criminal Code was put on hold and the administration of criminal justice on the island continued under the archaic system that Andrew Jameson had been employed to revise. By late 1853 the British authorities decided that this could no longer be tolerated and that the Criminal Code of Malta must be introduced irrespective of the wishes of the Roman Catholic Church. This it did through an Order in Council and the new Code became effective from 30th January 1854. The question of differential penalties for offences against religion was settled by simply omitting all reference to them.[30]

Thus more than ten years had passed from the time Andrew

---

[30] In an attempt by the British Government to prevent what it saw as inappropriate use by ecclesiastics of their position on the Council, the Governor issued in 1857 Letters Patent excluding them from participating in elections for the Council. As would be expected, this was resented by the majority of the Maltese and the Letters Patent were withdrawn in 1870.

Jameson had first submitted a revised Criminal Code for Malta and its incorporation into Maltese law. By that time he had already accepted a similar commission with regard to the Code of Civil Law in the island. However, it is necessary to return to January 1846. He had recently taken up his new post of Sheriff-Substitute of the County of Edinburgh and had found a comfortable home for his family. All seemed to augur well for him and Lexy because his health had held up well and he was back in the familiar environment of the capital, very much at the centre of all that was happening in legal circles. Soon, however, tragedy was to strike both him and his surviving brothers, while George Gray was to find himself approaching the brink of total ruin.

APPENDIX A

Letter From Sir Patrick Stuart, Governor Of Malta

to

The Right Honorable W. E. Gladstone,
Colonial Secretary

Malta 22 Jany 1846

Copy No 6

Sir,

With Lord Stanley's despatch No 30 of the 9th November 1843, I received a report from Mr Jameson, the Sheriff-Substitute of the County of Ayr, which had been prepared by him on the projected Criminal Code for Malta, in consequence of communications which with his Lordship's sanction took place between Sir Hector Greig & that gentleman in the year 1842.

His Lordship was at the same time pleased to intimate to me that valuable as Mr Jameson's services had proved & extensive as was his acquaintance with the whole subject on which he had written it was impossible that his Lordship should so far defer to his authority or to his arguments as to adopt his conclusions without being first apprized in what light they might be regarded by the framers of the Code & by the Legislative Council of Malta.

I was therefore directed to move the Council to enter upon a revision of the draft of the Code with an especial reference to Mr Jameson's remarks upon it & to narrow the discussion within its proper limits by an enumeration

& a statement of the successive questions demanding an authoritative decision.

My first step towards giving effect to this Instruction was to cause both the project of the Code & Mr Jameson's report on it to be printed in full length in order that a sufficient number of copies of them might be had for the purposes of reference and discussion.

This being effected copies of both documents were transmitted in April 1844 to the 2 surviving learned framers of the Code with the view of my obtaining their opinion whether it would be expedient to adopt in part or in whole the alterations & amendments suggested by Mr Jameson, in order that I might submit that opinion to the Council.

These gentlemen however declined entering on the consideration of Mr Jameson's report in detail, assigning among other reasons their opinion that many of the proposed alterations & amendments would if adopted change the whole spirit & basis of the Code. Under these circumstances I gave directions in July 1844 with the concurrence of the Council that the projected Code & Report should be referred to Dr Antonio Inicallif, the Crown Advocate for his opinion how far it were advisable to adopt the proposed alterations & amendments, & how far such an adoption would alter the spirit & basis of the Code.

This learned gentleman having given to the whole subject a full & attentive consideration, & having in September 1844 furnished a compendious report upon the points in question came to the conclusion that the greater part of Mr Jameson's amendments might be freely adopted & approved & that such alterations far from having the effect of destroying the spirit & the basis of the project would render the new Criminal Code useful & salutary, & leading as he thought to that improved state of society at large which a new Code must always be intended to accomplish.

Every necessary preliminary having thus been disposed of I took the earliest convenient opportunity of submitting the points in question to the consideration of the Council, with the assistance of the Crown Advocate who was present at all their sittings on the occasion, & whose opinion was heard on every point introduced for discussion. After a very patient, attentive & minute examination of the various details adduced to justice, which through adjournments lasted from November 1844 to June 1845, the Council concluded with the adoption of Mr Jameson's alterations & amendments in their full spirit & with but few & slight qualifications in their letter & detail.

The alterations and amendments made by the Council of Governt in the original draft of the Code requiring to be translated from English into Italian or vice versa & to be adapted to the Italian & English versions, some time has been necessarily occupied in the translations & and in getting a transcript of the Code, so altered and amended, made in both languages & it is only at this period that I am able to transmit for your consideration & approval the accompanying copy of the Code in Italian with a translation into English.

The most promising amendments suggested by Mr Jameson & adopted by the Council are the following

The abolition of the arrest at home & of the penal process not to go out at night

The modification of the scale of punishments as regards imprisonment

The suppression of the theory of alternating circumstances

The addition of new articles to supply omissions of the original project in respect of the punishment of seditious offences & of tumultuous assemblies

The extension of trial by jury to all offences within the jurisdiction of H. M. Criminal Court

But in order to understand the extent & value of the amendments proposed by Mr Jameson, I would solicit your perusal of that learned gentleman's report, both as showing his propositions in detail with his arguments for their adoption and as giving an insight into the principles of the Code as compiled by the original framers.

I am far from undervaluing the labours of the deceased or the surviving Code Commissioners as much learning & assiduity have evidently been employed on their important task, to which Mr Jameson in his report has more than once borne testimony; but the Council of Governt differed in opinion with the surviving Commissioners (Sir Ignatius Bonavita & Dr Chapelly) as to the practicality & utility of embodying with the original project the amendment proposed by Mr Jameson & I am bound to say with all deference to the opinion of the learned Commissioners that I consider a very great advance has been made towards the improvement of the Maltese Criminal law & procedure, by the adoption of the suggestions of Mr Jameson who has undoubtedly exhibited in his report a most extensive knowledge of the provisions of the continental codes as well as an intimate acquaintance with the general principles of Criminal Legislation.

If the Code as now presented for your consideration should meet with your approval, I have to solicit your sanction that I may take the usual steps of having it previously published for general information preparatory to bringing it again before the Council of Governt for the purpose of being enacted into law.

In consideration I have further to state that those portions of the criminal law which have not been embodied with the present Code (having been deferred by the original compilers for separate ordinances) will be enacted by such separate ordinances after the Code itself is passed into law & from the nature of those portions, regarding which the existing law will remain in force, little if any public inconveniences will be felt in the mean time, as the crimes they refer to are of rare occurrence & if the law in its present state comes to be applied it is in the power of the Queen's Representative in the exercize of HM prerogative to mitigate any too great severity of punishment by a due extension of mercy.

I have & etc
(signed) P.Stuart

CHAPTER ELEVEN
Personal and Family Sorrows

As 1845 drew towards its close it must have seemed to Andrew Jameson that a fruitful and contented life lay before him. He was happily married, his career was prospering and his health, if not robust, was nevertheless sustaining him in the discharge of his professional duties. Moreover, he was living and working in Edinburgh, a city where he had many friends and interests that had been difficult to pursue in Ayr. Events, however, were soon to destroy this happy prospect. The next two years brought the death of both his father and his elder surviving brother and he and other members of his family were soon to experience trials and disasters that made 1848 an *annus horribilis*.[1]

As it turned out, his father and his father-in-law were able to make their first and joint visit in early January 1846.[2] At the end of February, Melville and his father had to go to London, where they spent several days. They visited Marion Jameson, whose inability to withstand the climate of Bombay had necessitated her return home. The main purpose of the journey, however, was not social but legal, because Sheriff-Substitute Jameson was there to give evidence before the House of Lords on the Crawford peerage case. Litigation on the disputed claim to the titles and estates of Crawford and Lindsay lasted

---

[1] Although cited by the *Oxford English Dictionary* as being in use as early as 1985, Queen Elizabeth II brought the phrase to prominence in a speech to the Guildhall on 24th November 1992 marking the 40th anniversary of her Accession, in which she described the closing year as an *annus horribilis*.

> 1992 is not a year on which I shall look back with undiluted pleasure. In the words of one of my more sympathetic correspondents, it has turned out to be an "annus horribilis".

The phrase may allude to John Dryden's poem *Annus Mirabilis* about the events of 1666. The Queen's "sympathetic correspondent" was later revealed to be her former Assistant Private Secretary, Sir Edward Ford.

[2] v. p. 318 supra.

from 1810 until 1848 and it appears his evidence was in regard to the Scots law on heredity. He entered in the Almanack on 6th March that he had enjoyed "a delightful passage of 39 hours" by boat from London to Dundee. Melville wrote on 9th March to his brother to say they had brought back presents from Marion including one for Mrs Jameson of Drums, which he sent on to Andrew with the following comment: "You are requested to get the latter (the present for Mrs Jameson) delivered or sent to Mrs Jameson free of any expence if you can manage it in any way without her Ladyship becoming acquainted with the fact that it has come through any of us, as this would no doubt much diminish the value of the present in her eyes." The background to this was some property adjacent to Drums called Ferrymire that had been claimed by their father, her brother-in-law, through some clause in the will of Captain Jameson. An interpretation of this clause had been sought through the courts and only a few days previously the dispute had been settled in Sheriff-Substitute Jameson's favour, to the great chagrin of the captain's widow.[3]

Melville states in this letter that their father was in excellent health and had thoroughly enjoyed his visit to London. By contrast Andrew's son was giving him and Alexa great cause for concern because he was reacting very badly to teething and croning[4] much of the time. Worse, the child was suffering fits and on one day he had three separate attacks. A Dr Begbie considered the case to be critical and advised a change of air, whereupon Andrew arranged for Alexa, their son and nephew to move for a short time to Newington, where they could use the house[5] of Alexa's brother-in-law, the widowed minister Dr Begg, who was now in Canada. It was not long before young Andrew Jameson recovered. Meanwhile Melville's wife Jessie, who was expecting a child any day, was running a fever. She, too, got better and her father-in-law was able to enter in the Almanack: "Mrs

---

[3] A railway company wished to purchase Ferrymire, and other correspondence shows that Sheriff-Substitute Jameson had immediately sold it for £700. Melville Jameson had been acting for his father in the dispute about Ferrymire and its subsequent sale.

[4] *The Scots Dictionary* gives this word as "wailing".

[5] 15 Minto Place.

M. Jameson delivered of a son." This was the last entry that he made in this record of Jameson family life and affairs because on 23rd March he was taken ill, although there was no immediate cause for concern.

Apart from the worry over the health of his young son in the early days of March 1846 Andrew had had to deal with a case of civil unrest to the south of the county. Today, this would be a matter for the police to deal with initially but it was not until 1839 that the Scottish counties were empowered to establish their own professional police services. Thus, in 1846, policing, as we know it today, was still in its early stages of growth and sheriff-substitutes were still carrying out a law and order function little different from what had been the case in the previous century. In his novel *Guy Mannering*, which is set around 1783, Sir Walter Scott explains the duties of a sheriff-substitute of that era in relation to serious crimes (in this case the murder of an exciseman).

> The Sheriff-depute of the county arrived at Ellangowan[6] next morning by daybreak. To this provincial magistrate the law of Scotland assigns judicial powers of considerable extent, and the task of inquiring into all crimes committed within his jurisdiction, the apprehension and commitment of suspected persons, and so forth.[7]

In a letter of 7th March to his father he gives the following account of what had been happening:

> We have had a week of very painful anxiety & excitement since last Saty. On Sunday morning I was summoned to Fushie Bridge[8] in the absence of the Sheriff. I had a march of 15 miles at the head of about 30 police in pursuit of the criminals concerned in the riot & murder of the night before. I got home late supposing all was quiet.

[6] The locus of the crime. Scott used this name for Carlaeverock Castle in Dumfriesshire, where the action in the novel takes place.
[7] *Guy Mannering*, Chapter X, first paragraph.
[8] Near Gorebridge, Midlothian.

Next morning more alarming news arrived & I again went out. As soon as I reached the Police station I sent an express for a squadron of Dragoons & rode off alone to Crichton Moss. I found there about 2,000 people scattered along the new line of Railway firing huts & searching for Irishmen. I feebly endeavoured to command attention, riding in among the rioters at various points, but in vain. Some of the most violent threatened to pull me from my horse but I was not touched. I surveyed the scene of outrage for two hours with indescribable pain – ever looking to the distance for the appearance of the dragoons. They did not come until it was all over – but assisted us greatly in securing some of the guilty parties.

Before their arrival I was waiting at an Inn, when an Irish contractor[9] was pursued & took refuge at the door. I had a dreadful personal struggle, being the only man in the Inn, to get him pulled in & secure the door. They got in at the kitchen door in numbers and I was then obliged to advise them to let him out at a window, whence he escaped with some bruises – & the police coming up, we got his life protected.

There is some scanty evidence from the surviving correspondence about subsequent happenings, but in a letter (undated, but clearly written no more than a few days later) he tells his father: "Matters are all quiet on the Hawick Railway. We have 30 prisoners & Sheriff Gordon is anxious to hurry on the trial."[10]

Elizabeth Thomson wrote on 25th March 1846 to say that her uncle was not well but she gave no reason to cause them alarm. On 1st April

---

[9] This was a term then in common use meaning a man who had contracted to do a certain amount of work for an agreed payment. It was still in use in the steel fabrication industry on Teesside, Co Durham, as late as the 1950s.

[10] Among the papers concerning the Fushie Bridge riots is one from a Joseph Grant. It does not add very much to what we know of the riots, but since it may be of some interest to local historians it is added to this chapter as Appendix A.

1846 Andrew wrote to his father on certain legal matters and merely included a paragraph hoping that he would soon recover his strength and that he "would endeavour to be over sometime soon". A further letter from Elizabeth, written on 4th April, reported that his father was no worse and added "you would hear of Ferrymyre being sold. The company have bought the whole of it at £110 the Imperial Acre. We don't know yet what Mrs J. is to do." That letter must have reached Andrew that same day because he wrote again to his father to say how pleased he was to learn "that you had been a longer time in the parlour on Thursday." The bulk of the letter, however, concentrated on the success of the campaign in Sind, wherein John St Clair Jameson was playing his part, and on the funeral of young William Begg, the son of the minister, who had gone out to Canada after the death of his wife.[11] At a later date Andrew Jameson wrote at the head of this letter: "This the last letter to my dear father."

Melville wrote on 6th April to say that he was going over from Perth to see their father and hoped that Andrew could come on Saturday. The following day he wrote from Cupar to say that their father's health was deteriorating and asked his brother to arrange for a Dr Alison of Edinburgh to come. Replying on Thursday, 8th April, Andrew told his brother that Dr Alison would be leaving that morning for Cupar but that his duties made it impossible for himself to leave Edinburgh until Friday evening or Saturday morning. A very short letter arrived later that day wherein Melville told Andrew that he was "anxiously looking for Alison". That same evening Melville sent an express letter stating: "An unfavourable change has taken place, which makes me anxious that you should not lose any time in coming to see our dear father. Hire from Burntisland or Kirkcaldy." Andrew must have left for Cupar on 9th April, and that evening Alexa, now back at 14 Carlton Place, wrote to her husband at 9 p.m.: "The man has just arrived & I am grieved to find our dear father has shown such unfavourable symptoms. I earnestly pray he may yet be restored if it please God. How thankful

---

[11] v. p. 316 supra. It is not clear if this is the boy to whom Andrew and Alexa gave a temporary home or a brother.

you must be that you did not delay going over my dear A. I feel much alarmed & will be most anxious to hear from you. May the Lord be with you all & prepare your dear father for all His Holy Will." She added the following postscript: "Little Andrew is quite well and was out today. The man is just getting supper. In haste AGJ." The man to whom she referred must have brought her an express letter from her husband.

Andrew Jameson, Sheriff-Substitute of Fife, died the next day, 10th April 1846. His funeral took place on 14th April, and as a mark of respect all the shops in Cupar closed during the procession from the house to the graveyard. The coffin was carried by members of the local militia of which he had been a lieutenant-colonel and the provost and town council along with many other local dignitaries and members of the legal profession were among the mourners. A full description of the funeral and the tributes paid to Sheriff-Substitute Jameson are given at Appendix B to this chapter.

There were many letters of condolence. Alexa wrote a comforting letter to her husband, who remained at Cupar for a few days. Dr Chalmers said, "He was a very old friend and your mother, whom perhaps you scarcely recollect, one of the most cordial and warm-hearted of all my acquaintances in other days." There is no information of what became of Elizabeth Thomson.

The death of his father had one important consequence for anyone researching the life of Andrew Jameson. As a son he had been a devoted and regular correspondent, and fortunately his father had kept many of the letters sent to him. These were preserved by his son and succeeding generations. It would have been impossible to write a history of Andrew Jameson to 1846 without them. Although family correspondence continued, it was never in the volume and detail that existed before the father's death and, moreover, very little has survived.

For the rest of 1846 there are few relevant documents, apart from six from Alexa Jameson to her husband. In June she was on holiday with her young son at Barnhill with her brother Robert. There are three letters to Andrew, which are virtually illegible on account of faded ink and cross-writing but in one it is just possible to read of a visit with Robert to Caldarvan,[12] where they met the Whites.[13] A fourth letter about her holiday is highly legible but deals with family matters only except where she writes "I was delighted to get your letter on coming down here yesterday[14] and to hear you were well and getting on with your book."

It is possible that this is a reference to the Criminal Code of Malta. It had now been printed, and Lord Lyttleton had written[15] to say that the Secretary of State for the Colonies, W. E. Gladstone, had expressed "a hope that you will allow the Code in its present shape to be referred to you with a view of ascertaining whether the revisions suggested by you have been made so as to meet your approval." If this was the "book" to which his wife was referring, his revision must have been very nearly completed because Lord Lyttleton had sent the Code to him on 6th March and we know that it was back with the Colonial Office by September. There is another possibility. This is that the book to which Alexa Jameson refers was the Memoir[16] for which he had already started to gather material.

Alexa and her son were invited to Bowerswell at the end of August, and a long letter on the 28th of the month from her to her husband provides information about his sister Sophia and his brother Melville.

My dearest Andrew,

I am so happy to tell you that dear wee Andrew and I arrived in safety at ½ 3 o'clock yesterday and found Sophia,

---

[12] Caldarvan House, near Gartocharn, about 8 miles from Dumbarton, was the home of her sister Susan, wife of Robert Mackenzie (1812–1909), a prominent lawyer in Glasgow.

[13] This is mentioned for purely family interest. Mr J. St. C. Jameson, Mrs S. St. C. Scott and Mrs S. H. Gourlay, great-grand-children of Andrew Jameson, each inherited silver candelabra with an inscription on the base: "In Memory of Mrs White of Overton." Mrs White was a sister of Alexa Jameson. She gave much hospitality, mainly during the summer, to her nephews Andrew and John and their half-brother James. On Mrs White's death, James Jameson decided to recognize the kindness that he had received from Mrs White by having three candelabra inscribed in her memory.

[14] They were back at Barnhill after a visit to Balloch on Loch Lomond.

[15] v. p. 333 supra.

[16] v. p. 438 infra.

Melville & Jessie all waiting for us and very kind. They think Andrew a fine wee fellow but do not see his likeness to you or Grandpapa. The children here are really fine little things and they are all very happy together but I think Andrew is a little bewildered and does not find his little self of so much consequence among so many. I was vexed to leave you dearest Andrew but enjoy the prospect of your joining us soon.

This is a lovely day and I am in great hopes we may continue to have fine weather now. I should have written you last night but Jessie came up and I could not well get it done. After leaving you I got very sickish and continued so till we got to Queensferry, but after coming out of the steamer one of the ladies very kindly changed seats with me and except for the heat I was quite comfortable after that. I could not get a seat on the top unfortunately but the driver was very attentive and baby was very merry and happy till near our journey end, when he got very sleepy and restless.[17]

This place is looking beautiful and I admire the house exceedingly.[18] It reminded me of our marriage trip dear Andrew and what cause for thankfulness we have for the many and great mercies with which we have been blessed although so unworthy of them all. Sophia is looking remarkably well[19] and is very kind as were all the others, Phemy looking well and George[20] very much grown and become like Melville. He and his friend set off for the Highlands on

---

[17] It would seem that Alexa went to South Queensferry, probably by coach, where she caught one of the little steamers that plied up and down the Firth of Forth. She would disembark at Perth and be taken by some horse-drawn conveyance to somewhere near Bowerswell.

[18] George Gray had recently carried out considerable alterations to Bowerswell.

[19] She was now 38 and had produced her twelfth child that April. Three more were to follow in 1847, 1850 and 1855.

[20] Euphemia was now 18 and George 16. Sophia's next six children had all died before this visit and another in 1847. Her last five children all survived into adulthood.

Monday and I believe Mrs Gray expects the Parkers[21] and several of their friends on Monday or Tuesday next so the house will be quite full and I think we will require to go west on Monday.

They were all sorry you were not with us but happy at the prospect of seeing you soon. I do not think Melville looking so well as usual and Jessie says he has been ailing a little. She wishes him to take a trip but he thinks he cannot get away from his business.

We are going down as soon as I am done writing to see Jessie & the children. They say Miss Baird has been from home and Jessie thinks she has not yet returned but I will call whenever I hear of her arrival. Poor body, she has a great anxiety to see baby and me. Mrs Gray is to have a dinner party tomorrow and we are to dine at Croft House[22] on Monday but I hope there will be no party. As you know I am fond of questions. How did your party go on yesterday, my dearest Andrew? I hope you enjoyed it and were none the worse. Get your papers over like a dear and then you will go away with comfort.

When does the painter begin his work on the nursery? And have you heard of Mary Orr and Marion's nieces? Sophia and Phemy think Marion[23] sadly fallen off in appearance, they scarcely knew her but she is a fine creature and it is very nice having her and baby close by my room. I have been thinking of you all alone, dearest, and I am sure you will feel the house so dull without me and please write me all your news. I would like you to ask one of the servants to call at Aitchisons[24] to thank them for sending the nursery maids but tell them one of them would have suited nicely

---

[21] Presumably the parents and their two daughters, who were friends of Euphemia at Avonbank School.

[22] The home of Melville and Jessie Jameson.

[23] Marion Jameson was also a guest of the Grays.

[24] This must have been a nursing agency.

but my sister had first got me one in Glasgow. It is right to let them know the place is filled in case they should send more.

I would like to continue further, dearest Andrew, but I have got a disagreeable headache. I think it is from the long drive yesterday and that it will go off.

With a kiss from wee Andrew and his mummy and love from all here, believe me, dearest Andrew, your truly affectionate wife,

A G Jameson

The only other correspondence that survives from 1846 is a letter of Wednesday, 2nd September from Alexa Jameson to her husband. She is still at Bowerswell and the letter is mainly about the sudden death from typhoid of a young Mrs McDuff, who was well known to Sophia Gray. However, there are two other matters of interest. The first is that Alexa had learned that Miss Baird was back home and on the previous Monday had paid her a visit with young Andrew. This had greatly pleased the old woman, and she was delighted to have Andrew for a few hours on the following day. The second matter that Alexa mentioned was, in light of later events, much more important.

Phemy had a letter from the Ruskins yesterday and it seems *eight* of a party expect to arrive here on Saturday but if they keep their intention, you and I[25] are to go down to Melville's and remain till Monday or Tuesday with Marion and baby. Melville will perhaps go the length of Dunkeld with us if we go that way.

Correspondence for the year 1847 can be divided into two categories. One relates to the death on 22nd March in Bombay of Major John St Clair Jameson. His wife, whose health had required her to return home,

---

[25] In another part of the letter we learn that Andrew Jameson is joining his wife and son the following Friday (4th September).

and other members of his family were to learn of this in early May. Major Jameson's final years in India and the manner of his death have already been described in the second appendix to Chapter Six. The other category is mainly domestic and of little interest.

There was, however, one event in 1847 that requires special comment and this was the death on 31st May of Dr Chalmers, the great scholar and divine. He was well acquainted with Andrew Jameson's parents, and since Andrew's mother was a Chalmers there may have been a distant family connection. Although there is no documentation that states this specifically, the words that Dr Chalmers used in his letter of condolence on the death of Betsy Jameson does hint at this.[26] He died suddenly and peacefully overnight and "had evidently passed away in a moment, without pain or even consciousness."[27] As would be expected, there was an immense attendance at his interment in the Grange Cemetery and Andrew Jameson was of the number. On the back of the letter that he had received from Dr Chalmers on the death of his father, Andrew Jameson wrote: "A sorrowing church this day followed the remains of their much gifted and honoured father to the grave. Most men seemed to mourn him as a father – he was so affectionate and yet so great. I lament his death personally as a friend – the honoured teacher of early days, the friend of my parents and as a great champion of truth and righteousness in our day."

Sometime earlier in this year Andrew and Melville Jameson had decided that they should honour their father by raising money for a bust to commemorate his contribution both to his profession and to his public life. They asked members of the family and close acquaintances to suggest suitable epitaphs. Patrick Stirling felt that he had not the skills necessary for this but nevertheless sent in what he called a "contribution". Sophia very sensibly commented that whatever was decided must include a reference to their father's work for the improvement of the salaries of sheriff-substitutes. Whether a bust was ever commissioned is not recorded in any surviving documentation.

[26] v. p. 33 supra.
[27] From *The Popular Encyclopaedia*. Blackie and Sons, Edinburgh, 1883.

In a letter of 17th April 1847 Melville informed his brother that he had been over to Cupar for a consultation with Mr Drummond, the solicitor who was responsible for the settlement of their father's estate. Melville advised that it should be wound up soon, especially the sale of heritable property. What is more interesting was what he wrote about their niece. "The Bowerswellites are in good health. Phemy is going to visit the Ruskins at London next week."

In June Andrew and Lexy had another son, Alexander, who almost immediately was given the diminutive "Alick". On 7th July Melville wrote to say that he and Jessie would be going to Aberdeen to see her sister and that "Phemy has returned from London." In a letter of 12th August Melville recounts in great detail the journey that he and Jessie took to Aberdeen and it is so interesting that it has been added to this chapter as Appendix C.

At the end of August and early September Andrew and his family enjoyed a holiday at Barnhill with Alexa's parents. He returned to Edinburgh to negotiate a move[28] from their home in Carlton Place to Newington, while she and the children continued to stay at Barnhill. During this time she fitted in a short stay at Caldarvan and wrote anxiously from there that she was "weary to hear about the house." She also reminded her husband that "some of your things are looking rather shabby and do take care of your stomach."

Whether he began to suffer from a stomach or some other complaint, her husband wrote to say that he was unwell. This drew from the normally sympathetic Lexy the somewhat acerbic comment: "I was vexed to find you had been complaining so much, dearest Andrew. I really think I must just remain at home after this as you always seem to get unwell when alone." He must have recovered because there is no more heard of this illness, and by October, negotiations for the move out to 10 Blacket Place, Newington, having been completed, they left Carlton Place. Melville wrote a long letter on 28th October. He approved of the move of his brother and family to a "more salubrious district" but warned that their former family home in Cupar "will

---

[28] It is not clear whether this was a purchase or rented accommodation.

not sell at present." We learn, too, from this letter that John Ruskin must have been the first guest of the Jamesons at their new home in Newington. "John Ruskin was much pleased with your kindness. He is a very excellent young man and I am sure your literati friends would admire him."

Ruskin's visit to Perth marked the beginning of a somewhat fraught six months for George and Sophia Gray that culminated in the marriage of Ruskin and their daughter Euphemia, still known in the family as Phemy. Ruskin's parents had hoped that their talented son would make a marriage that was socially advantageous and they had severe reservations about the suitability of his choice, not least because George Gray was teetering on the verge of bankruptcy. Between 1844 and 1847 the government had given permission for over 9,000 miles of railway to be built and this had prompted what became known as "The Railway Mania". Although totally ignorant of the problems involved in constructing railway lines, thousands purchased shares, often investing their entire savings in projects that were unrealistic. George Gray, the apparent epitome of a sound and financially adept Scottish businessman, was such a speculator. The Limited Liability Act was not passed until 1855 and until that time all shareholders, irrespective of the degree of their investment, were jointly liable for the debts of the company, whose shares they held. When Gray was called upon to meet his obligations, he found himself unable to do so and he survived solely through a stroke of great fortune. He had long been friendly with Archibald Burns, who had managed the Perth branch of the Central Bank of Scotland since that bank's formation in 1834. Burns arranged a loan that enabled Gray to absolve himself of his debts and eventually pay off the loan. John Ruskin (Senior) was highly critical of what he considered to be gross financial incompetence on the part of George Gray and wrote to say so. Nevertheless he and his wife reconciled themselves to the betrothal since they had genuine fears that any opposition on their part might result in their son having some form of mental breakdown.[29]

---

[29] v. Lutyens, M. (1972), *The Ruskins and the Grays*, p. 1. John Murray, London.

Melville wrote again to his brother on 17th November 1847 and mentioned the betrothal of their niece and John Ruskin. "Phemy, I believe, has made an interesting communication to you. I think we have all reason to expect much happiness to her. He is certainly one in every way worthy of her and from his habits and tone of mind will tend to improve her much. They and <u>he</u> in particular are devotedly attached which is also of great consequence." He continues with other family matters and adds the following postscript: "Phemy's affair is still to be considered a perfect secret."

On the last day of November Melville wrote again to tell him that Sophia had given birth to Melville Jameson Gray.[30] He also sympathised with Andrew, who was ill with influenza, and this was a harbinger of worse to follow. Patrick Stirling had also been ill, and on 14th January 1848, replying to a letter from Andrew, he remarked that "good health this winter has been the exception rather than the rule". After thanking Andrew for his kind inquiries he wished him a full recovery and added an encomium on the healing properties of cod liver oil, to which he attributed his recovery.

Did you ever try that fashionable medicine cod liver oil? I have been taking a little spoonful every morning before breakfast and I think myself greatly the better of it. It is vile stuff to the taste, but there are no other disagreeable effects. I advise you to try it. *The northern nations all use animal oils during the cold season.* On this I found my theory in favour of cod liver oil. There is a woman at Leith who makes and sells the best but you will get it from any of the apothecaries.

If Andrew Jameson did follow his friend's advice it had no ameliorating effect. Although he made the effort to travel to Perth to attend the wedding of his niece Euphemia to John Ruskin on 10th April, he was soon afterwards forced to seek leave of absence on account of ill health.

---

[30] Melville Gray lived until 7th June 1946, dying at Bowerswell.

He had consulted James Miller, Professor of Surgery at the University of Edinburgh, who certified on 21st April 1848 that he was unfit for work.

> I hereby on soul & conscience certify that Mr Andrew Jameson, Sheriff S., is under my professional care, affected with Dysphonia;[31] and that I consider it absolutely necessary, on account of his health, that he should leave Edinburgh, for a milder exposure; remaining, if possible, a month or six weeks, at least.

To what part of Scotland Andrew and Alexa went with their boys is not recorded, but after four weeks there was no improvement and he had to write to Sheriff Gordon on 19th May asking for further leave of absence.[32]

> At the urgent request of several of my relatives I have consulted Dr Begbie and Professor Miller in regard to the state of my health and I am extremely sorry to say that they are of the opinion that I must give up all business for a time and endeavour by country air and relaxation to recruit my strength, which has been so much influenced by the attack of influenza I had in winter. I enclose their certificate from which you will observe that they entertained a favorable opinion of the probable effects of such retirement.
>
> They concurred in their thinking that any attempt to continue as I had previously been doing & performing the quieter part of the duties might be prejudicial and calculated to prolong the weakened state of my system.
>
> In these circumstances I hope you will sanction my being relieved until the end of September.

---

[31] Difficulty in speaking.

[32] This letter was sent to the Reform Club in London, where Sheriff Gordon must have been staying at this time.

The letter continues with the arrangements that he proposed to cover his absence. A colleague called Dickson was prepared to undertake all his duties and Andrew Jameson informed his superior that he would make some payment to this man out of his own salary. He concluded by saying that his doctors advised him to pass some weeks in England then go with his family to the Highlands until the beginning of October.

The seriousness of Andrew Jameson's illness is made clear by his doctors' certificate that accompanied the letter to Sheriff Gordon.

We the undersigned having repeatedly visited and examined And. Jameson Esq Sheriff-substitute of Edinburgh are of the opinion, that he is labouring under an affection of the throat and air passages, which requires for its removal the complete suspension of all public duty, and retirement to the country for at least three months. We are further of the opinion that such relief and retirement may be accompanied by an amendment of health to the extent of enabling him to undertake the duties of his office at the beginning of winter without risk of further interruption.
Signed: James Begbie MD
          Jas Miller, Professor of Surgery in the university.
Edin.
May 18 1848

He must have written to Patrick Stirling about his illness and asked about accommodation on Lochearnside during the summer. Stirling acknowledged receipt of a letter on 24th May and replied that he was unacquainted with that neighbourhood. Nevertheless Andrew did find accommodation at Glenbeich near Lochearnhead and was there with his family during the summer months.

He and Lexy invited Sophia to visit them but in a long letter full of family news she explained why she felt that she must decline. Quite apart from the fact that she was pregnant, her husband "has been very dull for many weeks"; this was a euphemism for depression. "I wish he could think less about it but that seems beyond his powers. However, I got him to go with a party of ladies and gentlemen to Glamis Castle 2 days ago, a pleasure party, the Kerrs and the Thomsons and the Stuarts. He took Robert[33] who behaved well and was no trouble. Mr Gray was much the better of it and much the better of being fully occupied." She also commented on her brother's ankle that had prevented him from climbing the local hills. "I think you ought to come down[34] and take advice about your ancle [sic] if it is not improving fast as these things ought not to be trifled with." This must have been the same trouble that had its origins, according to Euphemia Gray in her letter of 9th February 1844,[35] when he had tried to see how far he could jump. It had also prevented him escorting her round Ayr when she visited him and Lexy in early 1845. Sophia ended her letter by telling him that Euphemia and her husband, John Ruskin, had managed to lease a house for three years in London's prestigious Grosvenor Square.

Andrew and Lexy Jameson were back in Edinburgh by mid-September but they had not left Perthshire when Jessie Jameson, his sister-in-law, gave birth on 20th August to a premature child, a boy that died the following day. She made a slight recovery but died on 26th September. According to George Gray, who wrote that evening to Andrew, "Her liver and kidneys became affected & refused to act; consequently dropsy intervened." We know that Andrew and Alexa wrote to Melville because, in a letter of 20th November, Melville acknowledged receipt of "your kind letters". The two brothers had always been very close and Andrew's letter would have been composed in terms that fully expressed his sorrow for Melville's loss. That letter, if it has survived, will be with Melville's descendants. Andrew attended the funeral, spending the night with the Grays at Bowerswell. Sophia went to stay at Croft House with Melville and his

---

[33] Robert was 6.
[34] i.e. to Perth.
[35] v. p. 297 supra.

three children and wrote to Andrew from there on 4th October saying that their brother, with the help of friends, some of whom had been similarly afflicted, was gradually coming to terms with his loss and was even beginning to take a little interest in his work. Sophia then inquired about Andrew's health.

> We are now anxious in turn about you & dear Lexy. She will be so vexed if you are the worse of coming here and I should dread it. Lexy would be delighted to hear of the steadfast faith of dear Jessie who had no fear in the valley of death – his rod & staff did comfort her as she expressed. You have told her fully about it all.

A postscript asks Andrew to "let us hear how you are as soon as possible".

In early September George Gray (Junior) had stayed a few days with his uncle and aunt and from his letter of thanks we learn that Andrew had visited Leamington for treatment, possibly from Dr Jephson, and that a Dr Riach of Perth had told Melville that his brother was now "more and more a hydropathic patient." This comment is supported by Andrew's next move in his attempt to combat his illness. He had returned to Edinburgh and resumed his duties but after a short while he had to seek and was granted another six months' leave. Since winter was approaching he decided Rothesay in Bute was a better prospect than Edinburgh. The period 1820–1880 experienced the development of spa towns, probably encouraged by the success of Dr Jephson at Leamington, and places as unlikely as Peterhead entered this competition to attract patients. At Rothesay an enterprising Dr Paterson had opened Glenburn House that was described in his promotional material as a "Hydropathic Establishment". Sir James Clark, whom Andrew had consulted on some occasions when he had been in London, had praised the climate of Bute as "mild and equable, and as resembling that of the south-west of England and France and the Channel Islands".[36]

---

[36] From the September 1882 issue of *Christian World*.

His sister Sophia wrote a very comforting letter to him on 23rd October:

> I have been thinking a great deal about Lexy and you since I heard from her of your *break down*. It is truly distressing but you must try to keep up and take things as cheerfully as possible for dear Lexy's sake, who is doing all she can to keep you up but I doubt not she requires to be kept up herself in her present situation[37] – as it requires no little nerve to leave home and all her home comforts with the prospect she has before her were it not made easy to her by her great interest for you.
>
> We were all glad to hear you had got another 6 months leave. Before the end of that time something may turn out for your advantage. I have no fear of you whatever. Your acquirements are so various and your friends so true so that if you do not get one thing you will get another. We cannot at present see what the end will be but we may be assured it is for the best. All this may be sent to bring about a change of situation to you which may be for your ultimate good and that of your family.

Lexy's father wrote to Andrew Jameson on 28th October 1848. "I had the pleasure of receiving this morning your letter informing of your safe arrival & comfortable settlement and I am glad that you affected your object in getting a suitable lodging[38] so expeditiously & I hope I may add, reasonably." From this we gather that the Jameson family must have crossed over to Rothesay about 25th or 26th October. Lexy received a letter about the same time[39] from her sister Fanny White and although their father had made no reference to Alexa in his letter Fanny wrote that "she was most happy that you have not felt the worse of all

---

[37] She was pregnant.
[38] The address was 8 Battery Place, Rothesay.
[39] Undated, but the context suggests that it was also written at the end of October 1848.

your anxiety and fatigue but you must really take care and neither be *stretching* or standing around on your feet." This was wise advice but in view of what happened before the year was out one wonders whether in their somewhat straitened financial circumstances Alexa was unable to employ the domestic assistance that was then customary for a family of their social standing.

As for Andrew, his health did not, at first, respond to the mild and damp air of Bute. It will be appropriate to reproduce at this point some lengthy excerpts from a letter that he wrote on 10th November to a Dr Robert Buchanan because they provide a very precise account of the position to which his poor health had brought him.

Andrew Jameson and Dr Buchanan appear to have had a mutual friend called Alexander Dunlop, and it was from this man that Buchanan heard that Andrew had been granted a further period of leave from his duties as a sheriff-substitute and was now resident in Bute. On 6th November he wrote to Andrew: "In these circumstances I venture to bring again before you the subject of my former correspondence – the Scottish Guardian. A lingering idea that circumstances might reopen this negotiation led the directors of that journal to hang upon their oars till now. Dunlop has been our interim supply. If you see your way more clear to entertain the proposition formerly made it is again at your service. It occurs to me that you might at any rate try your hand for a month or two. You could do this for a time at least, living as you are at Rothesay, without inconvenience. But meanwhile my first & more pressing object is to bring the matter before you anew with a view to learn whither (sic) you are disposed to look at it favourably."

Back in 1842 when Andrew had been seeking, unsuccessfully, a suitable position Buchanan had suggested that he might join this newspaper as its editor. Andrew had declined that offer but now with a wife and two children and a third on the way he had to give serious consideration to this second opportunity of becoming a newspaper editor. As Sophia had said in her letter, "Your acquirements are so various and your friends so true so that if you do not get one thing you will get another."

Andrew Jameson's letter to Dr Buchanan has survived as a draft that he prepared before giving this reply to the offer from the *Scottish Guardian*:

I regret exceedingly that I do not yet find myself strong enough to venture upon going up to Glasgow to see you at present. I must content myself therefore with writing. I wish frankly to explain to you my position & my views in regard to the proposal, which you have so kindly renewed.

The result of the recent attempt to resume my duties in Edinburgh as well as former experience in regard to the effects of my confinement on continual mental labour upon my health make me doubtful whether even at the end of my leave I can hope to go on in my present office with any prospect of permanence. The same objection, you will easily conceive, applies to any other employment requiring much exertion and even more strongly to a new sphere for which I may not naturally be well qualified. Several of my medical advisors appear to take the same view of the matter and have been recommending me to be looking out for some quiet situation in the country such as the sheriff-substituteship of a small district. This involves a considerable sacrifice in point of income & other advantages to a young family besides the giving up of those hopes of usefulness to the Church & especially the plans of evangelisation at home and abroad, which were the principal inducement that led me to leave Ayrshire. Yet after all that has passed it seems at present to be my duty to make the sacrifice rather than encumber the risk of being altogether out of employment.

I was accordingly preparing to take advantage of any good opportunity that might occur in the way referred to & I have been in hopes that through the good providence of God such [word illegible] might cast up in the course of time.

In regard to your proposal I still feel great doubts about my fitness to conduct the journal in a satisfactory and useful way, being always [a few illegible words] ceased to have any desire for keeping up even an ordinary amount of reading in the general or periodical literature of the day.

At the same time as you have again put it in my power and circumstances seem to point to a different occupation from that which I have been long pursuing the uncertainties of my present position seem to point to the duty of making every exertion I can for the sake of my family & while one door of usefulness is shut to try another which is opening.

I would gladly adopt your suggestion of trying my hand for a month or two while I am here as soon as I am sufficiently recovered to undertake any regular employment. To all appearances I could scarcely do this for six weeks to come. I fear this arrangement might not suit the directors but I beg you will have no hesitation in telling me if it does not. You will understand that for obvious reasons what I have explained to you in reference to my present office & prospects is in confidence. Whatever may be the result I assure you I feel deeply your kindness in this matter and that of the friend you formerly referred to.

Later that same month he must have written to Professor James Miller saying that his health was improving and asking if there were any truth in the rumour that the sheriff-substitute of Lanarkshire, Daniel Vere, was contemplating retirement. In a long letter (dated 22nd November 1848) that suggests their relationship went beyond that of medical adviser and patient (there are references to some debate within the Free Church of Scotland concerning the missionary Alexander Duff) Miller said that he knew nothing about the possible retirement of Vere but that if he wanted to return to work he should apply for "Lanark or some similar situation. I can see your prospects being very favourable of enjoying a long life of endeavour in such a situation, discharging the duties thoroughly, being otherwise of service in your day and generation as God gives you power and energy, while I see a prospect very cloudy as to your return to business here – great risk of breaking down and then a compulsion to resign or nothing. I think the risk of returning here too great." In short, his health might bear up if he became a sheriff-substitute in a quiet rural county but would be unable to sustain the pressure if he returned to work in Edinburgh.

Shortly afterwards Andrew heard that Sheriff-Substitute Vere was indeed contemplating retirement and had approached Mr Alison, the Sheriff of Lanarkshire. A George Skene wrote to Andrew to say that the sheriff considered him to be the best qualified candidate but required answers on two matters. One was an assurance that Andrew's health was equal to the demands of the position, while the other was his opinion of Vere's statement that his offer of resignation must be conditional upon his receiving a share of the salary. Andrew left the draft of his reply among his papers. This stated that the sheriff should have no fears about his health but that the financial demands that Vere was making about his salary were illegal. It is worthwhile to give Andrew Jameson's full answer on this second point because it demonstrates his command of the law of Scotland and of the language in which he could express it.

AB

This makes me the more regret the other condition – of making up Mr Vere's retiring allowance to the amount of his full salary, regarding which after much consideration my doubts are not removed. The pecuniary loss involved in Mr Vere's proposal would be a strong objection to any man dependant upon his salary. But it humbly appears to me to be the least difficulty to be encountered in acceding to it. The arrangement seems to savour of a *pactum illicitum* in reference to an office of public trust. It stipulates for the payment of an annual sum as the price of his resignation which B must pay in order to obtain the appointment. So far as it goes, this looks like a sale of judicial office. I do not say that there may not occur circumstances of extreme hardship sufficient to justify such an arrangement but certainly apart from any extraordinary speciality it appears to me to partake of a doubtful, if not an illegal, character.

He concluded by asking Mr Skene to thank the sheriff for his kind consideration of him as a candidate but that, for the reason he had given, he could not accept the condition that Sheriff-Substitute Vere was demanding. This must have ended any chance of his succeeding Vere, and in a letter of 5th January 1849 from Miller he learned that someone called Dyer had obtained the appointment and that "there has been a Transaction." From this we can conclude that Dyer accepted the appointment on terms not dissimilar to those which Andrew Jameson had refused.

On 2nd December Melville wrote to tell him that Sheriff-Substitute Robertson of Forfarshire had died and that Andrew should apply to be his successor. However, within a few days Andrew learned that the appointment had gone to Dickson, who had been carrying out the duties of interim sheriff-substitute of the county of Edinburgh on his behalf under an arrangement whereby Andrew had been making a contribution to the man's salary.[40] Dickson's promotion now posed problems for Andrew Jameson's tenure of office as sheriff-substitute of the county of Edinburgh.

The career of his brother-in-law, Neil Campbell, was now prospering, and he made it his business to represent Andrew Jameson's interests in Edinburgh. Fortunately he often met Sheriff Gordon in the course of his professional duties. Not surprisingly, Gordon was concerned about Andrew's continuing absence and the need to find a successor for Dickson and he asked Campbell whether it was correct that Andrew had no intention of returning to his post. Campbell was able to deny this rumour and assured him that Andrew would be returning to his duties in the spring because his health was improving. This was indeed the case, and in a letter of 8th December Melville wrote: "I am delighted to hear

---

[40] v. p. 362 supra.

you are so advanced again. May God grant continued convalescence."

Neil Campbell reported this conversation in a letter to Andrew Jameson of 9th December together with the information that the sheriff agreed with him that the salaries of interim sheriffs should be the responsibility of the Crown. Writing one week later, Campbell told him that Gordon had made inquiries about payment of interim sheriffs but had been told that the Crown had no obligation to pay their salaries. Gordon had also raised once more the matter of Andrew's resumption of his duties. He was worried that after a short while Andrew would need to take time off again and given Andrew Jameson's health record this was not an unreasonable concern. Nevertheless Gordon appointed an advocate called Tytler to succeed Dickson under the same terms.

At the end of December 1848 a terrible change took place in Andrew Jameson's life. Having arrived in Rothesay late in October, Andrew and Alexa Jameson had decided that in the interests of Andrew's health they would not return to Edinburgh, even though Lexy was expecting their third child. During mid-November Lexy was unwell for a few days but early in December Andrew was able to tell Melville that she had recovered and, moreover, that his own health was improving. Melville, still suffering grievously from the loss of Jessie, replied: "I shall be anxious to hear of Lexy. I trust you may never experience the anxieties that I have felt at such an hour and may the Lord spare her long to you. I am glad to hear you and she are well." Regretfully his trust in the Lord was to be severely tested.

Early in December "Aunt Mackenzie" and Lexy's sister Elizabeth (known within the family as Bessie) came across to Rothesay to assist in the confinement. "Aunt Mackenzie" could have been another sister, Susan, whose married name was Mackenzie, or an older generation of that family.[41] A son, John St Clair, was born on 8th December, and the letters to his family show that Andrew had no reason to have concern about either Lexy or the child since both appeared well. The normal

---

[41] Very confusedly, both Bessie and Susan were married to men called Mackenzie. Walter Mackenzie, to whom Bessie was married, played a prominent part in Lexy's funeral arrangements.

letters of congratulation arrived. Melville told him that Miss Baird "thought you must either have it John or James: both are family names entitled to a preference before any other." Fanny White was more worried about the abscesses on her husband's leg than anything else. Marion Jameson was delighted that the child was to have the same Christian names as her late husband and added the fatuous comment that her brother-in-law should approach John Ruskin to seek his assistance in finding appropriate employment. Effie[42] Ruskin did not send her congratulations to Alexa until 18th December. She had heard earlier of John's birth from her brother George in a postscript to a letter that had seemed to suggest that Alexa had given birth to triplets. Accordingly she waited until she had heard from her mother "in proper form." Andrew wrote to a Campbell relation that he hoped to come across to the mainland soon for some skating. Around 24th December there must have been some sudden and serious deterioration in Lexy's condition because Fanny White wrote on 26th December: "Your letter this morning again filled us with anxiety about dear Lexie. I fear the bleeding yet hope it may be on account of removing these stitches or passing through her body." It was, unfortunately, neither of these, and Alexa Jameson had already died before her sister wrote this letter.

How the doleful news reached Perth is best described by reproducing the letter that Sophia Gray wrote on 27th December. It was headed "Be ye also ready", which was not, perhaps, quite the message that her brother would want to hear.[43]

My dearest afflicted Andrew how deeply I feel for your awful loss! Mr Gray opened your note to Melville (in his absence in Edinburgh) as he feared from the look of the letter that something had happened and alas! it is too true that something sad, sad has happened. Oh the dear, dear creature to be taken from you who had so much need of

---

[42] She signed it "Effie C. Ruskin" and from this time abandoned "Phemy" or "Euphemia".
[43] "Wherefore ye also, be ye ready, for in that hour that ye think not the Son of man cometh", Matthew Chapter 24 verse 44.

her kindness & love & in your frequent illnesses to be supported by her charming & hopeful disposition. What a wife, what a mother she has been. We can never cease to mourn for our loss but we may rest assured that she is now with her Saviour whom she so much loved on earth and on her account we cannot have one single fear; but for you dear Andrew I have many. This is a dreadful loss to you and would have been so at any time but more especially just now when you are not strong. Oh may the Lord support you in this trying time & give the balm of consolation unto the wounded spirit. For the sake of your dear little children try to keep up & bear your grief.

I was so thankful to hear that Mrs Mackenzie was with her dear sister. She would see every thing done that earthly skill could do and as she is with you I will not offer myself at present. Melville, poor fellow, left home on Tuesday morning for Glasgow and was to be in Edinburgh today and home tonight. It will probably be late before he arrives – but if by any chance he hears of the sad occurrence in Edin he may be at Rothesay before my letter but if not, he will get your letter when he arrives tonight & start tomorrow for Rothesay. It will be a great shock to Mel as he thought dear Lexy out of all danger. I dined with him at Christmas when he talked of you both. Little do we know what is awaiting us and our dear Lexy often said of having to be ready when our call comes. At such a time, dear Andrew, it will seem selfish to talk of my own grief but what <u>2</u> dear sisters I have lost within these three months! I can write no more. I feel more for you than I can tell & so does [sic] Mr Gray & George. We all *loved* her, we all had shared in her hospitality & kindness and felt her to be one of the family. We all sympathise deeply for Mr Campbell, her sisters and Niel. They were all so kind and attached to each other they will all feel her to be a personal loss. Now, dear Andrew, I hope to hear from Melville that you are bearing up under this *great affliction* with Christian fortitude. Oh may you be strengthened is the sincere wish of your affectionate sister,

Sophia M. Gray

It is not known if Melville learned of his sister-in-law's death in Edinburgh or on his return to Perth, but it is clear from the following letter that he did go to Rothesay to support Andrew and had returned to Perth on 30th December.

I arrived here quite safely about an hour ago, and thanks to God I find my little children well. Eliza's cough is much the same, but it is not serious. I am just going up to see Sophia, who must be anxious to hear about you and of the last moments of dear Lexy. Sad will be the recital and yet how the mind loves to dwell on every incident connected with the few fast fleeting hours of her passing away into Eternity.

I trust my dear Andrew you have been supported today by the same Almighty arm, who embraces in love her glorified spirit and that you will be so throughout the sad duties which are still before you.

Walter Mackenzie agrees with me in thinking you ought to come to Dumbarton with the dear departed's remains on Monday & take them to Uncle Humphry's house.[44]

With most affectionate & deep sympathy, believe me, my dearest Andrew,

Your most affectionate brother,

Melville Jameson

My kind remembrances to Bessie & Mrs Mackenzie and a kiss to each of the dear pets.

---

[44] Humphry Campbell was Sheriff-Substitute of Dunbartonshire and brother of Lexy's father. He lived at Croslet near Dumbarton.

It is from this letter only that we have any information about the arrangements for the funeral of Alexa Jameson. We know from another source that it took place on 2nd January 1849.

Apart from members of his immediate family Andrew Jameson received 29 letters[45] of condolence from friends and acquaintances, all expressing their sympathy and drawing attention to the consolation that he would receive from his deeply held Christian beliefs. This was how bereavement was expressed at that time and the sincerity is none the less on that account. From the number of letters with their many references to her character and conduct, it is clear that Alexa Jameson had been greatly admired and that her passing caused much sorrow.

Two more letters deserve to be reproduced in total. One is from his niece Euphemia, now Mrs John Ruskin, and one from John Ruskin himself that has been described as one of the loveliest letters of sympathy ever written. On the day of his wife's funeral Andrew wrote to his sister Sophia: "Mr Ruskin has written to me a kind letter – one of the kindest I have received." John Ruskin wrote to Andrew Jameson on 29th December 1848:

Dear Mr Jameson,

I have not yet been able to convince myself of the truth and reality of the distress, which have come upon you for indeed we are in great sorrow for you as well as in great fear and we cannot tell what to do for you or to say to you for there is nothing we can say but must at present increase your pain or be to you as an empty sound. I dare not speak to you of her whom you have lost – nor tell you now what perhaps hereafter may be grateful to you – how much I regarded her, how fondly the thought of her was associated with my own dearest and most precious memories, how truly she was to all of us the type of gentleness to duty and piety – and there is no need for me to tell you anything

[45] He retained these and they are now among the documents from which this life of him is being written.

else than this – your trust in her exalted happiness needs no confirmation – your own knowledge of every source of consolation which is open to you is greater than mine; I said I was in fear for you and so I must be from the suddenness with which the stroke has fallen on you – you have not had time to take to you the armour of God & if you had been an infirm or a formal or a would-be Christian, you must have been now utterly crushed; but I know you habitually fixed your heart on the other side of the grave: and that you will not therefore be cast down as another would have been by God placing your chief treasure there too. Men call these unlooked for sorrows *strange* – when they fall upon those who trust in God – how sad a world would it be if they *were* strange – if it were not as clear as the written revelation itself that God will gather the wheat out of the tares, though he rarely rends the tares out of the wheat – that the blessing which he gave to Josiah is often that which he chooses for those whom he loves: and that for those whom they leave to go forth weeping – bearing their precious seed, there is still a light to be *sown* with it – that light that enables them to say as their Master said For this cause came I unto this hour and to know that God has glorified his name – when they that stand by say that "it thundered." You have much depending on you – though little, it will seem at present, remaining to you but I have no fear that a permanent acuteness of suffering can ever be the lot of one to whom it has been granted to be so faithful & useful a servant, both of God and man as you have been and I trust will still be. I know that you are *faithful* and that you have ever looked rather to the work before than the rewards with you – perhaps the time may be very near when that reward will come to all such is its fulness. Write to us when you can, do not pain yourself by dwelling on what has been but tell us about your present health – and about what it is to be – God willing – tell us what we can do for you, if there be anything: if change of scene would be of any use and you can bear to see Phemy – come to stay with us when Mrs Gray leaves us (we have only one room) but at any rate write as soon as you can, for poor Phemy is very anxious about you. I don't know if she will be able to write to you herself today for she has cold and is in her room – and very sick at heart besides, but she will as soon as she can – her general health is good – better even than it has been. We hope to see Mrs Gray as soon as may be after the 8th Jan, when we trust to be again in Park St – much need there is for her having the comfort of seeing Phemy.

God bless you and be with you and keep you my dear Friend,

Yours ever affectionately

J. Ruskin

His niece wrote to him the following day:

My dearest Uncle,

I was too unwell yesterday and felt for you too deeply in your sad bereavement to venture to express my sorrow and sympathy for you but I hope you have received John's note which far better than anything I can say will show you how much we both feel for you, and yet I can scarcely believe that the sad event has indeed rendered you now as desolate as poor Melville and the strange likeness to my beloved Aunt Jessie's removal from this world to another and a better are at once circumstances so startling and so uncommon that I can hardly believe it possible that my two dear Aunts are now gone from amongst us and the place and friends that once knew and loved them shall do so no more on earth. How Melville will feel for you having so lately lost his own treasure but all who either knew you or dear

Aunt Jessie will give you all their sympathy. I cannot write as I would speak to you my dear Uncle but I cannot but feel that both the death of dear Lexie & Jessie is their unspeakable gain and that it is the great consolation you now have and I should think there are, alas, very few who could leave this world with a hope of a better so well prepared for the speedy summons as my dear Aunt. You who long had your thoughts fixed on the other side of time will by this trial be brought nearer to him, who has only called back to himself what we had but for a few short years. We have all experienced the hospitable kindness of dear Lexie and seen her amiable character. I first became acquainted with her more closely on my happy visit to Ayr during the first year of your married life and afterwards this last spring when John and I had so much happiness under your roof and poor Jessie, Marion & I used to talk of Lexie often and her unvariable sweetness and piety were the subjects of our admiration and converse about her. I never saw a sweeter or more feminine character in every way, her home so well ordered, her duties so well performed, her piety so unobtrusive yet so not to be mistaken, her love for you and her little ones so womanly and so tender, all these and other rare qualities have been often subjects of meditation to me both before and since my marriage and John & I have talked together of your happiness with each other and I feel now as if another of the most loved of my home circle had departed to join with her so lately gone before in singing the praises of God & the Saints. Oh! may the Lord keep under the shadow of his wing your dear little ones and be mother, father and all to them and enable you to bear this heavy affliction (which he has seen fit in his wisdom to visit you with) with patience & resignation. I greatly wish that one could be of any use to you and after a time when you can write tell us anything that we may have the happiness in doing whatever is in our power to serve you. How glad and happy it makes me to think that dear Lexie approved of what I sent according to your direction in the beginning of the week to Glasgow. I hope that your health is pretty good, what a comfort it will be to you to think that Mrs McKenzie was with dear Lexie. My mother writes to me yesterday in great distress because hardly has she lost one sister than she is called to mourn the loss of another no less dear and I am sure never did sister love her brothers' wives better than did my dear mother Melville's and yours. Mr and Mrs Ruskin feel very much for you and believe my dearest Uncle that I mourn with you most sincerely in your heavy affliction and that I am your

ever your most affectionate niece

Effie C. Ruskin.

APPENDIX A

The Fushie Bridge Riots

Letter from Joseph Grant to Andrew Jameson

35 Great King Street
Edinburgh 24 March 1846
Dear Sir,

I trust you will excuse the freedom I take in repeating in this form what I mentioned to you verbally today as it occurs to me to be proper to do so in order to prevent any mistake.

Before leaving Currie House on Monday morning the 2nd inst I heard it reported that the English & Scotch Labourers on the Hawick Railway meant to meet that day in a large number and burn the Huts of the Irish Labourers. In my way to town I met the contractors Messrs Wilson & Moore & stated to them that I was going to Edinburgh and that I would be glad to take any message from them to the Sheriff if they wished it in reference to the report I had heard. The place where I met them was just on this side of North Middleton. They said in reply that they thought it unnecessary as they conceived there was a sufficient Police Force already at Fushie bridge and they added that they had previously sent an express to Edinburgh that morning. On coming to the neighbourhood of Arniston Bridge I observed a considerable collection of men on the line of the Railway not engaged in work & as that seemed to me so far a confirmation of the Rumour, I thought it right, on arriving in town, to call at the county Police Office where I saw Mr

List. I told him of the rumour adding that I had observed the men collecting as I have mentioned but I stated also, that I wished to avoid any appearance of giving an exaggerated statement & I repeated what the Contractors had told me. Mr List stated to me that he had had an express from them that morning – and that was all that passed between him & me.

I have since heard more than once, that it was in consequence of what I had stated that a sufficient military force was not sooner sent – but until you mentioned the subject to me today, it really did not seem to be necessary for me to notice this and you may perhaps think that I need not now say more about it. My only object in doing so – in addition to that which I have mentioned – is that if the matter should in any shape come again to be alluded to justice may be done me and to what I actually said or did.   I am

Dear Sir

Yours very truly
Joseph Grant

Andrew Jameson Esq
Sheriff-Substitute

It seems that this letter was either shown to Mr List by Joseph Grant before he sent it to Sheriff-Substitute Jameson or, more probably, was sent to Mr List by Sheriff-Substitute Jameson after he had received it because at the end of the letter there is the following statement:

Note from Supt of County Police

I do not remember Mr Grant saying anything about burning huts; to the best of my recollection he said that the labourers were meeting in large numbers to drive off the Irish, but he had seen the Contractors, who said they did not apprehend any danger as there was sufficient number of Police on the spot.

The conversation scarcely occupied five minutes and I immediately reported it to the Proc Fiscal.

[2 illegible initials] List

APPENDIX B

The Funeral and Obituaries of
Sheriff-Substitute Andrew Jameson

The following obituary appeared in the *Fifeshire Journal* of 15th April 1846

THE LATE MR SHERIFF JAMESON

It is with the deepest regret that we have this day to record in our obituary the death of Mr Andrew Jameson, who for the period of 45 years has filled the office of Sheriff-Substitute of this county. Mr Jameson was, we believe, a native of Dysart, where his father filled the office of town-clerk. He was in the seventy-fifth year of his age, and his death took place on Friday afternoon last at eleven o'clock, after an illness of little more than a fortnight. Both the public and private character of Mr Jameson were such as fully justified the high respect and the warm esteem in which he was held by all who were acquainted with him. He was most faithful and assiduous in the discharge of his official duties. Under the guidance of an earnest love of justice and a strong vigorous common sense, and great practical sagacity, he was able in the most difficult cases to arrive at a sound conclusion; and in those instances in which his decisions came under the review of the Supreme Court they were very rarely reversed. To the profession, he was, as a judge, invariably courteous and candid, and by them his loss will be much felt. In private life he was not merely esteemed and respected, but was truly a universal favourite. His kindness of disposition, his gentlemanly bearing, and politeness of manners, were felt by all who came into connexion with him; and he possessed, all his days, that frank and hearty youthfulness of mind which in so many men is overborne and lost amidst the cares of this world. To his habitual cheerfulness and overflowing good humour, although no doubt with a constitution originally strong, may be attributed the excellent health which Mr Jameson enjoyed, and which was evident in the fine appearance which he preserved at his advanced age. In this quarter of a century the loss of a man so well known and so highly respected is much regretted, and most keenly by those who by long friendship had become most intimately acquainted with his many virtues and the many amiable points in his character. The sympathy which is on all hands felt for his family must now prove to them some consolation under the loss of a kind and affectionately beloved father.

Mr Jameson, about the beginning of this century, occupied the situation of lieutenant-colonel in the Fifeshire Volunteers. The following letter, which has fallen into our hands, was addressed to him by his captain, Mr Thomson, at a time when every hour brought some new rumour of the French landing. It is highly characteristic of Mr Jameson:-

> Cupar, 12th January, 1804
> Dear Thomson – As I am going to Dysart for two days, I have to request that you will inform me by an express on horseback if the volunteers are called to arms, or receive any order which you may think requires the immediate attendance of the officers. In the event of an express, which is sure of finding me at Dysart, I think I will be in Cupar before the Craigrothie lads. I am &c
> A.Jameson
> PS – In the event of the French landing I will most likely hear the news before you, and when we march, it will in all probability be to the south, in which case I am so far on my road to the field of glory.
>
> To Captain J. Thomson

Mr Jameson having been appointed Sheriff-Substitute in 1801, has held that office under no fewer than five Sheriffs-Principal in this county – Mr Fergusson of Pitcullo, Mr Monypenny, afterwards Lord Pitmilly, Mr Anstruther of Airdit, Mr Clephane, and the present respected Sheriff, Mr Earle Menteith – to all of whom Mr Jameson proved himself an efficient assistant. We ought not to forget that in a very great measure to Mr Jameson's active personal exertions the Sheriffs-Substitute of Scotland are indebted for their present remuneration, so well deserved by the laborious and important duties which they have to perform.

* * *

The funeral took place yesterday afternoon at one o'clock. The whole of the shops and places of business in the town were closed from twelve. The assemblage was very large. The town-officers and the rural constabulary, four abreast, were in front. The coffin was carried by the militia staff, and beside it were the Sheriff's two sons – Mr Andrew Jameson, sheriff-substitute Edinburgh and Mr Melville Jameson, writer, Perth – and his son-in-law, Mr G. Gray, Perth; his brother-in-law, Mr Ogilvie, writer, Dundee; and his nephew Mr John Ogilvie; Mr Sheriff Menteith, Mr Sheriff Campbell, Renfrewshire; Mr Sheriff Barclay of Perthshire; Mr Duncan, Procurator-Fiscal, Perth; Mr Macdonald, Procurator-Fiscal, Dunfermline; Mr Henry Russell, Dunfermline; Mr Sheriff Henderson, Dundee; Mr Neil Campbell, Barronhill, Dumbarton. The procurators, headed by Mr Thomas Horsburgh, sheriff-clerk, followed in a body; and next to the Provost, magistrates and council. Amongst the large body of principal inhabitants of the district, we observed Lord Leven, Sir George Campbell, Mr D. M. M. Crichton, Major Anderson, Major Christie, Mr Wilson, Inchrye Abbey, and all the clergymen in the bounds and neighbourhood. The procession moved from the Sheriff's residence to the burial ground in the west end of the churchyard.

In the same edition of the *Fifeshire Journal* there appeared the following:

CUPAR TOWN COUNCIL

The Council met in the Council-room on Monday, Provost Nicol in the chair.

DEATH OF MR JAMESON

The Provost said the members of Council would all be aware that a painful dispensation had deprived them of Mr Jameson, who had been the chief resident magistrate among them for the long period of 45 years and who had given the utmost satisfaction in his discharge of his official duties. He thought it was their duty to make some manifestation of their deep sense of the loss that had been thereby sustained and he therefore moved the adoption of the following resolutions (which had been prepared by Bailie Mitchell) for the council's adoption:-

1 The Council take the earliest opportunity of expressing their deep regret at the death of Andrew Jameson, Esq., who has for the long period of 45 years filled the important situation of Sheriff-Substitute of this county, and who, from his active business habits and courteous, gentlemanly and upright conduct both in public and private, had gained the esteem and respect of all classes of the county, particularly of the inhabitants of the town and neighbourhood in which he lived, to whom his death will be a public loss, and they direct the clerk to convey to Mr Jameson's family their warmest sympathies under their present severe bereavement.

2 The Council, out of respect to Mr Jameson's memory, resolve, with the permission of his family, to attend the funeral in a body on Wednesday first, and to meet in the Council-room a little before one o'clock on that day. The Provost and Magistrates making all necessary arrangements; and they recommend that the shops within the burgh should be shut between one and two, and the bells tolled.

The resolutions were unanimously agreed to.

Bailie Mitchell, in connexion with this subject, wished it to be distinctly understood by all, whether members of the Council or not, that as it was quite impossible for those who had charge of the arrangements for Mr Jameson's funeral to send invitations to all who might wish to pay the last mark of respect to so valued a citizen, it was expected that they should attend whether having been formally invited or not. It was a tribute of regard which was well deserved from all in the burgh, as Mr Jameson had been long an amiable and respected inhabitant, and few men could have continued for a period of 45 years so capable of discharging their duties, and without having, he might say, made a single enemy.

OTHER MEMORIALS TO SHERIFF-SUBSTITUTE JAMESON

There are two further references to Andrew Jameson, both in the *Fifeshire Journal* of 11th June 1846. One is in the report of the introduction of his successor by Sheriff Menteith, who commended his life and contribution to the administration of justice in the county. Only two excerpts from this long encomium need be given.

> It is a great satisfaction to me to reflect, that during an intercourse of many years, there was not a moment's misunderstanding between us, nor did a single incident occur to which I look back otherwise than with satisfaction and pleasure.

> His venerable age, and the kind personal interest he always took in me and mine infused an element into the relation [sic] that subsisted between us that I can never hope to see supplied; for while I valued him most highly as my official substitute, I revered him as a father, and loved him as a friend. (During the delivery of these remarks Mr Menteith was more than once so deeply affected as to feel a difficulty in proceeding.)

The second reference is in the report of the meeting of the Sheriffs-Substitute of Scotland that took place in Edinburgh on 10th May 1846, their first meeting after the death of Andrew Jameson. Sheriff-Substitute Tait of Edinburgh (he must have been one of the colleagues of Andrew Jameson (Junior)) proposed and it was unanimously agreed that "before proceeding to business, the meeting record and express the great respect and regard, which they entertained for their late lamented convener, Andrew Jameson, Esquire, Sheriff-Substitute of Fifeshire, and their sense of the great obligations under which the Sheriff-Substitutes of Scotland lie to him for his long-continued, unwearied, and successful exertions in improving their condition and raising the *status* of their office, and of the heavy loss which they and the public have sustained by his recent death, after a very long and useful life. And they direct that a copy of this minute be communicated to the members of his family, with sincere expressions of condolence on the very afflicting bereavement which they have sustained."

THE FIFESHIRE BIOGRAPHY

In 1866 there was published by John C. Orr, Inglis and Black of Edinburgh the *Biographical Dictionary of Eminent Men of Fife of Past and Present Times Natives of the County, or Connected with it by Property Residence, Office, Marriage*. It was edited by a Matthew Forster Conolly (1789–1877) and its shorter title was the *Fifeshire Biography*. Despite the full title's claim that it was about men, women were also included. There is a long entry about Andrew Jameson, and the editor made the mistake of spelling his name "Jamieson". The entry is more reminiscent of an obituary than a history of his life and it is too long to reproduce here, especially since about one third of it is a description of his funeral. However, it does refer to aspects of his life that have not been previously noted.

Mr Jamieson was also a zealous patron of science and arts, and enthusiastic in his devotion to general literature. The extent of his information on all subjects, not only in questions of law, but also on matters of general importance, was a general feature of his character; and the ardour and activity with which he embarked in the examination of every detail in the questions submitted for his decision were such as to ensure a correct judgment.

He long held the office of president of the Fifeshire Literary Scientific and Antiquarian Society; the interests of which institution he forwarded to a very great extent. He also found congenial exercise to his mind, not only in the theoretical study of the science of botany, but carrying into practical effect the truths he was there taught. It was in this exercise, we believe, he spent most of his happiest and otherwise unoccupied moments, and which enabled him to fill the office of President of the Cupar Horticultural Society to the satisfaction of every member.

The entry also refers to his part in securing improved remuneration for sheriffs-substitute which had previously been "disgracefully inadequate as a recompense for the valuable services rendered by these gentlemen to the county".

APPENDIX C

Melville Jameson's Account of his Highland Journey
July/August 1847

We both enjoyed it greatly. On the whole we had good weather and although I had seen much of the same scenery before, it was now so long ago that they had almost the charm of novelty to me as much as to Jessie, who was very much delighted with them. The approach to the Trossachs, the descent on Loch Lomond and Inversnaid, the drive from Tarbet by Arroguhar and Glencroe to Inverary, the still finer drive from there to Dalmally, with the many magnificent views ever changing, of the cold Loch Awe and its frowning Guardian, the black Cruach Mhor – and yet grander, the pass of Awe, dark and precipitous opening on the view of Loch Etive and still further in the sunset over the blue hills of Morvern, resting on the old ruin of Dunstaffnage. We arrived at Oban on a Friday evening & next morning at 8 started in a very fine steamer to visit Staffa and Iona.

The sail was not pleasant in consequence of rain in the forepart of the day, but about ten miles from the Island it broke up most beautifully and we were all enabled to land and walk along the basaltine pillars to the cave of Fingal, which you have, I dare say, often read descriptions of, and which is tolerably well given in the little engravings you sometimes see in annuals and such books. But no description or picture can adequately convey to the mind the most solemn & impressive reality. Beauty is there too but grandeur is the predominating quality. It has the mighty stamp of the workmanship of the Maker of all things, a fit temple for His worship.

Some young lads from Glasgow struck up the 100th psalm, which had a fine effect. After silence, the words of praise to God were the most grateful to the impressd feelings. I forget whether you have seen this wonderful piece of rock work, the basalts so nobly fixed together bearing the immense weight of the superincumbent conglomerate. If you have not, you should take Lexy to Barnhill, thence to Oban by the Crinan Canal and as there is a steamer almost daily from Oban, you might do all this in three days from home.

After seeing Iona ten miles further on we came round the other side of Mull and relanded at Oban after a delightful sail about 8 o'clock in the evening. We spent a quiet and pleasing Sabbath at Oban and started on Monday by steamer to Ballachulish, where with a small party of gentlemen we hired a conveyance to the top of Glencoe and never could we have seen it in more glorious style – the flitting clouds of mist, which seemed to be generated in the very clefts of the rocky precipices, one after another chased away and often for a time concealing the bold fronts and pointed tops of these alpine masses. It was very grand. I may say, however, this was the last of our fine scenery. The Tuesday we were on Loch Ness but the day was bad. Then we were in Inverness and on the whole disappointed with it.

Wednesday we visited Elgin Cathedral; very fine, greatly improved of late years by the clearing away of nettles and collection of parts of the ruins from the various old walls which have recently been pulled down and to the building of which some of the finest mouldings of the cathedral had been taken. It is more perfect than St Andrews but not so extensive. On Thursday night we reached Aberdeen.

(This letter was published in the December 2008 issue of *The Scots Magazine*.)

CHAPTER TWELVE
Missionary Interests and Second Marriage

No documentation concerning the funeral of Alexa Jameson has survived. All that is known is that it took place on 2nd January 1849, possibly at the Campbell family's church in Dumbarton. George Gray and Melville Jameson came through from Perth by train and returned next day. Andrew went back to Rothesay.

In a letter of 4th January 1849 Sophia advised her brother to continue living at Rothesay and suggested that Susan Mackenzie be asked to dispose of Alexa's wardrobe. She regretted that Alexa had not left a daughter for whom "some trinkets and ornaments" could be left. She told him that her daughter Euphemia was suffering from a bad cold and that she would be visiting her the following week.[1] On the 9th January Melville wrote that he could sympathise with his brother because he, too, was still feeling the loss of his wife, Jessie. On a slightly less mournful note he asked for Bessie Mackenzie to send the "recipe for potatoes done as I ate them at your table", when he had come to Rothesay immediately after Alexa's death.

John St Clair Jameson was baptised on 18th January 1849 and Andrew's father-in-law wrote that "Bess tells me of the christening of the little boy and of your being attacked by cold as well as by the more overwhelming feeling of the solemnity." Since the grandfather had heard the details of the ceremony from his daughter, this indicates that the baptism had taken place in Rothesay.

In addition to the death of her two sisters-in-law in 1848, Sophia Gray now had to bear the loss on 1st March 1849 of her son Robert. He had been her ninth child and with his death the Grays were left

---

[1] It was during this visit that Sophia Gray first sensed the latent hostility of Mrs Ruskin towards Euphemia.

with their two eldest children, Euphemia and George, and four others under six. Even in an era when infant death was far more common than today, it was unusual as well as heartbreaking for a family to lose seven children in succession before even one of them had reached their eighth year. Sophia was now 40 but this indomitable woman went on to bear two more children. Her last six children all grew to adulthood, one of them, Melville Jameson Gray, surviving into his ninety-ninth year.[2]

Since Sophia wrote to her brother at Caldarvan on 7th March 1849 thanking him for a letter of condolence sent by him on the death of Robert, we know that Andrew Jameson had left Bute about the end of February and was staying with Susan Mackenzie and her husband. He was still there when Effie Ruskin wrote to him from Bowerswell on 19th March. She had been suffering from more than a bad cold and her mother had brought her back to Perth to recuperate, while her husband, together with his parents, went off to Europe to accumulate more material for his work *Modern Painters*.[3]

Effie wrote "I was sorry to learn from the letter Mama had from you two or three days ago that you were not coming to visit her, which we all thought would do you great good. I was thinking riding might be good for you require bracing and you and I, if you would still come, might have some delightful rides together." Despite this plea from his niece her uncle did not change his mind and, according to a letter of 24th March 1849 from Melville, addressed simply "Andrew Jameson Esq., R. D. Mackenzie, Writer, Dumbarton", he was about to spend a few days with his father-in-law at Barnhill.

Before returning to Edinburgh, he had given serious consideration to Dr Buchanan's offer of editorship of the *Scottish Guardian*.[4] Neil Campbell had written on 29th January that he had been approached by Dr Buchanan's acquaintance, Dunlop, on the matter.

---

[2] He did not marry until 1939, when he was 91. In 1945 Mr A. St Clair Jameson, grandson of Sheriff Jameson, and his wife and children met Melville Jameson Gray and his wife.

[3] John Ruskin took the opportunity of Robert's death to prevent Effie accompanying him to Europe. He claimed he wished her to avoid the heat of the continent and "he imagines my mother may be the better of having me with her after poor Bobbie's death".

[4] v. p. 366 supra.

"Dunlop has again been talking to me about the "Guardian." He says it has been kept open for you yet he is very desirous of an answer now. I presume you will adhere to your former resolution but whatever your resolution be I think you should write a friendly answer directly to Dunlop himself." He added a short postscript: "Write immediately about the "Guardian."

He must have done so because Campbell sent a reply (undated) to a letter from Andrew of 31st January. It would appear that Andrew had suggested to his brother-in-law some sort of joint editorship of the newspaper. Neil Campbell insisted that it would be quite incorrect to become associated in any way "with a political organ". Even if contributions were anonymous authorship would soon become known and this would impede his (Campbell's) practice at the bar. In any case his spare time was already fully occupied with his work on behalf of the Sabbath Evangelical Alliance, the Deaf and Dumb School and Dr Guthrie's Schools[5] as well as holding office as a deacon of the Free Church that he attended. "Indeed, I am forced to neglect some of the things I ought to do. Besides, I am not well qualified at present to take a responsible share of the Editorship. In short, I do not see my way in the matter. I am satisfied, however, that if you were taking up the Editorship you would find a great deal of assistance among your friends & I would contribute my assistance as far as I reasonably could."

This was a very sensible decision by Neil Campbell, and it is strange that Andrew Jameson, whose judgment on most matters was sound, had not seen the professional difficulties that would attend his brother-in-law's involvement with a newspaper. It is possible that the death of his beloved wife had affected his usual clarity of judgment but he should have understood that Neil Campbell could not have combined editorial duties of a newspaper with his work as an advocate. For his own part, Andrew Jameson may have seriously considered resigning

---

[5] Dr Thomas Guthrie (1813–1873) was the minister of St John's Free Church in Edinburgh. In 1847 he founded the first of his schools for children in need and these "ragged schools", as they became known, made a significant contribution to the care and education of children who would otherwise have been left in extreme poverty. There is a statue of Dr Guthrie in Princes Street Gardens, Edinburgh.

from his post of sheriff-substitute on account of the challenge that it was making to his health and accepting the editorship of the *Scottish Guardian*. That must be left to conjecture and all that can be said is that he must have turned down the opportunity because he resumed his shrieval duties at the beginning of April.

His domestic arrangements leave much to speculation, although we learn from letters that he employed a nurse and a servant to assist him with his three children, the oldest of whom was not yet four. It is possible that Alexa's sisters or other friends took one or other of his children into their homes at periods but there is no documentary evidence to support this. Sophia Gray wrote an undated letter (probably late March or early April 1849) advising him to engage a cook/housekeeper. She strongly recommended to him someone who had been employed by a Perth friend from whom she had received an excellent account. The woman was utterly reliable in every respect, a competent cook, attended the Free Church and although only 24 looked six years older. It is possible that her brother took on this person because the census of 1851 lists a Jessie Duncan, aged 30, as a member of his household. Sophia could have been mistaken about the woman's age.

We know that sometime in 1849 he gave up his house in Blacket Place and moved to 15 Heriot Row, the home of a lawyer, John Melville.[6] This must have been a temporary arrangement until Andrew Jameson found accommodation that met his needs and it is possible that he was distantly connected through his mother's family.[7] His second son, Alexander, was carried away with some fatal child disease on 19th September 1849, and the newspapers reporting the death give the address as 15 Herriot Row. The census return for 1851 shows that by that date he was living in Greenhill Gardens[8] with his two surviving sons, Jessie Duncan and two younger domestic servants.

No correspondence survives for about another two years, although we know from the newspapers that he was involved in various public

---

[6] Later Sir John Melville, Lord Provost of Edinburgh 1854–1859.
[7] v. p. 17 supra.
[8] At that date houses in Greenhill Gardens were not numbered but subsequent information suggests it was number 14.

activities. On 29th May 1850 the *Dundee Courier* listed him as an Ordinary Director of the Scottish Association for the Suppression of Drunkenness, and he had been a member since its foundation in 1847 of the Edinburgh Section of the Central Board for the Relief of Destitution in the Highlands and Islands of Scotland.[9]

There is a letter of 8th August 1851 from his sister-in-law Marion Jameson, who was now living in London. Correspondence reveals that he and probably his brother and sister kept in touch with their widowed sister-in-law.

Marion Jameson's letter is so curious in its terminology that it is given here in full.

59 Wimpole Street
Cavendish Square
London

My dear Andrew

Come to me:

I find you can have a room in the house and I hope I & my sister shall be able to make you feel at home and comfortable with us; you have only to drive to the door and we shall be ready to receive you. Wimpole Street is the next street to Harley Str, where poor Mrs [name illegible] lived, is very centrical and near where you can get omnibuses to all parts of London, so I hope if you are comfortable you will not think of changing to be nearer the object that attracts you south. I shall be so glad to have you with me and hope the change may benefit the outward as well as inward & that you may not find your strength thereby unduly tasked. It would never do to take your two sweet little companions south with you – but I long to see them. What a nicely managed ceremony your brother-in-law's

---

[9] The highlands and islands of Scotland suffered from the same potato blight that ravaged Ireland.

marriage must have been! You must tell me all particulars please God we meet; & I hope for sweet communings with you over holy things.

Come, dear Andrew in the power of the spirit and may you give and receive aid to help forward the heavenly cause. I am not very well today & write a short note but I hope to be able to enjoy much when you are with me. If there is anything *in particular* you require let me know before your arrival; and hoping soon to welcome my dear Andrew I am his very affectionate sister

M. St. C. Jameson

Marion Jameson was living in a very prestigious address and, although the letter does not reveal her domestic circumstances, since she uses the words "I find you can have a room" it seems likely that the house belonged to her sister. It may be that Andrew had written to her asking for advice on accommodation in London but her reply with its underlined heading made it clear that she wanted him to come to her home.

She refers to the "object that attracts you south" and this was, in all probability, connected with his revision of the Maltese Civil Code that he had agreed to carry out.[10] The "nicely managed ceremony" was the marriage on 27th July of his brother-in-law Neil Campbell to Mary Paterson, daughter of William Paterson of Montgomerie in Tarbolton, Ayrshire.

Sometime around 1851 Andrew Jameson began his interest in the Protestants of Tuscany and Piedmont. He was on a committee of the Free Church of Scotland that had started to raise money in support of Protestants in Tuscany, who were suffering disabilities, if not persecution, on account of their faith. In 1852 there are two letters, both concerning the position of Protestants in Tuscany, then still an independent principality. On Good Friday John Ruskin wrote from Venice, where he was completing the research for his monumental book *The Stones of Venice*. Andrew must have been on a visit to

---

[10] v. p. 341 supra.

Tuscany because the letter had been readdressed from Edinburgh to Leghorn and was a reply to one from him. Ruskin sympathises with the Protestants in Italy, who suffer harassment from the authorities, but he regrets that Protestantism has become associated with republicanism.

Fedele Betti, who appears to have been one of the leaders of Protestants in Tuscany, wrote him a very long letter on 9th November 1852. Although it is mainly a diatribe against the Roman Catholic Church, we do learn from it that there was a small congregation in Genoa, who were hoping to buy a house that would serve the dual purpose of a school and a place of worship. The letter ends with an expression of thanks "to our brotherly benefactors" and this must refer to the Free Church of Scotland fund mentioned immediately above. Perhaps Andrew Jameson had brought money with him, when he visited Piedmont in the previous August/September.[11]

Another long letter, dated 26th April 1853, from a correspondent called R. Maxwell Hauwe, explains the reason for Italian Protestants seeking safe accommodation in Genoa. Hauwe wrote from Florence, where it is clear that he was responsible for the storage of bibles and their distribution through colporteurs, who, if apprehended by the police, were imprisoned for up to one year. The house, which, by 1853, had been purchased in Genoa, where there was a more liberal regime than in Tuscany, is referred to as the Geneva Refuge. Here lived the wives and children of colporteurs and other adherents, whose husbands had been imprisoned. Hauwe also thanks the Free Church of Scotland through Andrew Jameson for providing the bibles (presumably printed in Italian) for use by Protestant adherents.[12]

Throughout his life Andrew Jameson sustained his interest in the struggles of minority Protestant groups. As John Buchan commented in the introduction to his book on Andrew's son, Lord Ardwall, Andrew Jameson "visited the Mediterranean countries, acquiring their languages and developing a keen interest in the flickering

---

[11] I am greatly indebted to the Rev. Dr Domenic Zanrè for translating this letter, which was written in very old-fashioned Italian.

[12] These letters from Fidele Betti and R. Maxwell Hauwe would be very useful for scholars studying this aspect of religious life in Tuscany at that time.

Protestantism, which lit their Papal darkness. To the end of his life his house was a kind of consulate-general for all foreign pastors who sought spiritual or material aid."[13]

We know that Andrew Jameson had been in Piedmont in the late summer of 1852, as well as in Tuscany around Eastertide, because he received at Paris a letter from his sister Sophia dated 18th September 1852. She tells him that she had enjoyed reading of his interesting time in Piedmont and then continues on two domestic issues.

She had recommended to him in March/April 1849 a particular person to act as his cook/housekeeper and was now continuing her sisterly concern for him by suggesting that he engage, as a cook, someone who was suitable in every way. It is worth quoting Sophia's words in full because they give a good description of the background to employment of women in domestic service in that era.

> I write to you a few lines to tell you that I have the prospect of a very nice woman about 30 years of age for a cook. Mrs Hope-Moncrieffe has just been up giving me her character. She is at present with Mrs Craigie, her daughter, where she has been two years. They are very sorry to part with her but she has left of her own choice. She is a very respectable woman and of poor respectable parents in the Carse,[14] has a sister with Mrs Macfarlane, is very goodlooking but never asks out, nor has she any followers, which will, I think, suit you. She is a very good cook & dresses & washes very well. She has seen a good deal of superior cooking as she was undercook in several country places, where she acted under a head-cook. I have desired Mrs Craigie to send her in again to me and I will engage her if she will take kitchen and washing with the assistance of the house-maid.

[13] Buchan, J. (1913) *Andrew Jameson, Lord Ardwall*. Blackwood and Sons, Edinburgh and London.
[14] The Carse of Gowrie is a very fertile area of Angus.

The second and more important reason for Sophia writing to Andrew concerned their brother Melville. Although the purpose of this book is to record the life and achievements of Andrew Jameson, a minor diversion can be excused here. Two of his three sisters had died before he had reached the age of 12 and his brothers James and Robert had both died in 1832. With the death of his oldest brother John in 1847, there remained only three children of the marriage of Andrew Jameson (Senior) and Euphemia Chalmers. Andrew and Melville, who was only two years younger than his brother, had been very close to each other since childhood. This was because their two older brothers, having been launched early into their careers, were not around in the family home at Cupar and their third brother, Robert, had health problems throughout his short life. Moreover, in 1848 their dearly loved wives had died in childbirth and they supported each other in their bereavements.

By 1852 Andrew had been back for over three years in his work as a sheriff-substitute and was engaging himself in voluntary work for charities and the Free Church mission to assist Protestants in Tuscany. By contrast, Melville was meeting difficulties in his career. After completing his legal studies at Edinburgh University, where he had carried off the Civil Law Prize,[15] he had entered into partnership with his brother-in-law, George Gray. In 1839 the Perth Savings Bank was founded with Melville appointed as its actuary and manager, a position he held for the next 45 years. At some point during the spring of 1852 his father-in-law, Thomas Duncan, invited him to join Duncan and McLean, a legal practice of which he was the senior partner. Somewhat hastily, as he later admitted, Melville accepted this offer and deposited much of his available funds in the practice's account at its bank. The firm registered its new partnership as Duncan, McLean and Jameson, Writers, Perth.

In a long letter of 3rd July 1852 to his brother, Melville regretted his decision to sever his partnership with George Gray. Andrew had written asking him to contribute to some charity, possibly the Free Church mission in support of the Protestants in Tuscany, a request Melville

[15] v. p. 202 supra.

had to decline because "my means are not improving". He explained that it was only after he had united in partnership with Messrs Duncan and McLean, that he had examined the firm's accounts. He discovered that his father-in-law's assurances of the sound state of the business were "baseless and erroneous". He blamed himself for this "too ready resolution which I formed to become one of Mr Duncan's partners before making a more searching investigation of their pecuniary position". He concluded his letter by saying that if he was able to "escape with my own money at present I will rather commence my professional career of new with a small income for a few years".

In that summer of 1852, Melville's business affairs were not his only problem. On 9th August he married Agnes Martin, a dressmaker. It would have been expected that a professional man, left a widower with three children under ten years of age, would, after a decent period of mourning, take a second wife. However, Melville's choice of Agnes Martin, fourteen years his junior and daughter of the blacksmith at Scone, attracted the censure of the citizens of Perth and the concern of his sister Sophia.

A large excerpt from Sophia's letter of 18th September 1852 makes clear how the Perth public and his sister viewed Melville's marriage.

> Poor Melville's position is not improving. The public cannot get over the fatal step he has made & and the great bar in his respectability is the bad character of the woman and his domestic inconveniences have already begun; the 2 strange[16] servants they have brought from fairly [word obviously missing – perhaps Sophia meant "far away" or something similar] gave up their places on hearing what she was and with considerable difficulty they have got one to remain till the term.[17]

Mrs Blaikie[18] is here and though she won't see Mel,

---

[16] Can this mean that they were unknown to anyone in Perth?

[17] A day in either May or November fixed for the start or end of a period of agricultural or domestic service.

[18] She was a younger sister of Jessie and thus Melville's sister-in-law by his first marriage.

she has asked out the children to the Hills[19] as she is to be only here for a short time and Mel has granted the request. Eliza[20] is better – her papa says she has been in such low spirits they did not know what to do with her. I thought she must be feeling her degradation but he said he was sure it was not that as she was quite happy. I am afraid he is thinking himself to his daughter's happiness, poor thing.[21] I have not asked the children here yet and Melville thought it as well not for the fear they might get the disagreeable truth told them by the children to one another, which might make quarrels. They could not come yet at any rate for infection.

I went and called on Melville in his new office and had a chat with him. I cheered him about the prospects of business but he seems to feel Perth very changed to him and he has much to bear from the shameful position he has placed himself in. She seems to feel it very much too. The servants who are with them say he is very kind & attentive to her so that looks as he was happy with her at the meantime. Mrs O.[22] says he has been a most extraordinary being in his amours all his life.

As far back as 1839 Sheriff-Substitute Jameson had written to his eldest son John that the intimacy of Andrew with Elizabeth Thomson

---

She had married "well". Her husband was a prosperous Aberdeen businessman, John Blaikie, whose father had been Lord Provost of Aberdeen. Qualified as an advocate of Aberdeen, he had also established with Anthony, a younger brother, a legal practice in the city. The business was sequestrated in 1862 with debts above £200,000. The Blaikies fled to Spain and then South Africa before returning to end their days in London.

[19] This is Barclay Hills outside Perth, the home of her father, Thomas Duncan, and her stepmother. The Post Office Directory of 1852/53 "List of Gentlemen's Seats in the County of Perth" includes Barclay Hills. It seems likely that it had belonged to her stepmother before she had married her father, Thomas Duncan, as his second wife. The house is still standing but is now called Barclayhill House. It is located north of Perth on the A93 about one mile and a half south of Guildtown.

[20] Eldest child of Melville and his first wife, Jessie Duncan.

[21] It may be that Sophia has missed out the word "not" before "thinking" for otherwise the sentence does not make clear what she is implying.

[22] Mrs Ogilvie (1780–1857), sister of Andrew Jameson (Sen.) and thus aunt of Sophia, Melville and Andrew.

was indiscreet and that he was "not far from being condemned like his brother Melville as a faithless lover".[23] His aunt's comment was in similar vein. Had Melville had some "affair" with Agnes before he married her? Apart from some speculation that she came as his house-keeper there is no evidence of any relationships Melville may have had before his marriage to Jessie or during the four years between her death and his marriage to Agnes.

There is no more documentation about this aspect of Melville's life. He gave up his partnership with Duncan, McLean and Jameson and opened a practice on his own account. It appears to have been successful because his appointment in 1867 as Procurator Fiscal of the Eastern District of Perthshire indicates he was well-respected in local legal circles. He retained this post for about three decades and was succeeded in the office by his son, Melville, his first child by his second marriage. His second son by that marriage, Henry, established with a Donald Mackay the legal firm of Jameson and Mackay that flourishes in Perth to this day. Melville's obituary notice in the *Perthshire Advertiser* of 27th August 1904 records his many virtues, achievements and interests but there is no mention of his wife, who died about 1893 and was mother to four sons and two daughters.

Perhaps it was simply that since the professional classes in Perth expected someone of Melville's background to marry a woman whose social status reflected that of his own, taking to wife the daughter of a blacksmith was looked upon as demeaning on his part. This was despite the fact that a blacksmith was regarded second only to a mason as the most skilled of artisans. In an age when the horse was the only means of independent travel on land (apart from the fixed route of railroads), horseshoeing was a vital skill and, in addition, blacksmiths made and repaired much farm machinery, not least iron rims for cartwheels. Two brothers of Agnes entered professions, one qualifying as a solicitor, the other graduating from St Andrews University and becoming a minister of the Church of Scotland. While it was not unusual for a "lad o' pairts" to rise from the status of life into which he had been born and

[23] v. p. 209 supra.

to become accepted by his equals within the profession to which his talents had secured entry, the same opportunity was seldom available for women for whom marriage was almost the only ladder to ascend into a higher social hierarchy. Agnes must have seen her opportunity and taken it.

Sophia Gray was an exceptional woman. She was a constant source of support not only to her husband, especially when his business narrowly avoided bankruptcy in 1848/9 on account of his investment in railway shares, but also to her two younger brothers. She had borne the loss of seven children with a composure that arose out of her deep Christian faith. We will probably never know the grounds on which she could report that Melville's marriage to Agnes Martin was "a great bar to his respectability" on account of her "bad character", although one must assume that she was reporting the general opinion of Perth citizens at that time. However, family loyalty was a strong trait in her character. For this reason it is certain that, while she would never feel as close to Agnes as she had been to Jessie and Alexa, Sophia accepted her as a sister-in-law and was influential in integrating her into Perth society, of which she, herself, had been so long a prominent member.

In total contrast to Melville's unexpected marriage to Agnes Martin, his brother was pursuing a path towards matrimony in a manner more in accordance with the social conventions of the time. In the late spring or early summer of 1852 he had met in Edinburgh Margaret Hart Hotchkis, known within the family as Maggie, third daughter of James Hotchkis, WS and his wife, Margaret Hart. A considerable amount of correspondence has survived from the twelve months over which he pursued his courtship, and at times it seemed as if he was not so much taking a wife as joining a family over which her mother ruled imperiously.

Thomas Hart, a major in the East India Company's army, had bought Castlemilk, near Lockerbie, Dumfriesshire, on his retirement from active service, but for the last fifteen years of his life he had been mentally deranged and thus had become incapable of looking after his affairs. The management of the Castlemilk estate had devolved upon his son-in-law, James Hotchkis, and not upon his son, Montgomery, an affable eccentric whose brain had been badly affected by sunstroke during his four years' military service in India.

James Hotchkis was a man of great personal charm but, as related by his grandson, James Jameson, "he had the misfortune to be born with a golden spoon in his mouth, which successively became silver, copper and finally pewter. In other words he was the heir of several great expectations, which were never realised. He never applied himself to the business of his profession and, after his father's death in 1824, he retired with his young wife to Castlemilk to look after that estate, which he did, I am afraid, with very indifferent success."[24]

Mrs James Hotchkis never forgot that she was the granddaughter of a baronet[25] and three cousins[26] of her mother had married into the English aristocracy. Her husband had considered that these aristocratic connections entitled him to adopt the life of a country gentleman without paying that attention to the management of the estate that was necessary for it to sustain his chosen way of life. After the death of Major Hart in 1840 the estate was found to be so encumbered with debt that it had to be sold. James and Margaret Hotchkis went to live first at Moat Brae House,[27] in Dumfries, and later took a lease of Woodlands, a house adjoining the park of Duddingston House, Edinburgh. In 1851, probably through some residual local influence, James Hotchkis secured an appointment at Dumfries with the recently founded Board of Inland Revenue. He took lodgings at Bridge of Traqueer,[28] on the

[24] Jameson, J. H., *Reminiscences*. p. 2. James Jameson (1855–1937), only child of Andrew Jameson by his second wife, wrote a highly informative, and at times very amusing, history of his mother's family background together with some accounts of his own early life. This was published purely for family consumption. A copy in the Archive Department of Perth and Kinross County Council, Perth has the date 1936. This seems rather late and may have been the date of the acquisition. J. H. Jameson died in 1937.

[25] Sir James Montgomery, younger brother of Sir William Montgomery, also a baronet.

[26] They were the daughters of Sir William Montgomery and were the models of "The Three Graces" painted by Sir Joshua Reynolds in 1773. Sir William Montgomery's only surviving son never married, thus extinguishing that baronetcy.

[27] Some 25 years later a family called Gordon lived in this house, which had a large garden. A son of the family became friendly with James Barrie, who attended the same school during the period he lived in Dumfries with his elder brother. Barrie often visited his friend and it is claimed that the garden helped to inspire the Peter Pan story.

[28] Now incorporated within the burgh of Dumfries.

left bank of the Nith but his family did not move from Woodlands to Dumfries until the autumn of 1852. From the correspondence that dates from mid-1852 it is clear that the status of James Hotchkis within his family was by then little more than a cipher, all decisions being taken by his wife, who understandably attributed their decline in fortune and social position to his monumentally incompetent management of her family estate.

It was at Woodlands that Andrew Jameson first met Margaret Hotchkis[29] and one would have thought that the mother would have welcomed the attention paid to her daughter by a man well-established in his career and highly respected in Edinburgh society. However, it is clear from a letter of 17th July 1852 from Andrew to Margaret's mother that she had become less than welcoming, when he had called. Andrew was sufficiently perturbed, even distressed, to write to both her and Margaret pleading his complete mystification as to how he had offended them. That he considered carefully what he wrote is demonstrated by his decision to prepare drafts of his letters to the mother and daughter.

My dear Mrs Hotchkis,

I have for some time perceived that your manner to me has changed & that instead of the kindness and charming cordiality, which marked the commencement & progress of our acquaintance, you seem now to regard me with coldness if not with displeasure. I do not complain of this change as you may have good reasons for it but I can't help saying that I feel it very painfully – and that I am not aware what I have done to deserve it. I do not allude to your not asking me to your house, for I think that is a prudent precaution against the risk of infection, which it is right to enforce; but to a marked difference of feeling & its expression, to your former kindness, not to feel acutely.

If it is a crime to be attracted by the uncommon union of

29 Jameson, J. H., op cit p.15.

natural grace and Christian principles & to admire & love,
perhaps too warmly, those who are so richly endowed, I
must plead guilty to the charge. I am sure your kind heart
will tell you that if I have erred unwittingly, the punishment
will be severe enough without any addition from you.

I cannot doubt that whatever may be the reason, you
wish to discourage my visits to you and your family. I will
therefore discontinue them. I am grieved to think that an
intercourse which to me was such a source of happiness
& all on my part was founded on a deep interest & regard
and for a sincere desire for your highest interest in Him[30]
& eternity, should thus be cut short. It is a sad conclusion to the pleasant hours at Woodlands & Melville St.[31]
which I can never forget, but I cannot help continuing to
hope that it is not forever, even on this shortlived scene.
I cannot, at least as yet, make up my mind to the thought
that this intercourse will not someday be renewed, if we
are spared.

If not, I at least will have the consolation to remember
you on the throne of grace & trust to meet, at least in these
mansions,[32] where there shall be no clouds nor misunderstandings nor estrangements & where the world's whispers
& wretched fashions will have no place and love will fill all
hearts – for God himself will fill them.

At what must have been only a short time later or even the same day
(this draft letter is not dated) he wrote to Margaret. This being a draft
and he emotionally involved with her, there are erasures and additions,
which render occasional words and phrases illegible.

---

[30] God.

[31] Mrs Hart, widow of Major Hart and mother of Mrs James Hotchkis, had lived in Melville
Street, Edinburgh.

[32] An allusion to the well-known passage in the gospel according to St John, Chapter 14,
verse 2. "In my Father's house are many mansions: if it were not so, I would have told you. I
go to prepare a place for you."

Dear Miss M,

I cannot leave Scotland[33] even for a little while without attempting to express to you how much grieved I am to think that I have vexed or displeased you. I know no one, whom I should feel more anxious to please than yourself and for that reason I would regret causing you any (word illegible). It is with pain that I have noticed your decided and sudden change of manner to me within this short time & which, I confess, I felt the more acutely that it was so different from your natural sweetness & kindness of disposition & simple grace of manner so inexpressibly charming to all who know you. I fear I may have done something to deserve the change tho I am not aware of it and yet I beg you to understand that I do not complain, though I feel very sad that anything that has occurred to chill or interrupt a friendship I cannot help valuing very highly.

I assure you no bitter feelings, however, can ever be associated with the recollections of you that will ever be dear to my memory. It will ever give me solid comfort to think that you have chosen the good [there follow several illegible words] and thus although I may be repaid the happiness of watching your progress in all that you aspire to and although we may not walk together in the narrow way,[34] we cannot be far apart & ultimately I trust will meet, where there will be no more misunderstandings or [illegible word], when the world & the whispers and fashions will have no power and all will be [several illegible words].

---

[33] He was soon to leave for Italy.

[34] An allusion to a passage in the gospel according to St Matthew, Chapter 7, verse 14. "Because strait is the gate, and narrow is the way, which leads unto life and few there be that find it."

I am sorry circumstances have prevented me paying my intended visit to Menteith[35] but I am sure you will forgive me often thinking of you, your dear mother and sister[36] in my [two illegible words] and seeking, what you have long had in mine, an interest & mention in your prayers.

Whatever had been the cause of what was clearly a misunderstanding will never be known. Within a fortnight Andrew was writing to Mrs Hotchkis to thank her for her "unmerited kindness". In this letter of 30th July 1852 he says that he is suffering from lameness. It will be recalled that ever since he damaged his ankle in the attic of the house in Cupar in May 1831[37] he had recurrent trouble with this leg. Mrs Hotchkis, now house-hunting at Dumfries, replied on 12th August with a long letter that was fuller of references to Christian principles than of information about family events.

She must have been aware of Melville's marriage and how it was seen by his sister and brother. Here is her comment on that union in a letter to Andrew Jameson: "Reading this evening in II Corinthians words struck me as applicable to your poor brother II. 7. The overmuch sorrow I would imagine is lest he fall into despair and doubt the mercy of God, the all sufficiency of the blood of Christ to wash out sins of the deepest dye. How many ways Satan has of embracing his victims." In the seventh chapter of his second epistle to the Corinthians, Paul reminds them that "godly sorrow worketh repentance" (verse 10). Poor Melville, to have his association with Agnes Martin, whatever it was before his marriage to her, described to his brother, by someone who had never met him, as a sin of the deepest dye. However, she does imply that true sorrow will bring repentance.

---

[35] James Hotchkis had no brother and only one sister, Isobel. She had married John Finlay, a director of James Finlay and Company, who owned Deanston Cotton Mill, a highly successful operation that employed about 1,000 persons in the mid-nineteenth century. Deanston House, where the Finlays lived, lies near the village of that name on the south bank of the River Teith between Callander and Doune. This is in the district known as Menteith. In contrast to her brother, Isobel Finlay and her family were very comfortably off.

[36] Mary, who had been unwell at this time.

[37] v. p. 121 supra.

On the 10th September 1852 she wrote an even longer letter mentioning a visit to Deanston House and recounting whom she had met and what they had been doing and though she mentions her daughter Mary, is silent about Margaret. Mary had been ill and there had been consultations with both Professor James Simpson and his assistant, Dr Matthews Duncan, who, in 1860, married her youngest daughter, Jane. She informs him that she has found a suitable house at Dumfries called Sommerville but since they cannot have entry until May, she has taken a small but comfortable dwelling in the centre of the town for the winter. A short letter from Maggie on 20th October is in much lighter vein. The family were now living at Dumfries and she recounts the journey of her mother and sister, Mary, now sufficiently well to leave Deanston, from Edinburgh to Dumfries via Lockerbie. We learn from this letter that Andrew had seen the two women off at Edinburgh and had provided them with grapes for the journey.

A few days later Andrew sent to Margaret two love sonnets written in Italian, a language which lends itself to romantic expression.

Sonetto I
Cara e bella Margarita,
La Dolce Stella di mia vita,
Stella-non mai perduta-
Il Gesù ha ben tolto la caduta.
Quando sono da te lontano
Altro piacer cercar è vano.
Son come quello che senza velo
Va in barca e non vede il cielo.
Ah che tristezza per il cuore mio
A te, diletto, per dir, Addio.

15 Ottobre 1852

Sonetto II
Donna gentil e bella, sai tu come?
I pensieri vaghi miei vanno all'intorno,
Cercando quella che già fu l'adorno
Di questo luogo, cogli occhi e chiome
Nere e il bel volto, di cui il nome
Mostra un'alma – il felice soggiorno
D'alta vertù. Tutte la notte e il giorno
Di speme e d'amor le dolci some
Porto sempre per te, rilucente Perla!
Cosi vuol dire suo nome diletto.
Iddio ti benedica! e la tua vita
Alla lode suo duca. Che piacer vederla
Alma Gentil con alto intelletto,
Gioia di mio cuore, dolce Margarita.
29 Ottobre 1852

Few young women could be insensitive to courtship couched in such beautiful language and Margaret Hotchkis was not among them. When precisely their engagement first became official is not known, but on 20th November Sophia Gray wrote to congratulate him, two days after Anne and Isobel, elder sisters of Margaret, writing from Deanston House, where they were staying with their aunt, Isobel Finlay, had welcomed him as a future brother-in-law. A brief account of the four sisters and three brothers of Margaret Hotchkis is given as an appendix to this chapter.

It is worth reproducing Sophia Gray's letter in its entirety since it provides an excellent example of how this remarkable woman could combine family affection with sound common sense.

> I hold out my hand across the Forth to wish you *much* joy on this happy occasion. I have not heard such good news for a long time. I rejoice that you have been successful in your suit and are getting connected so closely with such an amiable family. I have had an excellent specimen of what they are from their mother and I have no doubt we will be all good friends with one another and spend many happy days together.
>
> I think from all you say she is eminently fitted to make you happy. For both your sakes you should have the marriage as soon as possibly [sic] and more especially as she is rather delicate for it is such a trying time to be engaged!
>
> From what you say of her delicacy in the throat I have no doubt but she will be better after she is married as it sometimes is nervous [sic]. If not, the [word illegible] time would be good for her. At all events you can only urge them to have it soon and this you must do as the Gentleman has always to do so leaving the choice of the day to the Lady.
>
> I have already written to her as I thought it best to do so at once. I was astonished to hear about the cook. What could she mean? She knew the kind of place it was from

me perfectly and said she understood quite well what was required in a Gentleman's house.

P. S. I regretted you were unwell and unable to come. I hope you are better – do let me know. I will keep it to myself in the meantime. I think it better.

Over the next eight months Andrew Jameson received almost as many letters from Mrs Hotchkis as from her daughter. Inevitably they were concerned almost entirely with domestic matters of which two predominated. One was the difficulty experienced by the family with the small house that they were renting[38] until they could secure entry into their new home at the end of May 1853. This house was too small to accommodate the entire family and Mr and Mrs Finlay always had two of their Hotchkis nieces living with them at Deanston. James Hotchkis appears to have continued to lodge at Bridge of Traqueer. There are constant references to the cold weather and as late as 27th February 1853 Maggie complains of the "cutting wind and snow".

The second was the many visits the family received from two clergymen. One was a Free Church minister called Brown, whose parish was at nearby Lochmaben. The other was Dr Julius Wood, minister of the Free Church in Dumfries attended by the Hotchkis family. By a curious coincidence, this was the minister who went out to Malta in 1842 following Andrew Jameson's successful plea at the General Assembly of the Church of Scotland that a Presbyterian church be established in Valletta.[39]

Presumably Andrew Jameson would mention his family in his letters to Margaret and her mother but none of this correspondence has survived. We learn a little about him from a letter sent on 28th March 1853 from the mother, and it is worth quoting an excerpt since it demonstrates two traits that were prominent in her character. The first is the strong hold that religion had on her sentiments. These were sometimes expressed with less than Christian charity as in her criticism

[38] v. p. 410 supra.
[39] v. p. 258 supra.

of Melville's marriage to Agnes Martin.[40] In an earlier letter (24th August 1852), sent to Andrew in Paris, she had hoped "the change of scene and the interest in seeing so many of the churches of Christ will do you good and direct your thoughts from brooding too much on your brother's sad fate".

> My dear Andrew,
>
> I grieve to hear of your being still on the sick list. I had hoped you would have been yourself again before this but it is otherwise & we know it is in love our Father chastises us. Ah! It would not be good for us, were it all sunshine – who has not these trials. Their secret sorrow is not outwardly seen, a smiling face often covers an aching heart. "I know their sorrows" says God. How sweet it is to feel he knows every thought, hears every sigh, sees every tear. No sympathy like His, yet when on earth He sought human sympathy and He has hallowed Christian friendship. Dear Andrew, you are very much very often in my thoughts & in my prayers – and your dear gentle Maggie.
>
> I see by her letters your illness has called forth all the warm affection of a first love in her warm heart, her feelings lie so deep & so shrouded in diffidence & shyness. She is one that will only be loved by a few.

As the years passed Christianity, as she interpreted it, would begin to occupy her mind to a degree much greater than was then common even among devout members of her faith and it coloured her outlook on life.[41]

The second trait, which has been mentioned earlier,[42] is that, as far as she was concerned, Andrew Jameson was uniting himself as much with her whole family as with her daughter and that family

---

[40] v. p. 409 supra.

[41] Jameson, J. H., op cit p. 40.

[42] v. p. 405 supra.

was essentially her Hart/Montgomery ancestry rather than that of her husband. That ancestry involved acquaintanceship with local "county" families such as the baronet Sir William Jardine [43] and his wife, whose home, Jardine Hall, was near Castlemilk. This determination to retain what she considered to be her close affinity with the local aristocracy was communicated to her second daughter, Mary, "who had very aristocratic tastes and never thought that the marriages of my mother and Aunt Jane were quite worthy of the dignity of the Hotchkis family. She moved among the higher orders of the Montgomery families."[44]

Since the engagement had been announced in November 1852, it was now time to make arrangements for the marriage. Mrs Hotchkis wanted the event to be held in a place appropriate for someone of her family background and, although there is no documentation to support it, she must have been negotiating over the early months of 1853 with the owner of Castlemilk, a George Armstrong,[45] to lease the property to her over the summer. In a letter of early April, Maggie wrote to Andrew: "I have joyful news to give you today. Mama has just got a letter from Mr Armstrong giving her leave in the kindest manner possible for us all to go to Castle Milk. We are so very happy that we are to be at Castle Milk again – how strange it is – we can hardly realize it yet – but we can distinctly see God's hand in this as in every event in our lives." The correspondence over the next two months from both her and her mother is concerned almost solely with the move from Dumfries and settling in at what had once been their own home.

The only information that has survived about Andrew Jameson and his family at this time comes in a letter of 28th March 1853 from Mrs Hotchkis, in which we learn that his elder son, Andrew, was now at school and that the younger son, John, had been parted from his nurse.

---

[43] Sir William was the foremost British ichthyologist of the nineteenth century.
[44] Jameson, J. H., op cit p.30.
[45] He was one of the first four trustees of the Lochmaben & District Savings Bank, established 1847. Mrs James Hotchkis described him in one of her letters to Andrew Jameson as "a wreck through drink".

The day of the wedding was fixed for 28th July 1853.

Meanwhile, Andrew Jameson was continuing his career as a sheriff-substitute. That he was highly regarded by his fellow sheriff-substitutes is shown by a request from the Sheriff-Substitute of Aberdeenshire (signature illegible) that he approach the Lord Advocate and press him to show greater diligence in support of the Sheriff Court Bill. As his colleague wrote: "You seem to be the only *sub* that is allowed any amicable intercourse with the Lord Advocate." Since this letter was written on 25th July 1853, it is unlikely that Andrew Jameson found time to accede to this request.

Writing a day later, Sophia Gray gave much family news. Elizabeth Thomson had visited for two days and from her Sophia heard "such indifferent accounts of Willy Ogilvie's credit". His cousin was to be married on 27th July "and will take his wife to lodgings. I never thought much of Willy, his principles are too democratic." Also from this letter we learn that young Andrew Jameson had been left in the care of his Campbell grandparents at Barnhill till after the wedding and honeymoon. There is no reference to John. It is interesting to note that the Grays would not be attending the wedding, "as the Gentleman's relations, when at a distance are not looked for". However, two small sentences in this letter are of more than family importance, as events transpired.

> We have had a great deal of rain and the Preraphaelites are sadly annoyed with it as they can neither paint well nor catch any fish. There are too many anglers frequent that locality, yet John will not move and we have no hopes of seeing them here at present now.

Few holidays have been of greater historical interest than that taken in the summer of 1853 at Glenfinlas by John and Effie Ruskin along with John and William Millais. Here John Millais painted his famous portrait of John Ruskin with the background of a highland stream.[46] It was during these weeks spent at Brig o'Turk, that Millais noticed the indifference Ruskin showed towards his wife, Effie. This led to what became the *cause célèbre* of the century, when Effie left her husband in April 1854, secured a Decree of Nullity the following July and on 5th July 1855 married Millais in Bowerswell.[47] This tale has been told in many publications, but as far as it concerns Andrew Jameson, its principal result (apart from the happiness of his niece) was that there was no further correspondence between him and Ruskin.

Andrew Jameson could not possibly have foreseen the outcome of the Glenfinlas holiday. The Ruskins stayed with him for two nights, 30th June and 1st July, breaking their journey north in order that Effie could consult Dr James Young Simpson, who gave her chloroform pills[48] to combat her persistent sore throat. On the second evening Andrew Jameson hosted a party to which the Millais brothers were invited so that they could meet Noel (later Sir Noel) Paton, an Edinburgh artist, who painted in the Pre-Raphaelite style. Paton had studied at the Royal Academy, London, in 1843 and had met John Millais there. Another guest was James Young Simpson (created a baronet in 1866), who had pioneered the use of chloroform to relieve pain in childbirth. Millais drew a sketch of him from memory a few days later.[49]

Andrew Jameson and James Simpson were exact contemporaries, both born in 1811 and dying in 1870, and were central figures in the social scene of Edinburgh in the middle years of the nineteenth century. As has been mentioned several times previously, Andrew Jameson was a man whose social skills and great learning attracted a wide circle of friends, not least persons of high political and legal standing, as noted by his fellow sheriff-substitute from Aberdeenshire.[50] It was through his friendship with Simpson that Jane, youngest daughter of James

---

[46] Millais had "fixed on his place, a lovely piece of worn rock, with foaming water and weeds and moss, and a noble overhanging bank of a dark crag". Letter from Ruskin to a friend, James, W., (1947) *The Order of Release* p. 206. John Murray, London.

[47] The occasion was also used by the Grays to have their fifteenth (eighth surviving) child baptised with the name Everett. He was 26 years younger than Effie.

[48] Effie became increasingly reliant on them and was never able to break the habit.

[49] The original is now in the Birmingham Museum and Art Gallery.

[50] v. p. 415 supra.

and Margaret Hotchkis, met Dr James Matthews Duncan, principal assistant to Simpson. They married in 1860.[51]

Pre-nuptial contracts are not a late twentieth-century innovation and were common in Scotland at the time of Andrew Jameson's marriage to Margaret Hotchkis. The contract for their marriage was drawn up by Walter Jollie, the solicitor to the Hotchkis family. When Major Hart had bought the Castlemilk estate he had appointed as factor the legal firm of James and Walter Jollie because his sister, Christian, had married James Jollie. As James Jameson records: "Neither my grandfather nor the Jollies seemed to have exercised any careful supervision, but had let things drift."[52] The Walter Jollie, who drew up the contract, was the nephew of James Jollie. His letter of 26th July 1853 enclosed the contract together with the advice that "if you are to be at Castlemilk tomorrow, I would suggest that it should be signed of that date, which ensures it being an *ante-nuptial* contract." Originally, Walter Jollie had declined an invitation to attend the wedding but, since the bride's mother had later particularly requested his presence, he had altered that decision and would be at Castlemilk on 28th July.[53]

Andrew Jameson and Margaret Hotchkis were married at Castlemilk by Dr Julius Wood, whom the bride's mother seemed to regard almost as her personal chaplain. No written account of the ceremony has survived but, curiously, several sketches taken at the wedding have. There are comments attached to each sketch but, with one exception, they are so brief as to be uninformative. The exception is the difficulty experienced by some of the family and the driver in extricating the obese Mrs Finlay from the light carriage in which she had arrived. There is no documentation that tells us where the honeymoon was spent apart from the following excerpt from Sophia Gray's letter of 25th July: "I trust you will get your first stage to your [word illegible]

---

[51] The name Matthews Duncan was never hyphenated. Dr Matthews Duncan (1826–1890) ought to have succeeded Sir James Young Simpson in the Chair of Midwifery at Edinburgh but, according to James Jameson, there was some internal corruption and he was passed over. He was soon offered a chair at St Bartholomew's in London, where he attained the highest distinction. Queen Victoria sent his widow a telegram of condolence on hearing of his death.

[52] Jameson, J. H., op. cit. p. 7.

[53] There is no copy of the contract in the archives.

place made out comfortably and that you may get good weather to pursue your journey. I think that Margaret will be much better of the change and when she arrives on the continent you will see what her strength will be able to undertake and form no plans but be guided by circumstances."

APPENDIX A

The Sisters and Brothers of Margaret Hotchkis

Margaret, the third daughter of James and Margaret Hotchkis, was born in 1830 and, at the time of her engagement to Andrew Jameson, had four sisters and three brothers. Anne (born 1827) married John Loch, a civil servant of the East India Company and later of the Indian Civil Service. They had no family.

Mary (born 1828) never married. "She had very aristocratic tastes and never thought that the marriages of my mother and Aunt Jane were quite worthy of the Hotchkis family. She moved among the higher orders of the Montgomery families etc in the days at Castlemilk and later had a long connection with the Massie Beresfords, the Woodsops, the Walkers and others. She had a kind heart, but a rather domineering temper, which was sometimes the cause of trouble in the family. After 28 Greenhill Gardens was sold she lived in rooms first at 9 Coates Crescent,[54] afterwards in Alva Street where she died. To her also Providence has been unkind. We always called her The Duchess and she ought to have been one."[55] She was, thus, to some extent like her father in considering that her mother's antecedents conferred on the family a superior social position that had to be maintained.

Another unmarried sister was Isobel (born 1831), a hypochondriac, until she was told by Dr James Matthews Duncan, the husband of the youngest sister, Jane (born 1839), that there was nothing wrong with her. Thereafter she lived a normal life. The Matthews Duncans (the name was never hyphenated) had 13 children.

Two of the sons of James and Margaret Hotchkis had died in their teens before Andrew Jameson and Margaret first met. The eldest

---

[54] Her nephew, J. H. Jameson, lived at 16 Coates Crescent.
[55] Jameson, J. H., op cit p.30.

surviving son, Richard (born 1834), was an officer in the East India Company's army. Despite a family tradition that he was at the relief of Lucknow in 1857, Richard saw no active service in the Indian Mutiny and in 1860 he returned to Scotland. He was promoted to the rank of major and was appointed adjutant to volunteer regiments in the Glasgow area, first at Barrhead and then at Crookston. Having fathered five children by his first wife and ten by his second, it might have been expected that there would have been an enormous number of Hotchkis cousins but this did not happen. One reason might have been an unusual condition of service in the East India Company's armies. This was that the unmarried daughters of their officers received pensions on the death of their fathers, an engagement honoured by the British government, when the East India Company armies were amalgamated with the military services controlled by the crown.

By his first wife, Richard Hotchkis had four sons and one daughter. Only one of these four sons married and had children, and although the daughter married, she had no children. The second wife of Richard Hotchkis presented him with ten more children. Of the six sons, four never married and two married producing children. All four daughters remained single throughout their lives, and there is a family rumour that their mother advised them never to marry. It must be left to conjecture whether this was simply sound financial advice or a warning against the travails of constant pregnancies.

The two other sons of James and Margaret Hotchkis failed to take advantage of positions which were obtained for them through their close family connection with James Finlay and Company of Deanston. James (born 1837) and a Finlay cousin were appointed to traineeships with a cotton importing firm in Liverpool, but of their conduct there James Jameson said "the family were discreetly silent but I know that the Finlays attributed the ruin of their son to his cousin's malign influence".[56] James was despatched to Australia with the loan of a few thousand pounds from his uncle, John Finlay, to set him on his feet as a farmer. He made no success of the venture, never repaid the

---

[56] Jameson, J. H., op cit p.35.

loan and never married. The youngest son was Finlay (born 1843), who "exhibited in an intensified degree the futile qualities of the male members of that amicable and handsome family".[57] After losing two positions in industry, the first with James Finlay and Company, because "he had no capacity for business and no brains",[58] he had to flee to America to avoid his creditors. Somewhat surprisingly, he won the hand of "a rather clever and handsome American lady and she finally set him on his feet".[59]

After the death of her husband in 1865, Mrs James Hotchkis continued to live at Ladyfield, Dumfries, and moved sometime after 1870 to 28 Greenhill Gardens, Edinburgh, together with her two unmarried daughters, Mary and Isobel, and her brother, Montgomery. She died in 1876 and for about a decade the two sisters and their uncle continued to live there. Soon after Montgomery's death in 1886, the sisters sold their house. Mary moved to Bridge of Allan, where she died in 1900, and Isobel "lived in rooms first at 9 Coates Crescent, afterwards in Alva Street, where she died in 1902".[60] Jane Matthews Duncan's husband died in 1890, and she survived him until 1916, dying at Minstead, Hampshire.

---

[57] Jameson, J. H., op cit p.40.
[58] Jameson, J. H., op cit p.41.
[59] Jameson, J. H., op cit p.42.
[60] Jameson, J. H., op. cit. p.30. It is probably just a coincidence that at a later date James Jameson lived in Coates Crescent and his daughter, Elsie, in Alva Street.

CHAPTER THIRTEEN

Years of Contentment and Professional Fulfilment

As stated in the Bibliography to this work, the Jameson Archive contains few letters or documents relating to the last seventeen years of Andrew Jameson's life. We do not even know where he took his new wife on honeymoon other than it was somewhere in Europe. However, it is clear that for the last seventeen years of his life, Andrew Jameson enjoyed a happy domestic and professional life. He had a wife again and so was relieved of the responsibility of running a household and supervising the five or six servants that were in those days necessary to maintain a professional man's establishment. He had been living in Greenhill Gardens, probably at No. 14,[1] since 1850, and this remained his family home until 1856. The only child of this marriage, James Hotchkis Jameson, was born on 4th January 1855, and the following year they moved to No. 7 Church Hill. Since the Evaluation Roll of the city shows that this house belonged to a Charles Chalmers, it is clear that it was rented and not owned by Andrew Jameson. In 1861 he purchased 2 Bruntsfield Terrace, which was his home until his death in 1870.

Margaret Jameson cared for Andrew and John, his two sons by his first wife, with the same devotion that she paid to her own son. That the relationship between the boys was good is evidenced in a letter that Andrew sent to James, when he and John heard that James had been ill.

In the summer of 1862 James was struck down by typhoid, while on a visit to his grandparents at Ladyfield, their home outside Dumfries. His life was despaired of but Dr Matthews Duncan had been sent for and he arrived just in time save the boy. Meanwhile, the two half-

---

[1] Numbers were not allocated until 1859 but another researcher has deduced what was the probable number in Greenhill Gardens.

brothers of James, Andrew and John, had been enjoying a holiday. They stayed first at Caldarvan House, Gartocharn, the home of their aunt, Susan Mackenzie, and then at Garten. It has been impossible to identify this place, and it was surely not on or near Lochgarten, which is situated by Grantown of Spey. From there they came to Overtoun (now Overton) near Fintry, where another aunt, Fanny White, lived. Susan Mackenzie and Fanny White were sisters of their late mother. It is probable that the boys first heard that their brother had been unwell when they arrived at Overtoun, because the letter written by Andrew seems to refer mainly to their time at Caldarvan that is very near Loch Lomond.

My Dear Jamie,

I am sorry that you have not been well but I hope that you are better now. Johnnie and I have been enjoying ourselves very much.

We were at Caldarvan for some time with Robbie Mackenzie[2] whom you will remember. We caught some big trout in Lochend but not very many as it was not good weather.

We caught some rabbits with a funny little beast called a ferret, which is a kind of weasel and is something like this. [He draws a ferret.] We put this beast into the rabbit holes, you know that rabbits have a great many holes running into each other, so when they smell the ferret they bolt out of their holes and are caught in the nets that we put there.

After Caldarvan we went to Garten we went by Loch Lomond the same way as you went to Arrochar, when Grace[3] was so frightened at the boat. We had very good fishing at Garten. Johnny caught some fine trout in the Cruach burn, which has grown better fishing since we were there.

[2] Son of Robert and Susan Mackenzie.
[3] She was possibly a Mackenzie or White cousin.

The little bull calf that you and I used to chase round the house has grown a great bull that would chase us. [He draws a very good likeness of the bull.] We were at the Collessan burn yesterday. We caught a dozen and I lost a fine sea-trout at which I was *not* pleased at all. Here I am on. [He draws a sketch of a figure holding a rod with the line in the mouth of a huge fish.]

We were very nearly late for the steamer yesterday with Hugh Cameron not having his boat ready but after all we got here safe.

With kind love
I am your affectionate brother A. Jameson.

(At the foot of the page he draws a sketch of a small rowing boat pulling out from the shore to a paddle steamer.)

We learn very little about Margaret Jameson from correspondence, but her son described his mother's character in the following words:

Her seventeen years of married life with my good father were very happy but a few years before his death they were overshadowed by ill health, which continued afterwards till she died in 1897. Consequently she lived in great retirement at our house, No 2 Bruntsfield Terrace, facing the links. She was a pious lady but never forced her views, which were strongly coloured by Free Church principles, on others. Her gracious influence, sweet temper and quiet commonsense were admired by all who knew her and she was successful in softening the asperities of other members of her family and smoothed out many ravels among her sisters.[4]

She also, some thirteen years after her marriage, inherited some money

---

[4] Jameson, J. H., op. cit. pp. 42–43.

that augmented the family income. As stated earlier,[5] her father, James Hotchkis, had adopted a style of life based upon an expectation of inheritances that were never realised. His last hope in this direction had lain with a cousin, Richard Gardner. The mother of James Hotchkis had been an Isobel Gardner and her brother, William Gardner, had married an Anna Rankine, whose family owned the estate of Dudhope in Dundee. This property became increasingly valuable as Dundee began to extend its boundaries. Richard, the Gardners' sole surviving child, never married. He made James Hotchkis his heir but unfortunately for James Hotchkis, he died in 1862, pre-deceasing his mother, and the Dudhope estate reverted to the Rankines.

As James Jameson wrote, "on Richard Gardner's death, the last of these great expectations were buried with him in his [i.e. Richard Gardner's] grave".[6] James Hotchkis felt fate had dealt him a final blow; his health declined, he became "feeble and peevish"[7] and he died at Ladyfield in March 1865. One year later Mrs Gardner died at the age of 91 and a large amount of money came to the children of her nephew, James Hotchkis. Thus, within a year of his death, one of the inheritances upon which he had relied for so many years came not to him but to his children.

By this time the legal firm of James and Walter Jollie had passed to Thomas Strong, a nephew of the Walter Jollie who had drawn up the pre-nuptial contract for the marriage of Andrew Jameson and Margaret Hotchkis. Andrew Jameson used the occasion of this accretion to the family finances to remove the firm of Jollie and Strong,[8] as it was now designated, from any further connection with his wife's affairs. He had a very low opinion of this man's legal competence and fully recognised the irresponsibility of Jollie's father and uncle in the mismanagement of the Castlemilk estate.[9]

Andrew Jameson continued his professional life as a sheriff-

[5] v. p. 405 supra.
[6] Jameson, J. H., op. cit. p. 22.
[7] Jameson, J. H., op. cit. p. 22.
[8] The name of the firm was a cause of amusement in Edinburgh legal circles.
[9] v. p. 417 supra.

substitute of Midlothian. There are no references to his health and one must assume that the weakness in his throat that had earlier required recuperative visits to Europe was no longer impeding the performance of his duties. As the years passed he became a familiar figure in Edinburgh society. His friendship with the eminent James Young Simpson and the marriage to Jane Hotchkis of Simpson's equally distinguished principal assistant, James Matthews Duncan, meant that he walked in the higher echelons of Edinburgh's legal and medical circles.

His Christian belief and affiliation to the Free Church of Scotland remained an integral part of his life. In 1857 he was one of the signatories to an article published in the *Glasgow Herald* entitled "Contemplated Union between the Free Church of Scotland and the United Presbyterian Church" and he was involved in the negotiations between the two churches that began in 1863. These continued for ten years without reaching any conclusion other than that further discussions were fruitless.[10] In May 1865 he was appointed a trustee of the Free Church.

His commitment to the interests of the Protestant minority in northern Italy never weakened. He continued to communicate with and, on occasion, to visit representatives of these struggling Protestant communities not only in Tuscany but also, as we discover from a letter sent to him on 19th May 1854, in Savoy.[11] The letter acknowledges a gift of £80.

In February 1866 he received a letter from Dr Alexander Duff, one of the best known Scottish missionaries of the nineteenth century. He had met Dr Duff[12] at Dumfries during his courtship of Margaret Hotchkis and it seems likely that they corresponded with each other over the subsequent years. Duff's main area of interest was India, where he was successful in founding colleges that broadened the basis

[10] Union of the two churches came in 1900.
[11] The Waldensians are a small Protestant minority living in the alpine valleys of both Piedmont and Savoy. They suffered centuries of persecution from the rulers of Piedmont to whom Savoy belonged until 1860, when it was transferred to France, and only since 1848 had been granted full equality of civil rights. The appalling massacre of Waldensians in 1655 by Piedmontese troops called forth Milton's famous sonnet "On the Late Massacre in Piedmont" (1655).
[12] Duff was on leave from his work in India.

of education for the indigenous inhabitants. He left India in 1863 and went on what was virtually a world tour, visiting parts of South Africa, the United States of America and Europe. While in Europe he spent some time among the Waldenses and on 24th February 1866 (by now back in Edinburgh) he wrote about a meeting on "Italian missions" over which Andrew Jameson was to preside.

This is a very interesting letter because it unequivocally portrays the outlook of nineteenth century Protestantism towards Roman Catholicism in Europe, especially in Italy. It is also is clear evidence of Andrew Jameson's continuing engagement in support of the Protestant minorities of Italy. Consequently, it will be given here in full because it will not have been read elsewhere in print. Towards the end of the letter Duff refers to "your Jubilee meeting" and so this must have been the 25th anniversary of the foundation of the mission.[13]

My Dear Sheriff,

I notice that, on Monday next, in association with the Italian Missions, a public meeting is to be held, over which you are to preside.

Now, next to what I must ever hold to be *the* greatest of all Christian enterprises, i.e. the evangelization of the eight hundred millions of Heathendom, there is none in which I feel a livelier interest than in that which contemplates the evangelization of Popish Italy, now so marvellously thrown open by the overruling Providence of God, to a preached gospel And the interest is vastly enhanced, when I think of the Waldenses as the principal agents & instruments in carrying the message of grace & salvation to the descendants of their once savage persecutors.

It is truly a glorious – rather, a Divine mode of revenge.

I have again & again read the tragic story of the sufferings of their heroic forefathers, of whom it may be as truly

[13] This was the Committee of the Italian Evangelisation Society in Edinburgh for which Andrew Jameson was for many years the convener.

said as of the primitive Christians that they "Conquered by Sufferings".

I have pored, until my eyes have been sore with weeping, over the graphic pages & frightful pictorial illustrations of Cromwell's ambassador and other kindred works.

On the banks of the Ganges I have repeatedly read over the mighty letters of Cromwell's Latin Secretary[14] addressed to the Potentates of Europe respecting the Waldensian persecutions – letters containing passages, that have in them the ring & roll of England's greatest poem – The Paradise Lost.

I have enjoyed the privilege of visiting the Valleys – and being hospitably entertained by some of their humble but zealous pastors – of addressing the annual meeting of the Waldensian synod – & of standing on some of those heights, where the bones of God's "slaughtered saints" once "Lay scattered on the Alpine mountains cold". And now it appears to me as if Milton's sublime prayer were about to be gloriously answered – the prayer, in which he solemnly invokes Almighty God, saying –

"Their martyred blood and ashes sow
Oe'r all the Italian fields, where still doth sway
The Triple tyrant; that from these may grow
A hundred fold, who, having learnt thy way
Early may fly the Babylonian woe."

With such views & feelings, had health permitted, I should have assuredly been at your Jubilee meeting on Monday next. But, alas, though now, by God's blessing, convalescent from my last severe attack of illness, I am still too weak to venture on such an attempt.

But I shall be with you in spirit. And may the Lord send *his* heavens & make *his* presence felt in the midst of you!

---

[14] John Milton.

Meanwhile, on behalf of God's cause in Italy, kindly accept of the accompanying £5, as a small thank-offering to the Lord for his abounding goodness to me.

I remain, my dear Sheriff,

Yours very affectionately,

Alexander Duff

This account of his domestic affairs and Free Church activities must now give way to continuing the narration of his career as a sheriff-substitute. Among the few documents that are available for consultation is one dated 7th January 1854, signed by Duncan McNeill, Lord President of the Court of Session, John Hope, Lord Justice Clerk and James Moncreiff, Lord Advocate. Hope had been Lord Justice Clerk since 1841 and had recommended Andrew Jameson to his relation, Henry Hope, an Under-Secretary at the Colonial Office, as a suitable person to revise the Criminal Code of Malta.[15] These three senior Scottish judges reject the request by the Sheriff of Aberdeenshire and the Society of Advocates in Aberdeen for an appointment of an additional sheriff-substitute for the county.

It is probable that this document, written on fine parchment in immaculate copperplate script, was sent to Andrew Jameson because he was now the convenor of the Sheriff-Substitutes of Scotland,[16] an association that had been established by his father in the early years of the century, when he was their prime advocate for an increase in their salaries. When the association was in danger of disintegrating in 1844, Andrew Jameson had advised his father how it could be strengthened by arranging regular and properly constituted meetings. Perhaps he had persuaded the association to support the request from Aberdeenshire because he remembered that only nine years previously he had been

---

[15] v. p. 265 supra.

[16] This had become the official title of the association by 1846, as shown in the extract of the minute of their meeting held on 10th May of that year, which recorded their appreciation of the work carried out on their behalf over many years by Andrew Jameson (Senior). The extract had been specially written on vellum and presented to Andrew and Melville Jameson. v. p. 388 supra.

heavily overworked as sole Sheriff-Substitute of Ayrshire.[17]

In July 1862 Andrew Jameson was in communication with Leon Levi (1821–1888) concerning an incidence of jobbery, more commonly known today as corrupt dealing. Levi, born into a Jewish family in Ancona, Italy, had emigrated to Liverpool in 1844, where he obtained British citizenship and joined the Presbyterian Church of England. He was appointed to the Chair of Commercial Law at King's College, London, in 1852. Whether Andrew Jameson knew him personally or merely by reputation must be left to speculation, and it is impossible to gather from the letter in what manner Andrew Jameson considered himself to have been ill-treated. He had asked Levi to raise the matter with the Lord Advocate, but Levi regretted that "when it has been done it is too late and it becomes difficult to prove it".

In May 1865, almost fifty years after his father had first started to lead delegations to London in pursuit of improved salaries for sheriff-substitutes,[18] Andrew Jameson was representing his fellow sheriff-substitutes on the same issue, although in this case it concerned only the sheriff-substitutes of Midlothian. From the correspondence it appears that a meeting had been arranged with Sir George Grey, the Chancellor of the Duchy of Lancaster, but before travelling to London Andrew Jameson requested a meeting with the Duke of Buccleugh. The duke had been a member of Peel's government in the years 1841 to 1846 but although he had subsequently withdrawn from active political life Andrew Jameson must have considered that he still wielded sufficient influence for his support to be sought. The duke, who was taking the night train to London on 10th May, agreed to see him that evening in the New Club, Edinburgh, prior to his departure. He must have been convinced of the merits of the claim because he wrote from London[19]

---

[17] v. p. 304 supra.

[18] It is interesting that in the obituary of Andrew Jameson, published in the *Quarterly Journal of Jurisprudence* No 30(2) 1870–1871, this aspect of his father's life is mentioned.

[19] The Duke of Buccleugh had written his letter of 12th May from 37 Belgrave Square. He enclosed with it a torn-off page of his writing paper with the words "Admit Mr Jameson to see Montagu House. Buccleugh. 12th May 1865." This opulent mansion had been built 1859–1862 by the duke on the site of a previous and less attractive building of the same name. One may presume Andrew Jameson took advantage of the invitation when he went to London.

two days later saying, "it might be advisable for you to send to Sir George Grey a copy of the Memorial on Remuneration respecting the Salaries of the Sheriffs-substitute of Mid-Lothian before the interview with him that he may be prepared as to the objects of the interview". Sir George's department must have had at that time some responsibility concerning the payment of public servants. There is no documentation on the outcome of the meeting, although it is possible that as Senior Sheriff-Substitute of Midlothian[20] some enhanced remuneration may have occurred as a result of his meeting with Sir George Grey.

On 4th October 1862 there had been a meeting of the Sheriff-Substitutes of Scotland, in which they discussed their role in the Scottish legal system. A report of this meeting was subsequently published in January 1863.[21] Apart from salaries and increase in duties, the most important issue that was addressed to the Government (as detailed in points 9 and 10 of the report) was that there was no possibility of promotion regardless of their expertise and knowledge. Whether or not the Government gave serious consideration to the report is unknown but in October 1865 on the promotion of Archibald Davidson, Sheriff of Aberdeenshire and Kincardineshire to Sheriff of Midlothian, Andrew Jameson was appointed his successor. He was the first sheriff-substitute to be so honoured[22] and, until 1962, when sheriffs were designated sheriffs principal and sheriff-substitutes as sheriffs, remained one of the few to have been promoted to the senior post.

He received several letters of congratulation. He must have been very pleased with the address[23] sent to him by the Incorporated Society of Solicitors, wherein they record that throughout his years of service as sheriff-substitute "we have had abundant experience during many years, of your great ability as a lawyer, of your uncompromising impartiality and integrity as a judge and of your courtesy and

---

[20] He is so designated in the *Dundee Courier & Argus* on 27th October 1865. Previous documentation refers to him as sheriff-substitute.

[21] v. *Dundee Courier & Argus*, 28th January 1863.

[22] Nicholson, G. (2000) *The Sheriffs of Scotland 1829 to the Present Day* incorrectly states at p. 12 that John Cheyne, Sheriff-Substitute of Dundee, appointed in 1885 as Sheriff of Roxburgh and Selkirk, was the first sheriff-substitute to be promoted sheriff.

[23] Dated 24th November 1865.

urbanity as a gentleman". Sir David Brewster, now Principal of the University of Edinburgh, wrote a brief note congratulating him on his new appointment but only after hoping that he had "got a ticket of admission to hear Mr Gladstone's noble testimony to our Common Christianity". A few weeks later Sir David was writing to him again, soliciting support for the candidature of the son of a friend of his to the now vacant sheriff-substitute position of Midlothian.

As was customary until 1962, sheriffs lived and worked in Edinburgh, from where they exercised a supervisory role over their substitutes in the counties. Thus Andrew Jameson continued to live in Edinburgh at 2 Bruntsfield Terrace and made such visits to Aberdeen as required. Documents were sent to him in a special bag with his name and address written on a heavy brass tag.[24] There is, unfortunately, no documentation at all in the Jameson Archive concerning his tenure as Sheriff of Aberdeenshire or his family life during these five years. It is for this reason that it is necessary to move forwards to the sad events of October 1870.

In September 1870, Andrew Jameson and his wife were visiting Mrs James Hotchkis, who was still living at Ladyfield, Dumfries. His second son, John St Clair Jameson, who "was preparing for a mercantile career"[25] in Glasgow, wrote to his father giving an account of a holiday he had spent in Skye and the western Highlands. His father doubtless recalled the walking tour he had undertaken in that same area in 1831.[26] John describes his journey back from Skye by way of Glen Shiel, Invermoriston, Oban and Loch Awe to the head of Loch Lomond. From there, either on foot or by local steamboat, he reached the southern end of the loch and walked on to Overton, where he stayed three nights with his aunt, Mrs White. He spent these days shooting and on one day met his half-brother James, who "had come up from Bloomhill and had caught a juvenile whale in the burn; at least I believe it was very like one".

---

[24] This is currently in the possession of his great-granddaughter, Mrs Sheila Gourlay.

[25] From p.346 of obituary of Sheriff Jameson in *Quarterly Journal of Jurisprudence*, No 30 (2 1870–1871).

[26] v. pp. 129–30 supra.

There is also family news in this letter. He hopes that his stepmother "is keeping a little better now & recovering from her unfortunate attack. I am glad she is to be part of the Winter at any rate at home; I think it is much better so." He had met Melville's wife at "the station" (presumably in Glasgow). "She had been staying with her brother at Paisley – a minister[27] & I may add a poor looking fly. I was glad to hear from her as well as from you of Andrew's successful début." Andrew, the later Lord Ardwall, was now 25 and must have performed well in his first case as an advocate.

In the middle of October Andrew Jameson learned that John had contracted diphtheria, an illness from which at that time few recovered. He immediately went through to Glasgow and acted as a nurse to his son. He wrote the following letter to his wife. It is given in full since it was probably the last letter he ever wrote.

2 Charing Cross,
21st Oct. 1870
Glasgow.

My dearest Margaret,

There is no improvement tonight 9. pm but rather the worse.

He has complained more of his throat & vomited several times, chiefly quantities mucus blackened with the iron (no water passed since 8).

On the other hand he has had a good deal of [illegible word] & brandy & nourishment and has spoken to me more like himself, clearly and so sensibly. He was less drowsy this evening than I have seen him & not so restless as he slept.

Both doctors have been here tonight and seem to be concerned.

Our dear son is in God's hands, as we all are, & at all times. He seems to be in a critical state with a hideous

---

[27] v. p. 403 supra.

disease & he must look to the Goodness & Mercy of our almighty deliverer.

I will be very glad to see James again tomorrow.

I have been at times much unnerved today. I can't tell how.

I am sure James will be very sorry & the servants. I believe there will be many prayers for him, poor fellow.

Your affectionate husband

And Jameson

According to one obituary[28] John appeared to rally and his father returned to Edinburgh to resume his duties. However, he himself soon showed symptoms of the same disease and although attended by Dr Matthews Duncan succumbed to the malady at 3.00 a.m. on 30th October 1870. He never lost consciousness but was probably not told that on 28th October John had suffered a relapse and died.

There was no report of his funeral in *The Scotsman* and the several obituaries do not refer to it. However, he was an elder at St George's Free Church of Scotland, where the minister was the famous Dr James Candlish, who, although a much younger man than Dr Chalmers, had been closely associated with him in the disruption of 1843.[29] Dr Candlish would almost certainly have officiated at the funeral of so prominent and devoted member of his congregation.

Andrew Jameson and his son John were buried in Grange Cemetery, Edinburgh. Possibly there had been a joint funeral service. A large granite memorial stone marks the grave of both men, and Andrew's wife, Margaret Hotchkis, was interred there in 1897.

The Dundee Courier and Argus of 1st November 1870 published an obituary that gave a brief, clear and accurate account of the life of Andrew Jameson. It pointed out that his "judgments were distinguished

---

[28] v. footnote 25, p. 432 supra.
[29] v. p. 289 supra.

for their soundness, and the fastidious conscientiousness with which he gave his opinions in all cases added much to their weight". His long and continuing interest in the struggling Protestant churches of southern Europe was commented on and this obituary states that a few weeks before his death he was proposing to visit Spain "to confer with the leaders of the Spanish Protestant Church".

In Aberdeen on 4th November 1870 there was a special meeting of the Sheriff Court that was attended by most of the members of the Society of Advocates of Aberdeen. They were addressed first by the Sheriff-Substitute of Aberdeenshire and Kincardine, Comrie Thomson,[30] who said, "I have had the privilege of being on terms of the greatest intimacy with Sheriff Jameson for the past ten years" and, after an encomium on the manner in which he performed his public duties, added this personal tribute.

> I can scarcely trust myself to speak of his unvarying, almost
> paternal, kindness to myself. I am thankful to-day to be able
> to say that, during the whole time that we have been associ-
> ated here, there never has been even a cold look between
> us; and that we never ceased to work in perfect harmony
> and mutual confidence. Let not the good that he has done
> be "interred with his bones"; he has left us all a precious
> legacy, the example of a good life.

The sheriff-substitute was followed by J. B. McCombie, who spoke on behalf of the Society of Advocates in Aberdeen. In a much shorter eulogy the following words expressed the feelings of the members of the Society, who had known him only for five years. "The talent, uprightness, and painstaking attention shown by him in all his public duties, and his urbanity and kindness to members of the Society, are known and acknowledged by all. Everyone who had the privilege of knowing him in private life entertained for him the greatest respect and

---

[30] John Comrie Thomson (1839–1898) had been appointed to this post in 1866. He was later to become a sheriff and resume his practice at the bar.

affection. He also enjoyed a deservedly high reputation as a benevolent active Christian man, interested in every scheme for the welfare of his fellowmen."

The words spoken by Comrie Thomson and J. B. McCombie accord well with all we know about Andrew Jameson and serve as a fitting tribute with which to finish these pages on someone whose domestic and public life were beyond reproach.

BIBLIOGRAPHY

Ashby, Eric, (1963). *Technology and the Academics*. Macmillan, London

Batchelor, John, (2000). *John Ruskin*. Carroll & Graf, New York

Bewley, C., (1982). *Muir of Huntershill*. Oxford University Press

Buchan, John, (1913). *Andrew Jameson, Lord Ardwall*. Blackwood, Edinburgh

Cant, Ronald, (1946). *The University of St Andrews*. Oliver and Boyd, Edinburgh

Cockburn, Henry, (1909). *Memorials of his Time*. Foulis, Edinburgh

Cooper, Suzanne Fagence, (2010). *The Model Wife: the Passionate Lives of Effie Gray, Ruskin and Millais*. Duckworth Overlook, London

Dean, A. & Morrison, M. (c. 2000). *The Spanish Gordons and Huntly*. (Privately published: copy available from Aberdeenshire County Library, Huntly)

Ford, P. J., (1982). *George Buchanan*. Aberdeen University Press

Gourlay, Douglas, (2002). *Captain James Jameson*. Robert Gordon University, Aberdeen

James, Sir William, (1947). *The Order of Release*. John Murray, London

Lang, Peter, (1926). *Duncan Dewar, a Student of St Andrews 100 Years Ago, His Accounts*. St Andrews University

Lewis, George, (1870). *Letters of the Rt Hon George Cornewall Lewis, Bart, to Various Friends*. London

Links, Joseph Gluckstein, (1968). *The Ruskins in Normandy*. John Murray

Lutyens, Mary, (1999). *Effie in Venice*. Palas Editions, London

Lutyens, Mary, (1967). *Millais and the Ruskins*. John Murray, London

Lutyens, Mary, (1972). *The Ruskins and the Grays*. John Murray, London

Nicholson, Gordon, (2000). *The Sheriffs of Scotland 1829 to the Present Day*. Sheriff Court Service, Edinburgh

Smart, E., (1932). *History of Perth Academy*. Tannahill and Methven, Perth

Smart, Robert, (2005). *Biographical Register*. St Andrews University

Information on the Principal Sources Used in the History of Sheriff Andrew Jameson

The bibliography above is much shorter than would normally be the case in the writing of a biography. The reason for this is that the author had to rely almost entirely on manuscript and privately printed documents from the Jameson Archive.

There are two main manuscript sources for the first five chapters. These are the diaries that Andrew Jameson kept during his years at St Andrews and Edinburgh Universities and his eighteen months in southern Europe from April 1833 to June 1834. The second is the Memoir of the family written by Andrew Jameson. The location of the original, if it survives, is unknown, but there is a typed copy in the Jameson Archive. It must be assumed that one of his two surviving sons – or a grandson – arranged for the Memoir to be typed. The author learned during his research that the A K Bell Library in Perth holds a copy with an acquisition date-stamp for 1936. In this book the term "Memoir" will be used when reference is made to information taken from this family history.

It is certain that Andrew Jameson was working on his history in the summer of 1848, while he was on sick leave from his work as a sheriff-substitute, because he wrote to his brother Melville asking if he could contribute any material. His brother replied, "You must excuse me from any contribution to the family history. First, I have no material – Second, I have no ability – Third, I have no leisure." The typescript ends abruptly at page 175 when Andrew returns from Edinburgh University to spend New Year 1832 at the family home in Cupar and finds two of his brothers suffering from illnesses that were to prove fatal.

In later years Andrew Jameson must have returned occasionally to his family history because at page 155, following a comment that the Roman Catholic Emancipation Act had been passed in 1829, severe doubts are expressed as to the wisdom of this legislation. "*Discontent and disaffection* have increased with *each concession* to the *clamour* of the *Romish faction* and have at present (1867) come to a height in armed insurrection." This is a clear reference to the Fenian Rising of that year, an armed insurrection by some Irish nationalists that was easily suppressed in Ireland, although a bomb had been exploded in London.

The Memoir is infuriating because it is written in a manner so diffuse that it is often difficult to find and follow any coherent thread. There are diversions into religious controversies that have no bearing on family history and little care has been paid to chronological arrangement of the material. There are, however, two reasons that account for these deficiencies.

The first is that this history of the family was undertaken as a labour of love by someone, who was not interested in writing a formal history and had certainly no intention of publishing it. Andrew Jameson writes that he has "become the depository of the principal fragments of our family history" and that his account "is indeed scanty and imperfect." This leads on to the second reason. The Memoir is "imperfect" because the author's grandaunt, always referred to, almost in reverence, as Miss Jameson of Graycraig, had burned many of the family documents. No explanation has been given for this and we must assume it was some general clearing out of what she considered to be useless and unwanted material. One result was that her grandnephew had to rely to a large extent for much of the eighteenth-century family history on what he remembered, as a very young man, from his discussions with this nonagenarian, who, "though her eye was dim and her steep tottering, retained in a wonderful degree the original vivacity and force of her mental powers." She died in her ninety-fourth year, when Andrew was only 20.

There are four other documents which have made possible the writing of this book. Andrew Jameson (Senior) began in 1800 to keep a record of significant events in both family and national life. He called this record "The Almanack" and this term will be used when it provides provenance of a statement or fact. Sometimes there would be only one entry for a year such as 1812, when the assassination of the Prime Minister is recorded, or even no entry as in 1807. It is quite clear that his son, Andrew Jameson (Junior), made considerable use of it when writing the Memoir, because additional material in his handwriting has been added to some of the pages.

Two other documents are closely linked to each other. The first is entitled "Outline of Family History", a document that was certainly written by the memorialist, since it concludes "I trust to fill up this outline at my leisure. Dec 5th 1831. A. J." This date is just four weeks after the death of Miss Jameson of Graycraig. It cannot have been written by Andrew Jameson (Senior), also "A. J.", because the father's handwriting was never as legible as this. The text is written on the left hand side of sheets of foolscap paper with additional comments and notes on the right hand side. Those comments on the right hand side of each page are in different ink and very much in note form. They have been inserted later when other information about family forbears has come to light. It was in this manner that he was able to "fill up this outline." This document must have been a prime source for the Memoir.

The second is headed "Notes of Family Antiquities" and since it is written in beautiful copperplate the author (unnamed) is thus neither the memorialist nor his father. It may have been commissioned by Andrew Jameson. It is the least valuable of all the manuscript sources because while it mentions various Jamesons, very few have any established link with the family. An example is David Jameson, Dean of Newbattle Abbey, who was recompensed in 1529 for the theft by one of the royal servants of a gilt chalice during a visit by James V. Again, there is an attempt to trace the family's ancestry back to mediaeval times through their connection with the Murrays of Couland. A great-grandmother of the memorialist, the first wife of Andrew Jameson (1708–1782), had a sister, who married a Murray of Couland but there is no blood descent from that family.

The fourth document was written by James Hotchkis Jameson, the second surviving son of Andrew Jameson, many years after the death of his father in 1870. It is a highly informative, and at times very amusing, account of his mother's family and of life in Edinburgh during the last three decades of the nineteenth century. He gave it the simple title "Reminiscences." No date is shown and it could have been written at any time in the first two decades of the last century.

Although Andrew Jameson ceased to keep a diary from the spring of 1836, he fortunately retained a great deal of correspondence that pertained to his professional and domestic life. Without these letters and other similar material it would have been impossible to continue with a history of his life and they are almost the sole source for Chapters Six to Thirteen. Very little has survived from 1853 until his death seventeen years later and consequently the final chapter of this work can supply few facts about the period that was most successful in his professional life. Three reasons can be advanced for this dearth of material. Having three sons to bring up and a wife, whose life became overshadowed by ill heath, it may be that he did not have time to retain and catalogue much of his correspondence as he had previously been accustomed to do. A second reason is that much of the correspondence over this period may have fallen into the care of some descendant of his eldest son, Lord Ardwall. Finally, one cannot discount the possibility that correspondence has been lost or destroyed.

Since the name Andrew is so widely used across generations of the Jameson family, one of the terms "Andrew Jameson (Junior)", "author of the Memoir" or "the memorialist" will be used when it is necessary to avoid possible confusion. The father of Andrew Jameson, the subject of this book, will be referred to as Andrew Jameson (Senior) or Sheriff-Substitute Jameson, except when it is clear from the context that it is he.

All letters and documents, without which this book could not have been written, have been preserved in the Jameson Family Archive, currently in the care of Mr J. N. St C. Jameson, WS, a great-grandson of Andrew Jameson, the subject of this biography. The author is deeply grateful to Mr Jameson for permitting him unrestricted access to the Archive.

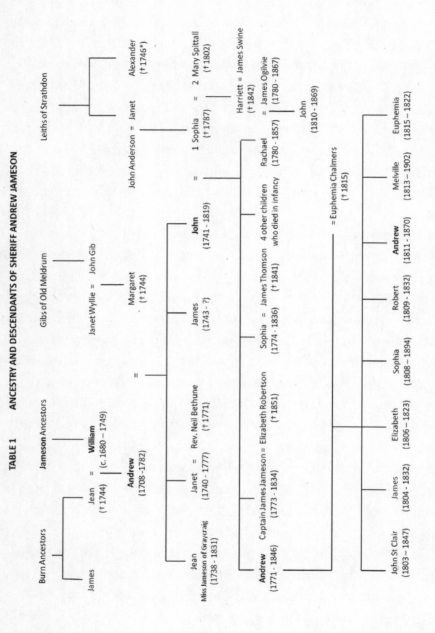

TABLE 1   ANCESTRY AND DESCENDANTS OF SHERIFF ANDREW JAMESON

* Hanged on Kennington Common, London, 29th November 1746, for adhering to the Jacobite cause in the 1745-6 rebellion.

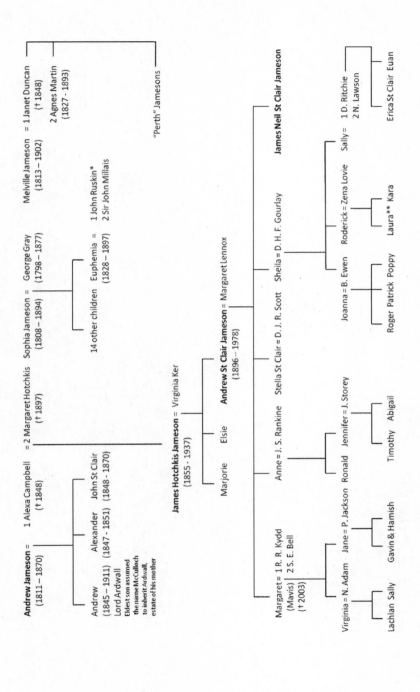

"Perth" Jamesons

**Married A. Machardie 27 August 2011

* Marriage annulled

TABLE 2   DESCENT OF JAMESON FAMILY FROM WILLIAM HOTCHKIS

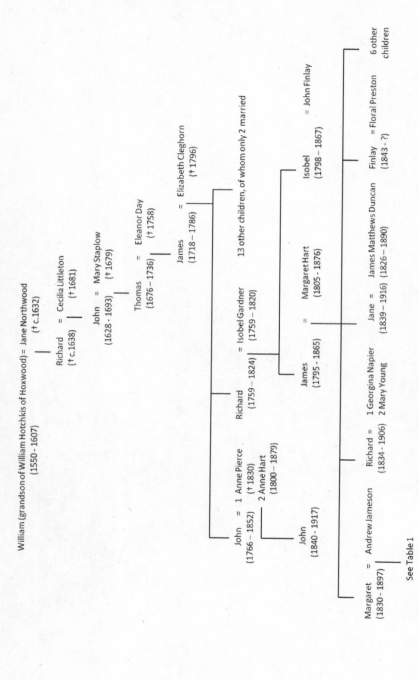

TABLE 3   FAMILY OF ALEXANDER CAMPBELL: SHERIFF-SUBSTITUTE OF RENFREWSHIRE

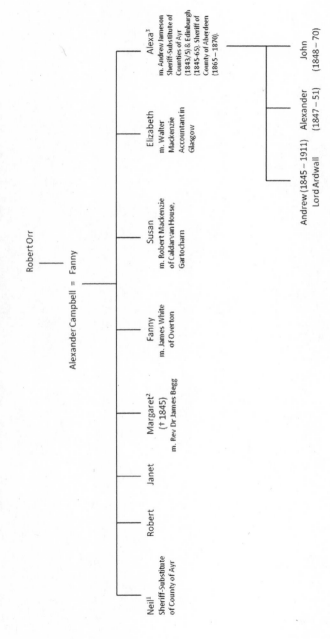

Robert Orr

Alexander Campbell = Fanny

Neil[1]
Sheriff-Substitute
of County of Ayr

Robert   Janet

Margaret[2]
(† 1845)
m. Rev Dr James Begg

Fanny
m. James White
of Overton

Susan
m. Robert Mackenzie
of Caldarvan House,
Gartocharn

Elizabeth
m. Walter
Mackenzie
Accountant in
Glasgow

Alexa[3]
m. Andrew Jameson
Sheriff-Substitute of
Counties of Ayr
(1843/5) & Edinburgh
(1845-65), Sheriff of
County of Aberdeen
(1865-1870).

Andrew (1845 – 1911)
Lord Ardwall

Alexander
(1847 – 51)

John
(1848 – 70)

[1] Married a Mary Paterson, who does not appear in any correspondence of Andrew Jameson.
[2] Died 1845 (miscarriage).
[3] Died 1848, a few days after birth of her third child, John.

445

TABLE 4   RUSKIN FAMILY TREE

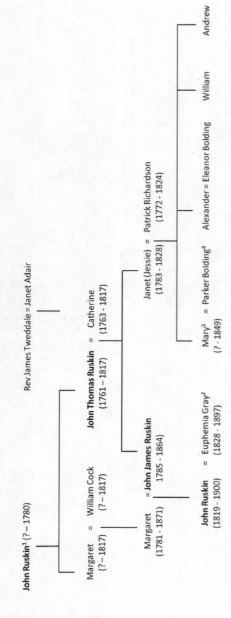

[1] Parish clerk of St Bartholomew-the-Great, London.
[2] Marriage annulled 1855.
[3] Adopted by John James Ruskin on her mother's death.
[4] Brother of the wife of Dr Alexander Richardson.

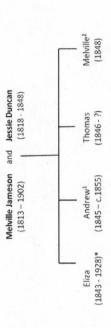

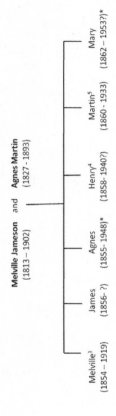

TABLE 5   MELVILLE JAMESON'S TWO FAMILIES

Melville Jameson and **Jessie Duncan**
(1813 – 1902)   (1818 - 1848)

Eliza
(1843 - 1928)*

Andrew[1]
(1845 – c.1855)

Thomas
(1846 - ?)

Melville[2]
(1848)

Melville Jameson and **Agnes Martin**
(1813 — 1902)   (1827 - 1893)

Melville[3]
(1854 — 1919)

James
(1856 - ?)

Agnes
(1855 - 1948)*

Henry[4]
(1858 - 1940?)

Martin[5]
(1860 - 1933)

Mary
(1862 – 1953?)*

[1] Emigrated to Australia.
[2] Lived only a few hours. His mother died a few days later.
[3] Solicitor at Jameson and Mackay. Succeeded his father as Procurator-Fiscal of Perthshire.
[4] Solicitor at Jameson and Mackay.
[5] Tea planter in Assam, India.
* All three daughters remained unmarried.

447

TABLE 6   ANCESTRY OF REVEREND ANDREW DUNCAN

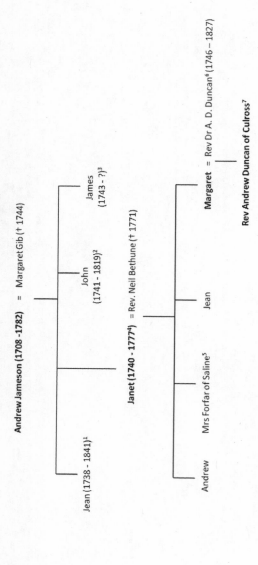

Andrew Jameson (1708 -1782)   =   Margaret Gib († 1744)

Jean (1738 - 1841)[1]

John
(1741 - 1819)[2]

James
(1743 - ?)[3]

Janet (1740 - 1777[4]) = Rev. Neil Bethune († 1771)

Andrew   Mrs Forfar of Saline[5]   Jean

Margaret   =   Rev Dr A. D. Duncan[6] (1746 – 1827)

Rev Andrew Duncan of Culross[7]

There married at Nagpur, India on 29th July 1825, Margaret, fifth daughter of Rev A. D. Duncan to Captain D. Bruce, Assistant Commissary General, Bengal Army and Susan, sixth daughter of Rev A. D. Duncan to J. Wylie, Madras Army, Surgeon in the Service of His Highness the Rajah of Nagpur

[1] Miss Jameson of Graycraig, the major beneficiary of the inheritance of her brother James .
[2] Father of Andrew, James, Sophia and Rachael Jameson. See Table 1.
[3] Major, Bombay Native Infantry. Died in India, unmarried, and left his fortune to his sister Jean.
[4] Approximate date. The Memoir merely states mid 1770s.
[5] Her husband was the minister at Saline.
[6] Principal Clerk (1807 – 1823) of the General Assembly of the Church of Scotland and Moderator of the General Assembly of the Church of Scotland in 1824.
[7] Inherited Graycraig and most of the fortune of his grand-aunt, Miss Jean Jameson.

INDEX